Major Reuben H. Fleet:

An all time Great for San Diego.
The man Who Put San Diego on the Industrial
Map. The man Who led the Republican
Party through its greatest San Diego
achievements. In short, "The Man
Who" for San Diego.

With highest esteem

Sincerely

Oscar W. Cotton.

Jan 17-1963

THE GOOD OLD DAYS

OSCAR W. COTTON

The Good Old Days

by

Oscar W. Cotton

ILLUSTRATED

EXPOSITION PRESS   NEW YORK

Exposition Press Inc., 386 Park Avenue South, New York 16, N. Y

FIRST EDITION

Acknowledgment

THANK YOU, JANE

I SUPPOSE nearly every egotistical male wants to write his Memoirs. Most of them never get around to it. I probably would not have done so, except for your request. Doing it has been fun. Brought back many pleasant memories. Makes me realize eighty years is a long time. Nearly half as long as the United States has been the United States. Somtimes it is hard to believe that the changes I have seen are facts, not fiction. The increase in San Diego's population from a quiet little horse-and-buggy town of 19,000 to a city of more than a half-million people! The national debt from one billion to nearly three hundred billion dollars—nearly 30,000 percent! The revolutionary changes in transportation, living conditions, medicine, our thinking and knowledge. It is fabulous, and if we allow ourselves to dwell on it—frightening. So I do not allow myself to dwell, but endeavor to live each day as conditions permit and to enjoy to the fullest the great privilege of living in this wonderful age and environment with our wonderful family and friends.

Again, Jane, thank you for getting me started.

DAD

In Appreciation

FIRST AND FOREMOST, I want to express appreciation in memory of my beloved wife, Violet, for her part in the production and rearing of our wonderful family; for the gracious atmosphere she maintained that made our home warm and hospitable to our friends, and for the happy life we all have had together over the years.

I use the phrase "wonderful family" advisedly. Our family is wonderful right down the line—children, grandchildren, and great-grandchildren. As they mature, I marvel at their individual accomplishments, and I appreciate fully their loving thoughts and actions. We have a family of widely diversified interests, valuable to the society and community of which it is a part and of supreme value, credit, and pleasure to Violet during her life, and to me. Each marriage of children and grandchildren has added immeasurably to our happiness.

Throughout all these years, our lives have been enriched by true and lasting friends. In times of prosperity and health our friends have brought us supreme happiness, and in times of depression, ill health, and bereavement, heart-warming comfort.

I want to express my appreciation to Laura for her love and affection throughout all of these years, and for her helpful suggestions in the preparation of this book.

I want to thank William for his constructive suggestions on the manuscript for this volume, and I want to express my appreciation to John for his help in "editing" many of my writings. While he was in Stanford University and majoring in English, I sent him for correction my six-month series of real estate articles for the San Diego *Union*. His revisions must have been good, since in the entire series the editors changd only one word and that one was not a correction in English.

I want particularly to express my sincere appreciation to Miss Margaret L. Wilmington, Assistant Secretary of our Cotton Mortgage Company, for her thorough and painstaking editing of this volume. Her assistance has been invaluable at all times and most encouraging.

OSCAR W. COTTON

Preface

AFTER READING about one-third through the manuscript for this book, a very close and dear member of my family wrote me: "You seem to be patting yourself on the back." Again, she thought parts of it "too frivolous" and also "too verbose."

She may be right, but such was not my intention. With all my opportunities, if I had been smart or clever my accomplishments could easily have been many, many times greater. Nobody knows this better than I.

I am, by nature, frivolous and verbose—but who wants to read all of any biography? My daughter Jane read every word and enjoyed it, but, primarily, *The Good Old Days* was written for men.

To any member of a Chamber of Commerce interested in the promotion of his community, the chapter "Lifting a City by Its Bootstraps" should be most stimulating.

For any group wanting to stage an Exposition in their town, the rather lengthy advertisement, the too-long speech on "Criticism," and much of the other detail in our "Second Exposition" might prove invaluable.

My series of articles on real estate promotion contains information that, to an active realtor, will be of material interest and value. One realtor, a stranger to me, from Los Angeles, told me he had made more than 150 deals by the use of one of the articles in this series.

Some of my golfing friends (both men and women) have been most enthusiastic over the articles and letters on "That Wonderful Game Called 'Golf.' " One reader of my manuscript (a woman) wrote: "Your slanderous golf battle is a riot."

Others have enjoyed most the stories of my early life in California, from Los Angeles with its population of 50,000 to the mining camps in the Sierra Nevadas.

When you come to a page that to you is not interesting—skip it. You won't hurt my feelings!

O. W. C.

Contents

THE GOOD OLD DAYS

CHAPTER I

Fun Is Where You Find It

I SPENT three months in San Francisco in the "Good Old Days" when life was free and easy; where a bar was a necessary adjunct to every corner grocery, and where there were from two to four "corner groceries" at almost every intersection. But I cannot truthfully say that San Francisco gave me any particular thrills. I was on a strictly milk diet, from which I did not deviate once during those entire three months. In May, 1882, when I was three months old, my family decided to move to Los Angeles. I came without protest.

Twelve years later, Mother, my sister Laura, and I returned to San Francisco for a considerable time. That was in the "Gay Nineties" and I did have fun. We three, Mother, Laura, and I, had been barnstorming the small towns from Los Angeles; Laura and I doing vaudeville acts, songs, fancy dances, swinging Indian clubs and dumbbells, giving readings and dialogues, all in different costumes. All of it was probably a poor excuse for entertainment, but being children (Laura was four years old and I was eight when we started in show business), the audiences and the press were generous, so we got by somehow, and Laura and I had a grand time.

During the "Gay Nineties" in San Francisco, among other frivolities, men's lodges were the thing. On Market Street, not far from where we lived, the "Odd Fellows"—I.O.O.F.—had built a huge building with many rooms or halls for their separate lodge meetings.

Around eight o'clock, about the time they were getting down to business, I would rap on the door of one of the lodge rooms and pass the word to the chairman that we would liven up their meeting by a thirty-minute program of songs and dances. Quite often it worked, whereupon I would hurry home and the three of us would bustle over to the particular lodge where I had made the date, lugging our Chinese bamboo baskets containing our bright costumes, change into them in the anteroom, and put on the show. The "Tyler" or some other club member would pass the hat, and we would return to our apartment with a pocketful of nickels, dimes, and quarters, and we had eats for another day.

Mother was the musician, playing the piano accompaniments for all our songs, and the Scotch tunes to which we danced the Highland Fling, the Sword Dance, the Shantrews, the Sailor's Hornpipe, a Chinese song and dance, and many others.

This I.O.O.F. building was a bonanza. Some evenings I would get two engagements in one evening in the different lodge rooms. Of course, we kids enjoyed it; all that applause, and sometimes money, would be thrown at us.

I loathed study of any kind and, not having been sent to school when I was seven, I was embarrassed to go into the second or third grade at twelve, when I could not even do first-grade work. On the stage, we were "professionals," or thought we were, which built up our egos no end.

Looking back on some of the happenings, I now realize in some ways Mother had good salesmanship and the nerve it takes to put over your sale.

When Laura was about seven, she played the Duke of York in *Richard III* at the Grand Opera House in Los Angeles with the then great Shakespearian actor, Frederick Warde. A year or so later, when Frederick Warde and Louis James were again in Los Angeles, Mother took Laura and me to pay a call on Frederick Warde at his hotel. He was most cordial and pleasant. He let us do a couple of dialogues for him, and then gave us the following letter, which Mother used profusely in all our advertising literature so long as we could claim the title, "Cotton Children."

Little Laura and Oscar Cotton are delightful in the extreme as entertainers. They have a wonderful amount of natural ability, and their work is singularly free from the mechanical methods of most child performers. They are bright and clever, without precocity, hence the charm of their performance.
Wishing them the greatest success, I am,

Faithfully yours,
FREDERICK WARDE

Life in San Francisco, even in the "Gay Nineties," was not all fun. I got a job as office boy in a stationery store on Mission Street. 7 A.M. to 7 P.M., six full days per week, for two dollars a week. That was one of my most depressing experiences. Even at twelve years of age, I realized that it was costing me more to eat than I was earning, and that I had better look for a better job. Finally, I got up the courage to quit. The proprietor said he was sorry, because he was intending to give me a raise. I have often wished that I had asked him how much the raise was to have been!

From San Francisco, we made barnstorming trips into the surrounding towns whenever Mother had an inspiration. Going to Stockton from San Francisco was great fun. It took all night to make the one-hundred-mile trip. We went by stern paddle-wheel steamer up the San Joaquin River. From time to time, the boat would shove its nose into the soggy bank and load and unload freight, then back out and head on upstream. Long tables were set in the main cabin for dinner, which seemed like a banquet to us, and after dinner, when the tables were cleared away, the chairs would be set up at one end of the room, and at the other they would roll out an old piano, and we would give a show.

It must have been in 1894 that we gave our show to help build attendance for a series of Farmers' Alliance meetings in Stockton and a number of the surrounding towns. We stayed for some time with some grand folks by the name of Merrill on a ranch nine miles from Stockton.

Mr. Merrill, or "Pop" Merrill, as he was known, was supposed to be running a grain ranch, but he was a great shot with a shotgun. One day he had a big Blue Rock or clay pigeon shoot right at the ranch. I operated one of the Blue Rock traps—exciting, with shooting right over my head!

There were two young Merrills—Frank, a young man (or so I thought, since he was sixteen!), and Nettie, a young lady just my age. After meals, it was Nettie's and my job to wash the dishes for ten people. I had learned to wash dishes when I was seven, standing on a soapbox in the kitchen, when Mother served her "Sunday Fish Dinners" at Redondo Beach. I had never thought of washing dishes as being fun, but at Merrill's it was tops! Fun is where you find it!

In Stockton, Mother worked up a theatrical company. She got out posters reading "The Celebrated Cotton Company," and advertised ten people in the company. One of the company owned a three-seat stagecoach and two good horses. I don't recall how we counted ten. Besides Mother, there was Laura and myself, and my older sister Florence had joined the company and played the piano. We had a young man violinist, and there were two little ten-year-old dwarf twins. Then there was the man who owned and drove the stage, and an advance agent. Possibly Number Ten was the wife of the owner of the stage.

This was a real adventure for us kids. The first day, we drove from Stockton to Oakdale, then up into and through the Mother Lode country, where money was supposed to flow like water (but did not); through Sonora, Columbia, Angel's Camp, Fiddletown, Jimtown, and a dozen other rough and ready mining camps.

In addition to doing my acts on the stage, it was my job to sit at the table at the entrance door and take in the money. I was twelve years old. When the customers came in singles and pairs, I got along fairly well, but when they came in bunches, I would get nervous trying to figure how much to charge twenty-five cents for grownups and fifteen cents for children.

Before going to the theater, or more accurately speaking, the hall, I would dress with one or two costumes under my street clothes. When it was time for the show to start, Laura would give two or three numbers. By that time, the audience would have all arrived, and I would go backstage, peel off my street clothes, and join Laura and the others for the next act. I cannot remember what happened to this "Celebrated Cotton Company." I do recall that the violinist did not last long, because Mother thought he drank too much—quite likely he thought he did not get enough pay!

We made two or three tours through this Mother Lode country, sometimes with only us three—Mother, Laura, and me, and an advance man. In that case, I handled all the financial transactions, settled for the rent of the halls, paid the hotel bills, et cetera, but the job in which I took the most pride was roping our trunk. I learned to do that pretty slick, and it gave me a grown-up feeling that was very pleasant.

One incident neither Laura nor I will ever forget:

The hall in this camp was half a block or so from the hotel and was reached by an old board walk. At eight o'clock we had an audience of not more than twenty, and we all felt pretty blue. I was at my table at the entrance, when suddenly, like a blast of thunder, we heard men running down the old plank walk toward the hall. I sat, rigid, wondering what was going to happen, when the front door burst open and thirty or forty miners in boots and overalls came stomping in, paid their money (fifty cents each), and took their seats. We started the show in a hurry and with enthusiasm!

The next day, we learned that this crowd had been in the barroom at the hotel, shaking dice to determine whether or not they would go to the show—we won!

In one town, our agent had arranged that we were to pay the owner of the hall 25 percent of our gross take, but when he saw that he had only a twelve-year-old boy to deal with, he said he could not take a percentage but must have a flat rent. I don't recall the amount, but there was nothing to do but agree to pay. Half an hour later, the house began to fill up and he came around and said that he had reconsidered and would take a percentage. I said, "No, sir, we pay a flat rent." And we did.

From the time I was six years old, Father was almost a total invalid. He could walk around, dress himself, and use several fingers on his right hand and one finger on his left hand. But Mother had to be the provider, and, since she had had no formal education or business training whatsoever, as I look back I marvel we did not starve.

Before we left our home in Pico Heights, Los Angeles, to make this northern tour, Father taught me how to figure percentages, so that I could settle with the owners of the theaters, halls, or barns, in which we gave our shows. I could not for the life of me understand why multiplying the total evening's receipts by 25, or 40, with a little dot in front of the last two digits, would give the answer we wanted, but it always did, so I boldly put it down on paper that way, just as though I knew exactly what I was doing. I don't remember anyone's ever questioning or disagreeing, so I came to the conclusion that there were some things in life that were just not made to be understood.

We missed out on one party that nearly broke my heart, and I expect the same was true of Mother and Laura, too. I think it was at Lompoc, on our way north. Somebody thought they would have some fun and help drum up a crowd for the show, so they met the train with a two-seated surrey, all decorated with big bunches of cotton, to advertise the "Celebrated Cotton Children." The sad part of it was that we knew nothing of this scheme and came in on a later train! We missed that beautiful ride all over town! You can imagine my disappointment, since I still think of it with regret!

Our long stage rides through the Mother Lode country stand out in my memory. Climbing the mountains, the roads would wind zigzag up the steep grades through the pine forests, and the drivers would have to walk the horses. Laura and I would hike on ahead of the stage and hunt for pine nuts. I can shut my eyes now and smell the wonderful mountain air and the pine fragrance. Those were some of the "Good Old Days."

I remember once coming down a zigzag road for what seemed like hours and then, all of a sudden, to my utter amazement, we got to the bottom and there, lo and behold! was a beautiful, wide, deep river and a barge to ferry us across! The water was as clear as crystal, and it seemed to me it was one of the most beautiful sights I had ever beheld. I still think so.

Sometimes in the cold weather, we would pick up two or three bricks or flat rocks and heat them in the fireplace at the hotel, then shove them into a gunny-sack and put them on the floor in the stagecoach, and take turns keeping our feet warm. One day the bricks got too hot, and after we were well under way the sack started to burn. The driver stopped the stage and grabbed the sack to throw it out, but the hot bricks remained on the floor. I do not remember what happened next, but I do remember there was considerable consternation among the other passengers, and much criticism!

CHAPTER II

I Learn to Read

BACK IN San Francisco after one of our trips, the Great Emporium Building, located on Market Street and extending through to Mission, was nearing completion. This building was to be leased out to different types of stores, which gave the Emporium the appearance of a mammoth (for those days) department store.

I had a friend two years or so my senior who worked for a piano store which was to occupy one of the spaces, and which needed a cash boy. For efficiency and economy, the cashiering was all done in the basement. The cash boy's job was to sit on a stool on a raised platform between two stores and put the money and sales slips into the "bullets" and send them down the air chute, returning the change to the proper salesman when it came back. I applied for the job, and got it. However, the next-door neighbor to the music store was to be a Chinese store, so I still had to go to Chinatown for an interview with the manager of the Chinese store.

The first thing the manager of the Chinese store asked was, "Can you tell good money from counterfeit?"

"Certainly," I replied.

He then took me to a back room and showed me a table about three by four feet, with a border of silver dollars around all four sides. Each coin was held in place by a heavy nail driven through its center. He asked me to tell him which dollars were good. As I walked slowly around the table, pretending to examine each dollar closely, the thought came to me that nobody would be foolish enough to drive a nail through a good dollar, so when I finished my inspection I said, "They are all bad."

"All right," he said, "you catchum job."

That is how I happened to help open the Great Emporium, in San Francisco.

I think my compensation was about four dollars per week, but it was a pleasant environment, looking down on a well-kept Chinese store on one side and a piano store on the other, with pleasant people in both stores, and I felt important, handling all their money.

The stores opened about 8:00 A.M., but customers were few and far between until 10:00 A.M., or so. About the time the Emporium opened, a notorious murder was committed in the bell tower of a San Francisco church. A young man was accused of the crime, and, with nothing better to do for two hours every morning, I would read the thrilling newspaper story of this great (and my first) murder trial. Generally, the articles were about a full column long, and it would take me just about my two hours to complete the article. It is not much of an exaggeration to say that that is where I learned to read.

In the "Gay Nineties," I believe every street in San Francisco was paved with heavy, oblong cobblestones. There were ruts where the stones had settled or been worn by use, and in some streets deep grooves had been worn from long use of heavy trucks. Street traffic consisted mainly of cable cars, electric cars, a few horse cars on Market Street, and trucks by the thousands. These trucks were drawn by heavy draft horses, moving at a fast walk or a slow, jogging trot. The clatter of their steel shoes and the roar of the steel truck tires could be heard for blocks.

The streetcar tracks were the exact width of the wheels on the trucks. The rails had wide flanges, and, when no streetcar was close, the truck driver would swing his horses over until the wheels of his truck would drop into the flanges of the rails. Instantly, the hideous noise of the wheels on the cobblestones would cease, and all you could hear would be the clatter of the hoofs, until a streetcar came up from the rear and demanded the right-of-way.

Boys of my age got about any place they wanted to go by jumping on the back of a truck. If the truck driver objected, I never saw any trace of it. I used to walk two blocks or so to Market Street, hop a truck, and ride in style to the Emporium Building.

One morning, at about 1:00 A.M., Mother awakened us kids and told us to get up quickly and dress. As I opened my eyes I thought the city was on fire. Giant flames were leaping uncontrolled into the air, and sparks soared skyward by the million. As we watched, we could see the fire was still several blocks away, but, in spite of the efforts of the Fire Department, it kept getting hotter and hotter. It was weird, sitting around in those old bedrooms and wondering if we were going to have to flee for our lives, and, if so, where we would all go at that hour. About 4:00 A.M., the Fire Department got the fires under control and we went back to bed, but with our clothes on, just to be sure.

Eleven years later, I came again to San Francisco, and saw this entire district where we had lived in ashes, from the great earthquake and fire of 1906.

I don't remember just why I quit my job in the Emporium. Possibly we were going back on the road. We never stayed "put" very long. I asked for, and was given, the following letter of recommendation from the music store:

136 Ellis St.,
San Francisco, Calif.
June 12, 1896

This is to certify that Oscar W. Cotton, 923 Jessie Street, San Francisco, was in our employment as cash boy at the Emporium Parratt Bldg., Market St., from the opening of the same to the above date and that he acquitted himself during that time to our entire satisfaction.

G. E. HEINE & Co.,
P. L. Beman, Mgr.

I probably did not ask the proprietor of the Chinese store for a letter of recommendation.

One day, to my surprise, I saw an Egelson Shirt Store on Market Street. I went in and told the boss I had distributed bills for their store in Los Angeles. He gave me a job folding and distributing handbills for his store. I think I worked myself out of a job here. When there were no more bills to fold, I sat down.

"Don't sit down," said the boss, "it wears the stools out. Take a duster; go behind the counter; keep busy."

I could not see any point in standing back of a counter with a feather duster, dusting boxes that had just been dusted. So that job did not last long.

The year was 1896. William McKinley and William Jennings Bryan were running for the Presidency. Both Republicans and Democrats were outdoing each other campaigning. It was a wonderful show. Torchlight processions on the big nights, a mile or more long, with four men abreast, coal-oil wick lanterns over their shoulders, marching the dark streets, weaving in and out through the city like great serpents, with bands playing and banners flying. At the street intersections, railroad ties were stacked ten feet high, saturated with coal oil, and lit to make huge bonfires. It was all mighty thrilling for a kid of fourteen.

Following up a "hot tip" I went to the headquarters of one of the political parties. I am mortified to say so, but I think it was the Democratic headquarters! I told them I was an expert at passing out circulars—which, incidentally, was true. I could always beat all the other boys at both folding and distribution. They gave me a job at three dollars per day! Oh boy!

On Election Day, I was hired by the San Francisco *Examiner* to go to four polling places and, as the voters came out of the polls, to ask each one how he had voted. You will notice that I refer to a voter as "he." This was long before any woman was permitted to vote! This report was to give the *Examiner* a forecast on how the vote was coming. I got three dollars for that job. I was sorry when the election was over.

When I did not have a job, I used to take a fishing line and a gunny sack and go down to the waterfront and fish for crabs. They were small, but they tasted good. In two hours, I would catch as many as I could carry. These crabs were fighters. The object of their fight seemed to be to deprive each other of their claw-legs; however, the loss of a leg or two was not serious, for I would frequently catch a crab with one full-sized claw and a tiny little one on the other side, just starting to grow out.

In one place we lived, there was a basement with a dirt floor, and I decided to raise squabs and rabbits. I built nests for the pigeons above-ground, and sank boxes underground, with a piece of stovepipe for an entrance, for the rabbits. I had one rabbit, but needed one more. I was told of a store in Oakland where I could buy rabbits for fifty cents, so I walked a mile and a half to the Five-Cent Ferry, and then another mile and a half to the store. When I got there, I found they had only one rabbit to choose from, so I said to the man, "Which is it, male or female?"

He said, "Which do you want?"

He sold it to me, but my rabbit venture was not a success.

One spring, we worked our way north from San Francisco to Eugene, Oregon, where we spent a large part of the summer with distant cousins of Father's. It was a beautiful summer, and Eugene was warm and lush with flowers, crystal streams of mountain water with wild blackberry bushes with delicious berries all along their banks, beautiful forests, and many China pheasants. I learned to swim in the millrace a short distance from Eugene.

An event of consequence to me occurred on our third return trip to San Francisco. My half-brother, Albertus Cotton, dropped in on us and stayed for a short while. That was wonderful. Bert was twenty-three, and he had just graduated with top honors with the graduating class of '96, from the College of Physicians and Surgeons, of Baltimore. Wet got along fine, and it was surely wonderful having a brother. One day he took me to a store and bought me a dandy suit of clothes. I wore that suit for everything until I outgrew it.

We must have lived in and around San Francisco for two years—possibly more. For a time, we lived in Oakland. Father and Florence came to live with us there. That must have been in the summer, because all of my recollections of Oakland are of beautiful, sunny days.

I used to walk to Lake Merritt from our rooming house on Twelfth

Street, close to town. One morning as I was starting out with a boy friend, Mother called us back, and told me she needed some money. I took out my purse and gave her what she needed, to the amazement of my friend, who asked, "Do you carry the money for the family?" I had never thought about it before, but since he asked the question, it did make me feel rather important.

We were in Oakland on the Fourth of July in 1895. I shot off small firecrackers, one by one, until it ceased to be fun. That night we went to Lake Merritt for some very special night fireworks, sent off over the lake from barges. Toward the end of the celebration, one of the barges caught fire and, before the fire could be extinguished, a man fell into the water and was drowned.

While in Oakland, Laura and I learned to ride bicycles. There was a bicycle store under the rooming house where we lived, and when "show business" was reasonably good, Laura and I would each rent a bicycle for an hour or two and ride around the suburbs of Oakland.

It was in Carpenteria that we picked up the twin dwarfs, Maude and Claude. They were ten years old. They were not identical twins; Claude was the larger. Standing, Maude's chin came level with an ordinary dining table. She weighed thirty pounds. Before starting our Chinese song and dance, I would carry out a bamboo basket hamper and set it in the middle of the stage. Claude, Laura, and I would start the number, and, at the appointed time, Maude, who was in the hamper, would raise the top and step out, clad in a bright Chinese costume, complete with cap and pigtail. That always made a hit.

I remember a year or so before we went to San Francisco—I must have been about eleven years old—we (Mother, Laura, and I) were giving a show at San Pedro. It was a warm, summer evening. The main entrance door was directly opposite the center of the stage. When it came my turn to do a monologue, I looked out the door and saw a house on fire about two blocks away. I went on with my recitation, but I wondered whether or not I should stop and tell the audience about the fire to save any possible stampede. I decided against it, and went on with my story, but before I had finished, some muttonhead outside yelled "FIRE!" and within three minutes the hall was empty! Within half an hour, half of those who had gone came back, so we completed the show, but it was rather flat after the interruption.

We learned our Scotch dances from a young man in Los Angeles whose name was Robert Burns. He had performed before royalty in England, and had a breastful of medals. I believe we really learned the prize Scotch steps from him, and he also taught us the Scotch Reel and the Reel of Tellock, which Laura and I danced with two boys, Dody and

Walter Cline. I think I was about ten years old, Laura seven, Dody nine, and Walter about seven. We four, all in smart little Scotch kilts, did these dances to a couple of bagpipes at the old Grand Opera House at First or Second and Main streets, in Los Angeles, and we made a great hit.

Dody's and Walter's father was a deputy sheriff in Los Angeles, and their mother was matron of the Los Angeles County Jail. Laura and I used to consider it great fun to go and stay for a few days at a time in the jail with the Clines. Quite a homey place to raise kids! While there, we had the run of the jail, including the kitchen, where the Chinese cook (an inmate) introduced us to the brown sugar barrel. We enjoyed being admitted and let out of the front door at will—a privilege not extended to all the other "guests."   •

We four kids went to Ventura with Mother and Mrs. Cline, to give a part of a show at some special club festivities. At lunch, we were seated at a big table and were served small steaks. Dody was working up a sweat trying to cut his steak when he finally blurted out with youthful emphasis, "Gee, Mom! This steak is tougher than we get at the jail."

Since we were in the midst of strangers, you can imagine what Mom's face looked like!

Laura and I also took some private dancing lessons from a Mr. Henry F. Cramer, who conducted the leading dancing school in Los Angeles for many years. We learned a supposedly graceful little dance termed "the Emerald Dance," which we did together, clad in pale green cheesecloth dresses to our knees. Laura was blond, with long, wavy hair. I wore a wig of long, dark curls. Laura had nice-looking legs for a girl of seven, but my legs were like pipestems, so Mother padded my black stockings with three or four hearts.

About this time, a book was written about a girl named Trilby, who was made to do a dance without shoes or stockings! So we changed the name of our "Emerald" dance to the "Trilby," and danced it right on stage in front of people, with no shoes on and with our legs absolutely nude almost to the knees! Shocking!

(Those were the days when all ladies, young and old, wore bathing suits with long sleeves, and skirts well below the knees, and shoes with cotton stockings—never silk.) I have no doubt our "Trilby" advertisements had some value on the "gate," but I felt more comfortable in stockings and hearts.

In one town, the hall was not much more than a barn with a floor and a stage at one end. We were told there were hornets' nests under the stage floor. We did not take this information seriously, until a hornet stung Laura on the leg, and I found one buzzing in my wig. After that show, Mother told us she had never seen us so light on our feet in our dancing.

We were in Fresno when I was eleven, and gave a number of shows. The December 5, 1893, issue of the Fresno *Expositor* gave us this write-up:

THE COTTON CHILDREN
They Meet With Success Wherever They Go

Yesterday's Madera *Mercury* says "A large audience greeted the Cotton Children at the Athletic Hall on last Saturday night. The little ones who were present at the show enjoyed themselves immensely. The show was a children's show and as such was a creditable one."

These are the same children who so pleasantly entertained a large audience in Kutner Hall, in this City, last Friday evening, and made friends of all who heard them. The little girl, especially, wins the praise of all who hear her, and she it is whom Fredrick Warde, the well-known actor, has pronounced one of the most talented children for her age he has ever listened to.

These children have been in this County several weeks giving entertainments. and everywhere they go they draw full houses and please everyone with the excellence of their performance. They took an active part on the programmes of the State Farmers' Alliance when in session in this city some weeks ago. The Grubb Brothers assist in the entertainments by furnishing music.

We stayed for a time at the ranch of some mighty fine folks by the name of Bowen. One of the older brothers, Will Bowen, a young man in his early twenties, played the harmonica. He had two friends, the Grubbs brothers, who played the guitar and the banjo. All three of these young men were itching to try out their charms in show business. The Grubbs boys taught Laura and me to play chords on the guitar; then Mother and the three young men made up a company, and we traveled south through the San Joaquin Valley, playing all the little towns where real shows never stopped.

Will Bowen was the advance agent. He would double back in time for the show when he could make it. For the opening number, we five would line up across the stage with our instruments—Will, with his harmonica, which he took very seriously, the Grubbs brothers with banjo and guitar, and Laura and I filling in on guitars. We made quite a lot of noise, and possibly some music. I would not be sure about that. Then the Grubbs boys, who were probably in their early twenties, would do a black-face act or two, mixed with Laura's and my numbers.

I believe this venture was a success financially; at least, so far as I can recall, we paid our hotel bills all the way to Los Angeles, where the company broke up.

CHAPTER III

Southern California

WHEN MY FAMILY first brought me to Los Angeles from San Francisco, my father was in the business of searching abstracts and locating prospective settlers on government land in the vicinity of Los Angeles. In his searching of the Records, he discovered a fifty-acre parcel of good land between Los Angeles and Pasadena that had been overlooked, so he filed on it at a cost of $1.25 per acre. Later, he proved up and built a fine house on it, at a cost of $3,000, which was a fine house in those "Good Old Days."

My memories of this ranch are rather dim, because Father lost it on a mortgage foreclosure and we moved to town when I was five years old, but the recollections I do have are all interesting, and most of them are pleasant. Laura was born at this ranch, on October 25, 1885.

The following are a couple of the incidents that were not so pleasant:

Once I was playing on the seat of our spring wagon and fell off. My dress (boys of four or five wore dresses in those days) caught in the brake and, when they got to me, I was black in the face. Another time, I stood at the wrong end of one of Father's favorite sorrel colts. For some reason, the colt objected to my being there, and he planted a hind hoof in the center of my gizzard. Father picked me up for dead about six feet from the point of impact. I vaguely remember being embarrassed because my clothes were wet. Had the said hoof been a foot or so higher, you probably would not be wasting your time reading this. When all is said and done, Lady Luck plays a strong hand in this world! I have often wondered whether that kick in the pit of the stomach has had anything to do with my digestive troubles for the past seventy-six years, but Dr. Churchill doesn't think so.

As was the custom in those days, Father had two houses built; one was a large house, where we lived, and the other was a very small, one-room affair in the rear, with a long seat with two holes, one for grownups and one for me. I went in alone one day and decided I would try the larger seat, and plunk! I dropped down to my armpits, and there I stuck until help arrived in answer to my frightened screaming. Life has its ups and downs!

It was at this ranch that Mother unwittingly played a mean trick on Father. Mother did not think that clothes and appearance were the big things in life. She had a beautiful head of dark, wavy hair, which took considerable time each day to brush and do up in the fashion customary for women of that generation. One day, she took the scissors and cut it off as close to her head as she could. I do not remember this, but I can nevertheless imagine what she looked like to Father when he came home that night. I have heard her say that he did not speak to her for a week. She claimed he told her that he had married her because she had such beautiful hair!

I remember our last Christmas there. Father cut down a tree, and it was so tall the top bent over and lay against the ceiling.

From the ranch, we moved to a two-story house on Olive Street, in Los Angeles, between Eighth and Ninth streets. I remember hearing Mother remark on how nice it was to be so handy—she could get on a horse-car right in front of the house, and ride clear to town for a nickel—"town" being First and Spring streets. Next door to us, there lived a man by the name of Sullivan, and I used to wonder whether he was the great "John L." Sullivan, about whom I had heard so much. He was not.

Three or four times a week, a big, tall Mexican would come walking along the street with a large bucket on his head, calling, "Ice cream!" We could hear him when he was still a block away. Sometimes Mother would bring out a dish, and we would have a treat. At least, I would. As I recall the taste and texture, it was more like milk, vanilla, sugar, and ice than ice cream, but it tasted good to me then, and I'm glad I had some.

One day we had some very special callers—friends of Father's from Ohio—a Mr. and Mrs. J. H. Holmes and their daughter, Angie, about my age, and son, John, about Laura's age. Mr. Holmes had come to take the management of a new hotel in Pasadena, called the Hotel Green. Anyone who knew Mr. Holmes in later years in San Diego, when he must have weighed nearly three hundred pounds, will be surprised to know that my first glimpse of him on that day was of a young man, not very tall, with a dark mustache, and of slight build. This was the picture as they came up to the front gate.

Our next home was at the corner of Figueroa and Jefferson streets, and it was here that I nearly blew my eyes out. One day while Mother was downtown, I discovered a horn of gunpowder in the basement, and I conceived the brilliant idea of pouring a teaspoonful on a large sheet of newspaper, lighting the paper, and seeing it go "PUFF!" My next older sister, Florence, told me I should not do it, so after three or four "PUFFS!"

I decided to quit, but before quitting, of course, I would set off just one more!!!

In order to have a good one for the finish, I tore a piece of paper about two inches wide by a foot or so long, and heaped gunpowder on it to within about two inches from the small end, where I was to light it. This was going to be a dandy! And it was. I lit it, and it went "PUFF!!!" all right, while my face was probably within a foot or so of the powder. The next thing I can remember, I was running, screaming, around the house, with my sister after me.

Florence was only about five years older than me, but she did about the smartest thing a kid could think of; she took a piece of cloth the size of my face, cut holes for my nose, mouth, and eyes, smeared it thick with vaseline and covered my face, which was, of course, completely blistered. I do not know how long the cloth and vaseline stayed on, but I do know that after a while I was in such agony that either my sister or I decided we should go to Mrs. Fisher, a neighbor. However, Mrs. Fisher had a six-year-old daughter, and I could not stand to have this young lady see me in that condition, so I insisted that Florence take off the cloth and vaseline and wash my face.

By the time Mother got to Fisher's the doctor had been there and gone. I looked more like an Egyptian mummy than ever before, or since. Fortunately, my eyes blinked before the gunpowder flashed, so while my eyelids were blistered, my eyes were not hurt. As has often happened during my life, Lady Luck was with me.

I had my sixth Christmas in this house. It wasn't much, but it was a thrill just to know it was Christmas. Also, it was here that Father finally gave up, and told Mother she would have to take over. His crippled condition, rheumatism, and lung trouble were so bad one wondered how he lived.

From there, we moved to a smaller house a mile or so away, surrounded by a Chinese vegetable garden, and, a few months later, we moved to Redondo Beach, where we located on a triangular lot where the main street of Redondo, facing the ocean, intersected with the next street, to the rear. We were now but a short distance from the ocean and a fine new bathhouse.

In those "Good Old Days" before Planning Commissions were thought of, everyone did as he pleased with any property he owned or occupied, so Mother had a sign made: SUNDAY FISH DINNERS. The dinners must have been good, because during the rest of the summer she packed the dining room with patrons.

That was where I learned to wash dishes, unfortunately, because I have been doing it ever since! My advice to young men and boys: "Never learn to wash dishes. If you have ever washed so much as one dish, you are sunk."

When school opened, I started to school with the other kids in the first grade. I always went barefoot, and one day I kicked a board and ran a nail under the toenail of my left big toe. It did not bleed, and the next day I forgot all about it, but the wound did not forget. Ten days later, or whatever length of time it takes for a dirty nail to get in its dirty work, the teacher sent me home crying with pain in my toe.

I was put to bed, and, as I heard Mother tell many times afterward, sometime during the afternoon I began to scream. Rushing in, she found me rigid, with set jaws and staring eyes. She ran to the drugstore, which fortunately was next door to our house, and the druggist ran over with a bottle of chloroform and put me out. I became limp; he took out his pocket knife and lanced the toe and, I suppose, cauterized the wound. The next day, Dr. Boal came down from Los Angeles, and pronounced the job O.K., so that time I guess I owed my life to a druggist.

The doctor who helped to bring sister Laura to live with us when I was about four years old, and who attended us in our various ailments, was Dr. J. Mills Boal. He was a religious man, of the old school, and I believe he was an excellent physician for those days. He had a big, powerful voice that made you forget you were in a quiet sickroom when he was present. Since there was no train back to Los Angeles until morning, Dr. Boal stayed with us overnight, and it was a night I shall never forget. He spent the evening telling us kids Bible stories, his big voice deep and sincere. There was one small lamp in our tented room.

While I was convalescing, I amused myself building a figure-four trap, which I set up about twenty-five feet from the rear steps. I put some scraps from the kitchen under the trap and attached a string to the figure four, and, when the seagulls would go underneath for the dainty morsels of garbage, I would pull the string and catch a seagull, or two, or three. Then I would raise the trap, turn them loose, and start over.

One day I caught a beauty. It had a purple neck, and it must have been a young male. I thought it would be fun to pet it, and possibly to keep it, but the seagull had other ideas. I got it out of the trap and while I held it gently in my hands, it reached around and took just one bite with its long, sharp beak. He peeled about three inches of skin, in a V-shape, off my right wrist. It left a scar for many years. Without further argument, I let my pet seagull go.

At the beach a block away, there was a young sea lion that was everybody's pet. We called him Dick. If he were in the ocean two hundred feet from shore, I would start calling, "Here, Dick! Here, Dick!" and he would raise his head to see where the voice came from, and then come in on a straight line. He was so friendly that if, on a Sunday afternoon, a lady sitting on the beach should call him, he would come and crawl right up in her lap, and if she petted him, he would lie down and go to sleep. Sometimes, a lady who did not know better would call him, and he would come leaping right out of the surf and into her lap. Not so good!

When the summer ended and the demand for Sunday Fish Dinners ceased, we moved, tent house and all, back over the hill a mile or so farther from the ocean. My fondest recollections of that sojourn are of learning to smoke cornsilk cigarettes, and of roaming freely through a large watermelon patch. The watermelon patch covered ten acres or so.

My companions included some older boys, two of whom were sons of the owner, so no matter what those two boys did, the rest of us followed suit without question. The favorite stunt of one of these boys was to select a fine-looking melon and say, "I have never tasted that watermelon in my life. It looks good." Whereupon, he would lift it up and drop it. If it was ripe, it would break open, and we would all divide the heart. Then he would go in search of another. It seemed rather extravagant to me, and I wondered what his dad would say if he knew, but it was fun. The melons we sampled were generally delicious. The summer days were warm and sunny, and we ate until we could not swallow any more.

Our tent houses (tent sides and roof and wood floors) were built adjoining each other on a slightly sloping lot. The floor of the last tent toward the rear was probably three feet above the ground. One day a few of us kids got a five-gallon coal-oil can and stood it near the back entrance, where steps should have been, and started jumping from the doorway over the can. Each time, we would push the can a little farther from the tent. Finally, I got the can too far away, and when I jumped my right leg scraped the edge of the can and I lost about two inches of flesh nearly to the shinbone.

This is not a good place to lose skin. Mother would bandage my leg, and then I would start to run and play and the bandage would slip down my spindly leg and pull the scab with it. I do not know how long it finally took to heal that wound, but I do know that I still have a two-inch scar for "permanent identification."

One Saturday, the U.S. gunboat *Charleston* came to Redondo to be there over the weekend. I suspect it was because the new steam train made Redondo the most accessible seashore out of Los Angeles at that time. It was estimated that five thousand people came to Redondo on Sunday, to see this beautiful white gunboat, with a gun so big a boy could almost crawl inside (that was the story, but vastly exaggerated), and a search-light such as we had never seen before, which played in our faces and over the hills and the town at night.

As a convenience to passengers, so that they would not have to walk too far, the trains used to stop and discharge their passengers on a road that led directly from the pier over the hill to our home. On the Monday morning following this big weekend, Father took me fishing. We walked over the hills, carrying our poles and tackle. When we got to the place where our road crossed the railroad track, Father, who had unusually keen eyesight, stopped, stooped over, and picked up something bright out of the dust. I asked what it was, but got an evasive answer. Later, I found out from Mother. It was a five-dollar gold piece. Did Father spend it fool-ishly? Certainly not. He ran an ad in our Redondo Beach newspaper:

Found small sum of money. Owner may have same by paying for this ad.

After three days, when no owner appeared, Father gave the money to Mother. To Father, right was right and wrong was wrong. The fact that thousands of picnickers had passed both ways over that spot the day before did not change his conviction that a sincere effort should be made to locate the owner.

I believe that Monday morning in 1889 was the day I caught my first fish. We fished from the end, or near the end, of the old Redondo Beach Pier, and the fishing on the whole was fairly good. Sometimes a school of porpoises would chase a school of large mackerel, and, when they happened to head for the end of this pier, the mackerel, from ten to twelve inches long, would bite like mad for from five to twenty minutes, in which time many fishermen would fill their baskets.

My first fish was a rock cod, about seven inches long. When he took my hook, I began to scream, "Papa, I got a fish! I got a fish!"

"Well," said Father, just as calm and collected as though this were an everyday occurrence, "pull him in."

Later, I was to catch my quota, but I shall never forget that first little rock cod.

Another day, we took Laura fishing. When we got home, she rushed to Mother. "Mama, I caught six mackerel, and one of them was a smelt!"

Our third and last move in Redondo was to Pebble Beach, about a half-mile or more north from the pier. Here, at high tide, the waves would sometimes wash clear up around the house. One morning soon after we located there, I got out early and caught several good-sized cor-vina, or "surf fish" as we called them. I cleaned them and Mother fried them for breakfast—yum, yum!

One of my favorite fish is sculpin, and I used to catch them when we lived here, often bringing home a half-dozen from one morning's catch. They are delicious—one of the best of all salt-water fish to eat—but they live a long time out of water, in fact, for several hours. They are covered with vicious, poisonous thorns. When one jabs a finger, you are in trouble for several days. I caught them by dropping my hooks and sinker on the sand close to the piling of the wharf. I suppose they were there to get bugs from the barnacles on the piles.

When the big mackerel were running, Mother would get a butter keg and salt them down. One layer of rock salt, and a layer of fresh mackerel, split down the back. They made pretty good fodder all winter.

I earned my first money at Redondo. Some of the women of the town were giving a fair of some sort and were serving ice cream. Nobody seemed to be interested in washing the dishes, so they put me on a soapbox and I went to work. According to Mother's story and my recollections, I kept three women busy drying, while I washed. I have no idea how long it lasted, but must have been several hours. When they gave me a half-dollar, I thought I was well paid. Mother did not think much of it, but that was not Mother's first half-dollar.

Before long, we moved to a rooming house at First and Broadway, in Los Angeles, across the street from the Los Angeles *Times* Building, and here I made a feeble beginning at earning money, selling the Los Angeles *Times,* and blacking boots. The *Times* sold for five cents and it only cost two and a half cents. Shines brought a nickel, and it was practically all profit. My paper route was from First Street to Third Street, on Broadway, and Spring Street. I never went south of Third Street because that was too far out of town—no customers. The newspaper sales came first, then after about 9:00 A.M., I would look for shine business. In the afternoon, we would go down to the *Express* office and repeat the performance, selling the *Evening Express.*

One night, Mother went to some lodge social and saw three youngsters who were about the same ages as Laura and me, who did some songs and dances. They were called the "Baldwin Children." That gave Mother an idea. Soon we started our dancing lessons.

While we lived at First and Broadway, I again started to school. This time, it was in the second grade. I was eight years old. It did not last long. Father had been a schoolteacher, and he thought we should go to school, but Mother thought it was better for our health to be out in the fresh air, rather than in a stuffy schoolroom. Mother won! But where she got it into her head that a schoolroom was stuffy and that a few hours a day in school would be bad for our health I do not know. The four or five schoolrooms

I remember were more like barns—big, airy, and only about half-filled with kids.

From First and Broadway, we made two uneventful moves, and one which was eventful. The latter was when we moved to an old barn of a house on Fedora Street, in Pico Heights, in Los Angeles. Almost directly back of where we lived was a fifty-foot vacant lot which was for sale for $200, and Mother bought it for $10 down.

By this time, we three, Laura, Mother, and I, with Mother at the piano, were doing our dances, songs, dialogues, and recitations, humorous and otherwise, at various lodges around town and in the small towns around Los Angeles.

In those "Good Old Days" in downtown Los Angeles, Mexicans and, later, Americans, would be on the street corners at night with steaming tanks of hot tamales. When our shows were in town, we would stop at a tamale stand and buy three hot tamales. They would be wrapped in heavy newspaper, and we kids would take turns carrying them on our laps to keep our hands and knees warm on the half-hour streetcar ride home. Then we would have a feast before going to bed. They were really mighty good eating. The price was five cents each, the same as the streetcar fare. Sometimes, the tamales would have an olive in one end—that was an extra special! Those were the Mexican tamales.

When the Americans started to make them, they made what they called the "Texas tamale," which was larger and made in three sections, each wrapped in a separate corn husk, and then the three made into one large tamale. I believe the price was the same, but we always preferred the Mexican tamale.

Even though Father had contracted tuberculosis during his short service with the Union Army in the Civil War, his conscience told him it was not right for him to apply for a pension. While we were living at Redondo Beach, a law was passed that all applications for pensions by former soldiers who were to apply for back pay must be in by a certain date. Father's back pay would have been around $8,000, but his conscience would not let him bend and apply.

I do not know what ultimately straightened out his thinking, but I do remember that after it was too late to obtain back pay, he finally did apply for a pension, and was awarded $25 a month.

CHAPTER IV

How I Happened to Be Born

POSSIBLY this would be a good time to go into a little family history.

My grandmother on my mother's side was Rochelle Rebecca Simmons. She was born at 26 Shaftesbury Terrace, Vauxhall Road, near Buckingham Palace, London, England. About all I know of her ancestry is that Mother said Grandmother was once taken into a big bank in London by her father, and introduced to a "cousin" by the name of Rothschild. (This "cousin" must have been the careless type. He did not leave Grandmother the Bank of England nor any part of it.) We have one picture of Grandma, as we called her, apparently taken in her late teens, and she must have been about as pretty a little Jewess as one would want to see. As told to our family by Mother, Grandma came to America to live with her sister, Elizabeth Read, in Ogden, Utah.

My maternal grandfather was Oscar Mortimer Jackson, and he was born in either Mississippi or Tennessee. Grandmother and he were married in St. Louis, Missouri, on January 19, 1856, and they were living in Houston, Texas, when my mother was born in 1860. Mother was christened Alice Victoria, presumably for Queen Victoria, of England.

Grandmother must have been popular as a young woman, because ultimately she had three husbands. Alva DeVere, Mother's half-brother, was by her second husband. As we knew her, Grandma had a most unfortunate disposition. She had a sharp tongue and spent so many of her waking hours reminding the family of their many faults that no one could live with her for very long. I suppose her first two husbands left her, and I know that both her children ran away from home—Mother at the age of thirteen. I think her third husband only lasted a few hectic months, or possibly weeks. I remember his coming to our house once when I was about six years old. Apparently, Grandmother had shown him the door and he was pleading with Mother to do something about it. I never saw or heard of him again. I believe his name was Smalley, so her full name would have been Rochelle Rebecca Simmons Jackson DeVere Smalley. DeVere was the name she always went by in later life.

Grandma used to teach painting, and also taught piano, although her hands were so small (she was a little mite) that she could not span an octave. As I remember her, she was very deaf, but as long as she was well, she managed to take care of herself with a little assistance from the family. She lived alone, grumbling that nobody cared for her, but as happy as one with that kind of disposition could be.

When Mother was thirteen, they lived in Sacramento and, having nothing better to do, Mother used to go to a blacksmith's shop and watch the smith shoe horses. In between times, she told him her troubles and told him she was going to run away from home. The blacksmith's name was A. W. Boggs. He came from Ewington, Ohio.

He told her that he was going to South America, and that if she was determined to run away from home, she could go with him and they would be married at sea. He told her she should talk it over with her aunt, who at that time also lived in Sacramento, and she did. The aunt tried to dissuade her, but to no avail. They took the ship, and after they were three miles out to sea from San Francisco the captain married them.

Mother, however, did not feel properly married. She had been reared an Episcopalian, and she thought that the only proper marriage was one performed by an Episcopal clergyman, so at the first port at which they stopped, which was in Mexico, they went ashore to be married again. The only church in the town was a Roman Catholic church, and the priest married them. Mother was still not satisfied, so when they got to a bigger port where there was an Episcopal church, they were married the third time, and the rector assured Mother that she was at last fully and properly married.

Their destination was a little town located very near the equator in Colombia, South America. Boggs built a sawmill to be operated by steam, and the first time he blew the steam whistle, it nearly scared the populace out of its wits. They lived in the home of a very fine Spanish family who were educated and who spoke, so Mother was told, pure Castilian Spanish.

Since no one spoke English, Mother had to learn Spanish, and learn it she did. She told me the people with whom they stayed, whose name was Gomas, owed a store which adjoined their residence. She said she spent most of her time at first pointing to this and to that and asking how to say it. She said she thought she learned all the Spanish she really needed in the first month or so. Back in the United States, she did not get along too well in talking to Mexican people, but when occasionally she would meet a family who, as she put it, spoke "true Castilian," she would beam with happiness and carry on conversations at a great rate.

Mother and Mr. Boggs lived there seven years. The seven years Mother spent in South America were, I believe, happy years. I never thought to inquire, and I never heard otherwise, so I assume they lived those seven years as a part of the Gomas household. Mr. Boggs must have done fairly well, as Mother never mentioned being short of money.

My two half-sisters were born there, Shellie in 1875, and Florence in 1877. Shellie was christened Alice Victoria after Mother, and Del Carmin for her godmother, the old Lady Gomas. Florence was named Florence Elizabeth.

Those were the days of "ladies" and "servants." I have often heard Mother say that if the old Lady Gomas, as she rather reverently referred to her hostess and companion, should drop her handkerchief, it would not even occur to her to pick it up—she would call a servant.

There was no mixing of races there. The Spanish people were very light, and the servants were all natives with very dark skin and with kinky hair. When a native girl was old enough to "hire out," she would be employed by an employer, given a place to sleep, fed, and I suppose clothed. Also, she would be given a very small monthly or annual wage, but—and here was the rub—if she broke a dish or damaged an article of furniture, the value of that article was withheld from her pay and, under the law of the land, she could not leave the employment of the household until she could pay up. Since the dishes and bric-a-brac broken or damage invariably added up to more than the small wages, most all house servants were virtually slaves.

As an instance of how servants were treated in that country in those days, Mother told a story involving the old gentleman Gomas, who was a man with a hot temper. One morning the cook set before him a platter of fried eggs and bacon. He looked down and, to his horror, there was a long, kinky black hair on the food. He stood up in wrath, picked up the platter, and threw it, eggs, bacon, and hot grease, at the cook's head. Today, with the shortage of cooks in San Diego, such a performance would not be deemed tactful.

One day, on one of those rare occasions when a boat came up the river, the captain sent a letter to Mother. It was from a sister of Mr. Boggs, telling of his death. He had gone to the States some months before to get larger equipment for his sawmill, and this was the first word Mother had had from him. She was always of the opinion that he had had tuberculosis. His sister advised her to sell everything and come back to the United States, and, acting on a quick decision, as Mother generally did, she sold or gave away all her possessions and came back on that boat, just like that.

For the most part, Mother was of an unusually happy disposition, but I believe those seven years in Colombia were "Good Old Days" for Mother. I doubt if she was ever happier.

When she got back to Sacramento, little, scolding Grandma was shocked and mortified that her grandchildren acted and talked "like Mexicans." They had lived near the equator and had worn little in the way of clothes, and I can imagine Grandmother's reaction. Mother said the only change in climate in the town where she had lived in Colombia was that it sometimes got hotter. Her blood had become so thin she could hardly ever be comfortable back in the United States.

Grandma issued an edict that those two "little Mexican brats" should not be allowed to say a word until they learned to speak English, and that is exactly what happened. In a very short while, they had forgotten all their Spanish, and they never learned it again.

I have often thought what a shame that was, since, with their start and with Mother to talk to, they could just as well have learned both languages. How fine that would have been for them and for Mother, and also for Laura and me. As it was, I learned only a few valuable, though rather youthful, phrases, such as: *Caramba!* and *Deme un beso, mi dulce corazon.*

Grandma also insisted that Shellie be named for her, so they prefixed Rochelle Rebecca to her name. When Mother married my father, the surname Cotton was added. Shellie eventually married Dell H. Harthorn, so her name was finally Rochelle Rebecca Alice Victoria Del Carmin Boggs Cotton Harthorn—Shell for short.

CHAPTER V

Father's Family

MY FATHER came from a long line of fathers. He had a father, his father had a father, and his grandfather had a father. I suppose we could go on and on.

In 1896, while Father was still able to punch the typewriter with his second finger on his right hand and to press the shift key with the thumb or forefinger of his left hand, he typed out the following "Family History" for Laura and me:

FAMILY HISTORY—COTTONS

WILLIAM COTTON—of Shenandoah Valley, Virginia, in Revolutionary times. My great-grandfather.

WILLIAM HARRISON COTTON—my grandfather. Lived in Nelson County, Kentucky. Died about 1825 at about seventy years of age. He was twice a member of the Kentucky Legislature.

WILLIAM W. COTTON—my father. Was born on a farm 9 miles from Bardstown, Nelson County, Kentucky, on the Louisville and Bardstown Turnpike road in August of 1806. Died in Los Angeles, California, December, 1879. He married Nancy Irwin, of Cain Springs, Bullet County, Kentucky, in 1829.

NANCY IRWIN—my mother. Born at Cain Springs, Bullet County, Kentucky, 1813. Died in Los Angeles, California, December 1, 1879.

MARION IRWIN COTTON—was born in Kentucky, 1830. Died at Sedalia, Missouri, December, 1868, of hemorrhage of the lungs.

MELVILLE M. COTTON—born in 1832 in Kentucky. Died at Nineveh, Indiana, December, 1859, of typhoid fever.

MARY E. COTTON—born in Bartholomew County, Indiana, 1834. Died the same year.

HENRY S. COTTON—born in Bartholomew County, Indiana, April 29, 1836. Died at Sedalia, Missouri, 1871, of hemorrhage of the lungs. [This brother married Sarah E. Smith, whose pet name was Sed and after whom Sedalia, Missouri, was named, the city being built on lands belonging to her and her sister.]

JOSEPH F. COTTON—born at Nineveh, Indiana, December 28, 1838. Died at South Mason, Illinois, December, 1860, of typhoid fever.

JOHN HANCE COTTON—born at Nineveh, Indiana, March 18, 1840. [Died
at Los Angeles, California, July 22, 1902, of tuberculosis of the lungs.]

MARY E. COTTON (2nd)—born December, 1841, at Nineveh, Indiana.
Died January, 1870, at Sedalia, Missouri, from pneumonia and lungs.

JEMINA L. COTTON—born at Nineveh, Indiana, August, 1843. Died
at South Mason, Illinois, October 1860, of typhoid fever and active
bowel hemorrhage.

WILLIAM W. COTTON, JR.—born at Nineveh, Indiana, December 18,
1845. Died at Stockton, California, June 17, 1887, of tuberculosis,
or quick consumption.

THOMAS H. B. COTTON—born at Nineveh, Indiana, December, 1843.
Now lives at Los Angeles, California, 1896. [I have copied Father's
dates but apparently he must have made a misprint, as I believe
Thomas was the youngest brother and therefore must have been born
later than the date indicated.]

MARGARET ELLEN COTTON (Rice)—born at Nineveh, Indiana, June
15, 1850. [Died April 11, 1934, at Alhambra, California.]

My mother's father, JOSEPH IRWIN, was born near Derry Beg, Newton,
Limit of Adda, North Ireland, of Scotch parents who were Scotch
Presbyterians, driven out of Scotland in the religious persecutions of
that time.

NOTE: My grandfather, Joseph Irwin, left Ireland at the age of sixteen years, came to America, and finally settled on Government land,
600 acres, in Bullet County, Kentucky, known as Cain Springs, where
he raised a family of fourteen children, all by one wife.

Father was twenty years older than Mother. He had been married
once before, and had one son by that marriage, my half-brother, Albertus
Cotton, who was about nine years my senior. When the family separated,
Bert went with his mother and grandparents to Ohio, and ultimately to
Baltimore, Maryland, where he became a highly respected orthopedic
surgeon.

It was my misfortune that our paths were so far apart, because, on the
few occasions I was with him, we had great times together. He was tall
and slim, like most of the Cottons, and far more studious than I. He took
after Father in that respect, while I must be more like my mother. Bert
passed away about 1950. Our son, John, was with him in Baltimore a few
days before he died.

As Father's condition grew worse and he was more and more con-
fined to his room or little short walks around the block, the family became
increasingly careful about washing his dishes and looking after him personally, with the thought in mind that we should be careful about con-

tracting the disease. As I have understood later (although we did not know it at that time), there are two types, or stages, of tuberculosis. During one stage of the disease, it is contagious; during the other, it is not. It must be that Father was in the non-contagious stage of the disease, for five other members of the family lived with him, and none of us became tubercular.

Nevertheless, I have always felt that because of Father's condition and the history of lung disorders in his family, it would be a natural tendency in either Laura or me to develop lung trouble, so I have always been scrupulously careful to try to avoid unnecessary exposure to the weather, to dampness or cold air. My care in this respect has certainly paid off, as even today, at the ripe age of eighty, I am still in possession (except possibly mentally) of most of my faculties. When I remember that Father was practically a total invalid from the time I was six years old until his death, when I was twenty and he was sixty-two, and then realize that today I am able to swing a golf club, drive my car, and generally lead a reasonably normal life, I consider myself most fortunate.

My Aunt Margaret Rice, Father's youngest sister, was a high type woman of great courage and "gray matter," who was admired and respected by all. Possibly twenty years after Father's death, our beloved Aunt Mag, as we called her, presented me with a little book for the family, and in the back she enclosed a synopsis of the family history, which I will copy verbatim:

BY MRS. MARGARET RICE

William W., son of William W. Cotton and Harrald Cotton, was born in Bullet County, Kentucky, August 31, 1804. In 1827, he married Nancy Ann Irwin, born in Nelson County, February 22, 1808. Their two first children, Marion Irwin and Melvilla Minerva, were born in Kentucky, and the family then moved to Bartholomew County, Indiana, near Columbus, where the parents were among the earliest converts to the Christian or Disciple Church, and were ardent and efficient workers in its growth.

The father taught school during the winter months and cleared and cultivated his farm in summer, while the mother spun and wove, cut and sewed and knitted the clothes, tended and reared the children.

Nine more boys and girls were given them: Henry Smith, Mary Elizabeth (who died at two years), Joseph Fassett, John Hance (your dear father), Mary Elizabeth, Jemina Louisa, William W., Thomas H. B., and Margaret Ellen.

No family was more respected in the community, and none more useful than your grandfather's, to the limit of their ability, in the development of the new country.

Father was most fastidious about his person and his clothing. Aunt Margaret, who also was a fastidious person, used to enjoy telling this family story on my father, which happened when he was ten and about the time Aunt Margaret was born:

According to the story, my grandmother, while cooking breakfast, handed Father a milk pail to take to Grandfather, who was out in the cow barn, milking. Father delivered the pail and started back to the house on the run. He tripped and fell flat on his face where the cows had recently been. He came to the kitchen door and stood, like a spread eagle, and, looking pitifully up at his mother, said, "Mother, I'm all 'amfubigated'!"

I note that there are some discrepancies, particularly as to dates, in Aunt Margaret's version or synopsis of the family's history and Father's. However, since Father's was written when he was in perfect mental condition, and knowing too how meticulous he was, I would be of the opinion that, where there is a discrepancy, his statement is correct.

This sister, Aunt Mag, was the only member of Father's family whom I ever remember seeing, and toward the latter part of her life she stayed at our house from time to time in San Diego. We got to love her very dearly. In her younger life, in Los Angeles, she took a great interest in the Ebel Club, the Women's Shakespeare Club, and other women's organizations, in all of which she was regarded most highly by all who knew her.

Her husband was George Rice, and they raised two fine sons, George and Hayes. Both of these cousins are now deceased. Hayes had one son, Paul, and one daughter, Irvine. Paul Hayes, who, I believe, lives in the San Francisco Bay region, I never happened to meet. I knew Irvine quite well as a delightful young lady. She died in her early twenties of tuberculosis. George had two sons, George Skidmore Rice, III, and David Webster Rice. Both are tops in every particular. They are now carrying on the old George Rice & Sons printing business in Los Angeles. That is not quite correct—it is really the new George Rice & Sons, as the original firm was reorganized some twenty years or more ago. The original George Rice Printing Company was started by our uncle, George Rice, Aunt Margaret's husband, in 1879.

CHAPTER VI

Father Studied for the Ministry

FATHER was given a grammar-school and a high-school education, which was considerable in those days, and then studied for the ministry. But as the time approached for him to take the final step, he found he could not believe all that he found in the Bible, which he had practically memorized from cover to cover. With Father, there was no halfway place to stop. It was all or nothing. Right was right, and wrong was wrong, and what he could not believe he could not preach. So in place of the ministry, he taught school.

I do not know when it came about, but as long as I knew him Father was a confirmed spiritualist, and with his disposition of believing all or nothing he was absolutely convinced that spiritualism was "it." He told fantastic tales of having gone to spiritualist meetings before marrying my mother. After the lights were out, the "spirits" would come through the medium, of course, and move the table all around the room and do the most extraordinary things.

One night, he was told to put his left hand behind a curtain in an empty corner of the room, and when he did so he could feel something touching his hand, and then a little "tinkle, tinkle," like a miniature hammer pounding on metal, and when he was told to withdraw his hand there was a gold ring on his second finger. It fitted perfectly, and he wore it for years. Finally, it disappeared.

There was no question as to Father's belief in all this. He was as sure of the spirit world as he was that we were all here in the present flesh and blood. He was the most gullible man I ever knew. I often have heard Mother tell of the time when he came home with some beautiful "Putana" tablespoons. She laughed at him, and said, "You mean 'pewter.'"

"No," said Father, "the man told me they were 'Putana.'"

An hour later, Mother was making some gravy in an iron frying pan. She stirred the gravy with one of the new spoons, then lifted the spoon to see if the gravy was thick enough, and more than half of the spoon had melted off in the gravy!

Father was a great reader. A few years before his death, he bought an Encyclopedia Britannica, thirty volumes. They were a great joy to him. He was an ardent Socialist, and he hated the Los Angeles *Times* because General Otis, the publisher, was an all-out Republican, but Father took the *Times* because it was by far our best newspaper!

When I was seventeen and working in a machine shop from 7:30 A.M. to 5:30 P.M., I would come into his room before or after dinner, and let him tell me the news. He had a good mind, and liked to talk, and I liked to listen. He was just six feet tall, and toward the last I doubt if he weighed ninety pounds, but, in spite of his terrible coughing and his crippled condition, he was almost always cheerful and hopeful that possibly he would get better.

I was in my teens when I appreciated my father the most. Sometimes we would take walks together, and when he stayed at the Soldiers' Home near Santa Monica I would ride over on my bicycle from our home in Pico Heights, to see him on a Sunday and to spend the day.

We gave a number of shows at this Soldiers' Home. At one performance when Father was staying there, Mother put on the printed program: "A Green Leaf Solo by John H. Cotton." Father would take a soft leaf from a tree or vine and, by holding it in a certain way against his lower lip, he could play any tune he knew. The notes were all clear, and always on key, and could be heard a half-block away. It was really very pleasing to hear. I tried many times to learn this trick, but I regret to say without success.

He used to have great fun with some of the old soldiers who were at the home, who had recently been converted and who felt it their pious duty to convert him. Father would let them read to him convincing passages from the Bible; then he would tell them to turn to a certain chapter, and while they read, he would quote (he had a wonderful memory) until he had them all mixed up.

When I was nineteen, I left our home in Pico Heights, Los Angeles, to go to seek my fortune in Bisbee, Arizona. The following summer, I returned home for two weeks. When I was leaving the second time, I remember so well his saying, "This is not so bad, son. Now that you have been home again, it will not seem that you are so far away." It was only then that I realized how hard it had been for him when I left the first time.

Before I returned again, he went to sleep, peacefully, one night. Mother told me he had been in great pain. Finally, she got him propped up with pillows to a half-sitting posture in bed, and he said, "There, Alice, the pain is all gone." A short time later, he stopped breathing.

CHAPTER VII

We Build a Home

I MUST HAVE been eleven years old when Mother made the first ten-dollar payment on the 50 by 150 foot lot on El Molino Street, in Pico Heights, Los Angeles. Soon after that, Dell H. Harthorn, who had married my oldest sister, Shellie, and I went to Redondo and started tearing down the old board and batten home at Pebble Beach.

The next day, a man whom Dell had engaged drove down from Pico Heights, and together we loaded the lumber on the wagon. The second night, we slept on mattresses on the open floor, and the next day, we loaded the floor, mattresses, and the gasoline stove on which Dell had cooked our meals, and the wagon departed. Dell and I returned by train.

As soon as the lumber arrived, we rebuilt the house into one room, 12 by 24 feet, and a lean-to kitchen about 6 by 12 feet. Looking back, I wonder how we all managed to live and eat and sleep in that size home, but we did, including Dell and Shellie, who, within a few weeks, presented Mother (then thirty-two years old) with her first grandson.

When I say "Dell and I" tore down the house at Pebble Beach and rebuilt it in Pico Heights, my part of the work must not be taken too seriously. However, I did try to help. I had fun, and I learned how to lay the shakes so that the roof would not leak, and by the time the job was finished I thought I was a carpenter.

We made one mistake in building this house. We made no provision to drain the water from underneath. In the long, wet winter that followed, I developed arthritis (rheumatism, we called it) in my hips so badly that Mother had to put a bath towel under me to turn me over in bed.

About that time, Mother received an invitation from our friend, Mr. J. H. Holmes, manager of the Hotel Green, in Pasadena, then one of the finest hotels in southern California, for Laura and me to come to Pasadena and stay overnight and give an entertainment for the hotel guests. Mother accepted the invitation, but decided to take only Laura, since I could not even get out of bed. Of course, I wanted to go the worst way.

"All right," said Mother, "if you can get into your clothes, I'll take you."

So I went to work exercising first my toes and fingers, then my wrists and ankles, then my elbows and knees, and, finally, my hips. Before it was time to leave, I was dressed and ready.

When we got to Pico Street, a long block and a half's walk in the rain, we found that because of the flooded streets the streetcars had stopped running. Mother hailed a man driving past in a single-seated, open buggy. She and Laura sat in the seat with him, and I stood back of the seat with my feet wide apart, on the springs, and he drove us the five miles to the Santa Fe Station.

I was getting better all the time. We took the train to Pasadena, and I went through all of my part of the program that night, including dancing the Sailor's Hornpipe and the Highland Fling. Laura and I had the time of our lives.

Mr. Holmes gave Mother the following letter:

Pasadena, California
February 16, 1894

Mrs. A. V. Cotton
DEAR MADAM:

I wish to express to you my sincere thanks for the splendid entertainment given by your children last night. I have heard expressions from a great many of the guests this morning as being well satisfied and more than pleased, and I would like voluntarily to recommend you to any hotel or society. We will be pleased to call upon you again in the near future for a repetition of the program.

Again thanking you and your little ones, I remain,

Respectfully,
J. H. HOLMES, *Manager,*
Hotel Green

After that experience, whenever I got a touch of "rheumatism," I started to walk and exercise until I got rid of it, and it always worked. I thought I had that malady licked until, forty-five years later, I developed a bad case of arthritis in my lower back from too many exercises to reduce my waistline and sitting by an open window in my office. For this, I had to stop all waist exercises, sleep on an electric pad, and wear a steel belt.

When Mother got the lot on El Molino Street paid for, she borrowed $225 from a Building and Loan Society and arranged with some carpenter friends to build us a four-room frame house on the front of the lot. This time, Mother decided to keep the house up off the ground, and she did, about three and half feet. They built three new rooms on the front of the lot and moved the old house up and fastened it to the rear for a combination kitchen and dining room. The lean-to made a bath and pantry. Here, we lived in fine style. When Mother, Laura, and I went traveling for a day or two, or for weeks or months, my second older sister, Florence, would stay home and take care of Father.

Once, when we were to be away for rather an extended time, we rented the house. Before leaving, I carefully nailed up all of our "valuables" in a rear closet. But when we came back, the house was in shambles, and our "valuables" were scattered all over the place. The tenants had moved out and had forgotten to pay the rent. Since that time, I have picked up a few pointers on how to manage rental properties.

CHAPTER VIII

Mother's Scrapbook

IN A WAY, Mother kept a scrapbook. I say, "in a way," because it had no beginning or end. Everything about it was helter-skelter, hit-and-miss. It is only about one-tenth what it should have been in size. In many cases, the most interesting events or newspaper write-ups are not dated, nor are the items pasted in, in order.

Father was methodical and meticulous; Mother was exactly the opposite. But as I look back and see how she managed to raise and support a family, I appreciate her far more than I ever did as a boy. As I browse through this old scrapbook, which Laura has taken care of all these years since Mother's death, I cannot see how she did it; how she kept us in food and clothing, paid the rent, and finally even built a home and got it all paid for! I can remember learning to dance, and giving entertainments and traveling over the state, but only as I look through this old scrapbook can I even begin to see how Mother accomplished what she did.

Originally, this scrapbook was an old leather-covered journal. She started using it as a date-book, to keep track of our engagements. Apparently, after the engagements were concluded, she would paste over the old memoranda the letters of recommendation from the heads of hotels or societies for which we had performed, along with newspaper articles, programs, et cetera.

On one page, I found pasted a large picture of the Hotel del Coronado. I believe it was made from a drawing, before the hotel was completed. Except for the name at the top, and under it, "E. S. Baback, Manager, Coronado Beach," one could almost mistake it for the two-blocks-long hotel at Banff Springs, in Canada.

On the back of this page, there is about a half-page of engagement dates which tell volumes. As in many other instances there is no mention of the year, but here is the list:

April 14 — People Party Hall
April 15 — Y.M.C.A.
April 17 — Moors Hall, E.L.A.[1]

---

[1] I do not recall what the "E.L.A." stood for.

April 19 — Pasadena—G.A.R.[2]
April 20 — Ventura—W.R.C.G.A.R.[3]
April 26 — Y.M.C.A.

May 5 — I.O.O.F., Spring Street, Los Angeles
May 12 — Olivet Church, Washington Street
May 26 — Harmony Hall

June 19 — Compton—Farmers' Alliance
June 21 — Ventura
June 24 — Monrovia
June 28 — Long Beach

The balance of this page is cut off and it is mutilated on the right-hand side, eliminating all but the dollar signs for the entries for the earnings per night.

On another page there is a list of eight leading hotels, from Redondo Beach to Riverside, to which she had written in two days, suggesting that the "Cotton Children" should come and entertain their guests. Mother must have been a born salesman, with determination and executive ability.

She had a small folder printed with a picture of Laura and me on the front cover in very pleasing, old-fashioned costumes. This picture was framed with headlines: "THE COTTON CHILDREN"—"DRAMATIC READINGS" — "HUMOROUS IMPERSONATIONS" — "EVERY-THING IN COSTUME"—and across the bottom, in black type: "LET-TER FROM FREDERICK WARDE" and then a copy of the letter. On the inside page was our "repertoire," and the third and fourth pages were devoted to press notices and letters from hotel managers and others. Apparently, this folder and Mother's letters did the trick, because we kept going and eating, and buying new costumes, from the time I was eight years old until I was fifteen.

The following is the "Repertoire" which appeared on the second page of the folder:

REPERTOIRE

DIALOGUES:
   Mrs. Brown's Mistake
   The Happy Little Wife
   The California Hayseeds
   The Brick Yard

---

[2] G.A.R. was for the "Grand Army of the Republic."

[3] W.R.C. was for "Woman's Relief Corps" (wives and possibly daughters of veterans).

Josiah Puzzles His Pa
Little William Henry Dimple FitzSimmons at the Dime Museum
When Ye Gang Awa, Jamie

FANCY DANCES:
Scotch National Highland Fling—genuine prize steps, taught by
  Bobbie Burns
Scotch Sword Dance—very difficult steps over the naked swords—in
  McDonald Tartans
Scotch Shantrews—most beautiful of all fancy Scotch dances—in
  Stewart Tartans
Chinese Comique and National Love Song—full costume
Sailor's Hornpipe
Erin's Favorite
Fairy Dewdrop
Emerald and Rose

READINGS AND RECITATIONS:
Tim, the Ragged Wharf Rat   The Elf Child
The Raggedy Man   The Man in the Moon
The Sale Extraordinary   Setting the Old Blue Hen
Smack in School   Muzzer's Bought a Baby
The Clown's Baby   Money Musk
Rock Me to Sleep, Mother   Our Folks
John Burns, of Gettysburg   Poor Little Joe
No Sect in Heaven   The Heart's Charity
    Three Songs of Life, from the "Songs of Seven"—Youth;
    Romance; and Old Age—Longing for Home

SHAKESPEARE:
Quarrel of Brutus and Cassius—in the Roman Togas
    (from *Julius Caesar*)
The Tent Scene
    (from *Richard III*)
Arthur and Hubert
    (from *King John*)

OTHER SPECIALTIES:
Indian Club Swinging
Blacksmith Dumbbell Chorus
Swiss Bell Ringing

A few of the letters and press notices Mother used in our advertising
leaflets follow:

REDONDO HOTEL

March 13, 1893

The entertainment given by the Cotton Children in the music hall at the Redondo Hotel, on Friday eve last, was appreciated in the highest degree, and, from present indications, I fear that we shall be compelled to call upon them for a repetition of their performance. Kindly advise me when you can come again.

Respectfully,

R. H. THOMPSON

MEMORIAL DAY, 1892—At Rosedale Cemetery, when the Decoration Services were over, Master Oscar Cotton stepped to the front and recited a very beautiful and touching address. He was followed by little Laura Cotton, who read a pathetic tribute to the soldier dead.

Los Angeles talent shows itself young. Little Laura Cotton as the Duke of York, at the Grand Opera House last night, fairly captivated the hearts of all present. Her imitation of Frederick Warde as crooked-backed Richard was wonderful. The little tot was captivating.—*Los Angeles Times*—March 4, 1892.

PEOPLE'S CHURCH—The special feature of the program was the performance of the Cotton Children, the popular Juvenile favorites.—*Los Angeles Times*—March 19, 1892.

CAMPBELL'S HALL—Last night the Cotton Children danced in their own inimitable style and were the recipients of much applause.—*Los Angeles Times*—December 5, 1891.

REDONDO—Little Laura Cotton captured the hearts of all present at the I.O.G.T. Hall last eve. Her recitation, "Tim, the Wharf-Rat," and the Highland Fling by herself and brother, were received with deafening applause.

BETHESDA CHURCH, LOS ANGELES—The Cotton Children, who have just returned to Los Angeles, captured the good will of the audience with their clever specialties. Their Chinese Dialogue and Dance was greatly enjoyed and loudly applauded.

The entertainment given at Malaga by the Cotton Children Friday night was a great success. Everyone expressed a wish that the entertainment might be repeated in the near future. The Scotch dances are especially fine, little Laura having won the prize when only four years old for the Highland Fling.—Malaga *News*

A large audience greeted the Cotton Children at Athletic Hall last night. All present enjoyed themselves immensely. The show was a very creditable one.—Madera *Mercury*

The entertainment given by the Cotton Children in Unger Opera House last night was well attended and gave universal satisfaction. The speaking and acting of the children is simple, inimitable, and the singing and dancing of little Laura was repeatedly applauded. Some of the costumes were artistic and pleasing to the eye, while others were ludicrous in the extreme. In the "Hay-Seed" play, both children wore faded overalls. Little Laura brought down the house by throwing back her baby shoulders and thrusting her tiny hands far into the depths of her overall pockets. The parts were well sustained throughout, and anybody who will go to see them will get a dollar and a half's worth of fun for fifty cents. —Selma *Irrigation*

The celebrated Cotton Children appeared the last two evenings at the Tabernacle and took immensely. Laura, a little Miss of seven years, shows surprising talent for one of her years, and some of her impersonations were presented in a manner so spirited and with such evident enjoyment of their humor by the young sprite as to be contagious, and she had the audience at her sweet mercy. Her brother, Oscar, is also great, and together they make a strong combination. They are well worth seeing and hearing.—Long Beach *Breaker*

The Cotton Children gave an excellent entertainment at the Christian Church yesterday eve; all were delighted. They are clever impersonators and elocutionists; they are excellent for so young artists. We can commend these youthful artists to people everywhere and they should meet with success—they deserve it.—Hanford *News*

The Cotton Children entertainment was worth double the price of admission, besides helping a worthy cause.—Tulare *Citizen* (Ladies' Auxiliary)

Occasionally, in one of the smaller towns after our performance the chairs would be moved to the walls, and the audience would have a dance. One night, before I had changed from a light green dress with fairly long sleeves and while I was still wearing the wig with the long, dark curls (which had once been Mother's hair), a young man came to the dressing room and asked Mother politely if he might dance with the young lady. Mother said, "Surely," and called to Laura. But the young man said, "No," that he meant "the older girl."

I felt a little foolish, but made no protest, and we danced a dance or two. I wondered what would happen if he found out with whom he was dancing. When we got back to the dressing room, Mother put her hand on top of my head and said, "It's time to get dressed, Oscar," and with that, she pulled off my wig. It seemed to me that that was a good time for me to beat it, so I ducked past Mother without looking up!

Mother's family was her life, and she devoted her life to the care of her family. After Laura was grown and "on her own," Mother went to Carmel, California, to live. There, as she had always done, she made many warm and lasting friends. I had a comfortable little home built for her on a 100 by 100 foot corner lot, where she raised flowers and gardened to her heart's content. She established the first flower nursery in Carmel. Her letterhead read:

Mrs. A. V. Cotton

MIL ARBOLES GARDENS

Specialties   Eleventh & Mission
Acacias
Native Ferns
Plants and Shrubs

Also, on a leaflet advertising the "School of Arts & Crafts—Carmel-by-the-Sea Summer Session, July through August, 1913," Mother is listed:

Mrs. A. V. Cotton—Teacher of Spanish.

6 Weeks Lessons: $5.00

Single Lessons: 50¢

Later, she filed on a piece of government land in the hills above Carmel, where she built another small home, and, as long as her health would permit, she divided her time between town and the mountain life, where quail and deer were her almost daily "guests."

Her last years were spent with Laura in San Francisco. After her death, Gertrude Price, a dear friend of the family for many years, expressed the sentiment of all who knew Mother, when she wrote me:

DEAR OSCAR:

I have just received your sad note. I phoned my mother about Mrs. Cotton a while ago, as she had been so anxious to know how she was. My mother feels heartbroken, for she was very fond of Mrs. Cotton.

We counted her among our real true friends. We knew her to be one of God's real gentle women with a heart of gold.

I can't understand why she should have to go so early. But I am oh so glad that she could pass out in a peaceful slumber instead of terrible pain.

I have been thinking of Laura and Florence all day. I wish that I knew how I could help them bear their sorrow.

Though I have not yet suffered at its hand I have always felt that death was the one fearful thing in life.

There is nothing I can say to you at such a time that will help, I know, except to tell you that I loved your mother and that her memory in my life is one of the sweetest and most uplifting I have.

To me, she was always the bubbling spring of energy and good cheer and kindliness, one who always sought the good in others, and shared her own happiness with all.

You, her children, were her life. And I know, from hundreds of things she has said, that your never-failing love and kindness and thought brought happiness and repayment to her in later years.

Please know, dear Oscar, that we mourn with you, for while you have lost the dearest possession of a son or daughter, we have lost the rarest, a friend.

With love to you all and heartfelt sympathy,

> Your friend,
> GERTY

On November 26, 1960, my brother-in-law, Dell H. Harthorn, nine years my senior and now a resident of Carmel, in answer to a letter from me seeking verification of dates, et cetera, wrote me as follows:

> Your mother was a wonderfully resourceful person, and a very loving and wonderful mother to us all. I especially loved her, and respected her advice and counsel. No sacrifice was too great for her to make if she saw the need. I attribute Shellie's and my long marriage success to your mother's advice and help in our early days, for we had a very rough road to travel the first few years. Times were hard and we were both but children. When I look back I wonder how we did manage.

Thanksgiving, 1960, Laura drove down from Berkeley to spend a week with the family. While she was here, I asked her to read the first part of this book to see how our memories jibed. Upon her return to Berkeley, she wrote me in part:

DEAR KID:

Your note awaited me on my return and I still have it on my dresser, because I, too, felt a joyous renewal of old-time ties in our happy visit.

It was a privilege to read your manuscript and I shall wait with impatience to see the rest of it. I am *so* glad that you are writing these things because your life was unusual in so many ways.

You and I have this in common: while we had no formal schooling, we did have parents who held the goal of knowledge and achievement and hard work ever before us. Also, our work gave us constant opportunities to see and experience a wide variety of things unknown to other children—such as going into mines; and being taken *all* through warships; and friendships with a wide variety of noted personalities of all ages; and learning to milk cows; and, *very* young, *teaching* others what we had been so fortunate as to learn from excellent teachers.

It was schooling of a different kind.

I wonder if you remember when, in Los Angeles, several times when a carriage with a driver and two horses would be sent to take us to give a program, Mother would say, "If you work hard and do things well, some day you will ride in your own carirage."

I have seldom entered my auto for forty years without hearing the echo of those words!

CHAPTER IX

Fun in Ontario

I WAS ALWAYS tall for my age, and skinny. At fifteen, I ceased to be "cute" in either short dresses or pants, so we quit the show business for the time being. When we came south again, we went to Ontario, California, I suppose because my sister, Shellie, and her husband, Dell, and their two sons, Laurence and Terrill, were living there. At first, Mother, Laura, and I stayed with them; later, Father and Florence came to be with us and we rented a little one and one-half story house on beautiful Euclid Avenue. Those were more of the "Good Old Days."

We made friends with some delightful folks by the name of Stone. I do not recall the parents' names, but the son, Oliver, and the daughter, Mary, were in their early twenties and they were wonderful company. During the spring of the year 1898, I worked on the Stones' fruit ranch, thinning peaches. That meant pulling off about 75 percent of all the fruit when it was very small and before the pits had formed, so that the fruit left on the tree would be larger. I remember that when I was getting instructions on how many little peaches to pull off, Ollie said, "If you pull off all you can find, you won't miss it far." He was nearly right. On a shoot three or four feet long, there might be a dozen little peaches, and we would take off all but three or four. I worked right along with the men, but of course I did not accomplish nearly as much. My wages were ten cents an hour (I believe the men got fifteen cents on hour) and I think we worked nine hours per day.

That is where I learned the value of a "cat nap." At noon, we would sit under a peach tree and eat our lunches, and then I would lie full length on the soft, warm, plowed ground, and sleep until time for the afternoon shift. All my life since then, and particularly of later years, I have found "cat naps" during the day, even if only for five or ten minutes, most refreshing. Starting to work again after a "cat nap" is like starting a new day.

When peach-thinning season was over, I used to go hunting cottontails and jack rabbits in the washes east of Ontario. I remember a time when about five of us, boys and girls, went in a one-horse wagon and we got quite a haul. About dusk, we started home. I was shooting at cans and rocks with an old revolver. Something got the matter with it, and the last shell would not go off. After several tries, I pointed it at my temple and started to call out to the other kids to watch me blow my brains out. Then I thought, "That would be a silly thing to do. Suppose it should go off?" I pointed the gun in the air, and pulled the trigger—and it did go off!

During this summer, I worked gathering apricots for drying. Note that I said "gathering" and not "picking." For drying, the fruit must be dead ripe, so the procedure was to go to a tree, pick up all the fruit that had fallen on the ground, and then spread a large canvas tarpaulin under the tree, climb up into the tree, and shake the limbs. It would literally rain ripe apricots, and boy! were they good to eat! Then we would gather up the fruit and put it in boxes and take it to the dryers, where mostly girls and women cut the fruit, removed the seeds, and placed in halves on trays, cup-side up, to be sulphured and dried in the hot sun.

In the late summer and fall, I tried picking oranges and working in the orange-packing house, but, except for "washing" oranges, which was accomplished by dumping a box of fruit into an old-fashioned washtub, and scrubbing the scales off with a scrub brush, I found work with oranges too heavy.

When I had a couple of free days, I would take my bike and ride to Los Angeles (about forty miles over old-fashioned dirt roads) and stay with friends. I once made the round trip in one day, but that was too much! Those long, carefree bicycle rides were wonderful. The air was warm and delicious, and the exercise was invigorating.

Returning one afternoon, I stopped to cool off in the shade of a beautiful eucalyptus grove. Looking back, I saw a man riding toward me, zigzagging across the road. As he approached, I could see he was literally covered with dust and dirt. When he was within about twenty feet, he twisted his handlebars too short and went sprawling. He got up, grinning, leaned his bicycle against his thigh, and said, "My wheel's drunk."

Once I visited Aunt Mag and family, and Uncle George said he would give me a job in his printing office. However, I had a feeling that he might be doing it because he thought he should do so, and therefore, when we finally returned to Los Angeles, I went to work in a machine shop. I do not know what Uncle George had had in mind for me to do, but he did say that he could not have me setting type, because he had discovered that I could not spell—I had once shown him my collection of birds' eggs and I had typed the names on a sheet of paper and then clipped and pasted them under each compartment.

Euclid Avenue, in Ontario, was a wide, straight street, seven miles long, extending through uplands to the foothills. The street was lined its entire length with six rows of beautiful trees. There was a streetcar line in the center between two rows of pepper trees, and on either side of the car line there was a smooth path for bicycles. Two mules pulled the streetcar to the top of the street—seven miles—then the motorman would have them turn the car around, and on the back was a platform where the mules could stand and ride back to town.

I never rode on the streetcar, but I used to ride my bike to the top of the hill, and then take off the chain to make it run smoother, and coast all the way back! Great sport! That was about as near to flying as was possible in those "Good Old Days."

Quite the popular thing to do in Ontario at that time was to have typhoid fever. Mother and Laura both came down with it at the same time and had it quite thoroughly. Florence and I had both had it when we were small, so we nursed and fed them, and looked after Father, and it all turned out "happily ever after," with no bad after effects insofar as I know.

One sport which I enjoyed in Ontario was shooting rabbits with a slingshot. I cannot remember when I did not have a slingshot, but, in Ontario, Dell made me a man-sized one out of a heavy tobacco-box slab, and I got some heavy rubber bands for it that would stretch my full arm's length. Like my mother before me, I used to hang around the blacksmith's shop. The blacksmith would let me pick up the chunks of iron cut off the ends of the horseshoes. These were about an inch long, with jagged edges, heavy and wicked, and they made splendid ammunition. Most of my shots, of course, went wild, but once in a while I would hit a cottontail in the head or in the middle, and when I did we would have rabbit for supper. Those little cottontails made good eating.

CHAPTER X

Growing Up

OUR NEXT MOVE was back to our home in Pico Heights, Los Angeles. I went to work in the shop of P. K. Woods—Deep Well Propeller Pumps. My job was oiler and handy boy for all the mechanics. The hours were from 7:30 A.M. to 5:30 P.M., and I rode my bicycle four miles to work and back, six days a week, for $4.50. I enjoyed it there. I liked the workmen. The head machinist got twenty dollars a week, but I must not have been much good. One day one of the workmen who was paid nine dollars a week told me he had a hunch that he or I was to be fired. His hunch was right. I was it.

I got on my bike and started looking for a job. It was summer, and fruits were ripening. A neighbor, a young lady about my own age who I thought was pretty nice, was working in a fruit drying and canning factory in Whittier, about twenty miles from our home. I rode out and paid a call, and might have gotten a job, but I decided forty miles per day plus a day's work would be too tiresome.

I finally landed a good job in a tin can factory, the Los Angeles Metal Works, later the American Can Company. My job was to take the bodies of the gallon cans which had been bunged up going through the header, and, with a small piece of scrap iron and an anvil, hammer out the edges so that they would go through again. My pay was ten cents a crate of about thirty-six cans.

This looked like an opportunity, and it was. I went to work with all the energy I had. My first weekly check was for about nine dollars, but before long I was making fifteen to eighteen dollars per week. One week, I got a check for $19.20, unfortunately, for it attracted too much attention. I was told it "did not look well on the books." So they changed the rate to seven cents per crate, but even at that rate I did pretty well.

Father was then at the Soldiers' Home near Santa Monica, and Mother and Laura were at Long Beach for the summer. I was living at home, alone. I cooked my breakfast there and put up my lunch. For dinner, I stopped at a little restaurant on lower Main Street, where they served a good meal for ten cents, with dessert five cents extra. All the money that I did not need for food, I put in a little round, tin box, in a big old redwood tool chest I had made.

When Mother and Laura came home, I brought out my little tin box and emptied it on the table—mostly twenty-dollar gold pieces. I do not recall how much it was, but it was enough to give the house two coats of paint, which made not only our family but all of the neighbors happy, for the house had never before been painted. One neighbor told me, "You have improved the whole street!"

Then Father got a raise in his pension to $75 a month, and $500 in back pay. The day his pension increase was due I went to the Soldiers' Home to bring him home. Together, we went to the office of the commandant, who personally handed Father the $500 check for his back pay. Father looked at it, said, "Thank you," and handed it to me. I looked at it, and put it in my pocket. To me, that was big business, by far the largest cash transaction in our family in my experience.

Mother got to planting and raising flowers in the yard; Father was at home where he wanted to be; my older sister Florence got a job in the Telephone Company, and Laura started taking lessons on the cornet. Those were "Good Old Days."

A little later, Laura was doing exceptionally well with the cornet, and I decided to learn to play the slide trombone, and I did. I played it like all get-out; practiced four hours a day, mostly out of doors, starting at 6:00 A.M.

About that time (I must have been eighteen) Mother decided that it was time for us "children" to get some schooling—whatever that was. She, herself, had never been in a schoolroom except to play the piano when we used a country schoolhouse for our show business. Some "nut" was conducting a private school evenings, upstairs in an old building downtown, on Broadway, where he would give you an education by the short method of learning: playing all kinds of games. He had a blank map of the United States, showing the states but without their names, and we would sit around a table and figure out what states we would have to go through to go from one point in the United States to another.

We did not get much education there, but we did meet Gertrude Redit, a very find young lady from England, about seven years my senior, who came to our house and stayed for nearly a year. During that year, she really taught both Laura and me considerable in English and in mathematics. I once figured that counting the tutoring we received from Miss Redit, plus the few short times I went to school, I did have the equivalent of possibly nine months of schooling, which was better than none, I can tell you.

Both Father and Mother spoke grammatically, so we picked up correct conversational English from them, but many is the time I have regretted all the years wasted when we might have been in school.

Miss Redit had a beautiful young friend, Eva B. Fowler, who was rehearsing with an elderly ex-Shakespearian actor who wanted to revive Shakespeare, and was training an amateur cast. His name was Samuel E. Wells. He was an actor of the old school.

The opening play was to be *Julius Caesar,* and it was to be put on at the Los Angeles Theatre. Laura and I joined the cast. As usual, I went all out for it. I memorized *Julius Caesar* from cover to cover, so that I could read any part without the book. The parts assigned to me to play were only bit parts: The "Leading Citizen," who led the mob scenes, and Trebonius.

As the rehearsing continued, jealousies among the cast crept in, and on the opening night one faction treated Mr. Wells to too many glasses of wine or something, presumably to wreck the show. There we were, the cast costumed and ready, and no stage manager to tell the stagehands how to set the stage, or when to raise or lower the curtain, and a paid audience on the other side of the footlights!

I took over and ran the show, and everybody, from top to bottom, including Wells, who played Cassius, took orders like gentlemen! By the second night, Wells was all right, but he let me continue to run the show. As I look back on the performance now, I am rather amazed that I got by with it, but at that time it seemed like the natural thing to do. For several years, I had been the head of our various little professional companies, so when this *Julius Caesar* cast needed a head, and I knew I was the only one left who could run it, I simply went ahead.

Rehearsals for *Julius Caesar* were conducted during the day on the stage of the old Hazard's Pavilion, at Fifth and Olive streets, where the Philharmonic Auditorium now stands. Among the requisites for a Shakespearian actor was that he must know how to fall, gracefully and naturally, when stabbed to death. The secret, of course, is to relax. So Laura and I practiced diligently at the Pavilion and at home in our front yard, to acquire the art of relaxing and falling to the floor naturally, yet without getting hurt. Sixty years later, I was to profit by these rehearsals in a manner I little anticipated at that time!

The newspapers were friendly and fair in their comments. The nearest thing to a compliment was: "Laura Cotton made quite a hit with her cornet solo and with her 'Roman Dance.'" In any event, we completed the performance as planned, and I made several good friends among the cast.

Following the *Julius Caesar* venture, I got in with another bunch of hopefuls, rehearsing a terrible melodrama called *Just Before Dawn*. This was to be a road show, and it was. We started out to play the "Kite." That was the trip around southern California advertised by the railroads at that time as "the Kite-Shaped Track." I think that all I need to tell about this experience is to quote from one of the press notices:

> The *Just Before Dawn* Company played San Bernardino night before last, Redlands last night. Riverside has yet to suffer.

Nevertheless, the head man of the *Just Before Dawn* company was an actor of considerable ability, and when we got back to Los Angeles, he went to work in stock in the Burbank Theatre on lower Main Street. He got me a job—small bit parts—and I spent some time at the old Burbank Theatre. This was good experience, because that was a good professional company with some very good actors and actresses. I was in one show with John Mason and his wife, Katherine Gray, and in another with Laura Nelson Hall. All of them were then, or later became, well-known stars on Broadway, in New York City.

I did not. The stage manager made me so nervous that I could not remember my lines. I was not afraid of the audience, but I could not see prosperity ahead for me, so finally I gave up my five dollars per week and quit.

After that, I joined the Stephens Fitzpatrick Company, a professional company which played all the small towns, showing *Ten Nights in a Barroom,* in which I played Mr. Romaine, the old man who comes in on the scene every ten years and comments on what has happened. We also played *East Lynne,* and several others. Laura, too, played small parts with this company. I worked as advance man, to travel ahead of the show and rent the halls, make hotel reservations and get publicity in the newspapers. I would then double back for the nights I was in the show.

When I ran out of cash (the most any of these folks got was their hotel bills and their railroad fares paid) I would quit the show and go back to work in the tin can factory. Quite a comedown, but more profitable. I think I was generally considered to be the most affluent member of the company!

In Mother's scrapbook, on page 187, I found the following:

(Oscar's first attempt at a write-up for the paper. Santa Monica.)

E A S T   L Y N N E
At the Auditorium This Evening

This play which was booked for Saturday last but which was postponed on account of the death of the President[1] promises to be the best of all the productions yet given in Santa Monica. The people of the Company are all exceptionally well fitted to the parts they play, which gives the performance a pleasing smoothness and naturalness which is so often lost in a performance not so well cast.

After a year of practicing four hours each day on my slide trombone and lessons from the best trombonist in Los Angeles, I decided I was just about where I had started, and I gave up music as a career. I did not ask anyone's advice on this. I was a grown man, or thought I was, and I made all my own decisions. As it happened, I was undoubtedly right. I would never have made a success in music.

Laura, on the other hand, was doing fine work on the cornet. She produced beautiful tones and had fine technique, and under an excellent teacher she was on her way. Ultimately, she became by far the best cornetist I have ever heard, anywhere. With her sweet tones, she made the cornet do things that simply thrilled her audiences. The cornet, and later the cello, and still later her voice, were a great source of pleasure to her, as well as to all who heard her, and she lived by her music for many years —but that came later.

---

[1] The death referred to was that of President William McKinley, on September 14, 1901.

CHAPTER XI

"Good Old Days" in Bisbee, Arizona

ONE DAY when I was nineteen, a letter came to me from Bisbee, Arizona, from a former friend in the *Julius Caesar* cast, one Havelock Morrow, a dignified "older man," possibly thirty years of age! Morrow was then a bookkeeper for the Bisbee Improvement Company, in Bisbee, Arizona, and he wrote offering me a job as office janitor and stableboy for seventy dollars a month. Wow!

Unknown to me, mother had asked him to keep an eye out for a job for me. I had sinus trouble very badly (catarrh, as we called it). My nose seemed good for two purposes only: as an ornament and to blow. I could not breathe through it. Mother thought that the dry climate of Bisbee might cure me. It did not improve my condition at all, as it turned out, but I would not have missed my year and a half in Bisbee.

Havelock lived with his brother, Harvey, in a small frame cottage several hundred steps above the town, and they took me in to "batch" with them. They were both good company, and Havelock and I would sometimes do some Shakespeare or other readings of an evening. He never had recovered from the show business bug.

My job in Bisbee proved interesting, and, as I mastered the technique of bedding down the horses and performing the less pleasing tasks for them, and how to mop the linoleum floor of the office and wash the plate-glass windows, I gradually assumed more advanced duties. The business of the company was furnishing ice and electricity and telephone service to the city of Bisbee. I finally became the bill collector, and collected practically all of the company's revenue. No one ever thought of mailing bills and checks in those days. Everything was cash.

There were two streets in Bisbee: Brewery Gulch and Tombstone Canyon, both former waterways, draining the large areas above. Tombstone Canyon was the main street, with the General Company Store, a bank, a number of restaurants, and many saloons. The only means of access to the residential districts was via one of these streets. The sidewalks were of wood, and built separately for each store. They were uneven, so the populace, whether afoot or in wagons, used the streets in dry weather.

In August, when the rains came, everyone got out of the streets and stayed out, while the muddy water, three feet deep, took over the entire street, bringing with it more cans and boxes than you would ever believe existed. At this time, there was no sanitation in Bisbee, no garbage or rubbish collections, of course. There were no gardens. Each house was perched on the side of a hill with a bird's-eye view over the tops of the neighboring houses. Very little fresh vegetables or fresh fruits ever got to Bisbee, so we all lived out of cans, and when a can was emptied it was thrown out the window. Period. Then, when the heavy rains came, you would hear those cans, by the tens of thousands, rattling down over those boulders and down to the main streets, and ultimately down to the wide canyon below. It was quite a thrill when seen and heard for the first time.

Water for all domestic purposes was delivered throughout most of the residential district by Mexicans leading a string of burros, each with two canvas bags of water, one on each side, for balance. I suppose each bag held about five gallons. The going rate was fifty cents per burro-load, so you may be sure we were careful how we used the water. I have no idea where the Mexicans got the water, but generally the residents of Bisbee were of two classes: those who had had typhoid fever, and those who were going to have it. The main business of the Bisbee hospitals, of which there were several, was typhoid fever cases.

The manager of the Bisbee Improvement Company decided to go into the business of selling distilled water, and I got the job of finding the customers. That was my first selling job. Besides my salary, which was then eighty dollars per month, I got twenty-five cents for each new customer. I soon had customers for all the distilled water I had time to deliver. That was good experience, and it gave me an opportunity to get acquainted with many of the "socialites" in Bisbee. There were many fine folks there.

I got acquainted with a young minister and his wife, who used to entertain a group of the younger set in their home. One night I came a little late to one of these house parties, and the hostess met me at the door with, "Oh, Mr. Cotton, I'm so glad you came! The party is dead! Come in and say something funny!"

For once in my life, I was utterly speechless. I could not think of anything to say, funny or otherwise. For years, that request has haunted me: "Please say something funny!"

Sometimes of a Sunday, Havelock and I went to bullfights in Naco, across the Mexican border below Bisbee. They made me sick at the stomach. I won't tell you why, because it would make you sick. One Sunday, everyone in the grandstand got a thrill: A bull caught a matador off guard, and tossed him bodily six feet over his head.

Before I had been in Bisbee many weeks, Harvey Morrow's wife came from Los Angeles to join him, and I had to be told I must find other quarters. I accepted this politely, but I was at a loss to understand why his wife was so fussy! At my home, and at Merrill's, in Stockton, and all the other homes I had been in, the more folks were around, the merrier. Some things in life were too deep for me.

I propositioned the boss for permission to put up a canvas screen in one corner of the stable. I bought myself a gasoline stove and fixed up a bed, and I was as snug as a bug in a rug. Of a Sunday, I would invite my friend Havelock out to lunch on fricassee of chicken, biscuits, and Boston Baked Beans.

My Boston Baked Beans made quite a hit. My mansion (the stable) was only a few hundred yards from the plant where we made the ice and distilled water, and generated the electricity. I would soak a pot of beans overnight, and in the morning, while getting breakfast, would boil them about twenty minutes with a small amount of soda, and then put them in a crock with a layer of salt pork, and then more beans, and salt pork. Over the top I would pour several tablespoons of New Orleans molasses, and then I would take the crock to the plant and put it in front of the boiler where the smoke and heat came through to the chimney. This was just about the right temperature to keep them simmering, and by dinner I had a dish fit for a king—if the king liked pork and beans. When I wanted to make an impression on a particular household, I would take them a crock of hot beans, about dinnertime.

One of the jobs I liked most was collecting bills in the outlying district, where I had to ride a horse over the hills and trails. I carried my bills and cash in a little black satchel, hung on a strap around my neck and under my left arm. One beautiful day, as I was riding at a gallop over a trail through the sagebrush, I looked back and discovered the catch on my satchel had sprung and the bag was wide open! That took all the joy out of the rest of that day. There had been several months' salary in that bag, and I was responsible for every penny. I had found that out to my sorrow only a few weeks before, when I had been short ten dollars, which I had had to make up. But this was my lucky day—my cash was all safe!

My first day as bill collector in town, I had a memorable experience. The Copper Queen Company had a big general store. A good stock supplied the needs of everybody, and all company employees could buy there on credit. So most of the other business houses on Tombstone Canyon were hash-houses, saloons, or gambling houses—usually a combination saloon and gambling house. On this first day of collecting bills, the first place I went into was one of the larger saloons with about four or five tables of roulette, craps, birdcage, and faro. I walked in, as big as life, about 10:00 A.M., and there was not a soul in sight. I stood looking around, and there were the tables all ready for customers, with $300 to $500 or $600 in silver dollars, all stacked neatly on each table—and not a soul in sight, I'm telling you! I suppose the bartender had stepped into the back room, and it was too early to man the tables, but it surely gave me a queer feeling. I contemplated the scene for a minute or two, and then decided that it was no place for me and I beat it.

With my new job and increased responsibilities, my pay climbed to ninety dollars. I moved from the stable and fixed up a bed in the back room of the office, but I had no place to cook, so I ate in restaurants. Out of my ninety dollars, I was banking seventy-five dollars per month.

Supposedly, people came to Bisbee to make a stake and get out, but I was told there were families who had been there for twenty years and were still financially where they were when they arrived. These were miners, working eight hours per day underground, like gophers. I let nothing interfere with my plan to save money; I did not know for what, but in those days the U.S. Government did not take care of people and there was no retirement pay for the aged. To me, Bisbee was a wonderful experience. It was unique, with its thousands of houses from the gulch a half-mile up the mountainside, with rarely a tree or shrub. The dry mountain air was often actually blue with fumes of burning sulphur from the smelters in the center of town, and every whiff would make you wheeze as though you had asthma. It was a thrilling place to see and to come to make your fortune, but to live there for twenty years and not even make a start . . . Horrible!

I had been in Bisbee about nine months when a telegram came from Mother telling of Father's death. Although I knew full well Father's condition, that telegram was a staggering blow. I had never before felt so alone.

That night, I drove Mr. S. W. French, the general manager of the Copper Queen Company, from his home on Knob Hill to a party at the home of George B. Ellisson, the manager of the Bisbee Improvement Company, about four miles, and home again after the party. Our transportation consisted of the one-horse truck I used for delivering distilled water. Mr. French was a very pleasant gentleman, whom I later got to know very well. His father had been ill and had recently recovered. When I told him of my father, he was most sympathetic and invited me to the party. I thanked him and declined, but the visit helped wonderfully to get me through that first night.

On Knob Hill, the Women's Club building was nearing completion, and I was invited to occupy a room there and act as caretaker, which I did throughout the remainder of my stay in Bisbee. At twenty, I had a sincere admiration for attractive women, and I enjoyed my role as the only male member of the Bisbee Women's Club. I did not attend any of the strictly women's meetings, but I was welcomed to all of the mixed parties and made many friends.

Sometimes at a dancing party, the men would come to my room for a "bull session," and would forget to go back to the party until the women came and routed them out. At the larger parties, Havelock Morrow and I would occasionally entertain, Havelock with more serious poems and I with comedy.

Now and then, on Sunday afternoons, I gave dancing lessons. Wherever you go, there are fine folks, if you are lucky enough to find them. The elite of Bisbee were the women of this Women's Club of Bisbee and their husbands.

About that time, Mr. M. A. Graham, who ran a livery stable in Bisbee, brought a bag full of ore samples from Mexico, which the assayer claimed would run $175,000 in gold to the ton. My friend, Havelock, who had graduated from bookkeeper of the Bisbee Improvement Company to a mining stock brokerage office, said he was going to mortgage his shirt and buy all he could. He said the stock could be bought for only part cash. I saw some of the ore samples; they had gold protruding from every crack and bulge. I thought it over for a day or two, and decided it must be good at $175,000 a ton. I had no idea how much stock was to be sold or anything about it, but I went to the bank and gave them my check for $500 and bought $1,250 worth, promising to pay the rest later, but there was a provision in the contract that, if I chose, could take only $500 worth.

Six or eight months later, after I had left Bisbee, Morrow wrote me that he could get me $1,000 for half of my stock, and I would own the other half clear. That seemed like a good idea to me, so I made the deal. A year or two later, while the company was going through reorganization, I sold my remaining stock for $250, netting $1,250 on my original investment.

That was my first, and one of my greatest, financial mistakes. Many years later, I learned from my friend, Lester R. Budrow, in San Diego, that had I kept the remainder of my original stock purchase, I would have had a fortune. It was a fabulously rich mine—the "El Tigre" of Sonora, Mexico. During its heyday, Budrow was its manager.

The Bisbee Improvement Company had two ice wagons, one for wholesale and one for retail. One day when the general manager was out of town for a week, the driver for the retail deliveries went on a drunk and turned up missing. I decided "the show must go on," as I had always been taught, so, without asking anyone's advice, I took over and became the iceman until the boss got back. That proved to be a most interesting and profitable experience, driving all over the steep, winding trails, delivering ice and making new friends.

One day, shortly after my iceman experience, I received a telephone call from one of my customers, who was also a member of the Women's Club, a Mrs. Folsom. Her husband was head of the big company store. She said a couple of very distant relatives were in Bisbee from San Diego. She was going to entertain them at dinner, and afterward with a game of High Five, and she needed a fifth man for the game. That is how I happened to come to San Diego!

I had been to San Diego when I was twelve. Mother, Laura, and I had stayed at the Coronado Hotel, where we were billed to give a "Concert by the Famous Cotton Children" at the Hotel del Coronado Theatre at 8:30 P.M. As usual, in the daytime, Laura and I went sight-seeing. We got lost, as you were supposed to do, in the Cypress Maze north of the hotel, and we had a ride on the double-deck electric car that operated for so many years from the hotel to the ferry site.

During the card party, I tried to pump the Folsom brothers about opportunities in San Diego, but, although they were real estate men, they would not talk about it. Early the following day, the younger of the two traveling Folsom brothers paid me a call at my desk in the office of the Bisbee Improvement Company; there he was not bashful, but opened up and told me all about San Diego and its real estate opportunities, and he sold me two 25-foot lots, overlooking Mission Bay at Pacific Beach, for forty dollars—twenty dollars each.

About that time, I was beginning to get restless. Although I was putting by seventy-five dollars a month out of my ninety-dollar salary, prosperity looked a long way in the future. Six months prior to that card party, I had decided to become a steam and electric engineer, and had purchased from the International Correspondence School a set of seven books that went with the course. I paid for the course and the books by selling several sets to other ambitious young men; a set of books on science to a man who ran a hash-house in a built-over wogan, and a set of history books to a minister. I worked nights on my course and finally mailed in the first lesson. When the papers came back corrected, I looked at them, then counted the pages in the book which I had completed (possibly five or six pages) and then looked at the beautiful set and thought how long it would take to finish, and then only get a job like our head engineer, at $125 a month. That was the end of my book-learning.

The two Folsoms needed assistance in the sale of these Pacific Beach lots, so I took a two weeks' vacation and went with them to Douglas, Arizona, to see if I dared to give up ninety dollars per month sure money for a commission job. I was just twenty-one years old. For me, this was no trivial matter. I was not spending much personally, but now since Father's death, I must be prepared to assist Mother, Laura, and Grandmother, if and when occasions required.

I will never forget my first day trying to sell Pacific Beach lots. The afternoon and evening of the day we got to Douglas was devoted to my education on what to tell the prospects, how to fill out the forms in the purchase of lots, et cetera. The Folsoms were both early risers, so by 8:00 A.M., we had finished breakfast and each started out in a different direction to canvass store to store and house to house. We met at the restaurant at noon. I had developed no prospects. We started again at 1:00 P.M., and met at 6:00 for dinner. Still no prospects.

After dinner, we started out again, and at about 9:00 P.M., I met an old codger about fifty-five years old, who was a "line rider" (a man who rode the boundary line between Arizona and Sonora, Mexico), who showed some interest. I went to work, and by 10:30 P.M. had him signed on a contract to buy two lots for forty dollars. He agreed to meet me at the bank at 10:00 A.M., the next day, to pay the money. I went back to the hotel feeling good.

The next morning, I took the older Folsom to the bank and when my purchaser came in, I introduced them, since Folsom had to sign the deed. Not knowing what to do next, I excused myself, which of course was not proper. Actually, I think I was scared and thought that Folsom might do better alone. Later, he told me that he was with him until noon, during which time he backed out several times, but finally Folsom had closed the deal for all cash—forty dollars. My commission was 20 percent, or eight dollars. That was my start in the real estate business. Before my two weeks' vacation was up, I made up my mind that it was safe to give up my job, so I went back to Bisbee for the balance of the month and cleared my desk, then I packed my bags and took the train for Bowie and Globe, to join the Folsoms.

Bowie was only a junction on the main line of the Southern Pacific. After waiting some hours, the train finally pulled out for Globe—ninety miles away. We made it in ten hours. I say ten hours, and I mean ten hours! It was a freight train, and we two or three unfortunate passengers rode in the caboose. I think it had one or two flat wheels, and there were no springs under, nor cushions on, the seats—for ten hours, mostly at night! After Globe, we worked Clifton and Morenci. Morenci was a mining camp high up in the mountains. To get there, we took a narrow-gauge train that wound in and out around the canyons and the hills, and finally made four complete loops to get to the little, dried-up town. I use the term "dried up" because it was dry and hot, and not a tree or blade of grass or a flower. At that time, no one was allowed to plant any growing thing of any kind, because of the shortage of water. The mining company owned the town—mines, utility plant, general store, and all the houses. It made the rules.

After Morenci, we divided up. The Folsoms went to Phoenix, Arizona, and I tackled Congress, Arizona, alone. In Congress, I sold sixteen lots in about ten days, earning sixty-four dollars in commissions—when and if I ever got them. Since most of the lots were sold on monthly payments, you were always bound to lose some, but my supposed success, alone in Congress, stimulated my courage no end.

We then went to Prescott, and then to Jerome, the burning camp. This was after the heyday of Jerome. The mines had caught fire and could not be extinguished. Here and there over the mountainside, smoke was oozing up through the crevasses. Of recent years, many of the houses and business buildings of Jerome have slid down the mountainside because of cave-ins in the old mines, and Jerome is mostly a ghost town. However, in 1903, it was plenty busy, although I have not one pleasant recollection of Jerome. Possibly one reason was that we had had good business, met some nice people, and generally had had a really good two weeks in delightful Prescott, which made Jerome a letdown for our spirits.

From Jerome, we took the train for Los Angeles. The senior Folsom had gone back to San Diego, and "W. A." and I were traveling together. When I got my check for a thousand dollars from the sale of my "El Tigre" stock, I told him about it, and he thought it would be a good idea for me to buy a thousand dollars' worth of Pacific Beach lots, but it seemed to me that I had better wait until I got to San Diego. From what I had learned, I felt sure that there would still be plenty of lots left when we got there.

On our way to San Diego, I stopped for a few days in Los Angeles for a visit with Mother and Laura. Laura was making splendid strides with her cornet. She had been in the Tournament of Roses Parade in Pasadena on January 1, 1902, to play bugle calls from one of the principal floats. Even at that time (she was just seventeen) her tones and music were superb. However, Mother thought Laura should have bigger opportunities, so she determined to sell our home and take Laura to New York for a theatrical career. This was before Hollywood was "Hollywood." In fact, I am not sure that that section of Los Angeles was called Hollywood at that time, but I do remember that, from our old home in Pico Heights, we could look directly across the lovely, rolling land and over what is now Hollywood, to Cahuenga Pass, in the hills beyond.

When I had nearly finished the first rough draft of the foregoing, I asked the typist if she thought anyone but me would want to read it. Her reply was spontaneous: "Write more about your love life."

CHAPTER XII

I Arrive in San Diego

I SHALL never forget my arrival in San Diego. It was about 1:30 P.M., July 2, 1903; a glorious day, with bright sunshine and a cool sea breeze. Smog had never been dreamed of even in Los Angeles, but the air was noticeably cleaner and fresher in San Diego.

The junior partner met me at the train and we walked from the Santa Fe Station, carrying my grips, up D Street (now Broadway) to the little half-office on C Street between Fourth and Fifth Avenues, opposite the old Brewster Hotel. D Street was paved with asphalt, and in those days the asphalt would get soft in the warm sun, so that the occasional horse and buggy or horse and wagon that passed had a muffled sound. There were electric cars operating on a single track on D Street, with a turnout for passing, at intervals along the track.

My first investment after I arrived in San Diego was the purchase of a one-third interest, for $5,000, in the two-thousand lot Fortuna Park Subdivision, at Pacific Beach, which we had been selling. On this deal, these lots cost me at the rate of $7.50 each, for lots in the same tract where I had made my first purchase at the price of twenty dollars per lot. O. M. Schmidt, the partner whom I bought out, was glad to sell, because he had paid $3.75 per lot, and he said that whenever he could make a "Dutchman's one percent" he would make a deal. I paid $500 down, or twenty-five cents per lot, and promised to pay the balance as we sold the lots. Those were "Good Old Days."

Following the closing of that deal, at the suggestion of the senior partner, I purchased a one-third interest in the firm of Folsom Brothers, for $250 more, paying another hundred dollars in cash, and giving my note for $150. Thereafter, the firm was known as "Folsom Bros. & Co."

In 1903, San Diego claimed a population of nineteen thousand, and "Tent City" Coronado, was the one bright spot. A large percentage of our own population, as well as thousands of summer visitors from out of town who were entertained there, looked forward to it from season to season. John D. Spreckels and his brother, A. B. Spreckels, owned Tent City. For a month or two before Tent City opened, John D. Spreckels would send his Tent City Band on a tour of southern California and Arizona, to drum up business, and this was wonderful advertising for the sale of beach lots! We had primed our customers and prospects in Arizona to spend their vacations at Tent City. We opened an office there. We met them upon their arrival and took them to see their purchases, and sold them more lots at twenty-five dollars each. During the summer of 1903, there was no fog and the famous and delightful Tent City, on the Strand at Coronado, was at its best, with nightly open-air band concerts, dancing at the old Casino (converted from a ferryboat tied to a dock) roller skating, swimming, boating—all kinds of fun.

Before they left for New York City, Mother and Laura came to San Diego to pay me a visit. Those were the days when vaudeville was still on the way up and "movies," as motion pictures were then called, were mostly crazy slapstick comedies. I took time out to get Laura a week's engagement with her cornet at a little vaudeville house on Fourth Avenue south of B Street, and on Sundays she played cornet solos at the First Congregational Church.

At that time, Pacific Beach was a beautiful area of tableland, nearly two miles across, extending from the foot of Rose Canyon to the Pacific Ocean, and from the foothills to Mission Bay. There were quite a number of five-acre and ten-acre plots which were in beautiful lemon groves. There was a hotel (vacant) and the college buildings (vacant, except that the owner and his family lived there), and a few scattered houses across the great expanse of level land.

O. J. Stough, an old resident and financier of San Diego, owned over three thousand lots and considerable acreage at Pacific Beach. He was impressed with our success, and wanted us to sell his property. He finally agreed to sell us his entire Pacific Beach holdings for $62,000 with nothing down and to be paid as we sold the lots. Together, we three partners (the Folsoms and myself) owed nearly $15,000 and all we had was a few contracts which might or might not pay out. The senior partner, M. W. Folsom, who was conducting the negotiations with Mr. Stough, was not sure that we should make the deal, but there was no question in my mind. At twenty-one, $75,000 in debits seemed no worse to me than $15,000. I was most enthusiastic and insistent that he close the deal, and he finally did, at an average price of about fifteen dollars per lot for scattered lots and acreage in proportion, much of it throughout what is now the central part of Pacific Beach.

We really went to work then, preparing for our fall and winter campaigns. I made a plaster of Paris cast about the size of a suitcase, of San Diego and the two harbors, and had it brightly painted to show what a wonderful city San Diego was to be at the southwest corner of the United States, already having the finest harbor on the Pacific Coast, and the finest climate in the world—and the cheapest beach lots! The younger Folsom opened a branch office in Los Angeles and put on a crew of salesmen. "Free Excursions to San Diego" were advertised for all purchasers of beach lots. The senior partner furnished the brains, and I was the office manager in San Diego.

By the summer of 1904, we were going high, wide and handsome! Our cheapest lots were selling at fifty dollars and others on up to $150. Contracts were piling up. We had moved our offices to 1015 Fifth Avenue, just north of D Street (Broadway) which was the very center of town and was where the Mortgage Department of the First National Trust & Savings Bank is now located.

From Los Angeles, there came a small but steady stream of customers, who were met at the Santa Fe Station and were driven over the city by horse and carriage. They were then taken to the La Jolla Steam Train Station and conducted to Pacific Beach, where a good lunch was served. Then they were ushered into another carriage and driven out to see the lots they had purchased. They nearly always bought additional lots. When possible, parties from Los Angeles were sent in groups, personally conducted by one or more salesmen for the entire round trip. Because of the promotion we were doing, our sales staff and members of the firm traveled on free railroad passes, but everything else was paid for, and as the money came into our office from sales it went out, like water poured into a sieve!

One day, a sure-fire promoter blew in from Los Angeles and sold us on the idea of selling our lots ten times as fast by mail, through magazine advertising. This was going to be big business, and we must have more lots to sell, so we really started on a buying spree. We bought the old Pacific Beach College property with its four blocks of 160 lots for $15,000; the old Pacific Beach Hotel at Lamont Street across from the railroad station (which burned down some years later); probably a dozen lemon ranches and unimproved blocks throughout Pacific Beach and, to cap the climax, we bought several hundred lots at Morena and nine hundred acres of beautiful grain land on the hilltops overlooking Morena, part of which now comprises the southern portion of Clairemont, for $65,000. Most of these deals were on purchase contracts, with no cash down.

We contracted with the J. Walter Thompson Advertising Agency, of Chicago to prepare advertisements and to place our advertising, and a fine job of it they did, as the immediate results proved. We took another office, across D Street and upstairs, for our Foreign Mail Department. Thousands of leaflets and booklets were printed. We started publishing a small monthly magazine on San Diego. The great national advertising campaign was launched with three-quarter-page ads in the *Saturday Evening Post,* full-page ads in other magazines, and to begin with a full-page ad in one of the Chicago daily newspapers. These ads told of the wonderful climate of San Diego, of the marvelous harbor, and of the stupendous growth which was about to start. Level lots were offered for as low as a hundred dollars each, with only ten dollars to be paid down. They were excellent ads. I still have copies of two or three of them in one of my scrapbooks.

Just about the time our national advertising was ready to start, another hot-shot promoter came to town and suggested that we launch a project to build a short-line railroad direct from San Diego to Yuma, Arizona. That sounded like a good idea, because almost every living soul in San Diego believed that, if we could get a direct railroad to Yuma, San Diego would soon become one of the great, if the not greatest, metropolises of the West. So we got back of the railroad project. One million dollars' worth of beautiful thousand-dollar railroad bonds was lithographed to start it, and on October 27, 1904, a full-page advertisement ran in the San Diego *Union*. It invited all San Diego to meet at 7:30 P.M., that evening, at San Diego's famous Isis Theater to consider a plan to build a "People's Railroad." The committee whose names appeared in the ad were: W. R. Rogers, Cashier, Merchants National Bank; F. W. Sterns and Judge A. Haines, Attorneys; H. G. Crow; M. W. Folsom; Philip Morse, and F. M. Elliott.

The advertisement had a beautiful picture of a steam train coming directly over the hills and mountains and headed for San Diego city and harbor, with Point Loma and Pacific Beach in the background. I attended the meeting and heard the speeches. They were splendid and enthusiastic. The only trouble with this "People's Railroad" was that the "people" did not buy so much as one of the beautiful thousand-dollar bonds!

I had plenty to do, however, without personally building a railroad to Yuma. The three-quarter-page ads in the *Saturday Evening Post* were bringing in actually thousands of letters from people all over the United States, who wanted to know more about our wonderful city of "Bay and Climate" and how they could get rich here otherwise than by buying our lots. Our "Foreign Mail Order Department" was a beehive of stenographers, and our postage stamps alone cost as much as thirty dollars per day, cash. We got deposits of ten dollars each from prospective purchasers of possibly twenty lots.

The *Saturday Evening Post* ads, alone, were costing $1,500 per issue, every two weeks, and bills for advertising were coming in on every mail.

After the first thirty days I could see we were sunk financially, but then it took another thirty days to stop the advertising campaign. By that time, $10,000 in advertising space had been contracted for; the bills for printing and advertising for the railroad had to be paid, and our promoters wanted compensation for their "valuable" services and advice! Their argument was that they did not know how much money we had, which was true—that was our affair. One of the owners from whom we had contracted to purchase a Pacific Beach block at $200 per lot, brought suit for $8,000 and won. All in all, those were not part of the "Good Old Days"!

Apparently, 1904 was a lush year for promoters, at least in San Diego. While we were working on plans for the national lot sale advertising campaign and the building of the railroad, a real "spellbinder" came to town. He was prepared to launch a project for building a $100,000,000 steel plant in San Diego! He had it figured out that the great iron ore deposits in Baja California would furnish iron ore to San Diego far cheaper than the present steel mills were paying for ore in Pittsburgh, and that it was much better ore.

After first stirring up San Diego, he went to Los Angeles. There, it was reported, he got a check for $10,000 from a prominent newspaper publisher, plus a few others for good measure. He then returned to San Diego and got either checks or signed subscriptions from the banks and leading business firms all around town. I do not recall how much he raised here, but it must have been more than $100,000 in promises, because our subscription alone was for $2,500. But why not? Think what a $100,-000,000 steel mill would do for a town of twenty thousand people, and think what it would do for the owners of seven thousand vacant lots!

Of course, within a few months or possibly a few weeks, this scheme blew higher than a kite and the promoter with it. However, in this case we were lucky. The man who was promoting our national advertising campaign was a lawyer, and at his suggestion we put a clause in our subscription that it was not to be used unless a certain aggregate amount was paid in, so the First National Bank of San Diego, which was the custodian for the subscriptions, handed ours back to us.

This steel mill promoter blew into San Diego every once in a while, but to the best of my recollection he never tried any other promotion scheme here. We would hear of him and his escapades elsewhere, from time to time. At the time of the earthquake and fire in San Francisco, in 1906, a story came to us that, as the fire was getting worse and worse, he went into an automobile agency in San Francisco and bought one of their biggest new cars, giving them a check for the full purchase price. He then spent several hours helping San Franciscans move their belongings out of the fire zone. When he got tired of being a Boy Scout, he drove off. The check, of course, was no good.

As I've said, it was a lucky break for us that our subscription for his steel mill project was returned to us, because if we had been forced to pay another $2,500 in cash on top of all of our other troubles, it might have been the last straw!

Fortunately, however, our Los Angeles office was producing a steady flow of business, so by deferring payments over a year or two, we finally put those two fiascoes behind us.

Fifteen years later, San Diego was to profit hugely, as a result of our mail order lot scheme.

Laura at the age of five, in costume for "Tim the Ragged
Wharf Rat."

Oscar at nine and Laura at six, in costume for "Chinese Comique."

Laura at six and Oscar at nine, in costume for the Highland Fling
and other Scottish dances.

Oscar at eleven, in costume for the Sailor's Hornpipe.

Laura at nine (*right*) and Oscar at twelve, in costume for the dialogue "Josiah Puzzles His Pa."

Laura at nine and Oscar at twelve. I am wearing the wig made of Mother's hair, under which the hornet once buzzed.

John H. Cotton, father of Oscar and Laura Cotton.

⟩⟩THE⟨⟨
Cotton Children

⟩ EVERYTHING IN COSTUME ⟨

LETTER FROM FREDERICK WARDE.

"Little Laura and Oscar Cotton are delightful in the extreme as entertainers. They have a wonderful amount of natural ability, and their work singularly free from the mechanical methods of most child performers. They are bright and clever, without precocity, hence the charm of their performance.

"Wishing them the greatest success, I am

"Faithfully yours, FREDERICK WARDE."

H. M. Lee & Bro., Printers, 140 N. Spring, Los Angeles.

Title-page of the four-page folder used extensively by Mother for advertising and mailing with letters soliciting engagements.

REPERTOIRE

DIALOGUES:

Mrs. Brown's Mistake.
The Happy Little Wife.
The California Hayseeds.
The Brick Yard.
Josiah Puzzles his Pa.
Little William Henry Dimple Fitz Simmons at the Dime Museum.
When Ye Gang Awa, Jamie.

FANCY DANCES:

Scotch National Highland Fling, genuine prize steps, taught by Robbie Burns.
Scotch Sword Dance—very difficult steps over the naked sword—in McDonald Tartan.
Scotch Shantrews—most beautiful of all fancy Scotch dances—in Stewart Tartans.
Chinese Comique and National Love Song, full costume.
Sailor's Hornpipe.
Erin's Favorite.
Fairy Dewdrop.
Emerald and Rose.

READINGS AND RECITATIONS:

Tim the Ragged Wharf Rat.   The Elf Child.
The Raggedy Man.   The Man in the Moon.
The Sale Extraordinary.   Setting the Old Blue Hen.
Smack in School.   Muzzer's Bought a Baby.
The Clown's Baby.   Money Musk.
Rock Me to Sleep, Mother.   Our Folks.
John Burns, of Gettysburg.   Poor Little Joe.
No Sect in Heaven.   The Heart's Charity.
Three Songs of Life, from the "Songs of Seven :"
Youth, Romance and Old Age—Longing for Home.

SHAKESPEARE:

Quarrel of Brutus and Cassius, in the "Roman Togas" (from Julius Cæsar).
The Tent Scene (from Richard III).
Arthur and Hubert (from King John).

OTHER SPECIALTIES:

Indian Club Swinging.
Blacksmith Dumbbell Chorus.
Swiss Bell Ringing.

Page 2 of the folder, giving our repertoire.

CHAPTER XIII

Stereopticon Lectures

EARLY IN 1905, after our liabilities for the previous year's fiascoes were behind us or the payments were deferred, I decided to try to stimulate lot sales by stereopticon lectures. I bought a stereopticon lantern and had San Diego's leading photographer, Herbert R. Fitch, make 225 beautiful slides, many hand-colored, of the city of San Diego: its homes, gardens, and business buildings; back country scenes, orange groves, country homes, our great water systems, harbor and boating scenes, the famous Hotel del Coronado, and fascinating Tent City.

We sent crews of salesmen back to Arizona, to northern California, and as far east as Oklahoma. The sales crew would rent a hall or opera house and would give out tickets to a "Free Stereopticon Lecture on the 'Beauties and Advantages of San Diego' by O. W. Cotton." I would arrive, give the lecture, and show the pictures. Then the salesmen would follow up the prospects for two or three weeks while I went on to another town. I gave my first lecture in Okahoma City.

I presented these lectures in style: I had an assistant to change the slides as I signaled with an electric buzzer, while I stood outside the picture in full dress and tails. I gave them in my best dramatic style, and kept the pictures changing fast enough to hold the interest of the audience. Both pictures and lecture began with San Francisco and worked south with the climax, San Diego. The lectures were always popular. I cannot remember ever lecturing to much less than a packed house, and I do not recall ever seeing anyone in the audience leaving before the lecture was finished.

These lectures were an excellent stimulus to sales, particularly in Los Angeles, where we would give a free trip to San Diego. To publicize the lecture and fill the house, the salesmen distributed a little leaflet entitled A FREE TRIP TO SAN DIEGO (via CANVAS)—the text of which follows:

SAN DIEGO

Is unquestionably the most delightful place in all southern California in which to live.

SAN DIEGO

Is growing rapidly and her population is increasing at a tremendous rate.

SAN DIEGO

Offers today to the businessman unparalleled opportunities.

SAN DIEGO

Investments are making by far the best percentage of profits on money invested of any section in the Southwest today.

SAN DIEGO

Possess today more and greater natural undeveloped resources and advantages than any other city on the Continent.

SAN DIEGO'S

Possibilites for satisfying the pleasure-seeker are practically unlimited.

SAN DIEGO

Is destined to become one of the great cities of the Pacific Coast.

THE REASONS WHY

These conditions do exist in SAN DIEGO today will be set forth in a very interesting manner by Mr. O. W. Cotton, of San Diego, in a stereopticon lecture to be given at the Dorris Theatre.

While Mr. Cotton is a businessman, and his talk on the industrial situation, financial conditions, and business opportunities and the superior advantages of San Diego as a home center are delivered right from the shoulder, he is also a natural and popular entertainer, and portrays his subject in such a manner that all may enjoy his every sentence.

To illustrate to better advantage the true conditions in San Diego, more than 200 views of San Diego will be thrown on the canvas from the latest improved stereopticon.

Write your name and address on the enclosed postal and mail, and

FREE INVITATIONS

will be forwarded to you.

DORRIS THEATRE
PHOENIX ARIZONA
October 17, 1905

We did some local advertising, so the newspapers were generous, sometimes profuse, in their comments. On October 18th, the *Arizona Republican,* of Phoenix, carried a full column, several paragraphs of which follow:

LECTURE ON SAN DIEGO
A Novel and Interesting Style of Advertisement

One of the most novel plans of advertisement that has ever been carried out in Phoenix was the illustrated lecture given at the Dorris Theatre last evening by O. W. Cotton, a representative of the firm of Folsom Brothers, real estate dealers of San Diego, Cal. The lecture was delivered to give publicity especially to Pacific Beach, a suburb of San Diego, owned largely by the Folsom Brothers' company, but all southern California was given mention, San Diego, the city, more than other points. Mr. Cotton, the speaker of the evening, has a most pleasing style of delivery, and talked with that enthusiasm that carried his thought and statements in a convincing way to his auditors. The views shown were beautiful and could not help but impress the audience with the beauty of the section described.

Over twelve hundred people had entered the theatre when Mr. Cotton began his remarks.

As a preface to the lecture, it was explained by the speaker that neither himself nor the company which he represents had any desire whatever to attempt to depopulate Phoenix, but that his visit to the city was made for the purpose of interesting Phoenix residents in beach property.

The views then shown pictured many of the busy thoroughfares of both Los Angeles and San Diego, some taken ten and twenty years ago and others as they appear today. Mr. Cotton, by the use of the stereopticon, then took his listeners on a trip from Los Angeles to San Diego and showed them different scenes en route. "Out in the harbor," said the speaker, "as you stand on the upper deck of your ship and look across the peaceful waters and notice the gentle rise of the land, forming space sufficient to accommodate the business section of a city of a million people, then rising in gentle terraces two hundred feet, making the most delightful sites for the residence section which could be imagined, you will say as all have said before you, 'What an ideal place for a city!' "

The audience was then given the opportunity to view the different sections of the city and Pacific Beach, in which tract the interest of those in attendance was centered. When finished there were very few if any present who would not agree with the speaker that a new era has dawned for San Diego, and that that city is just beginning to put on her cloak of prosperity.

Several of the views shown were of the establishment now owned by A. J. Bradley, a former resident of Phoenix, with whom many of those present were acquainted. Other views were familiar to Phoenix people, especially those of Coronado and the Tent City.

Following the lecture an explanation was made of the cost and manner of purchase of lots in the tracts near San Diego owned by the company. In this there was nearly as much interest taken as in the lecture of the first part of the evening.

In Sacramento, on Friday, August 18, 1905, which was the day following the lecture, the *Evening Bee* gave nearly a half-column:

PLEASING TALK ON SAN DIEGO
How Southern California People Advertise

Large Gathering Attends Lecture by O. W. Cotton, Who Advises
Investors to Look to San Diego for Good Opportunities

The lecture upon San Diego, delivered at the Ingomar Theatre last night, plainly illustrates the methods the people of southern California take to advertise their cities, and such methods might well be followed by the people of this locality. The lecture was delivered by O. W. Cotton before a well-filled house. It was interesting and to the point, and was illustrated by a series of handsome stereopticon views.

The lecturer said that while in the East he was surprised to learn the interest taken in California. One has but to speak the word "California," and everybody stops to listen. Nearly every Easterner expresses a desire to visit California at some time or other. In the larger Eastern cities the competition is keen, he said, and this is forcing the people of moderate means to come West to grow up with the country.

He showed pictures of San Francisco, saying that was the first city in the West to grow, and telling how people who invested their money in real estate in San Francisco thirty years ago had become rich. He then drifted to southern California, and showed views of some of the beautiful business blocks and residences of Los Angeles. He told of the remarkable growth of Los Angeles during the past ten years, and set forth the advantages of southern California.

He finally took up San Diego, and dwelt at length upon the resources of the city. He declared San Diego had not grown more rapidly, because it has not been properly advertised. Now it is being advertised, he said, and is destined to become a great city. Excellent views of the San Diego harbor were shown, which the lecturer declared to be one of the finest in the world. He told of the climatic advantages, and said that San Diego was the most delightful place on earth for homes. It offers the best opportunities for the real estate investors of any city on the Coast, he said, as lots purchased now are bound to double their value within twelve months.

On June 8, 1905, I gave a lecture in the Chickasha Indian Territory, in what is now Grady County, Oklahoma. The local paper gave this write-up the next day:

OPERA HOUSE CROWDED
To Hear O. W. Cotton's Splendid Lecture On
San Diego and Southern California

A VERY ENJOYABLE AFFAIR
His Talk Was Interesting and Pictures Were Beautiful

As was expected, a full house greeted Mr. O. W. Cotton last night at the Opera House to hear about and see southern California.

People began to arrive at 6:30 P.M., and by 8:15 there was standing room only and many who came later had to be turned away.

To say that it was an evening well spent would be putting it mildly.

Mr. Cotton is certainly an interesting talker and he handled his subject, "The Beauties and Advantages of San Diego and Southern California" in a way only possible by one who has familiarized himself with every detail and knows how to express his ideas in an intelligent and practical manner.

During the lecture he gave the poem of James Whitcomb Riley, "That Old Sweetheart of Mine," in a manner which thrilled every heart.

The stereopticon pictures were beautiful and, had we a little of the cool salt air Mr. Cotton told about, we certainly should have felt we were in the "Earthly Paradise" we read about.

The pictures dwelt on California from San Francisco to San Diego, being mostly devoted to the beautiful scenes in and around San Diego.

As a delightful place to live, San Diego certainly has no equal, with its magnificent landlocked harbor, its beautiful buildings, splendid old boulevards, and driveways lined for miles with palms and shrubbery, its homes literally covered with roses, and surrounded by almost every known flower every day in the year.

Mr. Cotton touched on San Diego as an investment, showed the growth of the city and the possibilities for making money, which as demonstrated last night are truly wonderful.

Aside from the intense heat which was almost unbearable, the affair as a whole was a very enjoyable one, and all who attended were more than repaid and they saw Beautiful California as never before. Mr. Cotton and his associates will remain in the city for a day or two and will gladly furnish literature and give any information desired regarding southern California to all who care to call on them. They are stopping at the Midway Hotel.

What the reporter had to say about the heat was not exaggerated, and, to make matters worse, there was not a particle of movement of air. While I was at the hotel desk signing the Register, a man rushed up to the clerk and demanded, "Where is your cyclone cellar?"

In 1906, I gave a series of lectures in Blanchard Hall, in Los Angeles. I presented a couple of tickets to one lecture to a Miss Violet Savage and her mother, Mrs. Caroline Church. At this particular lecture, the owner of the hall, Mr. Blanchard, was there. Afterward, as I came down the aisle to greet Miss Savage and her mother, he stopped me and was most enthusiastic over the lecture, but I was keeping an eye over his shoulder on a certain young lady and her mother, to see that they did not get away before I could get down to them. Finally, I made it, and, to my gratification, they, too, were most complimentary. But I am getting ahead of my story.

CHAPTER XIV

How Not to Make Concrete Building Blocks

ABOUT THIS TIME, someone had the idea of building foundations for homes and other buildings out of "Ornamental Concrete Building Blocks," and, when I returned to San Diego from one of my lecture tours, I found our company had rented an old car-barn on the seashore at Pacific Beach and had started a crew of men to making concrete building blocks. The idea, of course, was to promote Pacific Beach by establishing an industry there. It was surprising that no one had thought of this before, because the sand, which composed 94 percent of the product, was right there on the beach, and it was free!

In the next two years, I learned a great deal about concrete building blocks. Imagine my surprise when I discovered the men were putting mattresses in the wagon beds under the concrete blocks before they were hauled the ten miles to town. This was because the Pacific Beach sand was too fine-grained and would not bind, and, without the mattresses, the blocks would fall apart in transit!

Nevertheless, this looked like a good business venture, so I rented a warehouse at Sixteenth and N streets in San Diego, moved the plant, and started making good concrete blocks with coarse, river-bottom sand. Not only did we make the blocks, but we built the foundations as well. We built retaining walls, and did a really good business, but for some reason each job cost a little more than the price we charged for it. I did not realize it, but of course that is why we got so much business! The experienced contractors were smarter than we were—they bid to make a profit. We bid to get the jobs.

One day after a heavy rain, the manager of the concrete block business told me there was some trouble with a very special job we had finished just a few weeks before, at Juniper and Albatross streets. He would not tell me what the trouble was until we got there. This has been our finest job to date, using a new type of block which made an exceptionally classy wall —and there it was when we arrived, all spread out on the sidewalk.

That was the flood winter of 1905. The job at Juniper and Albatross streets was only the first of a series. On Eighteenth Street, one wall sixteen feet high fell out and spread over the entire sidewalk and into the street. What we had not learned was that we should have put "weepers" (holes to let the storm waters out) along the bottom of a wall, and anchors ten feet back with cables to hold the wall in place.

For reasons best known to ourselves, we got out of the concrete block business. When all phases of this venture were closed and we were definitely out, I asked the bookkeeper for a statement. When he brought it in, I sat and looked at it. We had lost just fifteen thousand dollars on this deal, and all in cash. It hurt, but not as badly as if it had come earlier—by that time we were getting used to losses. Moreover, we still had plenty of outstanding contracts on lots sold, and more lots were being sold every month.

All in all, 1905 was a good year, after we got out of the concrete block business and worked out, by payment and deferment, all of the obligations piled up by the mail order advertising scheme and the very short life of the railroad.

In the year 1901, two years before I arrived, the total building permits for the entire city of San Diego amounted to $123,285, but, beginning in 1902, they started getting better:

1902	$ 432,140
1903	710,123
1904	914,967
1905	1,194,370

nearly ten times the total for 1901!

Our lot sales progressed "steadily by jerks"—feast or famine—sometimes good, sometimes not. In the real estate business, you take the bitter with the sweet. The summers were always best.

In 1905, Mother and Laura came to San Diego to live. Laura took a position as hostess at Tent City for the summer. There she was right in her element. It was exciting and lots of fun.

I was enjoying the best health of my life. Except for a bad stomach, which I had always had, I really was in fine condition physically. The altitude and the dry air in Bisbee had not helped my catarrhal condition in any particular, much to my surprise and regret, but the San Diego climate had. Within six months after arriving in San Diego, the sinus trouble disappeared entirely. I had done nothing for it, had taken no medicine or treatments; it just dried up, and was I happy!

After the summer season closed, Mother, Laura, and I lived in a flat in town. Later, we all moved to our company's Hotel Balboa, at Pacific Beach. Mother ran the hotel for a time, and Laura acted as hostess.

We maintained stables at a barn on the old Pacific Beach Hotel grounds, with horses and vehicles for driving our clients over Pacific Beach to show them the lots they had purchased and sell them additional lots. I drove back and forth from the hotel to our downtown office in a light buggy with a rather spirited horse I called Rex. It took me exactly fifty minutes to make the trip.

In 1906, I bought a smart-looking little Ford runabout for $700. It was Ford's first mass-production car, ten thousand of that model being made that year. I drove back and forth in style. I gave Rex to Laura and she became quite a horsewoman, riding all over Pacific Beach and the surrounding hills, and at low tide galloping up and down the four miles of beautiful, wide, hard sand beach we advertised so thoroughly as one of the wonderful attractions of Pacific Beach.

There were some mighty fine folks living at Pacific Beach in the scattered homes among the orange and lemon groves from the ocean and bay front to the foothills. Laura got some young folks together and formed a dancing class. In addition to her job as hostess, she also acted as press agent, writing news items on the social events and other happenings at the hotel and throughout Pacific Beach. Mother and Laura made many good friends there.

CHAPTER XV

Street Lights for Downtown

SINCE I often worked late at night, I had a room at the Imperial Hotel a few blocks from our office downtown, as well as at the Balboa Hotel in Pacific Beach. About 9:30 P.M., one evening in December, I came out of our office on Fifth Street, locked the door, and started down toward the corner of D Street, and then I stopped. I looked ahead, and I turned and looked in the other direction, and then I just stood there.

In the next block south, an incandescent electric light of possibly thirty-two candlepower hung suspended from a piece of curved pipe in front of a saloon, and that was it. I walked to the corner. As far as I could see in any direction, there was not another light. A man was standing under the light in front of the saloon, but at 9:30 P.M., in the very heart of San Diego's business district, there was not another person nor a vehicle in sight. I said to myself, "Is this the kind of town we have been boosting to the skies?" I decided to do something about it.

The next morning, I went to see Mr. R. G. Hunt, the manager of the San Diego Consolidated Gas & Electric Company, to determine what could be done to get street lights for our downtown district. He proposed an agreement between the property owners and merchants and the Gas & Electric Company, whereby the company would install six arc lights in each block, if the property owners and merchants would pay the monthly charge. The San Diego Consolidated Gas & Electric Company prepared the contracts.

I got to work immediately, and signed up two blocks. Then others took it up, and by March 1, 1906, downtown San Diego was a blaze of light. In comparison to what downtown San Diego has today, that first street lighting was not much, but compared with one little thirty-two candle-power bulb for the whole downtown, it was wonderful!

The San Diego Chamber of Commerce had just elected its new Board of Directors for the coming year, and somebody on the Board decided they had overlooked a bet. Here was a young man who wanted to work for the community! They reconvened and enlarged the Board from fifteen to twenty-one directors, and invited six new men, including myself, to become members. That was the beginning of three strenuous but happy years. Through my association with the Chamber of Commerce, I became acquainted with practically all of the businessmen in town of that day. I soon felt at home and more a part of the community than would have been possible in many years, if this had not occurred. I did not think much about it at that time and did not even inquire at whose suggestion I had been invited to be on the Board. In later years, I have often wished that I had done so. I should like to have thanked him. It was one of the finest things that happened to me at that age. I was twenty-four years old.

I took my responsibilities seriously. I devoted from a third to half of my time and thinking to the Chamber of Commerce for the next three years. I served as chairman on many committees, and at the next annual meeting was elected second vice-president. During those three years, I carried most of the load for the Chamber, so much so that at last one of my competitors in the real estate subdivision business made the comment that the "Chamber of Commerce is being run for the benefit of Cotton . . ." which I thought was highly complimentary.

Had I been a politician and smart enough to go after it, I could probably have been its president, but in my inexperience I thought the job should seek the man, and I let my opportunity slip by. However, my not being president was no loss to San Diego. I worked just as hard as vice-president, and the Chamber of Commerce would not have accomplished any more, but I realized many years too late that it would have been fun to have had that honor at the age of twenty-five.

In those days, the total staff of the Chamber of Commerce consisted of a secretary and one stenographer. In the process of changing secretaries, there was to be a gap of thirty days before the new man could take over, and I offered to fill the vacancy for one month, without compensation, and was promptly installed. It had been the custom for the secretary to stand and read the correspondence aloud to the directors at the weekly meetings of the Board. During the mornings before our directors' meetings, I would go over to the Chamber and sort out the letters to be read, and would read each one several times until I had it about half-memorized; then, at the meeting, I would be careful to stand so that my knees would not touch my pants legs in front and thus expose my fright. Most of the directors were between forty and fifty-five years of age, and they were men I looked upon with great respect and, in some instances, awe. If any of them ever suspected that I could hardly read, I never heard of it. Some of them were among my warmest friends for many years.

During my second year, the officers and directors of the Chamber of Commerce were:

D. Gachenauer, *President*
Melville Klauber, *Vice-President*
O. W. Cotton, *Vice-President*
John S. Mills, *Secretary*

Directors

Edward Grove	F. S. Banks	E. A. Hornbeck
Barker Burnell	C. H. Wagner	Fred Jewel
Rufus Choate	William Clayton	C. J. Josselyn
Jas. A. Jasper	George H. Crippen	W. F. Luddington
J. S. Akerman	Ed Fletcher	J. B. Starkey
R. C. Allen	Ford A. Carpenter	E. E. Shaffer
	W. H. Halcomb	

One of the activities I enjoyed most during these first two years with the Chamber of Commerce was that of entertaining delegations of visitors from out of town, under the title "Chairman of the Excursion Committee." When these delegations came to San Diego, our Reception Committee would meet them at the Santa Fe Depot and escort them to a free lunch, and then give them a sightseeing trip around the city by tallyho, or a trip around the harbor in launches, taking them aboard a warship. When they had returned home, San Diego would then get a nice complimentary write-up of a column or two in their local newspapers.

The day after the return of one of these excursions which had been arranged by the Los Angeles Chamber of Commerce, the Los Angeles Sunday *Times* for October 7, 1906, carried the folowing story:

Friendship interlocked the handclasp of Los Angeles with San Diego yesterday. Three generations of the Chamber of Commerce of this City traveled to San Diego, on an excursion of good fellowship and met with a rousing welcome from the San Diego Chamber of Commerce.

San Diego learned that Los Angeles people move with a rush and have great appetites. When the Los Angeles delegation, 360 strong, surged from the streetcars on to the Santa Fe Railroad dock and attacked two heavily loaded tables of good things, O. W. Cotton, Chairman of the San Diego Reception Committee, gasped and then rushed to the nearest phone to deliver a hurry order for more reinforcements of eatables.

Those fruit-laden tables were good to look upon. The onslaught was fierce, but after all, a high compliment to the hosts of the day, for nothing but home products were served. Great piles of varicolored grapes, with Julian apples as a foundation, caught the sunlight with charming effect. Platters of rich black and green olives intermingled in tempting pyramids. Flanking the table at either end were deep boxes of ham sandwiches, Swiss cheese, and crackers. Nearby a squad of men opened soda pop of all shades with a zeal that discounted the dashing spray against the rocks at Point Loma.

Many Cars in Train

When 8:15 A.M. o'clock arrived, the hour of departure from Los Angeles, it was found that whole families whose papas were members of the Chamber of Commerce wanted to go. One coach was added, then another, and still a third, as the people kept coming. E. W. McGee, General Agent of the Passenger Department of the Santa Fe, was on hand to muster the best accommodations of the railroad, and the long train that finally left La Grande Station could hardly have been improved upon. Assisting Mr. McGee were H. H. Francisco and Thom. Chambers, of the Freight Department, and before the train reached San Diego, E. B. Stewart, Agent of the Santa Fe at San Diego, and J. A. Tulip, Agent at Oceanside, were aboard to assist in the hospitality.

A. W. Skinner, Chairman of the Executive Committee of the Chamber of Commerce, was busy ever in seeing to it that everybody was comfortable. He made speeches and his habit of moving about became infectious, so that, before Orange was reached, all the passengers were roving, too, and the train became one long reception room. White-coated attendants dodged back and forth in the aisles with trays of lemonade that came from three big barrels up in the baggage-car. Big boxes of savory Julian apples were loaded on at Oceanside and distributed with a freedom that made the "butcher-boy" shut up his sale-box in despair.

Stops at Stations

Wherever the train stopped the excursionists hopped off in large numbers from the cars, and, like naughty children, were loath to respond to the "All aboard!" cry of Conductor Jack Davis. At San Juan Capistrano, daring ones tried to see the Mission in thirty seconds and narrowly escaped being left. Judge Richard Egan, whose home at this place is famed for its forty-year record of hospitality, was at the station. Instantly, a white ribbon was pinned upon his coat, and he was shoved aboard the train, as he tossed his house-key to the station agent.

Oceanside had numerous carriages lined up at the depot, and the enthusiastic people of the place tried to elope to the hills with the train-load. As the Special was behind time only a five-minute stop was made, just long enough for the distribution of great armsful of red and white carnations, fresh picked from Oceanside's famous carnation gardens. A few risked the ride in the rigs, and were left behind. It was here that a committee from San Diego extended the first greeting to the Angelenos.

The gentlemen on the committee were: O. W. Cotton, E. H. Stewart, A. Moran, M. L. Ward, J. L. Doyle, and J. M. Ballou.

Cheers of Welcome

Cheers broke from a big crowd in front of the San Diego depot as the special train emptied forth its contingent of prettily gowned women, dainty little children and clean-cut men. The size and character of the delegation was evidently a surprise. It had been expected that few women would undertake the long day's jaunt. Cars in waiting whisked the visitor down to the wharf, where the "big feed" was basking in the sun and "seeing San Diego" was at last begun. Impatient steam yachts and launches were in position at the landing, and as soon as luncheon was over, they were loaded and dispatched on a trip about the bay. Coronado was visited.

All the badges of the Los Angeles Chamber of Commerce were honored as fare on the car-lines of the city, through the courtesy of the Spreckels' interests. The remainder of the afternoon was devoted to car-rides.

Everything Free

Informality was perhaps the secret of the success of San Diego's hospitality. Nobody was called upon to make speeches, there were no brass bands and no receptions. Except for the fact that everything was free, the visitors were treated just "like old residents," as one Angeleno put it. Another said that he had not been allowed to pay for a drink in a city barroom—and he wanted to remain—if the badge held good for more than a day.

The return trip was made at 6:30 o'clock in the evening, the train arriving in Los Angeles at 11:30 o'clock. O. W. Cotton and others of the Reception Committee acompanied the guests back to Los Angeles, seeing them safely home, so to speak. About 160 people of the delegation remained overnight in San Diego. For these, excursions will be run today to La Jolla; Tia Juana, Mexico; the Sweetwater Dam; Point Loma, and the Old Mission.

Later, the San Diego *Union* described the excursion as follows:

SAN DIEGO UNION
MAKES REPORT ON EXCURSION

O. W. COTTON GIVES STATEMENT OF RESULTS
TO CHAMBER OF COMMERCE

Votes of Thanks Extended Those Who Rendered
Valuable Help

At the meeting of the Directors of the Chamber of Commerce held yesterday afternoon, O. W. Cotton, Chairman of the Excursion Committee, presented his report of the Los Angeles Chamber of Commerce Excursion.

Among other things in his report, Mr. Cotton said:

"The Bohemian lunch was paid for by subscriptions from some of the businessmen of San Diego, as were also the launches, with the exception of the launch *Kate,* the use of which was extended to us without charge by its owner, V. Primrose.

"We would like to request that votes of thanks be extended to Mr. Primrose for the above service, to the San Diego businessmen who so generously contributed funds for the entertainment of our guests. Mr. A. Sensenbrenner for donation of portion of the cigars used, Fletcher-Doyle Company, Simon Levi, Nason & Company, fruits, and also to the San Diego Electric Company, who extended the free use of their entire car system, for the afternoon of the day the excursion arrived, to the Los Angeles visitors. The courtesy of the car company was especially appreciated by the Los Angeles people, and made a lasting impression with them.

"The excursionists expressed themselves as being very much pleased with their trip here, and we cannot but feel that this excursion will do much toward assisting in the elimination of the feeling which has in the past existed between our two cities."

During my activities with the Chamber of Commerce, I received a confidential letter from our old friend, J. H. Holmes, of the Hotel Green, Pasadena, California, asking me about San Diego and its prospects. I answered his letter fully and promptly, but I heard no more from him, and during the next several months often wondered what had prompted his inquiry.

CHAPTER XVI

I Learn to Smoke

LATE IN 1904, another nice thing happened to me. I was invited to join the Elks. In the early days of Elkdom, so we understood, many Elks Lodges were composed largely of actors, but when our San Diego Lodge B.P.O.E., No. 168, was organized, there were not enough men in that classification in San Diego to make up a club, so they took in bank presidents and cashiers, heads of corporations, stores, theaters, and occasionally a real estate man. I presume I was invited to join because my old friend, Havelock Morrow, who had come from Bisbee to join our office staff, told them of my former theatrical experience. He had formerly lived in San Diego and belonged to the Elks. In any event, as soon as I was initiated, I was called upon to entertain the lodge, which made me feel at home.

After I married, I did not attend meetings, but in those first few years it was good fun and good fellowship. Some of the prominent Elks of that day were: Patterson Sprigg, C. Fred Henking, John B. Osborn, J. M. Dodge, Eugene Daney, LeRoy A. Wright, A. F. Cornell, E. A. Hornbeck, Carl I. Ferris, Dr. Edward Grove, Frank S. Banks, A. H. Sweet, Alex Reynolds, Jr., W. C. Crandall, Carl H. Heilbron, Frank A. Frye, Montgomery M. Moulton, Dr. D. H. Elliott, John A. Gillons, A. L. Flowers, Dr. D. Gochenauer, Albert Schoonover, Duncan MacKinnon, Richard C. Benbough, and Russell H. Gunnis.

At the Elks Club meetings and at the Chamber of Commerce banquets, most of them smoked cigars. A few smoked cigarettes (coffin nails), but the proper thing was a large, fat cigar. I had had an experience with a cigar when I was sixteen which had definitely put all thought of smoking entirely out of my head.

When we were in Ontario, California, I had become acquainted with a small band of fellows my own age who got together evenings, playing "Run, Sheep, Run!" One evening, one of the fellows said there had been a marriage that day and suggested that we get some pans and cans and sticks and give the newlyweds a charivari. That sounded like a good idea, so we gather together some noisemakers and marched in front of the house where a party was in session, and opened up full blast. I felt that we were being highly improper and that I was into mischief, but I went along and did my part.

Within five minutes, the door opened, and instead of a policeman as I rather expected, or someone threatening to have us arrested, out came the groom with a broad, happy grin, and a box of cigars. We all took a cigar, and the charivari was over.

Someone in the gang had some matches, so we all lit our cigars and started to smoke. The other fellows all threw their cigars away after a few puffs, but this seemed to me to be not only wasteful but also rather discourteous after we had forced the groom to give us the cigars, so I continued to smoke mine. I did not like it much, but I kept smoking. When it was half-smoked, I began to feel light in the head, but I continued working at it until there was not too much left, and then threw it away.

Suddenly, I lost all interest in the game of "Run, Sheep, Run!" We were then at the Southern Pacific Station, and I climbed on one of the station baggage trucks and sprawled out full length. That did not help. The whole world started turning round and round, and over and over. I will leave the rest to your imagination.

The only other time in my life when I felt I would rather die than live was during a fishing trip off Coronado. I have always become seasick when aboard a boat, but after I've stayed away from boats for a few years I think that possibly I've outgrown the weakness and give it another try. Roscoe Hazard got up this party. I have forgotten who else was along, but when we could not catch any fish cruising, he anchored over a "hole" where they could catch yellow-fin, or some special fish, and they did, but not me. I lay flat on the deck while the boat rocked and rolled. My subconscious mind told me that it would be over sometime and that I would be glad I had not rolled into the ocean but drowned, but my conscious mind insisted that drowning would be a relief!

At the Elks' meetings, the Chamber of Commerce dinners, and other gatherings, to see practically all the other fellows (all older) smoking, made me feel youthful and not one of the crowd I admired, so I determined to do something about it. I started with small cigars about three times the size of a cigarette. I experimented with various brands labeled "mild." None of them seemed "mild" to me, but I studiously worked at it during off hours, so that it would not interfere with business. After several years, I got to the point where I could smoke two cigars a day without getting sick. About that time, the smoke began to hurt my throat, so I switched to a pipe, which was better, but soon even half a pipe of tobacco was too much. Fortunately, by that time, I was sufficiently "grown up" and established in business that I felt I could quit and still keep my self-respect.

As the years have slipped by and I have seen the grip which smoking has on some people, how it smells up a house, the breath, and the clothing, and the actual harm which it does some persons, I consider myself fortunate to be allergic to tobacco. I have one very good friend who, a few years ago, had an operation for cancer of the throat. When the "party" was over and he was OK again except for the loss of his voice, he asked his surgeon, "Why should this thing have happened to me?"

The surgeon could not answer that one, so my friend pressed the point with, "Would smoking cigarettes have had anything to do with it?"

The surgeon replied, "I could not say that smoking had anything to do with your trouble, but I can tell you that I have performed this operation a great many times, but never on a non-smoker."

My friend has never smoked since.

In December, 1906, two momentous things happened. At least, they were both of moment to me: John D. Spreckels announced that he would build the long-discussed railroad to Imperial Valley, to connect with the Southern Pacific and thus give San Diego a direct rail line to the East; and I organized the Pacific Building Company.

There had been many attempts, feeble and otherwise, to build a direct railroad from San Diego to Yuma, and there had been so much talk about it that, when I came here to live, most of our residents believed that San Diego would never amount to anything until we got that railroad. A common expression was that San Diegans had had "a railroad for breakfast every morning," referring to the numerous hopeful announcements which had appeared in the San Diego *Morning Union*. Years later, George W. Marston told me that he had once worked on a project trying to raise money to get a survey for such a railroad, and had one day made a talk to a group of businessmen, saying, "Gentlemen, if we could get a direct rail connection to the East, San Diego would grow to be a city of fifty thousand people!" He told me that story in about 1940, and our population then was two hundred thousand.

All previous attempts to build this railroad had come to naught, but when John D. Spreckels said he would build it, San Diego knew it would be built. At that time, Mr. Spreckels, in company with his brother, A. B. Spreckels, owned the Coronado Hotel, more than half of all Coronado, all of North Island, all of the land and shoreline from Coronado to Imperial Beach, the ferry system, our street-railway system, the San Diego *Union* and the *Evening Tribune*. They owned our source of water supply, the upper and lower Otay dams and reservoirs, and the dam site where later the Morena Dam was built.

For many years, John D. Spreckels and his family had lived in San Francisco, but after the great earthquake and fire there in April, 1906, he had moved to San Diego and had built a beautiful home across the street from the Coronado Hotel, and had made many other large real estate investments here. He was San Diego's outstanding citizen for many years, and a wonderful man he was. So when John D. Spreckels said he would build a railroad to connect with the Southern Pacific at Imperial Valley, everybody accepted it as a fact, and the town went wild.

San Diegans, who the day before would have scoffed at the idea of buying San Diego real estate as an investment, bought all they could pay for, quick! before prices started to jump. For nine months, the local real estate market was fast and furious. We even sold Pacific Beach lots to local speculators!

1905, 1906, and 1907 were "Good Old Days"!

CHAPTER XVII

The Pacific Building Company

THE Pacific Building Company started with a cash paid capital of $5,000. Its officers and directors were:

O. W. Cotton—*President and General Manager*
F. R. Burnham—*Vice-President*
G. H. Frost—*Secretary and Treasurer*
A. H. Frost—*Director*
W. R. Rogers—*Director*

The purpose of the Pacific Building Company was to build houses to be sold on the monthly payment plan—something entirely new for San Diego in those days. The fact that I knew nothing about the building business or the mortgage loan business did not worry me. I had known nothing about acting as stage manager for a Shakespearean production, nor about running an ice wagon, nor about real estate, but I had gotten away with it. The confidence of youth is unlimited!

At that time, there were only one or two small building and loan societies in San Diego; most of the money lent on homes was loaned by the savings banks, at 7 percent interest. The loans were for not more than 50 percent of the value of the house and lot. The entire principal was payable in three, or sometimes five, years, and the borrowers could not make monthly payments. Even the interest must be accumulated by the borrower and paid quarterly.

In Los Angeles, there was one large home-building company, and many contractors, building and selling homes on the small monthly payment plan, so I went to Los Angeles to find out how it was done. I found the secret of their financing was an instrument entirely unknown in San Diego at that time, called the "deed of trust" or "trust deed."

The old-fashioned "mortgage" demanded by our local savings banks was perfectly good security for the loan, but in the case of failure on the part of the borrower it would take the bank about a year and a half to get possession of the property, during which time the borrower would have free use of the house, and, of course, in most cases would let it run down badly. This new instrument, the deed of trust, could be foreclosed in ninety days, which put the lending agency in a much stronger position.

Whereas the banks would lend up to only 40 to 50 percent of value on a mortgage, the builder would lend up to 80 percent—40 to 50 percent on a first mortgage and the balance on a trust deed made subject to the mortgage. The mortgage would be made as the banks wanted them, payable in their entirety in three to five years, and the trust deeds would be payable in monthly payments.

With that setup, we were in clover with our Pacific Building Company. We started building small homes and found a ready market with our local banks for every one of our first mortgages, which made us carry only the trust deeds, a part of which represented our profits. The trust deeds paid 8 percent interest on the unpaid balance from the time the house was completed. The purchaser of the home liked it because he could pay monthly, like rent, and before he spent his money elsewhere, and it was good for us because every month our loan would become more secure.

We got the Pacific Building Company actively under way in 1907, and before we stopped building houses in the summer of 1914, because of World War I, we advertised that if all the homes we had built were placed side by side on fifty-foot lots it would make a street more than eight miles long. That was a record in home building for San Diego that was not broken by anyone until the building of Linda Vista by the United States Government in 1942.

During the entire life of the Pacific Building Company and even though we went through a very bad depression in San Diego during the years following the First World War, we did not have to foreclose on a total of more than half a dozen trust deeds. Nowadays, all banks and other institutions making home loans insist that all payments be made monthly, and in San Diego the deed of trust is used exclusively.

It was about this time that I had an opportunity, made possible by the senior partner, to sell my interests in Folsom Bros. Company, and that gave me my entire time to devote to the now rapidly expanding Pacific Building Company. When I arrived in San Diego in 1903, I had cash capital of $1,250. Four years later, when I sold my interest in Folsom Bros. Company, my cashable assets were a little better than $50,000. While relations between us three partners were at times strained because of our differences of opinion as to how the business should be conducted, we all profited equally up until the time I left the firm, and I am sure I earned my full share of the total profits.

I was most fortunate during my early days in San Diego to develop the friendship of so many very fine San Diegans. Through my membership in the Elks Club and my work in the Chamber of Commerce, I made many lasting friends. Outstanding among these gentlemen were: Dr. R. F. Burnham, one of our leading physicians and brother-in-law to George W. Marston; A. H. Frost, a retired bachelor from East Jordan, Michigan; and William R. Rogers, cashier of the Merchants National Bank.

I invited each of these gentlemen to become directors of the new Pacific Building Company, and they all accepted, which gave the company an excellent standing and reputation from the very start. It made a most happy situation for me. For secretary-treasurer, I invited George H. Frost, a nephew of A. H. Frost, and just a few years my senior.

As though it were yesterday, I remember Dr. Burnham's saying to me, "Cotton, habit is everything in this life. If you form good habits at your age and keep them until you are thirty-five, we can check you off the list, because that is the way you will carry on throughout your life."

To me at that time, Dr. Burnham was a middle-aged gentleman, probably forty-seven years old. Many years after he was gone I was chatting with his son, Marston Burnham, and told him of this admonition. I said that, because I had held his father in such high esteem, I had taken his advice and had followed it, and that I had always regretted it.

Will Rogers was a pleasant, friendly gentleman and a banker of the old school. I doubt if he paid much attention to financial statements. Either a man's word was good or it was not. If it were, he could borrow all the money he wanted, whenever he wanted and for as long as he wanted. If, in Will Rogers' judgment a man's word was not good, he got nothing. He was another wonderful associate.

Mr. A. H. Frost must have been sixty-five or more when I first met him. He was rather frail and delicate, but he had a most generous and lovable disposition. He was interested in real estate and was wonderful company for me. Many years after he was gone, I happened to see a little quotation in a magazine which described one of Mr. Frost's characteristics so well that I clipped it out and for these many years I have had it pasted on a small door in the front of my desk. It is not only a reminder of A. H. Frost, but one of the ideal standards of life that, if practiced by all men as Mr. Frost practiced it, would make for a happier world:

TOLERANCE

The most lovable quality any human being can possess is Tolerance. Tolerance is the vision that enables one to see things from another's viewpoint. It is the generosity that concedes to others the right to their own opinion and peculiarities. It is the bigness that enables us to let people be happy in their own way instead of in our way.

To start with, the Pacific Building Company had an authorized capital of $100,000—which I thought looked quite nice on our letterhead and in our ads. Our subscribed capital was $20,000 and the actual paid-in cash, $5,000. In the building business, even in those days, $5,000 did not last long. Within a few months, the first subscribers paid the balance of $15,000, but even $20,000 cash was not a drop in the bucket compared to what we needed. I bought more stock and sold more to some of the directors, and then started selling it around town to various businessmen, about $500 to $1,000 each; however, this was too slow, and it took too much of my own time, so I reorganized the company.

The new company had a capital of one million dollars, with one million shares at one dollar each. We had made a fine profit on our small capital investment, so we paid a stock dividend of 65 percent and exchanged the old $100 shares for the new $1 shares. I then advertised what we had done, and offered $50,000 of the new stock publicly at $1 per share. Boy! did it sell! We were financed.

When I was in Bisbee, there were about seven young men to each marriageable girl, possibly more. The reason for this state of affairs was that the high wages, which had attracted my friend Havelock Morrow and me, also attracted other young men from the cities of the West.

In San Diego at that time, when a young man finished school he went elsewhere for a job, because there was literally nothing for him in a financial way in San Diego. Here, then, young men were at a premium.

I saw and met a great many of the finest young folks in San Diego, but I was so busy with our business and the Chamber of Commerce that I missed a lot of the good times others of my age enjoyed. So many years of my life had been spent striving for so little, and it seemed I had such a long way to go now that things were coming my way, I felt I must make every day count. In those days, the rules were that a man must accumulate enough of this world's goods while he was young to take care of himself and his family when he was old, or else. It was claimed that 93 percent of the male population was broke at age sixty-five. That was not a very cheerful outlook, and it provided plenty of reason for me to keep my nose to the grindstone. Years later, I heard about the wonderful times some of my friends of those days had at Witch Creek, an old home in the mountains east of San Diego, about a day's trip by stage, operated by the Woods family. The times they told of having at that old ranch must have been great fun for kids in their early twenties; but in my early twenties, I was no longer a kid.

One day in 1906, while en route East by train I stopped over in Los

Angeles and had dinner at Aunt Mag's in Highland Park. The occasion was a birthday party for my cousin, George Rice, Jr., her youngest son, and to celebrate properly he brought home a bottle of champagne. For a number of us, it was our first taste of champagne. It tickled as I swallowed, but it tasted good.

At this party, I met a friend of the family, Miss Violet Savage, and was able to get somewhat acquainted before dinner. However, I must not have made much of an impression, since years afterward I was quite shocked to learn that she did not even recall it was I who had taken her home that evening! Taking a young lady home in those days meant walking her to the streetcar, transferring a time or two, and finally, in an hour or so, arriving at her street and accompanying her to her gate.

Miss Savage did make quite an impression on me.

She was a piano teacher, and her early life had been somewhat akin to my own. She had given her first paid concert at thirteen, and had begun her teaching at fourteen. When she was twelve, a friend, realizing her unusual talent, had taken her to Los Angeles to the outstanding teacher of piano, Herr Thilo Becker. Herr Becker had had her play for him and had immediately put her under the tutelage of one of his advanced pupils for one year, after which she was to come to him, which she did.

She had lived at Monrovia with her mother. She rode her bicycle to the train, hoisted it board, got it off again in Los Angeles, and rode uptown to take her lessons, then back home again. Between her practicing, her lessons with Herr Becker, her teaching and professional accompanying, she led a very busy life—a life largely wrapped up in music. But all of this hard work paid off. With her teaching, she supported her mother and herself in comfort and developed an appreciation for music that was of the greatest pleasure and value to her and to her friends and family throughout her life.

At the time I met her, she had forty pupils. She gave lessons to quite a number of her pupils at their homes, traveling by streetcar, and catching up with her reading en route. She played the piano wonderfully, with the most beautiful touch, tone, and interpretation I had ever heard. I have heard many fine pianists but not one whom I enjoy hearing more than Violet Savage.

Later that year, I boarded a streetcar with my suitcase and stereopticon machine, on my way to lecture at Blanchard Hall in Los Angeles, and there, sitting and reading a book, was Miss Violet Savage! I was always timid about women, and I still wonder how I had the nerve to do it, but I walked right across the aisle and sat down beside her. Before I got off the streetcar, I had given her two tickets to my lecture.

And that is how it all started.

Violet Savage and I were married in Los Angeles on the ninth day of May, 1907. We took a honeymoon trip to Santa Barbara, San Francisco, and Yosemite Valley.

San Francisco was a mess. There were no "Good Old Days" in the city then. Not only was it just one year since the great earthquake and fire, but also, to cap the climax, a streetcar strike was on.

Yosemite was wonderful. In those days, they did not open the Park until the snows had been cleared off the dirt roads. We arrived on the fifth day after the opening. It had been a wet year and all the streams were running full. We saw it at its best. We hiked to the tops of the trails and had a marvelous time—even got in one light snowstorm.

All this was in the very early stage of the life of the Pacific Building Company and, when I received a letter from the secretary of the company suggesting that, if I wanted to hold the company together, I had better get back to San Diego, we got. It was just as well we did. I had taken along all my spare cash, but my calculations as to how long money would last for two in place of one hadn't, apparently, been quite right. We barely got back in time. I had no cash—but my credit was good in San Diego.

CHAPTER XVIII

A New Life

THE NEW Mrs. O. W. Cotton made a wonderful hit. She was popular from the day she arrived in San Diego, and as folks got to know her better her popularity grew. Years afterward, she told me that, before coming to San Diego, she had had a mental reservation that after a few years she might persuade me to sell out in San Diego and go to Los Angeles to live, but by the time she told me that she thought there was no place for her to live but San Diego.

At first, we lived in a house which the Pacific Building Company had built on Diamond Avenue at Pacific Beach: "Job No. 1." Then we moved to a home I built on Fourth Avenue, between University Avenue and Washington Street, in Hillcrest. It was there our son William was born. When William was six months old, we sold our new home and moved to an old house I had acquired at the corner of Albatross and Juniper streets. Later, we moved to another new home I built in South Park, and there our daughter Jane was born. The next home I built was on Third Avenue, between Walnut and Brookes streets, and the next day after we moved in our son John was born. I thought it was about time to quit building homes!

Now, as I write this, and our family has grown up and each branch has given us the pleasure of parenthood, then grandparenthood, and now great-grandparenthood, all serving to make our lives so worthwhile, I am sorry we did not build a few more homes.

The Pacific Building Company made a reputation very early in its career by advertising that it would build a good, plastered, five-room house, for $895, complete with two bedrooms and bath, living room, dining room, kitchen, front and rear porches, electric lights, fireplace, and built-ins. These houses were well built and of good material. We did not make much profit on them, but they were a dandy ad.

There was a financial crisis in Wall Street in the early fall of 1907, and many of the banks throughout the nation had to stop cashing checks or paying out money, and used scrip. In San Diego, however, business had not really got under way after the long depression of nearly nineteen years, so we had no trouble except that money was tight for a few months and we had to slow down.

The real estate "boom," started in December, 1906, by the John D. Spreckels' railroad news, came to a sudden halt. In those days, when buying enthusiasm stopped, it stopped, and nothing anyone could do about it made any difference. The surprising thing is that those "flash in the pan" boomlets created as much buying interest as they did.

Picture the San Diego of 1907: A town of possibly twenty-five thousand people, and actually thousands of vacant lots in all directions, and countless thousands of acres yet to be subdivided! Imagine anyone, least of all a San Diegan, buying vacant property expecting that it would double in value!

After the great Stock Market Crash of 1929 I was on the witness stand in court on an appraisal, and an attorney said, "Mr. Cotton, you have some signs on some of your properties on Linda Vista Mesa?"

"Yes," I answered.

"One of those signs says: 'These lots will surely double'?"

"Yes," I replied, "but it doesn't say when."

Real estate business in San Diego in the days before World War II was always a feast or a famine. Properties sold fast and furious when enthusiasm was high, but when it died, that was the end. Not so with our home building program.

Before I was married, my personal expenses ran around $90 a month, $10 of which was for my room on the third floor of the Imperial Hotel on Broadway between Seventh and Eighth avenues. Six years later, I stopped by one morning at our new home at 3543 Third Avenue, and for a time I sat in the car. I pinched myself to be sure it was all true. Here was a truly beautiful home we had built. A gardener was working in the yard, a washwoman was hanging out clothes at the rear of the house. There was a cook, a nurse, a wife, and three children. There was also a $10,000 mortgage. I wondered if I were going too fast. That was early in 1913, just before the financial panic.

In 1908, I moved our office from Fifth Avenue to D Street (now Broadway) in the old Methodist Church property between Fourth and Fifth avenues. The next four years—until the financial crash of 1913— were "Good Old Days" for sure. The United States soon snapped out of the 1907 panic and was prosperous. San Diego had been getting some publicity, and it was getting more all the time. New people were coming, and there was an actual demand for new homes.

I bought all of the stock in the Pacific Building Company that I felt I could safely carry, at the starting price of a dollar per share. As we needed more money, we offered more to the public and generally sold our full offerings. As we made profits to justify doing so, we increased the price on the new offerings and also the cash dividends. Then we started to buy and to develop real estate subdivisions.

One of our first tracts was about one block north of University Avenue, on Utah and Idaho streets, west of Thirtieth Street. We built sixty homes of four and five rooms each in this tract, and each house and lot sold, complete, for from $1,800 to $2,200. Most of the lots were 40 by 140 feet. Terms of purchase were: $100 cash, and $25 per month. That was in 1909.

One of our head salesmen at that time was W. H. Taylor. Mr. Taylor sold many of these homes, either before or after they were built. Some thirty years later, in 1939, I was writing an article on "Depreciation on Houses" and I asked Mr. Taylor, who was still with us, to canvass those houses and find out how many were for sale and at what price. The cheapest home he could find in the tract was then offered at $3,600.

In October, 1960, I drove to this tract, parked my car on Idaho Street north of Polk Street, and walked around the block. I found one house, at 2817 Howard Street, for sale at $15,000. At 2820 Polk Street, there was a house on a small lot, which had recently sold for $14,500. Another house, in good condition, on a 50 by 140 foot lot, at 4012 Utah Street, had recently had a prospective purchaser, so the owner told me, whose offer of $17,000 had been refused.

After the University Heights tract, we got into large tracts, where we subdivided and sold the lots without building houses, but we did continue to build and to finance individual houses, scattered all over San Diego, wherever an owner wanted it.

The profits in the building business were not large, because the overhead required to run the organization was high. I remember we used to have a payroll of $6,500 a week, and that was when carpenters were paid $3.50 for eight hours.

D. C. Collier, another "old man" in his late forties, was a most able competitor in the subdivision and sale of lots in those days. He was elected to the presidency of the Chamber of Commerce in 1908. For a number of years, the presidency of the Chamber had been passed from one dignitary to another, as a well-deserved honor, but without regard to the particular ability of the individual insofar as the planning and execution of the development of the community were concerned. At this 1908 election, the Old Guard campaigned for a splendid, dignified, semi-retired gentleman. G. Aubrey Davidson and his friends wanted D. C. Collier. I sat at the back of the room, sizing up the two candidates, and made up my mind that we needed to get out of the old rut. I voted for Collier. He was elected by *one vote*. That was one of the most important votes I ever cast, as you will see.

G. Aubrey Davidson was a man of wide vision. He believed in San Diego and its future. He was in about the same age bracket as Collier. He had been auditor for the Santa Fe Railroad. In 1907, he had returned to San Diego and had opened a new bank. He came determined to do big things, and he did. His bank, the Southern Trust & Commerce Bank, started business in the basement of the new Granger Building, at Fifth Avenue and Broadway, right under the Merchants National Bank, which occupied the first floor.

Ulysses S. Grant, Jr., for many years one of San Diego's leading citizens, had acquired the famous old Horton House facing the Plaza on Broadway between Third and Fourth avenues, and had started construction of the nearly block square U. S. Grant Hotel. When the panic of 1907 hit us, all work on the hotel stopped and this naked, reinforced concrete skeleton stood, silent, for month after month, a blight on our downtown district. One of the first jobs Davidson undertook after he located in San Diego was to interest outside capitalists in working out a new financing plan for the hotel so that it could be completed. As soon as the work was far enough along, he moved his bank into its Fourth Avenue and Broadway corner, and stayed there until it was absorbed by the Bank of America twenty years or more later.

One day just after the bank had moved in and before the scaffolding was removed, I went in to see Davidson. Who should be sitting there talking to him but our old friend, J. H. Holmes, of the Hotel Green, in Pasadena. I had not seen Mr. Holmes since I was in my early teens, but I shall never forget his warm greeting, and his remark to Davidson: "You can depend on Oscar Cotton. He comes from good stock."

I realized then, of course, why Holmes had written me some months before, asking in confidence about conditions in San Diego. Mr. Holmes opened the U. S. Grant Hotel and operated it for many years, and a grand hotel it was. It was the pride of all San Diego, with a ballroom on the ninth floor and an excellent dining room on the first floor. Those were "Good Old Days" when chefs were chefs, and each chef was an individual "artist" and food was quality. It was expensive to eat at the U. S. Grant Hotel, but you got your money's worth. The atmosphere was good. Holmes told me once, some years later, that he sometimes lost $50,000 in one year on his dining room, but of course they made it up on their seven hundred rooms. J. H. Holmes became one of our leading citizens, and he and his wife and daughter, Angie, were beloved by all San Diegans whose privilege it was to know them.

CHAPTER XIX

Our First Exposition

IN 1909, Davidson was elected president of the Chamber of Commerce, and one of the first things he did was to propose that the Chamber promote the holding of an International Exposition in San Diego. Whew! That was the beginning of a real upswing in development that gave the city of San Diego an entirely new look. There was great publicity, a big increase in population, and an over-all growth that was a pleasure to behold.

Picture, if you can, Balboa Park as it was in 1908. The only portion that was developed as a "park" was a little strip along Sixth Avenue, south of Upas Street. On the mesa land north of what is now Laurel Street and west of the present Park Boulevard, a nine-hole grassless golf course, with twenty-five-foot sand "greens," had been laid out. Otherwise, the entire fourteen hundred acres of "park" land—hills, canyons, and level areas —were covered with greasewood, rocks, and hardpan.

To hold an International Exposition was a stupendous undertaking for a city of around thirty-five thousand in population, and in the final analysis it turned out to be fully as big an undertaking as it sounded. It was organized and promoted as the "Panama-California International Exposition," and the plan was to tie in the old Spanish days with the present.

G. Aubrey Davidson was elected president. The Board of Directors, officers, and Executive Committee were:

Officers

G. A. Davidson	President
John D. Spreckels	First Vice-President
F. J. Belcher, Jr.	Second Vice-President
H. H. Jones	Third Vice-President
George Burnham	Fourth Vice-President
C. L. Williams	Secretary
F. W. Jackson	Treasurer
E. J. Chapin	Director-General
C. H. Tingey	Auditor
H. H. Barter	General Superintendent

Board of Directors

R. C. Allen	M. F. Heller
Lucius R. Barrow	H. H. Jones
Frank J. Belcher, Jr.	W. F. Ludington
L. A. Blochman	Arthur H. Marston
George Burnham	J. W. Sefton, Jr.
William Clayton	W. A. Sloane
G. A. Davidson	John D. Spreckels
C. W. Fox	C. L. Williams
D. F. Garrettson	Julius Wagenheim
P. H. Goodwin	E. J. Burns
	C. H. Heilbron

Executive Committee

Frank J. Belcher, Jr., *Chairman*
E. J. Burns
G. A. Davidson
P. H. Goodwin
M. F. Heller
C. L. Williams
W. A. Sloane

The first campaign for funds had a goal of one million dollars, and they raised it. Bertram Grosvenor Goodhugh, one of the nation's leading architects, was employed. As his representative, he sent Carleton Monroe Winslow, who gave San Diego what is unquestionably one of the most beautiful groups of buildings ever designed. San Diegans who were not here in 1915-1916, should look at the beautiful pictures of these original buildings appearing in Carleton Winslow's book *The Architecture and the Gardens of the San Diego Exposition,* with Introduction by Bertram Goodhue. They are breath-taking.

It took five strenuous years and the time, thought, work, and money of many of our leading citizens, but when the "Panama-California International Exposition" opened, on the night of January 1, 1915, I can tell you that it was indeed a glorious sight to behold. I shall never forget that night. The entrance to the Exposition was across the new Balboa Bridge, since at that time most of San Diego's population lived west of Sixth Avenue. In company with some close friends, we took the streetcar and got off at Laurel Street and Fifth Avenue, and, after we passed through the turnstiles at Seventh Street, there before us was a solid mass of humanity, the full width and length of the bridge, surging toward and under the great arches of the California Building. Remember, as you visualize this thrilling scene and look at the pictures in Winslow's book, that San Diego's population was not over forty thousand people! As we walked along the avenues, through the Grand Central Plaza, through the patios and the gardens, and for the first time saw those gorgeous buildings beautifully lighted, it seemed almost as though we had been transported to another planet.

This Exposition cost a lot of money, many times more than they ever took in at the gate, and it was a tremendous job, but it was a wonderful advertisement for San Diego. It gave San Diegans an excuse to remodel and paint and refurbish old homes and other buildings all over the city. It spurred property owners and the city to pave the downtown streets and to do many other things to give us a "modern" city. It made our Balboa Park a thing of fame and beauty far ahead of our time.

After the Exposition, the buildings served many valuable purposes, as well as being used for recreational groups and for entertainment. Some of these old buildings and some of those from the last Exposition, in 1935-36, are now used daily by thousands of San Diegans and visitors and add wonderfully to the enjoyment of many people.

Ever since closing of this, our first Exposition, on December 31, 1916, the question has been asked and argued long and loud: "What shall we do with the obsolete Exposition buildings?" Again and again "experts" have advocated that the buildings be torn down and the ground developed as a park, in grass and trees.

Recently, a friend asked me what I thought. I answered, "Yes. By all means, tear the buildings down. Tear down the Recreation Center, where thousands play basketball, and the nearby halls where they hold the flower shows. Make the grounds into a park. Tear down the House of Hospitality, with its directors' room, cocktail lounge, theater, and beautiful dining terrace. Tear down the fine arts gallery, the California Building, the Museum of Man, and the zoo. Tear down the Old Globe Theater and the Ford Bowl where they have been having the summer symphonies and the Starlight Opera and, while you are at it, tear down the Cabrillo Bridge and then put the whole five hundred acres into grass and trees."

I must be losing my knack for salesmanship. My friend decided we had better keep the buildings.

It may be that since the advent of television it will never again be practical to hold another Exposition. This theory may or may not be correct, but it seems to me that we should continue to use these park buildings for their highest and best use as long as practical, and to tear one down only when the space can be used for something of more value to the people of our community. We have a lovely park between the Cabrillo Freeway and

Our mother, Alice V. Cotton, with Laura at the age of seventeen, the year that Laura played cornet solos at the First Congregational Church and in vaudeville in San Diego, before going with Mother to New York City.

Oscar W. Cotton, "lecturer," in 1905.

Miss Violet Savage of Los Angeles, taken in 1907 before our marriage.

Our office on Fifth Avenue north of D Street (Broadway), San Diego, in 1904. In the right-hand (south) window is an enlarged version of the relief map of San Diego I made in 1903 showing its two harbors. The north window exhibits an enlarged photograph of Pacific Beach at low tide and shows automobiles driving over the wide, hard strand. Seated in the White Steamer are (*left to right*) O. W. Cotton, Johnnie Gillons, proprietor of the clothing store adjoining our office, the chauffeur, and M. W. Folsom. Ordinarily we would have had a horse tied to one of the hitching posts, with a high, two-seated trap for driving prospective customers to show them the town.

Historical Collection, Title Insurance and Trust Company, Union Title Office, San Diego, California

The southwest corner of Fifth and D Streets (Broadway) in 1903.

Historical Collection, Title Insurance and Trust Company, Union Title Office, San Diego, California

McKie Block, the northeast corner of Fifth and D Streets (Broadway) in 1909, after I had moved our Pacific Building Company office one block west.

THE 1915 EXPOSITION: One of the many formal gardens. The beautiful California Tower, which has become a symbol of San Diego the world over, is in the background.

Historical Collection, Title Insurance and Trust Company, Union Title Office, San Diego, California

Historical Collection, Title Insurance and Trust Company
Union Title Office, San Diego, California

THE 1915 EXPOSITION: One of the lovely curving avenues.

THE 1915 EXPOSITION: Along El Prado, the main thoroughfare through San Diego's first exposition, showing how the ornate beauty of another era was recaptured in the architecture of the buildings.

THE 1915 EXPOSITION: Another view along El Prado.

Sixth Avenue, and, except for the one section devoted to games, how many people visit it daily compared to the tens of thousands who enjoy the various former Exposition buildings, the Zoo and the Bowl?

When I arrived in San Diego in the summer of 1903, San Diego was just beginning to recover from the collapse of the great Santa Fe Railroad boom of 1886-88. The only apparent evidence of "recovery" was the life at Tent City during the summer months. A few of us, who were trying to sell town lots, capitalized on every little thing that happened. The remarks made to me one day by Mr. M. F. Heller, then one of our leading grocers and later to become San Diego's first chain grocery store promoter, reflect the discouragement which was prevalent in the minds of most San Diego businessmen.

"Cotton," said Mr. Heller, "it is not a good idea to advertise for more people to come to San Diego until we have some factories here. There is nothing for them to do. No way they can make a living. The town right now has all the people it can support."

I simply could not go along with Mr. Heller's thinking. From the day I arrived in San Diego, I believed there were a great many people in the United States who could afford to live where they chose, and who would come to San Diego and build a city, and that all we had to do was to let them know about it. I did not have much of an idea as to how we could get our message across to enough of these people, and how we could convince them, but later I did conceive how it could be done, and we did it. Never, in my wildest dreams, however, did I visualize a San Diego half as big as it is today!

When I came here there were many empty stores in San Diego and many, many empty residences. If you took the steam train through National City to Chula Vista, you would pass rows of empty old store buildings. It was quite appalling. We were working, with our strenuous but meager methods, to bring people to San Diego, and while many bought lots, few came, except for a vacation at Tent City. But the year 1903 was a turning point for San Diego. An upswing began that was to show an almost continuous advance until the Wall Street Crash in the spring of 1913.

The years 1910 to 1912 were wonderful years. Work on the Exposition buildings was progressing and enthusiasm was mounting throughout the city. We did not realize it then, but actually we were enjoying a building and development boom of the first water. John D. Spreckels was the strongest financial backer of the Exposition and, as always, he led almost all subscription lists for every proposed project for civic betterment in San Diego. Further demonstrating his faith in San Diego, Spreckels had purchased most of the lots, and sometimes almost whole blocks, on the south side of Broadway, from Third Street west to the Santa Fe tracks, as well as considerable property on the north side of the street.

In 1912, he started construction of the Spreckels Theater Building, which was reported to cost a million dollars and which takes in nearly an entire block. He also began construction of the San Diego Hotel. This stimulated others into following suit, and soon new buildings were going up in all directions.

What with all that was done in city development in anticipation of the Exposition and what the Exposition did in developing and beautifying Balboa Park, there is hardly anything that could be said which would be too extravagant in praise of the building and holding of our 1915-16 Exposition. Let us not forget that our permanent California Building, with the beautiful California Tower, was an outgrowth of this Exposition, as were also our Museums, our Fine Arts Gallery, and our Zoo. During those boom years, I was giving my whole attention to our rapidly expanding Pacific Building Company, and I want to emphasize here that I, personally, had no part in the organization or management of this first Exposition.

In 1910, the Pacific Building Company purchased considerable acreage and about five thousand subdivided lots in east San Diego, a water company serving 350 residents scattered over thirty miles of pipeline, and, in addition to our subdivision business, we were building homes scattered throughout the city. Quite often, we would take out permits and start one new home every working day throughout the month. Since lots as well as homes were all sold on the small monthly payment plan and all material and labor was cash, one big job I, personally, had, was to keep the company financed.

In 1911 and 1912, lots in our east San Diego subdivisions of Fairmount, Bellmont, Eastgate, City Heights, and others, were sold like the proverbial hot cakes. In all our lot sales for the Pacific Building Company, I tried to hold the prices down so that the lots would sell fast, the idea being to make our profits on volume, and not on the individual lot sales. In our Fairmount tract, at Euclid and University avenues, we sold level lots, 25 by 100 feet, at $99 each, and sloping lots across the street at $49 each. I think the highest-priced lots were only $125. It was wonderful advertising and barrels of fun. On weekdays, sales would run from twenty to forty lots, and on Sundays around two hundred. We held some of the property for ten or twelve years, but we made a good profit on the whole deal. One business corner, 100 by 125 feet, which was set up on the books at a total cost of $40, was sold about ten years later for $15,000.

By the end of 1912, we had more than five hundred stockholders in the Pacific Building Company; assets of upward of a million dollars and liabilities of probably half that amount. Today (1962) that sounds like "peanuts" but in 1912, in San Diego, it was an establishment. At times, our company was the local newspaper's third largest advertiser.

In March, 1913, another financial panic hit Wall Street, but it did not bother us too much in San Diego. Our building activities were slowed down, and lot sales practically ceased, but we were not worried. The Exposition buildings were going up and the city was on a sound basis.

After the turn of the year 1914, I decided to make another lot sale attempt. Some of my friends in the real estate business tried to dissuade me. They argued that such an attempt would be sure to flop and that would be very bad advertising for the town. I did not believe that it would flop, so about June 1 we ran a double-page ad—an unusual splash for those days—and opened a big subdivision on Main Street just north of National City, which we called Arlington. It was a stupendous success, just as though nothing had happened. Lots sold "fast and furious" for two months. Then, suddenly, like a bolt out of the blue, something did happen!

On July 28, Austria declared War on Hungary; on August 1, Germany declared War on Russia; on August 3, Germany declared War on France; and on August 4, England declared War on Germany!

Every activity stopped. Just like that. Everything, except the completion of the Exposition buildings. That was the beginning of a most unhappy period. We could not sell at lot at any price, nor could we build a home. Hundreds of purchasers stopped payment on their lots. Nearly all of the houses we had built on owners' lots were secured by trust deeds, and we received our money on these regularly, but the houses we had sold on contract for $100 cash and $25 per month came back into our hands in many instances, and could not be resold. Fortunately, the Pacific Building Company had several hundred thousand dollars in outstanding contracts on lots sold, and while many of these were forfeited, there were also many purchasers who did not forfeit.

All building and other unnecessary work in San Diego came to a standstill. There were many idle men, and these idle men took their families to other cities where they could get jobs in war material factories. We disbanded our building organization and cut our forces to a minimum. We realized then for the first time that we had passed through a "boom," and when I say "passed through," I mean it. We were definitely through it then and for all of the foreseeable future. All we could do was retrench to the last ditch and hold the line, which we did, but it was no fun.

In the heyday of 1912 we had purchased a 100 by 100 foot corner at Fourth Avenue and C Street, where the California Theater now stands, for our expanding office. We had purchased at too high a price and we still owed $100,000 on it. Our stockholders were unhappy, which was easy to understand, when we suddenly and without warning had to stop paying our 16 percent cash dividends.

As the months dragged on and the tide flowed out, the war news grew worse and worse, and more and more families left San Diego. The end was nowhere in sight. There was always the possibility, too, that the United States would be drawn into the war.

The opening of the Exposition, on January 1, 1915, was the one bright spot. The war, of course, hurt the attendance badly, but nevertheless many thousands of sightseers did come who would not have thought of coming to San Diego otherwise. Everyone who attended the Exposition was delighted and left to sing its praises and the praises of San Diego as well. These thousands of visitors filled our hotels and spent money elsewhere throughout the city, so it was a wonderful boon to San Diego during those two depressing years, 1915-16, and the advertising it gave San Diego throughout the country was wonderful.

Many times during my years in Arizona or farther away places, when I was selling Pacific Beach lots, I would start to tell my supposed prospect about San Diego, and he would interrupt me to ask if I was talking about Santiago, Cuba! I was surprised to find how many people there were who had never heard of San Diego, California. That never happened after our 1915-16 Exposition.

Then, in 1917, the United States finally did declare War, and our San Diego picture changed again, overnight. I accepted an assignment on a committee of three (Montgomery M. Moulton, our county assessor, chairman, and my friend, Percy H. Goodwin) to secure leases for the United States Government on ten thousand acres of land on the Linda Vista Mesa for the establishment of a cantonment (Camp Kearney) to train forty thousand United States recruits. We got the leases signed up in record time. Other than that, and assisting in War Bond drives and Red Cross campaigns, there was not much at that time that civilians in San Diego could do for the war effort.

Most of the men who were free, and many who were not, enlisted. Others waited for the draft. Our company was in such a precarious position that I felt I must not leave, and so I waited, hoping my turn would not come. It came close. Another three months would probably have taken me; I missed it by just that much.

CHAPTER XX

We Build a Bridge

SHORTLY AFTER the United States entered the war, the San Diego County Board of Supervisors wanted to have a bridge built across the creek at Bernardo, south of Escondido. I took the contract for the company. Then my troubles really started.

This was in the late summer of 1917, and about the time we signed the contract to build the bridge the authorities in Washington, D.C., issued an edict prohibiting the sale of steel or cement for any purpose not specifically authorized by them. The Lake Hodges Dam was being constructed toward the Coast, several miles below the bridge site across this Bernardo Creek. When the winter rains came, the water from this creek would fill the dam. I asked for approval to purchase the necessary material to build this bridge, explaining that it was to be a quarter of a mile long and twenty feet high, and that it must be built now, while the creek was still dry, because after the first winter rains the water from Lake Hodges would back up and would be fifteen feet deep clear across the present valley. The answer was still "No."

We built the bridge, but it was a sad story; expensive and trying to the nerves. While it was building, I went back and forth from our home in South Park every day, arriving on the job before breakfast. This bridge was used as a part of Highway 395 until 1954, when the state made a cut-off and built a shorter and wider bridge. The old bridge is about five miles south of Escondido and stands now, naked and alone, west of Highway 395.

Violet talked a good deal about my working too hard. One Saturday, I took William, then eight years old, and a friend of his, out for the day. They made friends with the cook (who made delicious apple pies), roamed over the works, and had a fine time.

The next day William told his mother, "Mother, you don't need to worry about Dad working too hard. He doesn't work at all. He just walks around and talks to the men!"

As the United States got deeper into the war, it became almost impossible to get material for any local construction, whether private or for the city or the county, so I made a couple of trips to Washington, D.C., to get an assignment to do some building in San Diego for the United States Government. En route to Washington on one of these trips, I changed trains in St. Louis, Missouri. Since I had nothing to do for a couple of hours between trains, I decided I would go through the Anheuser-Busch Brewery and see how they made beer.

Back on the first floor after seeing most of the sights, we were taken to a room with a long bar, and offered a glass of beer on the house. I noticed that the bar was lined one or two deep with workmen, and inquired if there was any limit to the amount of beer an employee might drink.

"Oh, yes," said our guide. "It is all regulated by the Union. Each man is allowed twelve glasses of beer per day."

"Twelve glasses!" I exclaimed. "How much work will a man do if he drinks twelve glasses of beer a day?"

"Oh," replied the guide, "that's nothing. Good beer is good for you if you drink it in moderation. I drink twice that."

"What? You mean you drink twenty-four glasses of beer a day?" I asked in amazement.

"Why, certainly," he said. "Good beer is good for you if you drink it in moderation. We had a superintendent who drank sixty glasses of beer a day for thirty years and, when he died, his death was from an ailment that had nothing whatsoever to do with beer. Good beer is good for you if you drink it in moderation."

"Would you please tell me," I asked, "just how one would go about drinking sixty glasses of beer a day in moderation?"

"Why, certainly," replied he. "Drink your beer moderately throughout the day; not all at once!"

As a result of my two trips to Washington, we finally landed two contracts to build barracks for the government on Point Loma: Cost plus 6 percent. The first job was only $65,000 but it was a start. Just as we were finishing this contract, we were awarded another for $240,000, but before we got started on this second job, the war came to an end and the government, of course, canceled the contract.

I shall never forget November 11, 1918—Armistice Day. Everybody was all smiles and joy. The vice-president of our company was my old friend, Dr. F. R. Burnham. He came in to shake hands and rejoice; he was so happy he was literally effervescent, and everyone felt the same way. It was a great day.

I took stock: Our company's assets were mostly in dwindling, outstanding contracts and trust deeds and thousands of vacant lots upon which the taxes must be paid. There were about thirty-five hundred vacant houses and apartments in San Diego; in our then small downtown district, there were possibly three hundred empty stores. Our Exposition was over. We had no manufacturing to attract newcomers; we had no need for the carpenters or the mechanics to come back; and there was no sale whatsoever for any real estate, vacant or improved. The few houses that were sold from time to time brought less than half of what they had cost to build.

We had already been through four years of financial depression. How much longer could we take it?

CHAPTER XXI

Lifting a City by Its Bootstraps

BACK IN 1904, when Folsom Bros. & Company was persuaded to try to sell lots through national magazine advertising, the result had been a colossal failure financially, but it taught me, once and for all, the tremendous power of advertising. Although I would never again try to sell real estate by magazine advertising, the thousands of replies we received from our ads, telling what a wonderful place San Diego was in which to live, convinced me that, because of its matchless climate, its wonderful location, and its almost perfect harbor, San Diego had an opportunity for growth and development from a purely residential standpoint which far exceeded that of any other community in the United States.

I had carried this thought for fourteen years—ever since our expensive experiment in 1904. Now that we could see that the war was drawing to a close, I began working out a definite and comprehensive plan to again put San Diego on the up-and-up. As soon as the Armistice was signed, I went to work.

For many years, various cities had inserted a large ad or two in magazines or newspapers telling why people should locate there for industrial or other reasons, but all of these ads were merely a "flash in the pan." The city would run one or two ads and stop. To what extent the city profited, if at all, no one ever knew. About all the good they apparently did was to get the name of the city before the outside world.

The plan I worked out was complete to the last detail. I would get the San Diego businessmen to subscribe a large cash fund—$100,000 or more—to be spent in systematically advertising San Diego's marvelous advantages as a place to live. Each ad would carry a coupon asking for more information. Each person signing a coupon would receive a personal letter in reply, together with warm, friendly, alluring literature that he or she would not be able to resist reading. It was my belief that San Diego had something to sell that no other city in the United States possessed and that, as a city, we should go after people and sell San Diego, systematically, the same as any manufacturing enterprise sold its products.

With my plan completely formulated, I invited Carl H. Heilbron to a thirty-five cent lunch, and we talked it over, at Rudder's Grill in the the basement of the Union Building, at Third Avenue and Broadway. Carl was not only San Diego's leading electrical contractor and owner of an electrical fixture establishment, but he was also one of San Diego's foremost orators.

Carl jumped at the idea like a hungry trout for a fly. He suggested a $200,000 fund for a starter, and suggested further that we name our brain child the San Diego-California Club, tying that luring word "California" into every ad. Together, we called on G. Aubrey Davidson, and sold him easily. Then we called on F. J. Belcher, Jr., president of the First National Trust & Savings Bank. He did not jump so quickly, but after several visits, he agreed that the idea was worth a trial.

For six months, Carl Heilbron and I spent at least a third of his time, and practically all of mine, working shoulder to shoulder, interviewing our leading businessmen and selling them on the idea, one at a time. I could well afford to give all of my time, because all the Pacific Building Company could do at that time was to sit tight and continue to collect the money on its remaining outstanding contracts and pay its taxes. We could not build another house or sell a lot, until we got more people to come to live in San Diego. After six months of personal solicitation and persuasion, we at last got a group organized, with the following officers and directors:

Officers

Duncan MacKinnon	*President*
G. A. Davidson	*Vice-President*
Rufus Choate	*Vice-President*
W. S. Dorland	*Treasurer*
O. W. Cotton	*Secretary*

Directors

Frank J. Belcher, Jr.	Carl H. Heilbron
Wheeler J. Bailey	H. H. Jones
William Clayton	Wm. Kettner
O. W. Cotton	A. D. LaMotte
Rufus Choate	Jas. MacMullen
G. A. Davidson	Duncan MacKinnon
W. S. Dorland	D. W. Pontius
Ed Fletcher	W. H. Porterfield
P. H. Goodwin	Sam Porter
E. B. Gould, Jr.	John D. Spreckels
Geo. D. Easton	F. W. Stearns
Ed Davidson	F. M. White
	C. S. Holzwasser

We rented the Isis Theater for an evening, and mailed invitations to a meeting to be held June 10, 1919, to all of the businessmen of the county. When the meeting opened, seated on the stage were: Frank J. Belcher, Jr.; G. Aubrey Davidson; Carl H. Heilbron; Rufus Choate, member of the Harbor Commission; James MacMullen, manager of the San Diego *Union* and *Evening Tribune;* O. W. Cotton; C. S. Holzwasser of Holzwasser's, Inc., Department store; W. J. Bailey, of the W. J. Bailey Company, Building Materials; A. D. LaMotte of Thearle Music Company, and Ed Fletcher. In a box were Superior Judge Spencer M. Marsh, Edgar A. Luce, and W. A. Sloane, with W. J. Estep, secretary of the Manufacturers' Association. The first floor was packed and the first balcony had a substantial number of the overflow.

On June 11, the San Diego *Union* commented:

Preliminary talks were made by F. J. Belcher on San Diego's assets; Rufus Choate on harbor development and shipping; A. D. LaMotte spoke on U. S. Government activities.

In the absence of D. W. Pontius, G. A. Davidson spoke on the advantages to be gained by the new San Diego & Arizona Railroad.

Ed Fletcher talked on water and roads in our back country and the need of a comprehensive system of paved county roads in addition to making San Diego the terminus of at least one continental paved highway.

O. W. Cotton then made an explanation of the advertising plan. A résumé of his well-prepared address is as follows:

Advertising Plan for San Diego

What Have We to Sell?

In addition to the possibilities for business, commerce, and manufacture in San Diego, which are the main city-building factors for most cities, this community has an asset on which we should cash in every day in the year, namely: San Diego, a place to live.

Not only do we have a far greater variety of out-of-door pastimes, sports, and pleasures in San Diego than in any other city in the United States of similar population, but because of our climatic conditions, these pastimes can be enjoyed by us more days in each year than anywhere else.

When we realize the amazing number of days in any year that we can, in twenty minutes, go down to the bay and enjoy rowing, sailing, motorboating, fishing, or swimming; the number of days that we can enjoy the beauty of our park with its superb buildings, grounds, its walks and drives; the stadium and playgrounds, the rose gardens, the great outdoor organ; our beaches and our scenery—and then compare these opportunities with, for example, the opportunities afforded by any city of San Diego's size in any one of our Middle Western states, it is small wonder that all of us believe that the retired man or woman, who lives where he or she pleases, cannot fail to get far more out of life here than "back yonder."

Those who have traveled most speak with the greatest enthusiasm of the magnificent scenic beauty of the drive to the end of Point Loma; the drive to the rim of the desert above Mountain Springs, and the wonderful drives through our several hundred miles of mountains and back country, among the pines and oaks; our big lakes and farming country; and all this within two or three hours' drive of our city.

It is truly marvelous that one city should possess so many major attractions in so small an area.

There is a delightful opportunity here for the man of small income who wants a home, either in the city or suburbs or the back country.

What we have to sell, then, is "the most delightful place in the world in which to live," and our big outstanding permanent opportunity is for the man who has earned his rest and can afford to think of comfort and enjoyment for his family and himself in the city, by the seashore, in the country, or in the mountains.

To Whom Are We Going to Sell?

Shall we invite laborers?

Shall we tell carpenters and plumbers and other skilled artisans we have jobs for them?

Shall we urge businessmen who want a start to come and open more grocery stores, drugstores, clothing stores, meat markets, automobile tire stores, or fifteen-cent stores?

Do we want more hotel men to build more hotels?

Yes, when we can truthfully tell them that a need for their services exists here.

To create that need, what we want first is more families to patronize the stores and hotels we now have. We want to build up a permanent, stable population of people who are going to locate somewhere, just to live, and who might just as well come here.

The big outstanding opportunity that San Diego has to offer today is the opportunity to the man who has earned his pleasure and ease. To him we offer, at minimum cost, the greatest abundance of riches, the most charming place to live, of any city in the United States.

We can be honest with him, and in locating him in San Diego we are performing a service to him as great as to ourselves.

It is, then, to the man or woman of established income that we shall appeal; to the man or woman who wants a home.

Where Is Our Market?

The states from which the great bulk of our homeseekers have come in the past—the great Middle West states; because they lack the things we have to sell.

Is This the Time to Sell, and If So, Why?

Because of the enormously prosperous condition of the Middle West territory at this particular time, there are probably ten times as many people who can afford to come here to live as there ever were before.

The price of $2.20 on wheat, fixed by the government two years ago, has not only made more profits for the farmer in this district in the last two years than he ever expected to make in his life, but it has also increased the value of his land by two and three hundred percent, and more. Large numbers of these farmers are already profiting by this opportunity by turning over to others the burdens of the farm, and are selling their places at $400 per acre, and more. Some are moving to other parts of the country. Many are settling in the cities in their own districts.

This will be the last year of this guarantee in prices, and after a few years of high prices, when things come back to a more normal basis, the farmer will be back to the old grind. Nobody realizes this better than he, and probably more farms will change hands in the next twelve to eighteen months than in the following decade.

The industries of the Middle Western States also have been immensely profitable, and are so today. The business profits have been enormous. In fact, this whole country is teeming with wealth; the banks are full of money, and now, before this money has found a permanent investment, is San Diego's great opportunity.

There are enough people retiring annually in the United States to build several San Diegos every normal year; but to reach these people it would require a national campaign that would cost from a million to a million and a half dollars annually, which puts it away beyond our reach. But this year, owing to these enormous profits, there will probably be more people retiring, *in the Middle West district alone,* than ordinarily retire *in the whole United States in a single year*.

Inasmuch as we can cover this field for about 20 percent of what it takes to cover the entire country, we can accomplish far more for $200,000 in the next eight months than we could do in any other year by the expenditure of a million dollars or more.

The great outstanding opportunity San Diego has today is the opportunity to get these people *now;* while they have the money in the bank and before they locate elsewhere.

If we delay now, our opportunity is lost.

Too much stress cannot be put on the point that, to get the greatest benefit, we must strike *now*.

Another very important factor in this campaign is this: The people we shall appeal to are people who, as a class, will make very desirable citizens for our community.

What Amount Should Be Expended?

We are going into a district of 22,000,000 population and we want to talk to possibly one million people. That is, to the people who can afford to come.

To do this the field must be covered thoroughly. Today, in the minds of the people east of the Rocky Mountains, Los Angeles is "southern California." In probably ninety-nine cases out of one hundred, when people of the East or Middle West speak or think of southern California, they speak or think of Los Angeles. It is, today, without doubt, the best advertised city of its size in the United States.

Now, if we are going to accomplish any real results, *we must make San Diego symbolize California* in the minds of the people of this Middle ·West district.

This plan contemplates covering this district so thoroughly that we will reach, over and over again, the best class of people in the entire district.

The plan contemplates the total expenditure of $25,000 per month for eight months, about one-half of which will be for display space, and one-half for the follow-up system and the organization at San Diego.

At first glance this looks like a big sum of money. But we must remember that it is a big opportunity we have before us, and that we have a city of 85,000 people here, and that any publicity campaign, to be of very great benefit to a city of that size, *must be big*.

When we had 20,000 population, the mere *announcement* of the building of a new railroad was sufficient to increase our population by 25 percent, but to start a city of 85,000 people on a real prosperity and development era is a man-sized job; and $200,000 is not a large fund for a city of this size to raise, when we realize what it will do at this particular time.

How Should the Fund Be Expended to Reach the Particular Class of Homeseekers We Want?

After careful consideration it has been determined that the portion of this fund to be spent for display advertising space should be expended on *newspaper* space, for the reason that we can concentrate on a certain district by so doing; whereas, if we went into the national magazines, we would be paying for circulation, not only in the limited district where our best customers lie, but also for dead circulation in San Diego,

Florida, and all other parts of the United States, which cannot bring us the maximum results for the money expended.

This plan, therefore, contemplates the expenditure of about $100,000 mainly on newspaper display space in the Middle Western States. Abundant news and feature articles will accompany the "ads." The plan is to use probably quarter-page ads, running once a week in series. This will give us a total of thirty-two separate ads, each one of which will tell a different story of San Diego. Each ad will picture an entertaining and appealing scene. All will depict the attractiveness of our city from the home standpoint. The plan is to make all of these warm, "pulling" ads; to put into them an appeal that will make the reader want to know more about San Diego; ads that will build up the reader's interest to the point where he or she will sign a coupon and mail their address to us for further information.

We will reach, by the bigness of our campaign, the particular class of people to whom San Diego today holds out an opportunity, namely, the retired or retiring well-to-do class. And the only way it can be done with any real results is by a campaign so thorough that all of the reading public must see it, and by so wording the ads, news stories, and "follow-ups" that we shall attract the special class that we desire to bring to San Diego to live.

The expenditure of the $100,000 for display ads will give us a total circulation during the eight months of approximately 120,000,000 quarter-page ads distributed throughout a district containing 22,000,000 people. This means 15,000,000 total circulation per month, or 500,000 copies every day for 240 days. The object of all the ads will be *to get the class of homeseekers San Diego desires,* sufficiently interested to write *for information.*

These ads in themselves will, of course, do a vast amount of good; and they will go a great way toward making *San Diego, California,* to all who read the newspapers in the Middle Western States; but the real object of every ad will be to get a live prospect to send in his or her name.

This is a *direct selling* campaign. Its object is to attract the attention of the retiring man and to get his name; and then, by our "follow-up," actually to bring him to San Diego with his family. And then, when we get him here, we will make him want to stay. So that the display ads will cost probably one-half the total fund, and their appearance in the livest newspapers in the Great Middle West will start the great work going. The other half of the fund will be used for the follow-up system.

What Is the Best Method of Follow-Up?

The best method of "follow-up" for community advertising, such as we can do for San Diego, is a method that will make the prospective resident feel that not only have we what he wants in a home city, climatically and physically, but also that the people of the community want him with us. Not only for the money he will spend, but because we want our increasing population to consist of a class of people that we will all want to know.

To do this it has been determined to conduct this campaign under the auspices of the *San Diego-California Club.* This organization ought to comprise in its membership all of the other leading businessmen, bankers, professional men, and pastors; and in addition thereto, all of the citizens of San Diego, both men and women, who are interested in seeing the city develop along broad and progressive lines.

The first communication sent to every prospective homeseeker who answers one of our advertisements will be a leaflet describing this organization. In this leaflet he will be informed that this is a club of joyousness and welcome, organized for the purpose of promoting happiness for its members in San Diego and extending a welcoming hand to those who can come to our land of sunshine and beauty; to show the way and to make them feel at home.

With the first booklet we will send a card which our prospective resident will be asked to fill out and sign. This will give us a better understanding of just what his intentions are with regard to coming to San Diego. This card, when so filled out and mailed to us, will entitle him to honorary membership in the *San Diego-California Club,* and this membership will be complimentary to him until he arrives in San Diego, and for three months thereafter.

This booklet will be in the form of a message from this organization to a prospective member of the organization, so that he will be able to feel from the very beginning that every word in the message is true and sincere.

During all of our correspondence with him we will cause him to feel that we want him here, not only from a business standpoint, but from a social standpoint as well.

The power of this "follow-up" will be in the personality of the organization.

Before we get very far along, the local members of the *San Diego-California Club* are going to realize that this is not merely an advertising scheme, but that we have truly organized for the purpose of issuing invitations to the people who can afford to come to live with us; and that their coming to San Diego to live is more than a financial matter with us—it is also a social matter.

Among the last twenty thousand who have come to San Diego to live, we have found many delightful people and made many warm friends, and that is the spirit that is going to dominate our entire campaign. This feeling of fellowship will be the compelling factor that will pull our honorary club members around or through Los Angeles, and the controlling factor that will make them want to stay in San Diego when they arrive.

The *San Diego-California Club,* then, will be a Club of Welcome. It will be composed of all subscribers to the advertising fund, and should embrace all local clubs, societies, churches, etc., a business and social club.

How Shall We Keep the People When They Come Here?

We will maintain permanent headquarters and a standing reception committee. This committee will be paid men of such ability and personality as will make it a pleasure to the stranger to meet them; men who will make him feel the spirit of our welcome.

Every newcomer will be met personally by one of these committeemen, who will sit down with him and get acquainted, learn what his interests have been and what his desires are, and then acquaint him with the conditions as they actually are in San Diego. And before he has finished, he will give the newcomer a list of a half a dozen or so names of local club members, businessmen, or others whose ideas and tastes are the same as those of the newcomer. He will be told to call upon these gentlemen and that he will enjoy meeting them.

After the party has gone, the committeeman will call up these individuals and tell them of his arrival, where he is stopping, and of the fact that his interests are along the same general lines as those of our home citizen, and that it will be a pleasure as well as a benefit to the community for our local men to communicate with him, to call and make him feel at home. This work divided among several hundred members will not be an imposition on any of us, and it will be productive of tremendous results.

The newcomer or honorary club member will be instructed to use his membership card wherever he goes, and display it when going into a store or business house, and he will find that upon using it he will receive the same courteous treatment that would be accorded him had he been a resident of San Diego for the past fifteen years.

What Are the Results to Be Obtained?

This campaign will help to make San Diego a more livable city.

It will increase our population and lower the pro-rata tax rate.

It will put all local business on a more solid foundation, fill our hotels, apartment houses, flats, and residences, and start a home-building campaign such as we have not seen since 1912.

San Diego lies around a park one and one-half miles square. It is now built up on the south and west, but on the north and east there are thousands of building sites still unoccupied. The erection of homes on these vacant lots means the completion of our city; the beautification of it as nothing else *can* beautify it.

It will be more fun for us to enjoy our beautiful park if we are sharing it with more people. The same is true of our harbor, water sports, and our back country.

If there were more people here to enjoy our pleasures with us, we would enjoy them more ourselves.

And Now as to Factories

Even the so-called "geranium planters" are interested in seeing legitimate factories properly located in San Diego. We are all interested in seeing factories locate here. Most of us would unquestionably prefer to see the factories locate where they would not be objectionable to the residents of the city, but, be that as it may, we all favor legitimate factories in San Diego. The great question is *how to get them.*

This publicity campaign, as previously stated, is for the purpose of locating *homeseekers* in San Diego. It is not intended to directly hunt out the factory builder, nor the business builder. It is intended for the man of means, small or large, who feels that he can afford the comforts and pleasures of life. But when all is said and done we must remember that, in order to build factories in any city or in any place, there is one predominant factor which you *must* have, regardless of all other advantages of location or climatic conditions, raw material, market, or anything else, and that prime factor is MONEY.

If we are going to have factories in San Diego, we must have *money* to make it possible to get the factories here. If they are building fifty factories elsewhere while we build one in San Diego, it is very largely because they can finance fifty factories there while we can finance one factory here.

When a man or group of men determine to build a factory, they almost invariably desire or need to have at least a part of the capital furnished by the people of the community where the factory is to be built. It was because the business community was able and willing to finance the automobile industry that Detroit became the automobile center of the United States and has remained so.

For several years past the brokers, bankers, and those interested in the development of Los Angeles have made it their business to interest the tourist and capitalists who have come to live in Los Angeles, Pasadena, and vicinity, in the bonds and stocks in the home industries, instead of selling them town lots, as was the custom some years ago. By interesting them in their industries, they are giving them something to think about in Los Angeles, something to tie them to their community, something to do *at home;* and that is what we must do in San Diego. We must make up our minds to it.

If we want factories, we must have more money in San Diego and lots of it, with which to build factories, and the way to bring money to San Diego is to bring here the men who have the money.

If we are going to build a city we must grasp the whole situation and work out the problems we have as a whole, letting one factor determine another. We have a magnificent opportunity, and now is the time to begin; now, at the commencement of a prosperity era. Let's get together and organize San Diego as one big business unit to put our city over, and on a big, strong, permanent basis once and for all.

Previous to the meeting, I had my entire speech printed, and copies were distributed to each man as he left the theater. The next day, our three daily newspapers, the San Diego *Union,* the *Evening Tribune,* and the San Diego *Sun,* all gave us excellent front-page publicity. Thus, after seven months of strenuous work, our advertising plan was launched. Now it was up to Carl Heilbron and me to raise the $200,000.

Quickly, we got together a team of about forty businessmen and went to work. It was not surprising that every businessman had to be sold individually, because this was something that never had been done before and no businessman wanted to subscribe to a failure; besides, very few had money to throw at the birds. One of our great boosters was Dave W. Pontius, at that time the general manager for the San Diego & Arizona Railroad, which was then under construction. Pontius could see wonderful advertising value for the new railroad through our efforts, and he persuaded John D. Spreckels, backer of the railroad project, to subscribe 10 percent, or $20,000 toward our fund. Other businessmen came through handsomely, but not enough. Our town was still small, only about eighty-five thousand, and mighty hard up.

Our goal was $200,000 but, in fairness to all, we had a clause in each subscription to the effect that the campaign was not to start until at least $150,000 was subscribed. Work as we did, we got it up to $135,000 and there we stuck. It looked as though our whole nine months' effort was going to be thrown away, and, worst of all, San Diego was getting nowhere. The town was standing still.

Louis J. Wilde was then the Mayor of San Diego, and he was a colorful and spectacular promoter and politician. On the twenty-first day of September, 1919, Wilde called a meeting of our top businessmen to talk to them, as he put it, about a matter on which he wanted their advice.

When we had finished a good luncheon at the main dining room of the U. S. Grant Hotel, where all such meetings were held in those days, Mayor Wilde got up and said that, before he got into the matter he had invited them there to discuss, there was this matter of the organization of the San Diego-California Club that must be completed; that San Diego must have this advertising, and now. He reminded them that there was only $15,000 lacking to complete the minimum fund, and asked who in the audience would match the Mayor with $1,000 to complete the requirement.

Dave Pontius stood up and pledged Mr. Spreckels and the San Diego & Arizona Railroad for an additional thousand dollars. Then first one and then another in the audience came through, and our committee went after them for their subscriptions right on the spot—Mayor and all. When Mayor Wilde got all he could at $1,000 he dropped to $500, and then to $250, and so on down to $50, whereupon a lady's voice piped up and said she would sign. It was Violet, my wife. She figured she could save enough for the monthly payments from her household budget. Our Mayor was a good salesman.

That is how near we came to losing the chance for one of the greatest enterprises for putting over San Diego ever conceived, up to that time and for many years thereafter; an enterprise which was to be copied by Los Angeles, San Francisco, and 150 other cities, and states and nations throughout the world.

CHAPTER XXII

How It Worked

SINCE I had the whole plan in my head, the Executive Committee of the Board of Directors asked me to become general manager as well as secretary, and carry out the program. I was mighty glad they did, because I had been working the plans over and over, and had the general scheme figured out to the last detail. I wrote to a number of big advertising agencies throughout the United States and finally selected the H. K. McCann Company of San Francisco. They sent a topflight writer and executive to San Diego, C. E. Persons, who proved to be a wonderful helper and who fell right in with the entire plan with but very few changes.

We were tightly pressed for time. During the war, our great Middle Western wheat belt's farmers were rolling in wealth from the sale of wheat at the formerly unheard-of price of $2.20 per bushel. Many were selling their farms at $300 per acre, whereas they would formerly have brought only $40 per acre. There were also many people throughout the East who had made fortunes on "war brides" (large, quick profits made in various ways as a result of the war). Now was the time to reach these people, while they were newly rich, and bring them to San Diego.

There were two other reasons why this was just the right time: First, all travel had been restricted during the war and folks were ready to go some place; second, advertising rates, while higher than they had been during the war, were still comparatively low, so we could get that much more for our advertising dollar. All in all, the timing was "hot."

Our first ads appeared on the nineteenth of November, 1919. To our surprise, we got a few replies the day before! Some of our ads were in big Sunday newspapers which were printed and delivered to outlying towns several days in advance. Within a week, replies were pouring in. By early December, we were receiving nine hundred letters a day.

We had our office in the Spreckels Theater Building. The space was donated by the Automobile Club of southern California, who used the other half of the room and paid all the rent. I had a force of thirteen stenographers writing personal letters over my signature as secretary. In every letter, a personal membership card was enclosed inviting the recipient to become an honorary member of the San Diego-California Club, and he was told that in a few days we would mail him a very special little booklet, which was so fascinating he would read every word of it and then lend it to a friend and ask for it back. (Incidentally, our first booklet was just that—it was a "peach.")

The reason for holding back the first booklet for a day or two was so that they would read the letters several times and feel the spirit of our appeal. Later, we would send picture folders and leaflets on San Diego statistics, and last of all, a large, maroon-colored book entitled *Where Life Means Most*. It contained many large pictures of our beautiful Balboa Park, the waterfront, and beach scenes. It was a marvelous campaign, and it took like wildfire.

In all our letters we invited the newcomers to come first to our headquarters and register and get acquainted. In December, they began to trickle in. In January, we invited all new arrivals to meet with the San Diegans at a luncheon at the San Diego Hotel. The big dining room was filled, and we had many of the newcomers stand and tell their names and where they were from. It was thrilling for everybody.

February 7 was another big day. We had all the new arrivals come to headquarters, and we had about fifty businessmen drive up with their cars and take them out and show them the city and get acquainted. We all lined up in the Plaza at Balboa Park in front of the House of Hospitality Building; the Mayor made a speech of welcome, and photographers took their pictures. That was a great day.

Month after month, as the advertising and follow-up campaign continued, new families arrived in ever-increasing numbers. By the fall of 1920, one year after the first ads appeared, the thirty-five hundred vacant houses and apartments of the year before were filled; new homes were building all over the city, and the prices of old homes had nearly doubled. Most people who had wanted to sell a year before now took their homes off the market. That was the beginning of the great 1920-26 boom.

In December, 1919, when the advertising was less than a month on its way, a young man came in to see me one evening to get a story for the annual edition of the San Diego *Union*, which he was getting out for that newspaper on January 1. His name was Thomas G. Armstrong. We had never before met, nor even heard of each other, but he struck me as exactly the man we should have to run the organization, so that I could go back to my own office. Before he left headquarters on that first meeting, we had made a deal, and I got the services and cooperation of unquestionably the best executive we could possibly have acquired for that job. Armstrong came in to take charge soon after the first of the year and he carried the load for many years, all through the club's greatest successes. We were indeed most fortunate.

One day a friend wrote me that a professor of English at the University of California had read a copy of the first letter we would send to those who had sent coupons clipped from our ads, in class, and had stated that the letter was "100 percent in community advertising appeal." Here it is:

SAN DIEGO-CALIFORNIA CLUB

Mr. John Doe
57 Butler Street
Kingston, Pennsylvania

DEAR MR. DOE:

About eighty-five thousand of us here in San Diego, California, are so thoroughly suited with living in this delightful city that it gives me a great deal of pleasure to respond to your inquiry and tell you some of the reasons why we, and our thousands of visitors, feel this way about it.

There is, of course, much that cannot be included in a letter, even if I were to write at great length, and so you will receive, in a day or so, a little book different from any you have ever seen, that tells you more about us. You will enjoy reading it; you probably will read it twice and lend it to a friend and ask for it back. It's a wonderful story and every word is true.

When you consider that, in uniting ocean, mountains, and bay in one spot, Nature has done her utmost for beauty, you will realize the ideal setting we have for our splendid, modern city.

Add to this a climate free from winds and storms, never hot and never cold, with sunshine on 356 days of each year, and you will begin to see why there is no place in the world where you will enjoy life as you will in San Diego, California.

That is what we have—a perfect home city for those who have won a competence in a more rigorous climate and now are free to establish their permanent homes where life will mean the most to themselves and their families.

Our people live much out of doors the year round, among their rose gardens and shady lawns, motoring, swimming, yachting, playing baseball, tennis, and golf, and it seems to make them more joyous than where life is hard. We are spared the grim tragedies of heat and cold, and it is easy to live long and happily, and for less money than elsewhere. The city's population has doubled within ten years.

We should like to have you with us, and I am enclosing a card, which, when filled out and returned to us, will entitle you to honorary membership in the San Diego-California Club, an organization which now has a membership of more than one thousand representative citizens.

This honorary membership is complimentary and is extended to those contemplating coming to our city, that they may feel the spirit of our invitation and welcoming hand of fellowship.

At club headquarters, Second and Broadway, there is a standing reception committee, whose business it is to receive all honorary members, become acquainted, learn their preferences, and make them acquainted with other members of similar preferences. Your membership card will be your introduction to every member of the club and will serve as a guest card to others of our best clubs and organizations.

Please return the enclosed card as soon as possible after you have read your booklet, and write me fully if there is any subject upon which we can send you further information. The more you investigate, the better you are going to like San Diego, California.

When you arrive, we shall expect you to come directly to club headquarters, meet the members, and start with them your new and enjoyable life in San Diego, California, where every day is an adventure in happiness.

> Cordially yours,
> O. W. COTTON,
> *Secretary*

My *Annual Report* to the Charter Members of the San Diego-California Club, as of December 13, 1920, made some startling disclosures:

Total inquiries received as a result of advertisements were 46,151.

From these inquiries, 3,604 heads of families have returned signed questionnaire cards, stating definitely that they will come to San Diego.

In addition to this, from 15,000 follow-up letters, we have received 2,450 questionnaire cards, similarly filled out and signed, making a total of 6,054 families, of which we have record, coming to San Diego.

All of these 6,054 "Class 1" inquirers have been made honorary members of the San Diego-California Club and have been sent the regular membership card.

In many instances that we actually know of, they have voluntarily used the club literature over and over again, in directing their friends to San Diego.

Honorary members are now arriving in San Diego, and registering at club headquarters, at the rate of more than one hundred families per month, and we know that many who come do not call at headquarters.

Some of the individual letters we received were most interesting. A few examples follow:

Columbus, Ohio

Mr. O. W. Cotton,
San Diego, California

DEAR MR. COTTON,

Have received and read with a great amount of pleasure the little book describing San Diego, California. Will say after rereading same several times, and after several perusals of the accompanying views of your beautiful city and surroundings, I am fairly hungry for San Diego, and apparently my whole family are in the same state of mind.

Permit me to say that you people are doing things a bit differently in your town; and your invitation to strangers to partake of your hospitality; your unexpected kindness in conferring honorary membership in your San Diego-California Club to those contemplating visiting your vicinity, surely warms the cockles of one's heart. I am filling out the the card enclosed, and wish to thank you very much for same, also for the book and views.

Trusting I may at some time have the pleasure of meeting you personally, I beg to remain,

Very truly,
HERBERT THOMAS

Kingston, Pennsylvania

Mr. O. W. Cotton, Sec'y,
San Diego-California Club

DEAR SIR:

I think I have another convert for San Diego. . . . I have several others on the verge, but they are awaiting further information from me after my arrival.

I am planning to leave Wilkes-Barre Jan. 15. Leave Chicago 16th via Golden State-R.I.P. and go through to San Diego. As soon as I arrive I hope to have the pleasure of shaking hands with you.

Received your last letter and membership cards. Thanks.

Very truly yours,
W. P. JONES

Kansas City, Missouri

Mr. O. W. Cotton,
President, Pacific Building Co.,
San Diego, California

MY DEAR SIR:

Pardon this direct reply to you in your business capacity of the literature forwarded by the San Diego-California Club, but I want you to know how I view and appreciate it. It all is good, but the letter possesses exceptional merit, for it was more like a communication between very dear friends concerned in each other's welfare than a bureau document.

Brimming over with sincere hospitality, setting forth the attractions of your locality in such a frank and convincing manner, the reading of it caused me to let the furnace go out. "Come all ye that are heavily burdened and I will refresh you" should be your slogan. I can now easily comprehend why "Cotton" has dethroned "Wool" as "King."

The author of your communication is an expert on both selection, blending, and composition, and I will wager he was never a member of the George Creel U.S.A. publicity committee during the late Hohenzollern fiasco. I am not jesting, for your declarations are borne out by old neighbors who recently became your evangels, so I guess that San Diego must be heaven, for the paeans come from there.

Missouri is quite a state and so is Ohio, where I got the Irish blood and the vitalizing American air from good old Lake Erie. Kansas City, my home for thirty-three years, is not lacking in many things and leads in a group of important ones, but it would seem that God in His wisdom finished His work of six days in San Diego and there took His seat.

Thanking you most heartily for the old-fashioned welcome vouchsafed, I am with sentiments of deep and lasting gratitude,

Very truly yours,
JOSEPH P. McGUIRE

36 High Street,
Aston, Birmingham,
England

MY DEAR MR. COTTON:

I am at last writing to answer your letter to me of September 15th last, in which you enclose my membership card in the Club. I can only thank you once more for this and for your letters, which, I assure you, were greatly appreciated. It was most kind of you to take the trouble for me and other strangers.

The reason I have delayed in answering you was that I have been waiting to see some people from this town who have now returned from San Diego.

I have therefore had a good chance to get more information and the fact that they are returning to your city in a month or two has been the deciding factor, and as soon as I can clear up my affairs we shall follow them.

Again thanking you, and trusting to make your acqauintance soon,

Yours faithfully,
H. B. ELCOCK

Since I had practically given my life to the organization and promotion of the San Diego-California Club for two years, the results were most gratifying, as were also the many letters I received from business executives throughout the country. A "sampling" of them is quoted here:

THE CHICAGO, ROCK ISLAND AND PACIFIC
RAILWAY COMPANY
Passenger Traffic Department

L. M. ALLEN,   CHICAGO
Vice-President and Passenger Traffic   February 18, 1922
Manager

MY DEAR MR. COTTON:

I have been favored with copy of President MacKinnon's circular letter to charter members of the San Diego-California Club which contains your report to the Board of Directors dated December 12.

This is to me most interesting reading and confirms the impression that you have been doing a splendid job of community advertising. The results cannot but be satisfactory to your members, but, of course, must be continued to get the maximum results.

With personal regards and best wishes for your continued success, I am,

Sincerely yours,
L. M. ALLEN

LESLIE'S ILLUSTRATED WEEKLY NEWSPAPER
Seattle, Washington

Advertising
Department   March 23, 1921

Mr. O. W. Cotton
c/o Pacific Building Co.,
San Diego, Calif.

DEAR MR. COTTON:

I certainly have enjoyed reading the article in March 10 *Printers' Ink,* summing up the results you have secured for the San Diego-California Club.

Permit me, Mr. Cotton, to take off my hat to you. I do so with a great deal of grace and make you a very deep bow. Any man who can take a community thing and make the big success of it that you have deserves the compliments and good-will of the entire community in which he lives. You certainly have done a very wonderful work and let me wish you continued success.

Very truly yours,
W. F. COLEMAN,
Pacific Coast Manager

DALLAS ADVERTISING LEAGUE
Affiliated with Associated Advertising Clubs of the World
DALLAS, TEXAS

June 16, 1921

Mr. O. W. Cotton, Secy.,
San Diego-California Club,
San Diego, California

MY DEAR MR. COTTON:

From several different sources, there has come to me comment on the most excellent campaign conducted by your organization, to interest prospective homeseekers in your wonderful city.

Moreover, I have read a few figures concerning the number of inquiries received by you, as well as the number of families removed to San Diego or pledged in that direction.

I am convinced that your campaign has been a most extraordinarily successful one, from the standpoint of results, as well as from the standpoint of the impressions created generally by your advertisements.

For this reason, I would like to give the Study Club of the Dallas Advertising League some information on the campaign as a whole. The Study Club is composed of the livest members of the League, who meet regularly to LEARN MORE about the business to which they are devoting their lives.

If you will provide me as Chairman of the Study Club, with any figures you are willing to dispense to a group of advertising men, as well as proofs of the ads, with your booklet and other literature or information you may feel would be potent, I will devote either one or two whole meetings to such material.

You may be assured that any courtesy you may extend us in this manner will be fully appreciated, and credit will be openly and whole-heartedly given you for the cooperation you may see fit to grant us.

Incidentally, I am sure that consideration of this matter before the Study Club will not only create a bunch of boosters for you personally for your kindness, but also will make some San Diego enthusiasts on the spot.

Trusting that this request will not cause you undue inconvenience in gathering material if you see fit to accommodate us, I am,

> Cordially yours,
> C. O. BEDELL, *Chairman,*
> Study Club,
> Dallas Advertising League

A. H. COPLEY
   AGENT

THE DENVER AND RIO GRANDE RAILROAD COMPANY
Pueblo, Colorado

Aug. 6, 1921

Mr. O. W. Cotton, Sec'y
San Diego-California Club
San Diego, Cailf.

DEAR SIR:

Your letter of August 2 received with pleasure and in reply will say that I have been to your city and have made an investment of $20,000 in two lemon groves located at Chula Vista, and although we have had a bad year for lemons yet I have no regrets in the matter, and as the market is picking up now I feel very confident in regard to it and will make that place my home as soon as I get it paid for or at least where I can handle it with the proceeds from the lemons.

I am very sory that I did not call on you at the time of my trip there, and will be sure to see you when I come again, which I hope will not be long in the future.

I found San Diego and the country around there just as you wrote me and am perfectly satisfied with it and know that I will enjoy spending the rest of my life there. I not only found the climatic conditions as you stated but the hospitality made a lasting impression upon me.

Will be very pleased to hear from you in regard to land values, that is, if the trend is upward and the city is growing as was predicted last winter. What do you think of the lemon prospects now?

> Yours very truly,
> A. H. COPLEY

Robert E. Hughes
Louisville

Address: D&RG Minnequa
Pueblo, Colorado

March 3, 1921

DEAR MR. COTTON:

The coupon clipped from the *Literary Digest* and mailed to the San Diego-California Club promptly brought me your letter and, after a few days' delay, the club's publications. Permit me to compliment your organization on the subject matter of both. It has certainly served to most materially increase an interest that was long since awakened in a community that must be the "Asparagus Bed of the Garden Spot of Creation," a name given Blue Grass Kentucky by Senator Jo. C. S. Blackburn, but Senator Blackburn had never received letters and literature from the San Diego-California Club.

My present plans call for a visit to San Diego within the next three or four weeks, with the purpose in view of locating there with my family—wife and daughter 15. I am hoping that I will find the business development such that I can make an active connection for myself and my money. In any event I shall be glad to call at your headquarters soon after my arrival.

Yours truly,
R. E. HUGHES

TREASURY DEPARTMENT
Internal Revenue Service
Reno, Nevada

June 16, 1921

Office of
Federal Prohibition Director
Nevada

San Diego-California Club
San Diego, California

SIRS:

Honest to goodness—tell me: How does the world REALLY look to you fellows down there? Especially your own little world—San Diego? From your advertising campaign "I don't guess" you ever have even a bad dream about anything.

Now, your optimism is catching, I confess. You intend it to have just that effect, and it surely has me coming—not going. So far as you boys are concerned, I know I like you already. Personally, I am convinced you are an irresistible crowd. It takes big fellows to stand up on the rim of the universe and command attention clear through to the center, and I've a notion to come your way.

Born in New Jersey in 1880—been in Reno ten years—admitted to the Bar of Nevada in 1917—have a family and all that and am Federal Prohibition Director for the State of Nevada and the counties of Lassen, Modoc, Plumas, and Sierra, California. But (no, really, this is not a secret) this is an "open season" for Democrats, and at sunrise most any bright morning now a sharp crack will split the air and my spirit must find a new repose. Reno is all right, but it isn't right enough. So I'm reaching out for a new sprouting ground.

Send me some of your newest literature and any additional personal expressions you think would interest me. And tell me—I most always hear of your town as a fine place for those who have acquired a competence and want to spend the balance of their days quietly. Now, I'm not in that class—yet—I want to do a lot of wriggling the next ten years—I've got to. What about that?

Sincerely,

JONATHAN PAYNE

Advertising Department

THE LITERARY DIGEST

NEW YORK

August 12, 1921

Mr. O. W. Cotton
San Diego-California Club
Spreckels Building
San Diego, California

DEAR MR. COTTON:

I sincerely wish to thank you for your kind letter of August 2 and regret exceedingly that I could not hear from you personally the good words about the *Literary Digest*. At any rate, you may rest assured I appreciate what you say in your letter.

You may also rest assured that we are going to do all we possibly can to favor the San Diego-California Club, just as much for sentimental reasons as for business reasons.

The writer has had considerable experience in the advertising of Chambers of Commerce, Boards of Trade, etc. I must state that your advertising is the most consistent and the best compiled of all that has appeared over a period of a great many years. The great trouble with most Chambers of Commerce advertisers is the fact that they lay out a certain amount of money and spend it all in one year, spreading it in a dozen or fifteen magazines and then wait to see what is going to happen. Your advertising has been so consistent, so well prepared, and copy so interesting that it cannot but have the same result that any well-prepared advertising campaign would have.

The best indication of what advertising will do is in our own organization. Before September 1916, the *Digest* used to advertise in a more or less careless way, but commencing that year we started to advertise consistently all over the country in newspapers, streetcars, etc. When we started we had less than 500,000 circulation. This September the circulation will be 1,500,000. To our advertising we are adding the efforts of boy salesmen, which we govern very closely, and expect to have between 30,000 and 50,000 boys handling the *Digest*. An average of only ten copies each would add considerable circulation. I like to tell you these facts because this fall we are going to give you 500,000 or 600,000 more circulation than you had in the spring and at exactly the same price.

If at any time we can be of service or if at any time the *Literary Digest* can do anything to further the interests of your beautiful city, be sure to call on us.

With best personal wishes, I am,

Very truly yours,
ARTHUR B. CUDDLER

ABC/MKH

Every letter received that required a personal or individual reply got it. In the beginning, I personally dictated all of the individual letters. From carbon copies of these, I had paragraphs clipped out and put in loose-leaf notebooks, indexed to cover various subjects. After the first month, I gradually turned over the established routine to Armstrong, who was heartily in accord with my ambition to make this the most personal, friendly, and irresistible campaign ever presented.

The entire campaign procedure was something new from start to finish as a community building project, and it was a success beyond my most optimistic hopes and expectations. It was gratifying to see Los Angeles, with ten times our population, and a year or two later, San Francisco, following in "little old San Diego's" footsteps. But most of all to me was the satisfaction of seeing San Diego make a definite and quick right-about-face and start on another strong upswing of prosperity.

CHAPTER XXIII

"Bay and Climate"

DURING THE first four years, the San Diego-California Club spent the bulk—possibly 90 percent—of its funds for display space in publications east of the Rocky Mountains, where the climate was more rigorous. We kept accurate records showing the cost per inquiry, and the cost per family arrival, for all publications, so that those of us who were spending the money knew where we received the most for our advertising dollar.

There were some subscribers, however, who were not convinced and who were of the opinion that the bulk of the money should be spent in Los Angeles. They reasoned that it would be easier to bring people from Los Angeles the 135 miles to San Diego than to bring them some two thousand to thirty-five hundred miles from the Middle West or the East Coast. Our own reasoning was that it would be far more difficult to get people to leave Los Angeles and come to San Diego, because aside from "Bay and Climate" Los Angeles had almost every advantage and attraction San Diego could offer, and many more besides. Our records of advertising results proved conclusively that we were right, but we could not convince some of these subscribers.

Some of them thought, too, that our advertising account should be placed through a local advertising firm instead of the H. K. McCann Company of San Francisco and New York City. I knew they were wrong, but we had to have the subscriptions, so for the fifth campaign we made concessions on both counts. We employed the local advertising firm, Western Advertising Agency, and agreed to spent 25 percent of the entire fund in Los Angeles.

At the height of the great Santa Fe Railroad boom in 1885, San Diego had a population of possibly thirty-five thousand. When this boom burst in about 1888, many of the newcomers had no means of support and had to leave. The Census of 1900 gave San Diego City a population of 17,700.

Los Angeles had experienced a boom at about the same time—namely, the years 1885 to 1888, but when their boom had burst, Los Angeles had not experienced the disastrous reaction San Diego had had, for several reasons. Los Angeles was the terminus of several converging railroads. It also had vast lakes underlying much of the surrounding fertile valleys, so that abundant water could be pumped for domestic and farm use. The Census of 1900 gave Los Angeles a population of 102,479 and another "boom" was in the making. When I stepped off the train in Los Angeles in 1903, on my way to San Diego, I was quite startled at the changes I could see in downtown Los Angeles from what it had been when I left for Bisbee, Arizona, in 1901. There were more people on the streets, and there were more and better streetcars. Additions were being made to downtown buildings. There was an air of movement and prosperity that had not been noticeable two years before.

The Santa Fe Railroad had orginally planned to make San Diego its Western Terminal. As an inducement, San Diegans had donated $25,000 in cash, and seventeen thousand acres of land in the "Rancho de la Nacion." The Santa Fe sent its chief engineer to San Diego in the fall of 1880, and early in 1881 construction was under way. Rails were shipped to San Diego around the Horn from Belgium and Germany. By January, 1882, the new ra'lroad was operating as far north as Fallbrook; by March, service was extended to Temecula; and in September, 1883, the first train from San Diego arrived in San Bernardino.

Unfortunately, however, the road bed through Temecula had been laid too near the creek. The heavy winter rains washed out the bridges and miles of track, and San Diego was again isolated. The Temecula route was abandoned, and a new road was extended along the Coast to Oceanside, Santa Ana, and then to San Bernardino via Corona.

The first Pullman train arrived in San Diego from the East hauling a Missouri Pacific sleeper, November 16, 1885, and the great boom of the eighties was under way! San Diego was at last the Western Terminal of a transcontinental railroad, with railroad shops and all that went with it. The boom was fast and furious. Newcomers poured into this wonderful new "Earthly Paradise," with its marvelous climate and perfect "land-locked harbor" until the population was estimated at more than thirty-five thousand. They stood in line all night to be the first to get a chance to buy lots in subdivisions many miles from the new town—lots they had never seen and never did see.

While this great boom was in progress, the Santa Fe started building a line from San Bernardino west to Los Angeles and then to Redondo, for a second Pacific Coast Terminal. They built a road from Los Angeles to connect with the San Diego line at Santa Ana, and moved all their vast shops and terminal facilities from San Diego to San Bernardino.

Thereafter, all through trains terminated in Los Angeles, with only an occasional local train operating between Los Angeles and San Diego, making San Diego the "Tail of the Kite," so to speak.

CHAPTER XXIV

A "City of Blighted Hopes"

BY 1903, when I arrived in San Diego, the consensus of opinion in Los Angeles was that San Diego was a "City of Blighted Hopes." It was just a little, dried-up town on the Mexican border, with no capital assets but "Bay and Climate"—a town that took itself seriously, but could never amount to anything because it was too far from Los Angeles—five hours by either of the two more than half-empty trains per day. It became quite the thing for Los Angeles people to make fun of San Diego. Any would-be comedian at the Orpheum Theater in Los Angeles had only to mention that he was from San Diego, whereupon he would always get a good laugh from the audience.

Angelenos heard so much about our lack of rainfall (we had years then as we have them now, when the total rainfall would be about four inches plus) that many of them believed San Diegans hardly had enough water to drink!

This "knocking," as San Diegans termed it, became increasingly hard to take year after year, but nobody could think of anything that we could do about it. Even when San Diego had doubled in population, the people of Los Angeles were unimpressed because, while our population in 1910 was 39,578, theirs had increased to 319,198! This ridicule was not malicious; it merely expressed the belief, based on hearsay, of the Los Angeles people. But it was just as damaging to San Diego, and it hurt the pride and feelings of the residents of San Diego, just as much as if it had been malicious.

When the fifth campaign fund of the San Diego-California Club was raised and it was time to make allotments, the new advertising firm came to me with a real problem. They knew, from our carefully kept records, that if they spent 25 percent of the fund in Los Angeles, they would not make nearly as good a showing for their expenditures per family arrival as had the McCann Company. I had foreseen this, and I was ready with the answer.

I told them, "We will use that appropriation to change the sentiment of the thinking population of Los Angeles from ridicule and abuse to a realization that San Diego is a fine, live, growing city, and a wonderful place to live, and a wonderful addition to Los Angeles' back country."

I told them I believed we could accomplish this objective with five full-page ads in the Los Angeles *Times*. That sounded like a big order, and they asked me if I would write the ads—which was exactly what I had hoped they would do! The idea, from the outset, was for San Diego to compliment Los Angeles; to show our admiration for their wonderful city and then let them know that we had quite a wonderful city also in San Diego, and that we were important to them. The ads made a really super-fine series, and they worked wonders.

The first ad ran on November 25, 1923, starting the campaign. It carried a large picture of San Diego County showing the harbor, with Coronado and the city, and in the background, all of San Diego's reservoirs, full of water! Here is the text of that first ad:

LOS ANGELES—SAN DIEGO

Twenty years ago Los Angeles had a population of 175,000. Today it has probably 850,000—an increase of nearly 500 percent.

The businessmen who began with small establishments in Los Angeles in 1903 have large business houses today. Those then in the larger establishments today have colossal buildings to house their institutions. The men who owned even a lot or two near the business district twenty years ago are rich today. And during all of these years their lives have been pleasant because they have lived in southern California.

One hundred and thirty-five miles south of Los Angeles is southern California's second city, San Diego, which twenty years ago had a population of 20,000. Today the population numbers 125,000—an increase of more than 500 percent. Pioneer businessmen in San Diego in 1903 are the heads of strong business institutions in that city today. Bankers, merchants, real estate owners, and professional men have profited in proportion to the steady growth and development that has taken place in San Diego. To these men and their families life has been sweet because they have lived in southern California on the shores of a beautiful harbor, with every advantage of southern California's most delightful year-round climate, scenic beauty, outdoor sports and recreations.

Half a century ago a small stream of people commenced to trickle into southern California from the East and Middle West. Because they found this to be the land of their heart's desire, their enthusiastic and sincere messages to friends back East brought others here, and they in turn influenced even larger numbers to come, until today the tide of immigration to southern California has assumed undreamed-of proportions, and yet this great inflow of new population has actually only begun. It is destined to continue and increase until every available foot of land has been developed, and this richly endowed section of California lying south of Point Conception, west of the Coast Range, and north of Tia Juana, is filled to overflowing.

There is no more delightful place in all the world to spend a week, a month, a year, or the rest of your life, than in San Diego. Here you will find a quality in the air that will fill you with vigor; from every vantage point is unfolded a panorama of unsurpassed beauty to charm you— the sparkling bay and ocean, the noble promontory of Point Loma stretching to sea, the mountains nearby and in Mexico, alluring Balboa Park, its myriads of flowers and mammoth open-air pipe organ, where free concerts are given every afternoon.

There is always somewhere to go, something to do in the out-of-door life here—motoring, golfing, tennis, yachting—all made the more pleasurable because of the abundance of sunshine and balmy sea air.

San Diego is growing in a definite, substantial manner—faster than ever before. It is today a modern city with 25 percent more population than Los Angeles had in 1900.

If you would enjoy the hospitality of cordial residents, and the pleasure of living in a most delightful community while it is growing from 125,000 to 300,000 or 500,000 population, San Diego beckons you.

If you would spend a time where life means most in the sheer joy of living, San Diego beckons you.

Come down and stay a while, play a while, look around, live and smile with us, enjoy our many recreations—trips to our back country, to our mountain peaks, to the border towns, to the great valleys, through wondrous deep gorges, to our old missions, to Coronado, Point Loma, La Jolla—spend a few joyous days or weeks here first, then make up your mind where you want to make your permanent home.

Our commodious, yet reasonably priced hotels, apartment houses, and cafés, will surprise you. Come and look us over. You have not seen southern California until you have seen San Diego. We want the pleasure of welcoming you. Write us a letter and we will send you a fascinating story of San Diego, and pictures that will make you want to come. Mail the attached coupon and you will hear from us in a manner that will make you glad you wrote.

Drop in at our Los Angeles office, in the Chamber of Commerce, and we will tell you more.

Mail the coupon now.

SAN DIEGO-CALIFORNIA CLUB

The headline for the second ad was: BUILT AROUND A PARK —SAN DIEGO. Nearly half of the top of the page contained a gorgeous photograph of a portion of Balboa Park taken from the air, showing some of our beautiful Exposition buildings and the Spreckels organ in the fore-ground.

WHERE THE NAVY GATHERS—SAN DIEGO was the title for the third ad, which had a striking photograph of a destroyer fleet headed almost straight for the camera and making a most spectacular smoke screen. This ad also had actual comprehensive photographs of the then new Marine Base buildings, with Marines marching in the foreground and the city on the hills in the background.

The fourth ad, headed THE FIRST MISSION, started:

> On the edge of one of the beautiful valleys near San Diego, with a view looking westward to the sea, Father Junipero Serra, in 1769, laid the adobe cornerstone of the first California mission.

The fifth and last ad, with a large photograph of San Diego from Point Loma, taken with a photostatic lens on a clear day and showing a large passenger ship sailing in the harbor and the new large buildings on North Island with the city and the mountains beyond, made an excellent setting for the caption:

ALONG THE WATERFRONT—SAN DIEGO

> Rising from the very edge of the harbor are the tall buildings which mark the heart of the business district of San Diego.
>
> Up easy grades, at vantage points on surrounding eminences and mesas, are blossom-covered homes on contoured drives and palm-lined avenues looking down on the sparkling bay, the white beaches, and the calm bosom of the Pacific.
>
> Back of all this, as mighty sentinels guarding the harbor and city, rise the majestic peaks of the Coast Range. Between the mountains and San Diego are fifty square miles of man-made lakes affording sport and pleasure, and unlimited, pure, sparkling rain water for our rapidly growing community.
>
> In the center of the residence district is fourteen-hundred-acre Balboa Park, with its groups of sately buildings in a setting of semi-tropical shrubs and foliage, more beautiful than in the days of the Panama-California Exposition. Here some of the best exhibits remain intact and, like the daily afternoon concerts of the great outdoor organ, are free to all.
>
> At the Zoo, the birds enjoy our out-of-doors in the largest cages ever built, and even the lions and bears are housed in open grottos without bars or screens.
>
> Hour after hour one will delight to stroll through this fairyland amid the bloom and fragrance of thousands of roses, to bask in the sun in the formal court of La Laguna de las Flores, or to enjoy the shade

of the great Cork Oak surrounded by all manner of new and tropical verdure.

Then, too, under the pergola overlooking beautiful Mission Valley with the first mission in the distance, you will enjoy your ease, and wish as have all who have come before you that you might remain here always.

One hundred and twenty-five thousand of us enjoy the exceptional advantages of San Diego throughout the year. On every train and every boat, new families are arriving to join the happy throng.

These new arrivals are adding to their capital to develop the opportunities existent here. Some are financing large office buildings; others are developing industries. One man built a cottonseed oil plant and the world's largest seed warehouse to store cottonseed grown in the great valleys back of San Diego. His profits have been enoromus.

One man became so enthusiastic over the possibilities here that he interested the Southern Pacific Company, and together they spent eighteen million dollars building the San Diego & Arizona Railway, opening a new transcontinental route through gorgeous mountain and valley scenery and giving San Diego a new rail connection to tidewater.

The U. S. Government has spent more than twenty-five million dollars in San Diego for great training schools and other establishments, because of the extraordinary climatic conditions.

Does your opportunity exist here? Frankly, we do not not know. We do know that newcomers with new capital are finding opportunity here. They are also finding the finest place on earth for everyday happiness.

So we say to you as we have said to them, come to San Diego and look around. Come and browse about; spend here a few of the most delightful days of your life and see what you shall see, come for a week if you can, or a month or longer, but come. No one but you will ever know what opportunity awaits your discovery in San Diego. Your sojourn here, be it long or short, will be an adventure in happiness you will never forget. The splendid service and moderate prices of our modern hotels and apartments will delight you.

Come tomorrow and let's get acquainted. Come by railroad, by boat, or by motor over paved roads—and when you arrive, come direct to San Diego-California Club headquarters at Second and Broadway, San Diego, and afford us the pleasure of welcoming you. Complimentary honorary membership will be extended to you during your stay.

If you cannot come tomorrow, mail the coupon and we will send you the most interesting story ever published by any community—you will read it twice in the first twenty minutes.

Mail the coupon NOW.

SAN DIEGO-CALIFORNIA CLUB

After that series of ads, the "ribbing" and poking fun at San Diego dried up, and we never heard it again. After twenty-five years of belittling and ridiculing San Diego, the sentiment of the entire city of Los Angeles was changed and San Diego was given its rightful place in the minds and thinking of the people of the larger city. They were our friends and "pals"— all as a result of five full-page ads in the Los Angeles *Times*. Another splendid demonstration of the power of advertising. If the San Diego-California Club had done nothing more than that its existence would have been well worth while.

Recently, I wrote to Don Thomas, managing director of the All-Year Club of Southern California, as follows:

Mr. Don Thomas, Managing Director
All-Year Club of Southern California
628 West Sixth Street,
Los Angeles 17, California

DEAR MR. THOMAS:
I am getting together for future reference some data on things that happened in San Diego forty or fifty years ago and, in working on the history of the San Diego-California Club, I wanted to make mention of the All-Year Club of Southern California, which has been such an outstanding success. I called our Information Department at the San Diego Chamber of Commerce and was delighted to learn that you are still the managing director of the All-Year Club. Congratulations to the Club! I have watched its progress from time to time and naturally have been delighted with its accomplishments.

Your advertisements still carry the same appeal that seems to me most logical for southern California, and your appropriations have been such that you have been able to display your ads so that they have been compelling. Your institution has been a fine thing for all of California.

Specifically, what I would like you to tell me is:
The date the All-Year Club of Southern California started.
The amount in dollars of the first year's appropriations.
What was your largest year in advertising expenditures, and the amount?

Trusting I am not imposing on you, and with appreciation, I am,

Sincerely,
O. W. COTTON

Four days later, Mr. Thomas replied, giving me some most interesting information:

ALL-YEAR CLUB OF SOUTHERN CALIFORNIA
628 West Sixth Street
Los Angeles 17, California

March 7, 1960

Mr. O. W. Cotton, Realtor,
524 B Street
San Diego 1, California

MY DEAR OSCAR COTTON:

Hearing from you again brought a flood of pleasant memories. Our contacts were always so pleasnat, and I have always thought a lot of you.

To answer your specific questions, the All-Year Club was started in May, 1921. The initial appropriation for national advertising was $60,000. The largest appropriation we have had is the current one of $710,970, which is spent exclusively for national advertising.

You will be happy to know our campaign is going better than ever. Our Board of Directors is considered the top one in the area. Also, the reputation of the campaign seems to have spread all over the world. Next week, a foreign delegation (I believe it is the 14th) referred to me by the U. S. State Department, will confer with us to find out "how we do it."

So nice to hear from you.

Warm personal regards,
DON
Don Thomas, *Managing Director*

The *Thirty-Eighth Annual Report* of the All-Year Club of Southern California is fabulous: "Nearly four and one-half million visitors brought to southern California in the twelve months ending July 31, 1959. (Comparable to attracting the entire population of the State of Missouri to southern California.)"

In May, 1939, the Los Angeles *Times* made the following comment on its editorial page:

THOSE TOURIST DOLLARS

State after state is taking a leaf from California's book and advertising its charms to attract the tourist dollar. It has paid them, too. North Carolina's gasoline tax income increased $1,250,000 the first year it told the world about its attractions, according to the *American Business* Magazine. Nebraska is realizing more from tourist travel than from corn since it tried the same plan, a leading state official says. Wisconsin has balanced its budget from tourist spendings since it let all and sundry know of its scenic marvels and good fishing.

These are some of the newer evidences of the pull of community advertising. It is certain that California, which started it all, has had the biggest drawing power of any state since it yanked its light from under a bushel. And southern California, with its All-Year Club in continuous functioning, has long attracted more tourist visitors than any other section of the country.

The following is from the editorial page of the San Diego *Evening Tribune* of June 10, 1950:

SAN DIEGO-CALIFORNIA CLUB MAKES VALUED CONTRIBUTION

San Diego claims a unique distinction which today gives it an anniversary to note.

For it was 31 years ago today that farsighted leaders organized the San Diego-California Club and originated the idea of community advertising.

Since that day in 1919, cities, counties, and states throughout the nation have utilized the idea. It is now no uncommon thing to see community advertisements in the country's most costly magazines, as well as in newspapers. Foreign countries also use the paid advertising appeal to attract tourists from this nation and on occasion we go abroad with display lures for those planning to travel.

But in 1919 the venture was distinctly an experiment, and there were those who approved it with fingers crossed. The reason they finally approved was that conditions here were desperate and no one had a better idea.

The originator of the idea, it is worth noting, was Oscar W. Cotton, whose vision quickly caught the attention and support of the late Carl Heilbron and of G. Aubrey Davidson. These men were pioneers in the movement.

It is also worth noting that in 1 month after the campaign started, the Club was receiving 900 tourist inquiries a day. During 1920 and 1921, 74,000 persons answered the Club's advertisements; 2,007 families arrived in San Diego and registered at the Club office; 800 of these families arrived in San Diego and settled here. Tourist expenditures amounted to $135,000 a month or $1,620,000 a year.

The Club has never let its interest lag. During its lifetime it has spent $2,000,000 in attracting 10,000,000 visitors who spent $500,000,000 in the county, its estimates show.

"Very conservatively," the Club office reports, "the county has received $250 in 'new wealth' for every dollar spent."

And that, in our opinion, is a very good footing for the profit and loss account.

The San Diego-California Club continues to function under the name San Diego Convention and Tourist Bureau. Its current appropriation (1960) will be in the neighborhood of $292,000, of which $113,000 will be spent for display ads and booklets.

The San Diego-California Club was organized and its first campaign started in 1919. The first organization to follow San Diego's leadership was the All-Year Club of Southern California in Los Angeles. As I am writing this in 1960, you cannot pick up the *National Geographic, Holiday,* or any other travel magazine, as well as many not devoted to travel, without finding alluring advertisements by cities, states, and nations, exhibiting their advantages. San Diego's advertising plan has gone around the world.

CHAPTER XXV

The 1921-26 Boom

IN THE DAYS before we had a politically controlled economy in the United States, politically stimulated inflation, Social Security, and 92 percent taxes on incomes—in short, before Franklin Delano Roosevelt was elected President—we actually lived under a system of Free Enterprise. The nation, the states, and cities had "booms" and "busts." During boom periods the blue sky was the only limit to which enthusiasm or overenthusiasm carried optimistic speculators. When a boom had burst and the excitement was over, optimism turned to pessimism, and investors in stocks, business ventures, and real estate became so depressed they wondered why they had ever been so foolish as to put all their cash in equities at the former ridiculously high prices.

In a city like San Diego, situated at the southwest corner of the United States, with the Pacific Ocean on one side, two hundred miles of mountains and desert on the other, not much but grain land for one hundred miles to the north and the Mexican border on the south, with nothing beyond that but land and ocean for a thousand miles, when a real estate boom burst, it really "busted!"

When I arrived in 1903, San Diego city and county were still near the bottom of the depression that had hit in 1888. The rather modest boom that began in 1910 carried land values far beyond the boom prices of '88, so that, when the bottom fell out again as a result of World War I, it had a long way to go. Real estate values zoomed down faster than they had zoomed up, much faster, and when they hit bottom they stayed there.

While working on the details of the advertising and follow-up campaign for the San Diego-California Club, the idea came to me of making a chart showing the rise and fall of San Diego real estate values and prices over a fifty-year period. I thought such a chart might awaken investors to the unparalleled opportunity to make investments in San Diego real estate, for it would show that at that time realty prices were at their lowest ebb in many years and the prospects were that they were in for a tremendous advance.

Early in 1920, when we could see that the campaign of the San Diego-

California Club was going to accomplish even greater results for San Diego than we had anticipated, I employed an engineer for the Pacific Building Company and had him make a chart, beginning with the year 1867 when "Father" Horton had purchased all of the present downtown San Diego property for twenty-six cents per acre. It showed the sale prices and value lines of San Diego real estate, skyrocketing and then dropping, plummet-like, with the booms and "busts," and it showed values in 1919 far below the peak of the boom in 1912, with real estate prices far below the value line.

The value line was based on population figures, assessed values, building permits, bank clearings, general business, municipal expenditures, and kindred figures, while the price line was based on actual sales prices according to deeds recorded. When completed, this chart made an excellent ad for our company, and also for the general real estate market in San Diego.

By the time we got the booklet to the printers, about June, 1920, the house market was already booming, but general real estate was scarcely moving. The booklet made quite a hit in real estate circles and was used for many years by appraisers, amateurs and professionals, when determining values on specific parcels of real estate during that period. I titled the booklet *Realty Values in San Diego, California, for the Past Fifty Years.*

In August, 1920, I gave a talk based on my booklet and showing the graphic charts to the Rotary Club. The next issue of *The Rotator* carried the following comment:

Thanks Mr. Cotton

The meeting last week was still another of those home talent affairs that have proven again that we do not need to go out of San Diego in order to get men big enough to give us something worth while. It is indeed seldom that we have the opportunity to learn so much about our fair city in such a short time, a matter of mere minutes, as we did at last week's luncheon. O. W. Cotton has well deserved his success as a realty dealer and home-builder, for any man who so definitely and systematically follows the causes of the rise and fall of the volume and values of his business cannot help but succeed, and it is to be hoped that everyone of us will doff our hats and say a good word at every turn for men of this caliber, and more especially for this type of men who are here with us and are citizens of our community and neighbors individually. We are much stronger for giving bouquets to the living than in shedding tears for the dead, and it is a real pleasure for us to thank O. W. Cotton for his splendid address, and can be frank in stating that it was one of the best business information talks every made before the San Diego Rotary Club.

The last three paragraphs of this booklet read as follows:

We now have our direct eastern railroad, which makes possible the development of commercial enterprises here, manufacturing and harbor development heretofore impracticable. The city has been organized into a unit for the purpose of advertising our advantages and bringing people here from every part of the United States to share with us the delights of the most wonderful place in all outdoors in which to live and work and to develop our natural advantages in commerce and industry with which the city is blessed. We have also another factor, which has never been seriously considered in the past, namely, the U. S. Government, which will probably spend in the next decade more money than the total combined expenditures to date for all buildings in the city of San Diego. The cost of upkeep and maintenance of these buildings, payroll, and supplies which will be expended here as the result of this work, is beyond our present ability to calculate.

Just how long it will be before the awakening to real estate opportunities comes and the market price makes a jump to catch up and again passes the real value line, it is impossible to say. If we knew, we would be justified in waiting until the last day before making our investments.

Of one thing we can be sure. Those who take advantage of the present situation, and make their investments while the prices are at low ebb, will reap deserved and noteworthy reward from their foresight in the coming advance.

There never was a truer or more timely forecast of coming events. New people literally poured into San Diego, until, by the fall of 1920, there was a housing shortage. The sale price on homes actually doubled in twelve months and all realty values started to climb.

That was the beginning of the boom that transformed downtown San Diego from a small town to a city. Among the buildings erected during those years (1921 to 1928) were: the Bank of America Building; the San Diego Trust & Savings Building; the Commonwealth Building; the Fox and the California Theater Buildings; the Pickwick Hotel; the Medico-Dental Building; the San Diego Club; the El Cortez Hotel, and many smaller buildings. Downtown San Diego took on a "new look" that was not to change materially for thirty years.

As an instance of how dead real estate was during the early stages of World War I, a man who had done considerable work for the Pacific Building Company as a subcontractor came in to see me one day and bought, for cash, several thousand dollars' worth of lots as a speculation. This was the first and only sale we had made of vacant real estate in many months. After we had closed the deal and he had gone, I remarked to Mr. Taylor, "Do you suppose he is crazy?"

Some months later, we saw by the newspaper that he had been declared insane and sent to an asylum. As it turned out, he was about the sanest man in town!

As a shortage of homes developed, new homes started to spring up, and again the musical sound of the hammer and saw could be heard all about town. However, I did not go back into the building business.

The Pacific Building Company owned thousands of vacant lots and had several thousand more on contract for sale. So while San Diego doubled in population and new buildings were going up on every hand, I sold lots. For ourselves and for clients, I sold about forty subdivisions, ranging in size from a few hundred of several thousand lots each, and located from National City to La Jolla, East San Diego, and Bostonia.

One of the Point Loma subdivisions we marketed was Plumosa Park. The owner of this tract, the San Diego Securities Company, was land poor. It owned many fine tracts of land on Point Loma, but had no income to carry the tax burden. I went to Frank J. Belcher, Jr., who was a member of the Board of Directors of San Diego Securities Company and who was also at that time president of the First National Trust & Savings Bank of San Diego, and told him that if the securities company would give the Pacific Building Company a contract, we would subdivide their properties, install water, sewers, gas, electricity, pave and sidewalk the streets, and sell the properties, and the owners would not have to put up one dollar. It sounded like magic.

Mr. Belcher invited me to a directors' meeting. My proposition was that I would divulge my plan of operation to the Board on the understanding that, if the Board determined to carry out the program as I outlined it, I would get the contract. They accepted my plan, gave me a contract, and I sold the first unit of several hundred lots within forty-five days after the subdivision map was filed.

After this first stupendous demonstration, other subdividers, large and small, wanted to do it, and they did—all over the county. San Diego had the biggest land boom for the next five years since the Santa Fe Railroad boom in 1885-86.

The plan was to have a map made subdividing the property, and then offer the land for sale "as is," but to have each purchaser sign a petition to the City Council for all street and utility improvements to be put in, and the property to be bonded to pay the costs. By this sales plan, the purchasers got the lots at a minimum price, because they did not have to pay a promotional profit on the street improvements, and they could pay for their improvements over a period of ten years.

The prices at which we sold these Plumosa Park lots (one of the choice locations on Point Loma as of that time) averaged about $750 for a 60 by 125 foot lot.

CHAPTER XXVI

"Good Old Days" of the Twenties

As SAN DIEGO again started on the high road to prosperity, material things other than business began to take the attention of some of our leading citizens. One was the promotion of the San Diego Country Club, at Chula Vista.

There had been two previous attempts at developing country clubs in San Diego. In 1896, a group of golf enthusiasts obtained permission from the City to lay out a nine-hole golf course in Balboa Park on the high, nearly level land between Laurel and Upas streets, east of the present Cabrillo Freeway. The members cleared off the brush and made sand "greens" twenty-five feet in diameter. A clubhouse three hundred square feet in size was built near Park Boulevard and Upas Street, and the first recorded official meeting of the San Diego Country Club was held at the home of Charles P. Douglas, on March 5, 1898. In 1911, these quarters became inadequate so they built a larger clubhouse across from the Park, on Upas Street. Soon after they were comfortably installed in the new clubhouse, the City notified the club that the golf course land was needed for the coming 1915 Exposition.

In the meantime, A. G. Spalding, who was promoting Point Loma, and particularly Loma Portal, through the San Diego Securities Company, had built a most pretentious clubhouse north and east of Chatsworth Boulevard and Rosecrans Street, and had laid out an eighteen-hole golf course with dirt fairways and sand "greens" extending from a portion of the present Marine Base east to the present Highway 101. When the San Diego Country Club had to give up its course to the City, Mr. Spalding's invitation to consolidate with the Point Loma Golf Club was quickly accepted.

However, as World War I developed, the government purchased the Marine Base site for training Marines, and that, with other encroachments, new streets, and other improvements, soon reduced that course to nine holes.

On April 7, 1920, the San Diego Country Club was incorporated with the intention of developing a permanent eighteen-hole golf course, with grass greens and fairways, and an adequate clubhouse, all to be developed and owned by the members. This was a big order, but it was success-fully carried to completion. Among the leaders of this project were F. J. Belcher, Jr.; H. H. Jones; Alexander Reynolds; Ed F. Chase; Robert C. Vroom; Scott E. Watson; N. E. Barker; Frederick W. Stearns; V. P. Morgan; M. B. Fowler; George S. Pickrell; Lester G. Bradley; E. B. Gould, and D. C. Hazelrig. The present Chula Vista site was chosen; a beautiful golf course was developed, and a most comfortable clubhouse was built.

The first officers and directors were: E. O. Hodge, President; L. A. Ellis, First Vice-President; E. B. Gould, Treasurer, and M. L. Ward, Jr., Secretary. Directors: Mrs. H. C. Oatman; Mrs. C. M. Fox; Charles P. Douglas, and Bently W. Sinclair. The membership of the club embraced most of the active younger and middle-aged social set of San Diego. Socially, and from the standpoint of the golfers, the club was an outstanding suc-cess—a wonderful and congenial crowd.

Most of San Diego's golfers were among the club's many members. On the opening day, I was paired off with Walter Whitcomb, vice-presi-dent of the First National Trust & Savings Bank. I don't remember Walter's score (I think it was probably around 100), but I remember mine very well indeed! It was 141 gross—which exactly equaled my weight in pounds on the day I was married—not very, good, in either case, since I am six feet tall!

The opening of this San Diego Country Club marked the beginning of many "Good Old Days." Golf in the daytime and parties at night. The club had a good chef; and we always had good dance music—the new tunes of the day made just about everybody want to dance—which we did, week after week, for many years.

After the club had been operating for a year or two it was decided that the club should publish a monthly magazine. It was called the *Golf Partner*. One day "A Member" wrote a letter to the editor of the *Golf Partner,* complaining because some of the golfers (so she claimed) used profane language near the clubhouse. I then wrote the following letter:

Editor
Golf Partner:
    I was immensely pleased to read the article in your magazine from "A Member" complaining of the profanity about the Clubhouse.
    Although I always look with more or less suspicion on anonymous letters, and would have been more favorably impressed in this instance had he or she signed "its" name, at the same time, the suggestion ex-pressed therein, namely, the prohibition of profanity at or near the Clubhouse, or in fact anywhere upon the course, is most excellent.
    Swearing is not good—in fact, it is bad. It befouls the air, increases

the bad temper of the swearer, teaches an unwholesome vocabulary to the caddies, grates on the sensitive ears of the fair sex, and I have always suspicioned that, indulged in to excess, it causes the brown spots to appear on some of the more unprotected greens.

However, this profane evil in man is of such long standing that if we are to eradicate it we must not mince matters, but must call a spade a spade and strike at its very vitals.

I recommend that every member interested in this new movement for the suppression of profanity shall constitute himself a committee of one to report to you, Mr. Editor, in a signed letter for publication the name of each offending member, the exact words used, the particular green or tee at which the specific offense is alleged to have taken place, and the name or names of those whose sensibilities seemed to have suffered most from the shock.

As an example, I shall start this great forward movement by specifically naming Jay Gould as the first offender. Jay, with three others, was on the 8th green; I was in a foursome on the 9th tee. Jay evidently made a bad shot, because suddenly, and frankly to my great surprise, I heard him vehemently exclaim, "Rats!"

Of all disgusting animals one could think of to compare with a poor golf shot, I think the rat is the worst. If he had said, "Mice!" or if he had wanted something larger to express greater displeasure, he might have said, "Kangaroo!" but the rat is such an unclean sort of being; it carries deadly germs; in fact, there is nothing good I can think of about the rat; therefore, the first rule of etiquette on the golf course should be that the profane expression "Rats!" is taboo.

Why would it not be a good idea to name a committee of three, to include C. M. Hosmer, chairman, and to act with him, Dempster McKee and Harry Folsom, which committee would censor all language used on the course?

This committee might make up lists of permissible expressions to be used to fit each type of shot, slice, hook, for head up, etc., selecting such gentlemanly terms as "Pickles," "Fudge," "Well, well," "I do declare," "Gracious me," etc.

My son John took me to a Fathers' and Sons' lecture one evening at the First Congregational Church. The speaker, the Reverend Roy Campbell, was exhorting the fathers to attend church at least once each week.

He said, "A lot of you fathers may think you can worship God on the golf course on Sunday morning just as well or better than in a damp and musty church, but I want to tell you that no man can worship God on the golf course on Sunday morning when he misses a short putt."

Yours for purity in Golf,
OSCAR COTTON

The "Committee" I suggested were members who might almost be considered "professionals" in the use of profanity.

Dr. Hosmer was a most quiet and refined gentleman, but when he made a bad shot, the blue sky was the only limit to his—shall we say, "adjectives." A favorite stunt of his, when he was invited to play in a foursome who had not played with him before, was to accept the invitation most courteously, but with the provision that no profanity be indulged in during the game. The use of any foul language, he would claim, was upsetting to him to such an extent that it invariably spoiled his game. It was a most unusual request, but, coming from such a refined gentleman, the other golfers would acquiesce and the game would proceed. After three or four holes of most dignified golf, regardless of bad shots, Dr. Hosmer would fail to get out of a sand trap, or would finally miss a putt; then he would cut loose with his whole vocabulary!

The *Golf Partner* was published monthly for several years. I wrote a series of articles which provoked varying comments. One member said, "Mr. Cotton has the unique distinction of being a humorist who writes things that are funny." A woman remarked, "When I finished reading your article on 'Diet Number 13-13,' I said to my husband, 'The darn fool!' " Another woman said, "Every month I grab the *Golf Partner* as soon as it comes and find your article and laugh till I cry."

A few of these articles follow:

GOLFING HINTS BY A GOLFER WHO "THINKS HE KNOWS"

Last month I read a lot of blah in San Diego's favorite magazine, *Golf Partner,* by a golfer who admitted knowing all about putting and other types of golf, but I noticed he did not dare sign his name, probably because he is stoop-shouldered from carrying around a thirty-six handicap, all of which he deserves, I have no doubt; in fact, since in his article he stresses mostly the effeminate art of putting, I am suspicious that he plays most of his games on our miniature courses, which is all right if he has a girlish figure and a boyish bob, and does not need the physical benefits as do some of us; because playing miniature golf for exercise is like riding horseback with the same object in view, only in the last-mentioned instance it is the horse that gets the exercise, whereas in miniature golf it is only the golf ball, which does not count much.

However, since the anonymous article sounded as learned as a college professor, I gave it a workout; took it to the course with me, and before each putt I would pause and read it through once or twice and then let the old pill have it square and flat like it said.

Far be it from me to criticize a fellow sportsman golfer, anonymous though he be, but frankness compels me to admit that the theories expounded may be O.K. on a miniature course, but on the putting green they won't work, or else I overlooked something in my interpretation of the "hints," because I took sixty-seven putts on the first nine holes and got the other fellows all hot and bothered because I was holding back the game somewhat.

So I decided that if what our golfers need is "HINTS" I could set down a few myself which would mean more to the average golfer because my suggestions would come from someone in particular, and not just by "One Who Knows."

Also the writer of this article (I mean myself, personally) has played golf from more specific points on and not on our course than any other golfer.

While some of these suggestions are strictly original, others are ideas developed by observation, but all are made with the same object as our last month's anonymous contributor, which is that of playing par golf or better.

Incidentally, I would like to call to the reader's attention that by following my suggestions he will not have a page of rules to read on the green before making his putts or any trouble of that kind. My method simplifies the game to a point where all players may get equal pleasure out of it.

When driving off the Number One Tee take a full, easy swing, hitting the ball squarely like Bobby Jones; next take your midiron and drop the ball on the green about ten feet to the right and west of the cup, then take the putter and carefully sink the ball for a birdie.

Pursue the same tactics for the other seventeen holes, using iron clubs to drive with on the short holes and wood clubs on the fairways on the longer holes.

Control your temper so all members of your foursome can enjoy their game.

If you must swear, say something original.

Count all strokes.

Knock all balls toward the cup.

Keep out of traps and hazards. Play ball as it lies when other other players are looking.

Judge all distances and directions correctly.

Sink your ball in one putt.

Utterly disregard the length of skirts in mixed foursomes.

Keep your eye on the ball.

Play the nineteenth hole last.

If these "Hints" do not reduce your score to par golf, or better, possibly you have missed your calling. Honors may come to you on a miniature course!

One foursome who played together quite regularly consisted of George W. Marston; Julius Wangenheim; Milton A. McRea, and M. F. Heller. One day someone dubbed this group "The Millionaire Foursome," and the title stuck.

When one of this foursome was out of town, some other club member would be invited to fill the vacancy. It was a most congenial group so they never had any trouble filling the ranks. This foursome, regardless of the personnel for the particular day, always played for a cash stake, but, no matter who won, the pot was always turned over to Mr. Marston to be given to his daughter, Mary, for her pet charity, Neighborhood House.

For the August, 1930, issue of the *Golf Partner* (or to better describe the date, it was about nine months after the 1929 Stock Market Crash) I wrote the following article:

THE MILLIONAIRE FOURSOME

From time to time we have seen in the *Golf Partner* honorable mention of the Millionaire Foursome.

Even in these days of billionaires, and bread lines, there is a certain alluring fascination about a million dollars, or ten million, as the case might be, that is little short of irresistible, especially to a real estate man. So when one of this foursome went on a vacation and I was invited to substitute, I accepted with alacrity.

There are several reasons why I accepted. In the first place, a prospector only strikes it rich when he prospects where the gold is, and while everybody knows that no real estate man would take advantage of a friend on the golf course, unless he got the chance, it seemed a good bet, at least.

Then there is the advertising. Other club members and prospective investors will say, "I knew Oscar Cotton when he only weighed 140 pounds and now look at him, tips the scales at a tenth of a ton and plays golf with the millionaires; there must be money in real estate."

My bankers have not called me on a single loan since I have been playing in this foursome, and several times club members have introduced me as "Mister."

The immediate results have not been so good financially. These supposed controllers of currency play rather a better game than I anticipated, and they are very clever at mathematics, handicaps, etc., but the worst of the business is that when I lose, I lose, and when I win, I lose, because it seems that all winnings go to the Neighborhood House, which place is so exclusive I have never even been invited there for supper.

The low man in the foursome—in score, not in intelligence—buys the lunch. When I say the low man, I mean the high man; I mean the poorest man, not the poorest financially but golfically speaking. The one who messes up the most sand traps, jerks his head up and tries to kill the poor little ball; the rottenest player for that particular day. Sometimes the richest man plays the poorest and the poorest man plays the richest, at least it is "rich"—if I may be permitted to use a slang expression—watching some of the shots.

I have one advantage. I can say or write what I please about their golf shots and they can't strike back, because if they did I could sue them for libel. I purposely shall not say anything nice about their golf games because if they should hear about it, coming from me with my vast knowledge of the game on account of having taken 400 lessons, it would make them vain and they are hard enough to get along with as it is, temperamental, etc., always expecting to do better. But there is one member, a merchant, who can swing a wicked wooden club. When he keeps the bean down and follows through and the white pill drops in the middle of the fairway, a distance of 250 yards, we all get a thrill.

Another member is worthy of honorable mention because of his ability to find his ball in the rough. I think that is because of his early training in driving a grocery wagon around our canyon roads before the streets were paved. He seldom buys the lunch.

The other member is, I think, frankly, better in philosophy than golf, and until recently has devoted more attention to reconciling himself to his game than vice versa. "However,"—as he would say—recently I have noticed him eying the merchant enviously, then holding his own head down, and making some worthy shots; there is latent talent there if we can bring it out.

In my youth, I was taught that I should exercise and get an appetite, but in this foursome, the men who exercise the least eat the most. I am appalled to see what the aforesaid merchant can eat after taking only 93 strokes in 18 holes, by comparison with what I order after playing 119 shots, and having to sign checks for one lunch and three banquets.

There seems to be a lot of human nature in human nature.

I Can't Please No One

Certain members of our club have severely critcized me for selecting one special group of members and advertising them as millionaires; thereby embarrassing the other members who were not included.

To make matters worse, one of the other three members of this millionaire foursome—not counting myself—complained bitterly because, he said, the advertising had increased the financial demands made upon him to the point where his title is weakening under the strain; with the Community Chest still ahead of us.

To make amends for having committed this social error I put on some swell clothes in order that my friends would not recognize me, and parked for a week at the Number One Tee. As the golfers, near golfers, and others, came up to drive off, I singled out each player individually, and asked this simple question:

"Are you a millionaire?"

I was surprised how few answered "Yes" without hesitation. Also, it was interesting to see the expression on their faces. While some few apparently have been sounded out on that subject before by social workers, bond gentlemen, real estate sharks, and other crooks, to this great majority, I feel certain, it was an entirely new experience.

Those few of the first-named classification became very formal and looked as though they thought me a fool, which I feel is underrating my mental faculties somewhat; while most of those of the latter class seemed complimented, as though being a millionaire was not anything to be ashamed of especially, which made it seem to me that they were honest fellows and had honest thoughts about how they would go about getting their last $999,864 to be a millionaire.

On the other hand, when a man appeared offended by my simple question—and I am sure it was simple—I became suspicious that he was guilty, and I wondered how he had come by his millions that it so mortified him to be found out.

In the next issue of the *Golf Partner* I may print a list of the names and their answers—it would make interesting reading.

Neither those who admitted they were millionaires nor those who reluctantly admitted that they were not, seemed to be offended at my last article, so I have come to the conclusion that those who made the complaints were themselves "would-be-millionaires," that is, fellows who would like to be millionaires but could not think just how to go about doing it.

As I have already intimated, the poll showed that the majority of our members were not yet millionaires. I suppose that is on account of our membership dues, betting on their own game instead of their opponent's, lost golf balls, and the high cost of prescriptions,[1] or, possibly, like real estate men nowadays, they are too busy to bother about it. Although those who brazenly admitted to the disgrace of being millionaires seemed to have very little bother about anything. Theirs appeared to be quite a refined life. I rather think I should enjoy it, myself, provided, of course, that I could acquire my millions—seems funny to be saying "my millions"—I am not used to it yet—by real estate transactions or some other honest means.

If all the members of our club, except, of course, the members who criticized my last article, could be as satisfied with their respective golf

---

[1] This was during Prohibition.

games as they appear to be with their financial standings, our club would
be a symphony.

Regarding the gentleman who, because of my aforesaid article, feels
that he has been injured both financially and socially, I can only hope
that time will cure the social wound, and I think his financial losses
will be offset on account of my buying the lunches, which I am continuing to do quite regularly.

Have You a Past?

A famous magazine publisher once said, "The thing which most
interests man is himself."

Broadly speaking, he meant: Men like to read about other golfers,
J. Pierpont Morgan, and Brigham Young; while women want stories of
others of their sex who have become outstanding in spite of matrimony;
undercomforted wives; he-heroes, and other myths.

Obviously, the pages of a high-class magazine like the *Golf Partner*
cannot be devoted to the frivolities of fiction, but, in order to give this
publication a gripping human touch, the Editor has made up our mind
that we should publish a series of biographies of the living members of
our club; depicting the events of their pasts in such illuminative style
as will stimulate the mentality of our readers to the extreme of their
imagination.

Writing biographies of the dead is simple. An historian can go to the
library and get enough facts to fill a bookstore. If he makes a mistake in
his verbiage or adjectives, there will be no lawsuit.

In writing of live, virile golfers, there are many possibilities of error
which might prove costly; also there is no reference library, except the
the "Blue Book" and "Who's Who in California," which publications
maliciously, or otherwise, leave out all of the details of our golfers'
pasts, which I particularly want to write about. I mean, incidents which
they never expected to see in print.

In looking over our Club Roster, I find quite a number of members
whose pasts appear to be outstanding. Often, however, appearances are
deceiving. The very person who looks like he had enjoyed a colorful
past may not have had one at all, in which case an article about him
would be as insipid as near-beer, or a blowout on a spare.

In order to save time and separate the lambs from the goats; I
mean, to enable me to select quickly the members with pasts and elimi-
nate those drab souls whose games uniformly range between 82 and 83,
I should like each member of our club to write me a letter, telling in
simple language that I can understand—words of one or more syllables—
of all the incidents that have happened to them in their pasts, or
thoughts which they have had, if any, awake or asleep.

There are no special rules to this, like there would be in a contest
of bathing beauties. Write briefly of each adventure or thought. Do not

try to hold out anything. I will do the editing. If you were to try to do that, you would probably leave out the very incidents in your past that would make the best reading.

Use one side of the page only. Send letters to the *Golf Partner,* with my name printed impressively on the lower left-hand corner of the envelope.

All letters will be treated in strict confidence. Only the name by which a member is known locally will be used. Women members are eligible. I am hopeful that some of our most colorful letters will be from the fair sex. There again one can never tell, the lives of some of our most vivacious women of today, before their husbands made them what they are, may have been drab.

Do not delay. It is imperative that we waste no time in getting started. The chairman of our handicap committee figured out for me, trigonometrically, that with our present membership of 450, and the *Golf Partner* appearing monthly, to complete the full set of biographies will take exactly six months and thirty-seven years.

Sleeping With a Redheaded Woman
(As intimately related to me by a member of our Club)

Before getting into this first biography, I must say just a word to our members at large who have not as yet written me letters on their pasts.

Please write shorter letters. Five or six pages is quite sufficient. Leave out such items as the fact that you never loved but once. The number and sex of issue, by marriage. How, in business, you always place your customers' interests ahead of your own, etc.

The lives of George Washington and Sir Galahad are fine examples for our children's textbooks during the fourth grade, but the other members of this Golf Club are like you. They crave a stick in their limeade.

Frankly, what I want in these letters are little items of the big moments in your lives. Write me less about more. I will rewrite it into more about less.

I had planned to write this first biography on the past of our newly elected president, H. D. Stalnaker. He has the appearance of possibilities. So far, he has been elusive. When he did not write me, I telephoned him, but he claimed he could not see me—had to go to Agua Caliente with three other birds for golf—"You know how that is, Oscar," he said. To this day, I have not been able to figure out what he meant by that remark. I don't admit knowing anything about Agua Caliente.

The next time I telephoned him, he was in a rush to go to Sacramento. "Another stag party," that is what he said. He promised surely he would see me on his return. If he were a real estate man, I could believe him. However, I let him go because what I want is a colorful memoir. It is possible that such a trip would be a help. It might add a zip to his past—possibly two zips.

As it turned out, I am glad our new president went to Sacramento. His absence gives me an opportunity this month to present to the members of San Diego Country Club a narrative illustrative of the exact type I need from other members for these biographies. So far, out of fifty letters from members, the following memoir, "Sleeping with a Redheaded Woman," is the only one I have received which has such irresistible "It-ish" appeal as will distract the golfer's mind from his beastly game, his business losses, and his home life.

At the request of this member whose autobiography follows, I am omitting the name; although from his boldness of expression on what would ordinarily be considered a delicate subject, I am sure the other members of our club will have no trouble in identifying him. I shall quote the letter verbatim for the benefit of those of our readers whose lives are drab and who get their thrills mostly from Balzac and *Tales of the Arabian Nights*.

He wrote:

"The last time I slept with a redheaded woman was about two weeks ago.

"We were in a certain large, centrally located hotel in a fair-sized Pacific Coast city, close to the Mexican Border. I had known the girl for a number of years, so everything was perfectly proper; I mean, it was not just merely a chance acquaintance.

"The girl has a pleasing personality, class, etc., full of fun. Nice disposition; likes to keep a fellow entertained while he is awake, yet does not crab if, perchance, he should fall asleep.

"On this particular occasion, I did not realize I had dropped off to sleep until suddenly I heard a heavy male voice, not two feet away. I awoke with a start, I can tell you! Involuntarily, I tried to get free, but it is not always as easy to get away from a redheaded woman as one of less experience might hope. In this case, the girl still had hold of my hand. As I looked up, what should I see but a large, grim-looking man standing there towering over us, with an opened razor in his right hand. I remember him well; he wore light pants, no coat, and his sleeves were already rolled up.

"Naturally, I was embarrassed, for the moment, until I could think up something to say. It seemed to me that conversation was appropriate, but my mind would not function.

"Then things began to happen! The Big Fellow, with his free hand, jerked off the sheet from around my neck and called, 'Next!' The redheaded manicurist released my hand, and I climbed down from the barber's chair."

Those were "Good Old Days." I played rotten golf, but I enjoyed immensely the companionship and the thrill of an occasional good shot. We enjoyed the sociability of the evening parties and the dancing. We almost forgot there had been a war, and a depression. The future looked bright indeed—not a cloud on the horizon.

In the early days of the San Diego Country Club, many of the wives took as keen an interest in golf as did their husbands. On November 19, 1923, the San Diego *Union's* Sports Section carried the following news item on its front page, in heavy "caps" and twelve-point type:

MRS. COTTON AND MRS. CHILDS WIN LEGS ON TROPHY

Mrs. C. F. Atkinson yesterday won the Class A Golf Sweepstakes play at Chula Vista, scoring 101-14-87, while Mrs. Childs was Class B winner with 109-22-87, and in Class C, Mrs. O. W. Cotton and Mrs. Mrs. R. M. Pray tied with 39 net for nine holes. Legs on the trophy now being contested for each week were won by Mrs. Cotton and Mrs. Childs, the former making 86 net.

Next day (Tuesday, November 20) the *Union* ran a five-column cut showing Mrs. O. W. Cotton in a happy pose, in golf outfit, holding a driver and standing beside Mrs. Bert Levi in front of the San Diego Country Club. It bore the title: PLAYING IN TITLE TOURNAMENT AT CHULA VISTA, and under the picture was the following caption: "Mrs. Bert Levi and Mrs. O. W. Cotton, awaiting their turn yesterday morning to drive off Number One Tee in the second annual San Diego Country Club's Woman's Championship Tourney. The Class C prize went to Mrs. O. W. Cotton."

After the first few years, Violet gave up golf, devoting her time and thought to raising a family, her music, and our friends, but she has always been most encouraging to me in my—shall we say—"Golfing Exercise."

May 19, 1925, was a Red Letter Day for me. I had a most delightful "Good Old Day" playing golf at our San Diego Country Club with Senator M. L. Ward. I shot a 92, which was by far my best score to date. When I told Senator Ward how thrilled I was, he smiled and expressed his pleasure, and told me that a number of his friends had made their best scores while playing with him. Then I realized what had been going on. Senator Ward was a most friendly gentleman, of even temper; nothing ruffled him. Even on a 5-par hole, a 10 did not frustrate him in the least. He played golf for enjoyment and companionship, and possibly exercise. He kept the score (I still have the card) but not even that bothered him.

For two years, while I was most active in the Chamber of Commerce,

Senator Ward was on a small committee of which I was chairman, so I had the pleasure of his acquaintance for many years, and never, in all that time, did I ever see him show displeasure.

He reared a wonderful family of three sons, John, Paul, and Luther, and a daughter, Martha. They all inherited this lovable characteristic and passed it on to all of his grandsons whom it has been my privilege to know. After the Senator left us, I used to play with John, and I found him a wonderful and congenial companion. Senator Ward, like J. Jessop and Senator Ed Fletcher, left San Diego a rich heritage in his descendants.

At the very end of the year 1930, one of the famous "Millionaire Foursome" sent me the following letter:

GEORGE W. MARSTON
San Diego, California
December 30, 1930

MY DEAR COTTON:

Here is my belated thanks for your note of November 20. I was in the hospital then but came back nine days ago and am gaining rapidly every day. I can dictate for about a half an hour and am able to read a good deal, and have already started walking about the garden.

Of course, this is all preliminary toward golfing days when I expect to outdo you all in accurate driving. In order to keep my incision closed I shall have to depend upon my arms and wrists. This with keeping my eye on the ball (and I have been thinking about that and concentrating my mind on it for sixty days) will enable me to shoot a very straight and snappy ball. It is little doubtful whether I can make a score of 80 to correspond with my recent birthday, but in the course of time, say when I am 90, I may be able to do that, I feel quite sure.

Thanking you for your remembrance and with happy New Year wishes.

Sincerely yours,
GEORGE W. MARSTON

Mr. Marston lived to be ninety-five, respected and admired by everyone whose good fortune it was to know him. He attained and far surpassed his ambitions in most of his undertakings. I do not believe he ever shot his age on the golf course, but he had a lot of pleasure and healthy exercise trying.

I did not realize it at the time nor for many years later, but ultimately golf was to play a major role in my life.

CHAPTER XXVII

The Great Valleys of Yuma

EARLY IN 1923, a real estate promoter from Yuma, Arizona, came into our office and told me of the wonderful opportunities for land development in the Yuma, South Gila, and Mohawk valleys, adjacent to and north of the town of Yuma. A few days later, I went with him to Yuma to have a look. We stopped at the Juch Ranch, near Santa Ysabel, to pick up William, who was staying at the ranch for a vacation. I had been through Yuma from time to time on the train, but had never stopped over.

This trip was by auto, through our beautiful mountain country, then down the gorgeous Mountain Springs Grade and through the Imperial Valley continuing east to the end of the paved highway, then for a mile or two through the sand to the dunes, then via the narrow, one-way, old plank road, twisting over the sand dunes, and finally, after six hours, over the bridge across the Colorado River to the old Southern Pacific Hotel in Yuma, to park in front of an enormous sign thirty feet or more long, reading FREE MEALS EVERY DAY THE SUN DOES NOT SHINE.

The real estate promoter who brought us over was O. T. McCoon, a thoroughly desert-seasoned man of possibly fifty-five years, who really knew Yuma, its possibilities, and its people. McCoon was correct in everything he told me. The opportunities for thousands of people to come to Yuma and make their fortunes were there, just waiting to be taken. For me, one three-day visit was enough. I saw the land and what it produced, and the vast profits that were possible. I met the farmers, farm advisers, bankers, and others "in the know."

I appointed McCoon our agent to option land in all three valleys; returned to San Diego, and wrote a booklet, *Gold,* describing Yuma and its wonderful possibilities for profits. In due course, I put on a newspaper advertising campaign, and started our sales staff driving our prospects to Yuma, over the same interesting route I had taken.

Yuma was as different from San Diego as any community could be. San Diego, as a place to live, was tops, but almost all farming had problems—the high cost, and lack, of sufficient water, and both soil and climate suited for raising only certain crops. Yuma had abundant water at (to us the unheard-of rate) $1.75 per acre foot, and soil and climate which would actually produce nine crops of alfalfa a year, and no rain to spoil the crops. It all sounded wonderful to us, and it was.

I wrote a second booklet *Twelve Years to Riches,* telling in detail, and illustrating with pictures, how a farmer could start with a moderate capital on a forty-acre ranch at $75 per acre, and in twelve years be independent for life. This second booklet was so good and factual that it was used for many years as a sales book by many Yumans.

We worked like the dickens and kept the roads hot between San Diego and Yuma for possibly a year, but results were most unsatisfactory. It was one thing to advertise San Diego to the folks in the East and the Midwest as the grandest place in all the world in which to live; they would fall for that and come, but to persuade people to leave San Diego and live for twelve years in Yuma, where the temperature often soared to 105° and occasionally to 120°, just to get rich, was another story.

I finally wrote one more booklet, *Yuma's Marvelous Growing Climate,* and had a rotogravure folder made up which had some twenty or more pictures and was entitled *What Yuma Will Do for You,* but even this did not help. Folks just did not want to leave beautiful San Diego and go to live in Yuma, and least of all the housewives did not want it.

Yuma has grown from a town of 4,300, when I first went there in 1923, to a city of 23,811, according to the U. S. Census of 1960. The great valleys and mesas surrounding Yuma have been developed as forecast thirty-seven years ago, all without my help and, I am quite sure, without a very large percentage of new residents drawn from San Diego.

Although they did me no good personally, my books on Yuma all made quite a hit. I received many highly complimentary letters from individuals and associations, government bureaus, and libraries, requesting copies. A few of them follow:

HARVARD UNIVERSITY
Graduate School of Business Administration
Cambridge, Massachusetts

December 18, 1924

Pacific Building Co.,
San Diego, California

For the purpose of instruction in this School, we should greatly appreciate your contribution of the material listed below to our Library:
Oscar William Cotton
Twelve Years to Riches.

CHARLES C. EATON
Librarian

THE JOHN CRERAR LIBRARY
Chicago

Oct. 29, 1924

Mr. Oscar W. Cotton
San Diego, California

My attention has been called to the publication noted below and
I beg to be informed how it may be obtained.
Twelve Years to Riches. 1923.

C. W. ANDREWS
Librarian

DEPARTMENT OF AGRICULTURE — CANADA
International Institute Branch
West Block, Ottawa

Aug. 22, 1924

The Manager,
Pacific Building Co.,
San Diego, Calif.

I beg to request the favor of a copy of the publications indicated
hereunder for my official library which is the Department's authorized
depository for official publications.

Assuring you that we shall appreciate the courtesy, I am,

F. K. DOHERTY
Institute Commissioner

Twelve Years to Riches, by O. W. Cotton.   1923.   30 p.

NATIONAL BOND & MORTGAGE COMPANY
Subscribed Capital $1,000,000
San Francisco, California

August 18, 1923

Pacific Building Company,
San Diego, California

ATTENTION: Mr. O. W. COTTON

Wish that you would send us three or four of the booklets entitled:

Gold
What Yuma Will Do for You
Yuma's Marvelous Growing Climate

Several of the directors wanted some of the pamphlets. They are
fine advertising and somebody must have given the work a great deal
of careful thought.

BYRNE A. BEAM

SALT RIVER VALLEY-ARIZONA CLUB
Phoenix, Arizona

July 27, 1923

DEAR MR. COTTON:

Kindly accept thanks for your booklet *Gold,* which I enjoyed very much. Would be pleased to receive a copy of the booklet dealing particularly with the climate of Yuma, and hope that when same is received from the printers you will mail me a copy. Also accept thanks for the folder *What Yuma Will Do for You,* which came today.

We also owe you considerable thanks for the assistance you gave us last summer when we were forming our advertising club. We are now preparing our winter campaign, and I have in preparation a new booklet, the *Romance of Phoenix,* and when same is received from the press, will be glad to forward you a copy.

FRANK A. JEFFERSON
Secretary

YUMA IRRIGATION PROJECT
Yuma, Arizona

July 18, 1923

Mr. O. W. Cotton,
San Diego, Calif.

I have just read your booklet *Gold,* giving an account of your day's ride in the Yuma Valley; and, as a resident and landowner here, I want to thank you for putting forth in such a compact readable form the simple truth about our locality.

I know every one of the farmers you talked to, your only deviation being that you changed their names.

This story to be complete is too immense for you to get it into one booklet. I am hoping that you will come over here again soon and write the story fully of just one of these ranches—the thirty-acre fruit ranch. Just tell that story in detail as honestly and clearly as you wrote this story about your trip, and I believe you will then have the most inspirational story you have ever written; and it might do a world of good pointing out to some people who are looking for real homes just the kind of a country they are thinking about.

C. W. INGHAM
Secretary

DEPARTMENT OF THE INTERIOR
Bureau of Reclamation
Denver, Colorado

May 23, 1924

Mr. O. W. Cotton, President,
Pacific Building Co.,
San Diego, California

Recently, while on a trip to Yuma investigating the proposition of advertising the valley lands with a view to more intensive settlement and development, I was handed your publications, *Gold, Twelve Years to Riches,* and *Yuma's Marvelous Growing Climate.* I was pleased to note that you had written up your observations in a very attractive manner and had stated the case of the Yuma country conservatively and clearly.

I have been connected with the Yuma Valley as an owner for more than 23 years and am particularly interested in seeing that district developed to the highest possibility. I have been during a good many years with the Reclamation Service and am now preparing a booklet on the Yuma district to use in our settlement work.

I am writing to you to ask whether you have any objection to my copying certain parts of your booklets in the preparation of my own. I should like to copy the talk by Mr. Heineman to the Kiwanis Club, as quoted in your *Twelve Years to Riches;* also, a part of your personal observations as given in *Gold.*

I should be very much pleased to hear from you in this regard at your early convenience.

B. E. HAYDEN
Industrial Agent

I never regretted my Yuma experience. It was most interesting and educational and I, personally, enjoyed the climate, particularly the low humidity (during the warmest part of the day, about 10 percent), and I loved driving through the mountains north of Yuma.

Sixty miles or more east of San Diego, almost on the rim of the mountain range overlooking the vast deserts, we have our beautiful Cuyamaca Mountain, 6,500 feet high, with a peak rising from the center of its dome. The historian at our public library will tell you that the old Indian word *Cuyamaca,* translated into plain English means: "No rain beyond"; or "It rains behind"; or "Rain yonder"; or several other interpretations by famous historians. All translations are more or less vague.

In the low range of mountains north of Yuma, one beautiful, rounding dome stands apart from the rest, and from the center of this dome rises a short, jagged peak. I have not been able to verify this, but my old desert friend and associate in Yuma told me that the Yuma Indians of his day called

The Pacific Building Company's tract office at about Thirty-fifth Street in East San Diego in 1921, where William O. Cotton made his first sale.

(*Top*) The clubhouse of the San Diego Country Club, about 1925. (*Center*) Playing in the
tournament at Chula Vista, Mrs. Bert Levi (*seated*) and Mrs. O. W. Cotton, waiting their
yesterday morning to drive off number-one tee in the second annual San Diego Country C
Women's Championship Tourney. (*Bottom*) Players on the eighteenth green (*left to ri*
Arthur Childs, Nelson Barker, P. Victor Morgan, and Roy Pickford.

Historical Collection, Title Insurance and Trust Company, Union Title Office, San Diego, California

Fifth Avenue at B Street, looking south, in 1924.

Historical Collection, Title Insurance and Trust Company, Union Title Office, San Diego, California

The northwest corner of Fifth Avenue at Broadway in 1925.

Historical Collection, Title Insurance and Trust Company, Union Title Office, San Diego, California

Broadway looking east from First Avenue in 1926.

A portion of the only highway between San Diego and Yuma in 1923, between the easter terminus of the paved road and the western end of the plank road over the sand dunes. was driving.

Sand dunes in the California desert between the Imperial Valley and Yuma, Arizona.

A portion of the original plank road that wound its way over the continuously shifting sand dur

the mountain "The Squaw's Cuyamaca," meaning, of course, that it looks like a squaw's "cuyamaca"!

In the *Cuyamaca Club News* of April 1962, a monthly bulletin to members, Rodney Sprigg, son of Patterson Sprigg, one of the founders of the Club in 1887, said:

> The Cuyamaca Club came about one afternoon in my father's office when he and two other men—Heber Ingle and Charlie Flower—admitted that they wanted to have a place where they could get together for lunch and visits. So they decided to form their own private club with no strings attached.
>
> They took the name from the mountain, because they wanted something with local identification that would also be impressive. I have a ranch up there, and for years I've been observing or in touch with the little Indian tribe whose language includes the word *cuyamaca*. They're a peculiar Indian tribe, called the Inajas, and you have to know them for thirty years before they'll even say hello to you. As far as I know, there are only about 300 Inajas left now.
>
> But the Inajas have told me that *cuyamaca* means "twin peaks"— more in the sense of the way female anatomy, in heroic proportions, might suggest the most impressive or highest terrain in the area. That's how the mountains were named, at any rate, so it may surprise some to learn that the etymology of our club name reaches back to the Inaja Indian tribe and the way these mountains north and east of us apparently resembled some well-endowed Inaja squaw.

CHAPTER XXVIII

My One and Only — Cup

In 1921, I took the division chairmanship of a campaign committee to raise $75,000 to buy 650 acres of industrial lands along the harbor frontage of National City and Chula Vista from the San Diego Land Company. We raised the money and bought the land, and had it deeded to the Chamber of Commerce.

My team secured the largest number and total amount of subscriptions, and, as chairman, I was presented with a sterling silver cup, inscribed:

Presented to:

OSCAR W. COTTON
as Commander,
Winning Division,

Industrial Lands Fund Campaign,
San Diego Chamber of Commerce,
September 20, 1921.

The funds were pledged on the understanding that, when the lands were sold, the subscribers would be reimbursed for their original subscriptions plus 7 percent interest and all residue would belong to the Chamber. That was in 1921.

On May 7, 1928, the Chamber of Commerce sent the following letter to the subscribers of the Industrial Lands Fund:

SAN DIEGO CHAMBER OF COMMERCE
Organized 1870
San Diego, California

May 7, 1928

TO THE SUBSCRIBERS OF THE
INDUSTRIAL LANDS FUND:

In 1921 or 1922 you, together with about 270 others, subscribed a total of $68,734.61 to the Industrial Lands Fund of the Chamber of Commerce, for the purpose of purchasing approximately 650 acres of land in the Chula Vista and National City districts.

At the time this money was subscribed, it was the belief of all con-earned that these lands could be sold out in approximately ten years for a sufficient price to pay all subscriptions with 7 percent interest and leave a net profit of some $200,000 to be used as a building fund by the Chamber of Commerce.

The matter has not worked out as planned. During the past seven years only $21,936.50 has been received from sales. During this same time, taxes amounting to $34,403.79 have been paid.

There is no prospect at the present time of an appreciable increase in the rate of sales of these lands.

There are, at present, $8,861.66 delinquent taxes on this land and the 1928 taxes, which will be due in October, 1928, will amount to approximately $8,000 additional.

Three possibilities have been considered by the Industrial Lands Trustee. The first is to attempt to find a purchaser for the entire re-maining 615 acres of land. It is possible that such a purchaser can be found, who will be willing to pay a price sufficient to enable us to re-fund all subscriptions with 7 per cent interest.

The second possibility is that the lands may increase in value to such an extent during the next four years that this increase will offset the taxes which will accrue during that time. If such increase in value did not occur, the subscribers to the Fund would be faced with the necessity in 1931 of subscribing an additional $40,000 to pay off the accrued taxes or lose the entire 615 acres of land, plus their original subscription.

The third possibility considered by the Trustees is of asking the subscribers to contribute the $17,000 necessary to pay off the 1927 and 1928 taxes.

The Trustees believe that the matter requires the serious attention of the subscribers to the Fund and is withholding action until the opinion of the majority of the subscribers can be obtained.

We are attaching hereto a Ballot on this matter, which we request that you properly mark, sign before a witness, and return to the Indus-trial Department of the Chamber of Commerce at the earliest possible moment.

> Respectfully yours,
> THOMAS F. BOMAR, *Manager,*
> Industrial Development
> Department

I do not remember any discussion of a ten-year plan for holding the land; however, that is immaterial. When the Ballot was presented to me as one of the subscribers, I was most distressed. I definitely felt that the Cham-ber of Commerce should keep the land and that ultimately it would prove a fine investment for all concerned, although at the time the Ballot was sent out, there were no "factories" in sight for San Diego in the foreseeable future.

May, 1928, was close to the end of a seven-year boom period. This boom had given most of San Diego a "new look." The downtown, especially, had overbuilt with many fine buildings, including four skyscrapers. Definitely, a readjustment period was ahead. Much as I hated to do it, I went along with the majority and signed the Ballot. The Chamber of Commerce sold the balance of the land to the Santa Fe Land Company for $135,000. This paid all of the delinquent taxes and left about $100,000. The Chamber then made out two checks to each subscriber, one for the principal he had subscribed, and the other for seven years' interest at 7 percent per annum.

The checks were all delivered personally by a member of the Chamber of Commerce staff or Committee, who suggested to the subscribers that they endorse the checks back to the Chamber of Commerce for the purchase and improvement of a 100 by 100 foot corner lot on Broadway, and for the remodeling of the building into a permanent home for the Chamber of Commerce. In most instances, this procedure was followed.

So the ultimate result of our Industrial Lands deal was the acquiring for the Chamber of Commerce of a permanent home, remodeled and free and clear. It has made a fine home for the Chamber since 1929, and would have a present worth of possibly $200,000.

The 615 acres of Industrial Land would have a present minimum value of $3,000,000.

CHAPTER XXIX

My Life in Rotary

In 1923, I was invited to join the Rotary Club. It was pleasant, having luncheon once a week with that fine group of San Diego's top businessmen. It seemed extravagant to take two hours at noon every Thursday instead of forty-five minutes, but after a few meetings I forgot about the extravagance and enjoyed myself. I may have been a little stale from so many years of mostly work and little play, and Rotary seemed a friendly, cheerful enjoyable break.

For some luncheon—I do not remember which—shortly before joining Rotary, I had been asked to make a speech on astronomy. A friend had prepared the speech, and it had gone over all right, so after I had been in Rotary long enough to feel at home, I walked past the head table one day and handed a typed sheet of paper to the president, Ed Davidson, and suggested that if he could spare four minutes we might have some fun. Ed looked at the paper, and said, "O.K." When luncheon was finished, he stood up and called me by name, and when I arose, he said, "Oscar, I understand you are an authority on astronomy."

I replied that I did not claim any such distinction, although I had given the subject some study. Whereupon the chairman asked me if I would give an impromptu five-minute talk on the Psychology of Astronomy as it pertains to Trigonometry. I answered that I would be glad to do so, but that, in discussing a scientific subject of this nature without preparation, it was difficult to couch one's speech in the terms of the layman. Therefore, if in this discussion I should occasionally revert to scientific terms, I would like the audience to bear with me and understand that it was only because I had had no time for preparation. I then said:

"Trigonometrically speaking, the atheneum, athermanus as revealed by the astronomical clock, with the astrophotometer, produces an interesting spectacle to one familiar with this science. To make myself clear, by the coordination of the astronomical, trigonometrical, atheneum conditions, illimitable and immeasurable in its scope, with the use of the magnetograph, with its metaphysical, neontology, the vicissitude or unusual Zenith is illuminated across the heavens."

Simultaneously with the last phrase, I waved my right arm across the horizon, which was the signal for Davidson to slam down the gavel and state that the Club would wait for further discussion of this subject until such time as I was better prepared.

After I had been a Rotarian for a considerable time, the chairman of the Entertainment Committee called and asked me to represent "Andy Gump" at the Annual Banquet. I had never heard of "Andy Gump" but, as he described him it sounded as though he had possibilities, so I went over to the office of the San Diego *Union* and looked through the Comic Section.

The year was 1924, and "Andy Gump" was running for President of the United States and making political speeches on his own behalf. Our annual party was to be on October 30—one week before Election. Also, at that time, "Andy" and his wife, "Min," were on the outs, because Min thought Andy was having an affair with another woman.

I made careful preparations. I practiced my speech before a mirror, gesticulating with one or both arms with open palms and thumbs erect. I got a costume with tight-fitting pants and short jacket and short sleeves; covered my then rather profuse head of hair with a totally bald wig, and reshaped my nose with nose putty.

At that time, Rotary meetings were all held in the Banquet Room of the San Diego Hotel. At the Annual Meeting, when it was time for my appearance, Rotarian Sam Porter, manager of the hotel, asked the chairman for permission to introduce a very special guest who had just arrived at the hotel. He then told the Rotarians and their wives that one of the Presidential candidates had just arrived and that he had invited him to come to our meeting and say a few words, and he particularly requested that, regardless of the political beliefs of those present, we give this candidate the respect which was his due. Whereupon, I was duly ushered to the head table.

"Andy Gump's" reception was little short of a riot. The speech was as follows:

My Dear Friends:

Words can scarcely express to you my appreciation of the privilege of being one of this noble assemblage on this auspicious occasion.

San Diego is famous around the world for its matchless climate, its glorious sunsets, its scenic grandeur, its magnificent harbor, its proximity to Tia Juana, its energetic businessmen, and its adorable ladies.

In the founding and building of your wonderful city, when I call to mind the small part the Gumps have played, my bosom swells with pride.

My ancestor, the great Philip Gump, was the Captain on the good ship *San Salvador,* which first sailed into the peaceful waters of your silver gate in 1542, under the bold and fearless Cabrillo.

In 1903, I first came to your beautiful city, and since then your population has increased from 20,000 to 150,000. You have built factories, skyscrapers, wonderful parks, and a five-, ten- and fifteen-cent store. [*Note:* Guilford H. Whitney, of Whitney's 5¢, 10¢ & 15¢ Store, was in the audience.]

While extreme modesty on my part prevents me from taking credit to myself for all of this prodigious growth, I cannot refrain from noting in passing that San Deigo's beginning and all of its great prosperity has taken place since these two notable events.

In 1912, another great event took place which was destined to focus the eyes of the world of love and friendship on San Diego. In that year, your keen, farseeing businessmen organized the San Diego Rotary Club.

Tonight we have the crowning glory; we are here in this wonderful city, in this palatial banquet hall, feasting as the kings of olden days, gathered together the most intellectual audience it has ever been my pleasure to meet and all members of this great organization of Rotary that will some day rule the world.

I want to say to you, my friends, that it brings from my heart of hearts a warm glow of mingled pride, friendship and love to see such men and women as you, flocking to my standard, such organizations as this Rotary Club, such cities as this wonderful city of San Diego, with its suburbs of National City, Oceanside, Escondido, Los Angeles, and Watts. [*Note:* Watts, at that time, was a very small town near Los Angeles.]

To realize that tonight the eyes of our nation are upon this fair city in this most favored state, that tomorrow will be printed far and wide the story of my great ovation.

You may wonder why I have waited until the last before coming to your city; I'll tell you, it is because I have been holding San Diego in reserve, as the climax to effectually turn the tide of this great campaign—because it is well known in national politics that "as goes San Diego, so goes the nation."

And now, folks, about Babe Summers. As man to man, positively, there's nothing to it; she's just a friend, as I told those reporters. I tried to explain to Min, but she wouldn't listen. she was worn out from this campaign and all wrought up. I even repeated to her those little verses so full of human sentiment:

> Her lips were so near,
> Her lips were so near,
> I'll explain it, my dear,
> Her lips were so near.

So you see, there's just nothing to it.

I'm for the people 100 per cent—I am for San Diego 100 per cent.

I feel as much a part of your city as though I had lived here every day of my life. If I am elected President you will not need to spend large sums of money maintaining a lobby at Washington; you will have me, Andy Gump, and to get whatever favors you want for your fair city or for any Rotarians will be but to let your wants be known. And I pledge you my word that my first official act will be to make San Diego the capital city of the United States.

Thereafter, I was known to Rotarians not as Oscar Cotton, but as "Andy Gump."

Some months later Violet and I were returning to San Diego by boat from San Francisco. I sent the following wire:

ALBERT E. SCOTT, PRESIDENT,
ROTARY CLUB
SAN DIEGO, CALIF.

ON BOARD RUTH ALEXANDRIA SOMEWHERE IN BLUE PACIFIC SORRY I CAN'T LUNCH WITH YOU THURSDAY AM ALL AT SEA ON A DIET NO AP-PETITE ANYWAY CAME HERE TO LOSE WEIGHT HAVE LOST MOST EVERY-THING WEIGHT COLOR STRENGTH AMBITION MONEY NEW STRAW HAT AND LAST THREE MEALS NEVER AGAIN LEMUEL GULLIVER CAPTAIN KIDD AND OAKLEY HALL CAN HAVE SEA I WILL TAKE SOMETHING SUBSTANTIAL TO LEAN ON GIBRALTAR OR LAMP POST

ANDY GUMP

The day after Election, I received the following letter in a small white envelope with a heavy black border, from one of our Rotarians:

To:
The Honorable Near-President Andrew Gump
San Diego, Calif.

DEAR ANDY:

It is with feelings of profound depression that I now address you with regard to the unfortunate termination of your political activities, and I can deeply sympathize with you in your consequent disappointment. You certainly had the presidential office by the tail with a strong down-hill pull, and, but for the unfortunate accident of your name being omitted from the ballot, you would have won in a walk. I say this ad-visedly, for your eloquent speech before the Rotarians and their *managers,* on a recent occasion, elicited the most favorable expressions from the *latter* and we well know that "As the women go, so goes the Country."

When the four votes which the foot of my table controls arrived at the polls yesterday and found that your distinguished name did not decorate the ballot, we were, to say the least, dumbfounded and knew not which way to turn. However, after some family argument, we finally decided that the only remaining thing to do was to vote the Prohibition ticket; so you may console yourself with the thought that in this case at least, your successful rival for office did not gain in the slightest degree from the contemptible trick played on you. We had hoped it was an accident, but there is now a rumor to the effect that it was never intended to put your name on the ballot but that Min had arranged the whole business with your campaign manager in order that she might get a caboose joy-ride over the country and that her occasional objections were merely the results of feminine inconsistency. If this be true, it would require asbestos paper and a tin envelope for me to properly express my feelings in the matter.

Wishing you the success you deserve next time, I am,

Rotarily yours,
CHAS. M. ARMSTRONG

My last year in Rotary, I was chairman of the Program Committee, and I arranged with Dr. James F. Churchill to give, as a twenty-minute talk, a "lecture" he had given me about a year before I was invited to join Rotary.

I had gone to Dr. Churchill's office for a check-up. After the general routine business was out of the way, he looked at my card and then across the desk at me, and said, "Oscar, you are forty years old."

"Yes," I said, "I know that. It is not a condition I particularly like."

Dr. Churchill then proceeded to give me a twenty-minute lecture, which I realized at that time and have realized many times since, was one of the most valuable twenty minutes that had come to me in all my forty years.

Back in Chicago, where he had formerly practiced as a physician and surgeon, Dr. Churchill had made a study of what happened to businessmen after age forty. His studies developed the fact that, for the normal human being, in our American way of life, forty was the turning point. Until we reach the age of forty, we are building up our bodies. After the fortieth year, we are on the downhill side. So the fortieth year is the crucial year. It is the time of life when the businessman in particular must begin to put health first on his program if he would live in comfort to old age.

Dr. Churchill said that prior to reaching the crucial age of forty, a man could eat too much, drink too much, do with too little sleep and exercise, and it did not seem to matter because the body was continuing to build. But after forty, the picture changed and the healthy businessman who continued to live as he had always lived, who continued to eat and to drink as he pleased, who did not take regular exercise and rest and recreation from the daily grind—he was the man to watch. Not occasionally, but very often, between fifty and sixty, without any warning, he was gone.

He then shocked me by saying that the businessman most likely to live to be seventy, eighty, or more, was the man who developed some incurable ailment or condition at the age of forty and had to learn to take care of himself, becoming moderate in his habits, taking ample exercise and recreation and keeping his mind free from worry. It was an outstanding lecture, and since I had not one, but two, incurable ailments, I took in every word and made up my mind then and there to follow this advice.

When Dr. Churchill gave this lecture before the Rotary Club, boy, did it go over! It was one of the best and most appreciated talks ever made in a Rotary meeting in San Diego. In presenting Dr. Churchill, I said in part:

> I have the extreme pleasure of introducing to you today a man whom San Diego is most fortunate to number among her citizenry and professional men.
>
> Alfred LaMotte inveigled me into playing golf every two weeks; this man frightened me into playing it three times a week.
>
> He is a man who has given a great deal of time and research, in fact, has made one of his professional hobbies the study of MAN after he reaches the age of forty; what a man should and should not do and the rewards and penalties therefor.
>
> He has a message today that will be interesting in the extreme, in fact, one which is vital to everyone present, because I can see, as I scan your handsome faces, that every one of you is on one side or the other of the age of forty.
>
> It is my extreme pleasure to present to you a man who needs no introduction to a San Diego audience—Dr. James F. Churchill.

The next day, the San Diego *Union* reported:

ROTARIANS HEAR NOTABLE TALKS
AT LARGE MEETING

Dr. Churchill and International Director Norman Contribute to Program

San Diego's Rotary Club yesterday had one of its best programs and biggest treats of months, two notable addresses being delivered to a large meeting. The first was by Dr. James F. Churchill, well-known local physician, on "After Forty, Then What?" The other was by John E.

Norman, a Rotary International Director, here on a visit from the East.

Oscar W. Cotton was chairman of the day, and he soon launched into an introduction of Dr. Churchill by reading one of Mark Twain's talks on health and what to do about it. The famous humorist's precept, at least as outlined in his humorous talk, was to do about everything that he wanted to in the way of eating and sleeping. The chairman, however, admitted that recently he had gained some more profitable advice from Dr. Churchill. The physician then told what he thought about it.

"There are three things which I consider the best business policy for a man to observe when he has passed forty years," said Dr. Churchill. "One is to keep the weight normal, or as nearly so as possible. The second is to keep the muscles in good shape by exercise. The third is to maintain a regular time for recreation."

Dangerous Age

Dr. Churchill said in the beginning that the human body was such a wonderful machine that, in its youth, its owner could do lots of things to it without apparent harm to that machine, but as the man grows older, he finds that things are different. From forty to fifty years he called the "dangerous age." At that time, he said, the machinery of the body is reaching such condition that it has to receive a little better care than before forty years. He said that the man who causes the doctors most worry is the one who has remained close to his business practically all his life until forty or fifty, then begins to feel bad, and comes into the doctor's office and says, "Why, I never before had a sick day in my life."

Dr. Churchill laid stress on the necessity for getting exercise and recreation regularly, and said it was much better to take two half days off every week than to take two or three weeks together once a year. His address was heartily applauded.

In 1926, I was nominated for the presidency of the San Diego Rotary Club, but I had to decline because the luncheon meetings were being held in the basement dining room of the San Diego Hotel. The air-conditioning was too strong for me. I would go to a luncheon feeling fine, and would invariably come away with a cold.

CHAPTER XXX

Our Trip to Alaska

BY 1926, our slate was clean. The Pacific Building Company's properties were all sold. In our safes we had book after book of contracts, representing the balances of payments to be paid before deeds were given. Also by 1926, it seemed to me that real estate and building developments were going too fast to be safe. Real estate prices had increased, in many instances, several hundred percent over the depression prices of 1919. Although other corporations were being formed, for example, on Point Loma, and large acreages were purchased for future development, I advised closing out the Pacific Building Company and returning the capital assets to the stockholders. This was done, and so the life of the Pacific Building Company was exactly twenty years: 1906 to 1926.

I made a deal with the directors to personally take over the business, make all future collections, relieve the Pacific Building Company of all further expense of operation, and to disburse the capital to the stockholders. After the meeting closed, and I sat alone in my office, I felt as though a great weight had been lifted from my shoulders. I had not realized it before, but the responsibility to five hundred stockholders during so many trying years had been a burden all my waking hours.

During the early years, while we were paying 8 percent dividends and increasing them year by year until we reached 16 percent, everybody was happy and it was lots of fun, but, when World War I broke out and all operations stopped, we were heavily in debt and had to conserve every dollar, and it was necessary to stop dividends entirely. It is not hard to understand that many stockholders were mighty unhappy, including myself.

One evening at the dinner table, shortly after I had personally taken over the business, our son William, who was then sixteen, said, "We should take a trip to Alaska, via the 'Inland Passage.' "

As he described what he had heard, it sounded like a good idea. I did not comment on his suggestion, but the next day I made inquiries and found that the boat trip from Seattle, Washington, to Skagway, Alaska, was rated as a delightful trip of nine days up and back, all but three hours of which was as smooth as sailing on a lake, with beautiful scenery all the way. It sound like a trip to a new world.

We left San Diego June 20, 1926, in an old seven-passenger Packard, with two extra tires. In Seattle, we stayed for a week at the new home of our former San Diego friends, the C. Edwin Davises, in the Broadmore Country Club tract. They had a family of three only a little younger than ours. The weather in Seattle was like San Diego summer at its best. Fruits and flowers were luscious. The new Broadmore Country Club's golf course was not yet playable, but Ed and I played another beautiful course. They and their friends took us on a boating party one afternoon and evening. All in all, it was a wonderful week.

One night at a party, someone asked me to dance the Highland Fling. They pinned a sash on me, and hung a coat backward around my waist to represent a kilt, and someone played "The Irish Washerwoman," which is the same 4/4 time as the Highland Fling. To dance the Highland Fling, the dancer must jump in the air with every beat of the music with one foot, while the steps are performed with the other. As kids, when Laura and I would do two or three Scotch dances in too rapid succession, we would sometimes develop a "goose egg" on the right side, but I had forgotten about that. Also, I did not stop to think that, in the twenty-eight years since I had last danced a Scotch dance, I had changed somewhat.

There are ten steps to the Highland Fling. I had not finished the first step before I realized that I was not as young as I had once been. I finally got through seven steps, but by that time I was so winded I could hardly get the breath in and out of my chest fast enough. I made my bow and dropped (literally) into a chair. I don't think I got back to normal breathing much under half an hour. Never again!

While in Seattle, we drove our two families up to Mount Rainier, and had the glorious fun of sliding down the mountain snow slide on "Tin Pants"—pants which had been paraffined on the seat. Half a dozen at a time would sit down in the snow (all wearing the "Tin Pants"), holding each other's feet. Then the lead man would take his heels out of the snow, and down we would go for a quarter of a mile, like greased lightning, all piling up in a mess at the end of the trail. Fun? Wow! I was thirty-four; Violet, the Davises, and all our children, were younger, but I am sure I enjoyed the fun as much as anyone in the party.

In Seattle, we parked the car and boarded the American Steamship Company's *Dorothy Alexander* for Skagway and thrills never to be forgotten. Imagine four and a half days on a comfortable steamer, with ample staterooms, good food, entertainment in the evenings and all the long, bright days, weaving in and out around gorgeous, towering mountains, with enormous pine trees right to the water's edge! Again and again, the boat would be headed straight for the end of the passage; then, as we approached the bluff or the mountainside, the boat would move around slowly to the left or right, and there before us was another passage, as delightful as the one through which we had just passed.

Then, on ahead a mile or more, we would see one of the most picturesque little villages, climbing from the water's edge up the side of the cliffs, with many of the houses partly on stilts and with just enough of the beautiful pines cleared to make room for the houses. The pilot would blow the great steam whistle, so that all within miles would know the boat was appoaching, and a small crowd would start gathering at the wharf.

Later in the day, or it may have been the next day—it did not matter, Time was of no consequence now—the steamer pulled up to within half a mile of one of the many glaciers along that scenic inland waterway, and as we looked at this awe-inspiring spectacle the Captain again vigorously blew the steam whistle, and down came an avalanche! Hundreds of tons of ice from the face of the glacier were jarred loose by the vibration and tumbled into the still waters. Again and again the whistle blew, and each time the blast was followed by a stupendous crashing of ice as it plunged into the arm of the sea. It was a thrill to see such a spectacular sight in a movie, but to be actually on the spot and see it in real life is an experience one will never forget.

At Wrangell, we learned we would be docked for several hours. John got some fishing tackle and—he struck a jackpot—pulled in more big fish of various varieties than most of us had ever seen before. Just before leaving port, we learned the reason why the fishing there was so good: John had been fishing at the outfall of the town sewer!

Those were "Good Old Days" of relaxation. It was summer. The days were warm, and each day was longer than the last until the night of our return trip, when we had daylight around the clock. William and Jane stayed up "all night" just to be sure. Was that fun for teen-agers? And was it fun for their parents? I give you three guesses—right! It was fun for grownups as much as for kids.

Skagway in 1926 was almost a ghost town, but for a one-day stay it was delightful. Doors and windows of most of the buildings were boarded up, but here and there would be a home that was occupied, and the flower gardens at some of these homes were just out of this world in brilliance and beauty.

We traveled by narrow-gauge railroad over the old "Whitehorse Trail" to Lake Bennett, the "jumping-off place" for Nome. Here we saw a large sign which read NORTHERN CITY LIMITS OF LOS ANGELES.

I must tell you about the trees. As we left Seattle, the dense forests on every hill and mountain were of beautiful pine trees that looked to be a hundred or more feet tall. But day after day, as our steamer moved farther north, the trees became shorter and shorter until finally, when we got over the Whitehorse Trail and edged our way slowly over the great plateau, the trees were full grown, with heavy trunks, but crooked and spread out over the ground and rocks and only from three to five or six feet tall. We did not see any gnomes, but these dwarfed pine trees, around miniature lakes, looked like pictures in the old books of fairy tales.

I am sure we all enjoyed every hour of this trip, but as I stood on a mound of broken bottles overlooking Lake Bennett, where the row of saloons had been in the Gold Rush days of '98, and looked at the lake and the vast emptiness as far as the eye could see, I felt we were a long way from San Diego, and I was not sorry that this was the end of the trail and that in an hour we would be starting back.

CHAPTER XXXI

Five Brown Pills

OUR HOME on Third Street above Walnut Street, where our son John was born in 1913, was large and comfortable. The architecture was pleasing and there was ample yard for lawns, flowers, fruit trees both ornamental and bearing, and a croquet court. It was near most of our friends and it was just the place for young folks to live and raise a family. All our recollections of this home are of happy days and many, many gay evenings.

Violet was a musician by nature, and fortunately had studied for ten years under southern California's outstanding pianist, Herr Thilo Becker. On our evenings at home when there were no parties, she loved to sit at the piano and play favorite compositions by Chopin, Brahms, Schumann, MacDowell, Liszt, and many others, by the hour, and while her audience consisted of only one, I enjoyed every minute as much as she did. Good Old Days.

Sixteen months after we moved into this lovely home, World War I broke out. All building and real estate sales stopped, and first one and then another activity ceased, but, generally speaking, life moved along more or less serenely although with growing apprehension. The war news was horrible from the beginning and it grew worse from month to month, so that, by the time the United States finally declared war, we were prepared for the shock. After that, all but really necessary business came to a standstill. I reduced our company's staff to a minimum, and I helped on Red Cross campaigns and War Bond drives.

One day shortly after the United States had entered the war, I stopped for a glass of orange juice at the lunch counter in the Orpheum Theater Building on B Street. (That was before I gave up all hard liquor.) When the young lady brought me my drink, she said brightly, "Have you enlisted for the war yet?"

I thought, "My goodness, I must look young!" So I said, just as brightly, "Yes."

Whereupon she asked, "Which war—Spanish-American, Civil, or Revolutionary?"

One day an American from Mexico decided he would like to own our home and would give us, clear, his seven-room home in South Park on Fern Street beyond Thirtieth Street, for our house, subject to a 60 percent mortgage. Since I could not see how I could ever pay the mortgage and it was more than a 50-50 chance that I would be drafted, we made the swap. As it turned out, the war lasted less than two years and we could have gotten by, but I could not foresee that.

In 1920, when the first wild scramble for houses was under way and prices were up 100 percent, we sold our South Park home and rented an eight-room house on Front Street near Laurel Street, back in the part of town where our friends lived, and here we stayed for twenty-six years, first as tenants and later as owners while our family grew up and went to college and finally all started homes of their own.

The eight-room house on Front Street was convenient enough while our young folks were young folks, but as they grew older we needed more and larger rooms. As soon as we returned from our Alaskan trip, we moved to a rented house two blocks away and remodeled the old Front Street home.

I spent most of those two months in bed with a cold. After five weeks, I wrote the following letter to Dr. David R. Higbee:

DEAR DR. HIGBEE:

I have five brown pills left. Yesterday, Mrs. Cotton told me you said that after a time one would become immune to the beneficial effects of a drug and that I should not take any more of these brown pills. She inferred that you think I am on the high road to recovery and that you are not coming to see me any more.

I do not doubt but that you are entirely right, and Dr. Churchill seems to concur in your opinion as he is about to check me out, too, so to speak.

All of this is very nice really and I appreciate it. I am glad to get well, of course; in fact, the main advantage of getting sick is to get well.

However, there is one point on which I would like your advice. Understand, I am not worrying about this. I never worry because I went to a nerve specialist once who also cures insane patients, and he told me what was the cause of worry and I was very much mortified over all the worrying I had done, but the point I am asking you is this—

We have a large medicine cabinet nearly filled with old bottles of partly used prescriptions, little boxes containing remnants of tablets, capsules, powders, pills, salves, ointments, and all manner of drugs one could think of. Each bottle and box has been carefully kept against the possible recurrence of the same disease, which, of course, never happens. After twenty years and with a family of five who boast of fifty operations and nine hundred illnesses—not counting minor colds and sicknesses which require only one doctor and a trained nurse and keep the patient in bed less than a week—you can readily see that this medicine cabinet is quite an institution.

I once heard of a white aunt, who, during slaves times, would call in the "little "pickaninnies" and feed them the remnants of castor oil, paregoric, and other medicines left in the spoons by the sick white folks, but of course times have changed—anyway I can see certain objections to that system. But you can appreciate that we cannot go on year after year accumulating a stock of this kind. It is not a thing one wants to leave to one's heirs; in case of a fire, it is always one's neighbor's house that burns and he probably never has been sick and has no collection of medicines anyway.

I was always taught economy in my youth, and I have tried to so raise my wife and family. One cannot deliberately throw away good pills and then thrash his child for buying an all-day sucker after 11:00 A.M.

If Mrs. Cotton's appointment with you had been one day later, the five brown pills would have been gone, or if she had returned home five minutes later, there would have been only four brown pills left, but she got home at five minutes before one, which was the hour to take the next pill, and said I was not to take any more, and since the medical advice costs more than the pills, I could see at a glance that it was a three to one better bet to take the advice than the pills, but it was most unfortunate that it happened that way, because, instantly, his whole extravagant business flashed through my mind and the first thing I did was to reach over and get the box and count the pills and found there were five left.

Of course, I know you could not take them back because in a way they are secondhand, but what shall I do with those five brown pills?

                                        Faithfully yours,
                                        OSCAR W. COTTON

P.S. Mrs. Cotton thinks one box per day of Kleenex papers for my nose at 35¢ a box is too expensive; handkerchiefs, of course, are out of the question. She suggests a couple of corks—what do you advise?

Dr. David R. Higbee
Watts Building
San Diego, California
October 27, 1926

The next day, Dr. Higbee paid me a personal call to pick up the five brown pills.

Thirty-two years later, I was highly complimented to have Peg Higbee tell me they had kept the letter, and now had it pasted in their copy of our Christmas Book, *Europe 1957*.

Little did I realize as I wrote that letter, what the balance of 1926 and 1927 held in store for us. After we returned to the Front Street home and were settled, William had a bad automobile accident and still later, John developed double mastoiditis.

Those were tragic times, and I marvel that we all came through as well as we did.

CHAPTER XXXII

Happy Days at Corte Madera

EARLY IN 1928, we bought a share in the beautiful Corte Madera Ranch, above Pine Valley. During that summer, we again packed our suitcases and this time put them in a new five-passenger Lincoln, and took a five-thousand-mile trip to the Grand Canyon, the Petrified Forest, Boulder and Denver, Colorado and Yellowstone National Park. Such a trip! We will none of us ever forget it. Every day was a new adventure in gorgeous scenery and happiness.

One thought I secretly had in mind, during our travels through the beautiful Rocky Mountains with their many lovely resorts, was to get ideas for the new cabin we were going to build in Corte Madera. To my surprise, as it turned out, I got only one idea from the entire trip, but that one idea gave our family and many of our friends joy and delight for sixteen years.

At the South Rim of the Grand Canyon, the old hotel was set back a considerable distance from the edge of the Canyon. To get a view of the Grand Canyon, one would leave the hotel and walk to the edge of the gorge and stand back of a rail; then possibly take a stage or other vehicle and drive along the rim to see the wonders of the canyon from many different vantage points. But at the North Rim, the hotel was built at the edge of the canyon, and most of the end of the beautiful living-room-like lobby on the south was of plate glass, right to the floor. Large, comfortable couches were placed in front of this enormous plate-glass window, and here one could sit in the greatest comfort, luxuriously enjoying miles of the Grand Canyon, to the left and right, in all its gorgeous colorings, and then look almost straight down to the winding, muddy, Colorado River, a mile below. To sit there and enjoy this marvelous and spectacular view was one of the most thrilling experiences of my life.

Later that year, when we built our cabin in Corte Madera, on a knoll overlooking the lake surrounded by beautiful pine and oak trees, for every room we built large plate-glass "picture" windows. From the end of the living room, which was almost entirely glass, one looked out on the lake and surrounding hills; from the east window, beyond the pine-covered hilltops rose the majestic Long Valley Peak, while in the foreground from both windows could be seen a beautiful meadow which in the spring was a solid carpet of buttercups. From the kitchen, we projected a dining nook right out in the pines and oaks, with three sides almost entirely of glass. Today, in town and in the country, many houses and cabins are built largely of glass, but in 1928 no one had ever done such a thing, and our friends were as thrilled as we were.

The entrance to the "shack," as I dubbed it, was over a wide, irregular terrace, surfaced with slabs of stone built around four seventy-five-foot native pine trees. The interior woodwork was of straight grain pine, wire-brushed throughout. The living room ceiling was open, following the contour of the roof. The plaster in the living room was put on by hand. We had begac floors, and rustic interior finish throughout to the last detail, with specially made electric fixtures to harmonize with the walls, ceilings, and furniture. We furnished the cabin entirely with the heavy, Spanish-type furniture just coming into popularity at that time and Indian rugs. Richard S. Requa, our architect, remarked to a friend, "If I never build a more pleasing mountain cabin, I will still be satisfied."

Our fireplace was quite an institution. Built for utility, as well as for decorative purposes, it comprised about half of the west wall of the living room. It was faced with natural Corte Madera rock, most artistically laid so that no mortar was visible. It had a swinging crane, with a thirty-six-inch, swordlike skewer for broiling chickens and filet roasts and, on the right-hand side, a Dutch oven for baking "Beans à la Bisbee." Above the long, heavy mantels were racks to hang shotgun and rifle, and above that the head of a seven-point buck I brought back from a deer shoot in Baja California.

On other knolls scattered around the lake were cabins built by Mr. and Mrs. D. F. Garretson; Mr. and Mrs. Frank J. Belcher, Jr.; Mr. and Mrs. Herbert L. Sullivan; Mr. and Mrs. Percy H. Goodwin; Mr. and Mrs. Guilford H. Whitney; Mrs. Lilly Weggeforth; Dr. and Mrs. E. H. Crabtree; and Mr. and Mrs. A. J. Dulin. Later, Mr. and Mrs. Frank G. Belcher built an elaborate home with pool and private stables, half a mile south and east of the Central Valley. The duck lodge on the lakeshore made a comfortable, homey place for New Year's Eve parties and other gatherings. The Corte Madera Ranch itself enbraced some thirty-four hundred acres, and was surrounded by many thousands of acres of forest reserve, so for a dozen families it was like owning an empire.

For amusement, we rode horseback, or hiked over the many mountain trails, shot ducks in season, or just sat indoors or on the terraces enjoying the views and the dry, mountain air. At four-thousand-feet elevation and fifty miles from the Coast, it is a delight to merely sit and breathe the invigorating, dry, and fragrant air.

The moon and the stars in this clear air were marvelous. On clear nights—and most of the nights were clear—we nearly always went out of doors for a few minutes for one last look at the gorgeous moon and stars before going to bed. One little six-year-old girl said, "Mama, there are more stars in this sky!"

A polo field was laid out in the meadow of buttercups, and sometimes of a Sunday fifty or more members and guests would enjoy a game and then hie to the various homes for refreshment and lunch and a lazy afternoon.

In those "Good Old Days" help for running the home was plentiful. Host and hostess and other members of the family could play bridge after dinner, or ride horseback, or go for long hikes through the beautiful forests and meadows in the daytime.

We built our house for fun and comfort, and comfort and fun we had. We put a double coil in the fireplace and piped hot water through a radiator in each bedroom and bath so that, when it snowed, we just let it snow, and up to ten guests were warm and comfortable. Christmas; New Year's; and other holidays and Sundays throughout the summer were big get-togethers for families and friends. Good Old Days. Wonderful for grownups and coming generation as well.

For our 1929 Christmas card, I took a picture of the "shack" from the valley east of the knoll, so the "shack" with its peaked roofline was nearly hidden by the tall pines and oak trees surrounding it. Our message read:

> Snuggled under the pines and oaks,
>> On a knoll in the Corte Madera,
> Rests a friendly hut that grew out of the hillside.
>> It's made of scraps of this and that,
> But filled with welcome and Good Cheer;
>> And all kind thoughts for you and yours,
> This Christmas and the Coming Year.

> *—Violet and Oscar Cotton*

Here are a few "quotes" from our Guest Book:

All the charm and freedom of the country; all the comfort and hospitality of the City—what a delightful combination!—*Julius Wangenheim, Laura Wangenheim*—June 28, 1931

> There's nothing better for a man's insides
> Than atop a horse to joyfully ride.

There's nothing more restful to man's tired brain,
Than the charm of the Cottons' delightful domain.

> —*Guilford H. Whitney*
> *Grace D. Whitney*
> June 14, 1930

Why don't I apply for the cook's job, so I can come every weekend?
—*Florence Utt*—July 3, 4, 5, 1931

Wishing the Cottons long years of happiness in their mountain home where I have found peace and happiness in the enjoyment of their gracious hospitality during my too short visit.
—*Florence E. Ellis*—July 3, 4, 5, 1931

You were wise in building your beautiful home on a rocky foundation, but more wise in choosing God's landscaping for its surroundings. Thanks for the pleasure it has given us on this 8th day of February, 1931.

> —*Arthur S. Church and*
> *Margaret Church*

A winding trail for a merry ride,
To our smiling hosts and doors flung wide.
A sturdy house with rough-hewn rafter,
Peace that is spiced with happy laughter.
Clear windows wide that look afar
On mountains, meadows, on blazing star!
Great pine trees where the wild bird swings!
A lake where pelicans stretch their wings!
Oh! we look and we lounge in soft deep chairs,
And snap our fingers at silly cares,
With a roast on the spit, and a leaping fire,
Oh! this is the place of heart's desire!

> —*Rose Marie Rice*
> *George Rice, Jr.,*
> *George Rice, III*
> May 1, 1932

A surprisingly beautiful and restful place. The Sierras, like friendships, become more precious the further explored.

> —*Janice Church Lloyd*
> *Harry Lloyd*
> October 2, 1932

We are preparing to leave this beautiful home in this glorious mountain country after a wonderful visit. Our enjoyment of your hospitable home has been too good for words. We sincerely hope that we may again be permitted to enjoy such a wonderful visit at Corte Madera.

—Albertus and Florence Cotton
April 6, 1930

(Brother Bert and Florence were here for a visit from Baltimore. When we arrived, I took Florence into the living room and sat her down in a comfortable chair in front of the large window. When she was seated and wondering what this was all about, I pulled aside the heavy drapes and there before her, in the bright sunlight, was a fifty-acre carpet of buttercups, a beautiful lake surrounded by pine and oak trees, and the towering mountains in the background. She said she did not ever want to get out of that chair!)

Roast Beef	—	3 slices
Pancakes	—	9
Crumpets	—	4
Pounds Gained	—	3 or 4
Who Cares?		

—Helen Peterson
February 25, 1933

Down under the hill,
There is a little still,
And the smoke goes curling to the sky.
You can easily tell, by a sniffle and a smell,
There's good Licker in the air close by!
For it fills the air with a perfume so rare,
And it's only known to a few,
So wrinkle up your lip, and take a little sip,
Of the good old mountain dew.
—An old school song of mine, that I now dedicate to
Corte Madera.

—J. Harold Peterson,
February 25, 1933

June 9, 1932

DEAR OSCAR:
Enclosed herewith is the key to the gate at Corte Madera. More particularly I am writing this to tell you and Mrs. Cotton again what a wonderful visit we had with you at your beautiful mountain home on last Saturday and Sunday. It is the first relaxation I have had for

many days, and your wonderful hospitality and kindness to both Lotta and myself will be one of the unforgettable incidents in our lives.

CHESTER ALLISON

Cuyamaca Club
San Diego, Calif.

My DEAR OSCAR:

Enclosed you will please find your ranch key—thanks for the pleasure of bringing my friends to your "shack."

I had prepared my fastidious friend, Mrs. Noble, with a description of a recluse living in a shack, made cabin, away from the habitations of the genus homo. So that her pleasure was intensified by contact. Both an eye full and heart full were the result.

With best wishes for the Cottons.

UNCLE WHEELER [1]

HALF-MINUTE INTERVIEWS
WITH FOLKS HELPING TO MAKE LIFE WORTH WHILE
From the SAN DIEGO UNION:

by—Forrest Warren

I arrived in San Francisco in 1882 as a tourist. Twenty-one years later, I was a registered voter in San Diego. Since then I have traveled; I have been to Los Angeles and Agua Caliente. I have learned considerable about real estate, our local water situation, and other problems, but not much about snow. So when last week Dean Blake advertised a blizzard in prospect I climbed into my "chugy," [Navajo for used Ford] and drove the thing up to my mountain cabin at Corte Madera, which is 4,000 feet nearer heaven than most real estate men ever expect to get, to loiter in snow. However, I soon found out that one does not "loiter" when the chugy stalls in a snowbank on the hillside, and I had to wade through snow up to my knees and pack freight on my back to the cabin like the other jackasses I have seen. The chugy loitered for a week where it stalled, and as we rode away on horseback it looked a little sad and cold, half-hidden by the drifting snow, like Commander Byrd's ship when he sailed off in an airplane for the South Pole. This was a new experience to us both, but collectively we learned more about snow in two days than I have learned in 50 years about my other problems.

Hospitality Plus—and I lost my boyish figure on Oscar's Diet!

—Jas. D. Forward

---

[1] Wheeler J. Bailey

Alas for him who has never seen
Corte Madera's artistic dream.
Where the Cotton Family's charming way
Makes the happy hours fly away.

—Lenore Forward

CHAPTER XXXIII

1929

ON OCTOBER 29, 1929, the Stock Market Crash nicked a lot of us and our friends. The fun went on; but the years that followed got tougher and tougher.

For the first time in twenty-five years, I moved my office from the ground floor to an upstairs location, in the Commonwealth Building—now the Orpheum Theater Building. Those were the days when building managers asked prospective tenants how much rent they could afford to pay, and that was it. For three large, outside offices, our rent was $65 per month. All business in San Diego during the years 1930 to 1933 was bad.

We took over the management and sale of the Timken-Bridges properties, which were mostly downtown business properties; the management, appraising, and sale of possible 150 houses which had been acquired under foreclosures by a life insurance society of New York; and another hundred or so for the Home Owners Loan Corporation. Also, Frank J. Belcher, Jr., appointed me "Real Estate Consultant" for all of the Spreckels Company's local holdings—at that time by far the largest privately owned real estate holding in San Diego. These jobs were all interesting, because each property had its individual problem to be solved.

We also sold several hundred one-acre and half-acre lots at Bostonia for a former mortgagee, acquired under foreclosure. Sale prices were so low it was actually sickening. Level, half-acre lots in Bostonia, with water piped, sold for $99. Good, five-room houses right in town, went for $3,000 to $4,500 with 10 percent down, and others not so good for $2,500. Occasionally, a smaller house would bring as little as $1,500. Business properties were just as low in proportion. It was all most depressing, but the town had been much overbuilt and overexpanded during the lush twenties, and here we were again, absolutely stranded with thousands of properties for sale, and only an occasional prospective buyer.

In 1928 or 1929, I had subdivided about two hundred acres on Linda Vista Mesa for my partner, A. H. Frost, and myself. We had the city build a big water tank and put in a pipeline from Morena Boulevard. We also had graded and paved, under a bond plan, Sixth Street Extension, from

Sixth and University avenues across Mission Valley to this "Chesterton" property, connecting with the paved Linda Vista Road. We had just gotten nicely started marketing this property when the 1929 Crash stopped everything flat, so we had bonds and increased taxes to carry, and only a meager income from the few contracts that the purchasers had not forfeited.

CHAPTER XXXIV

My Greatest Error

In 1932, I committed an act that ultimately turned out to be—putting it politely—the greatest error of my life.

Of course, if I could have had the slightest idea of the consequences and of the far-reaching damages it was to produce, I should never for a moment have dreamed of doing such a thing. But, like many of our worst errors in life, at the time the act is committed we are under some strain or a crisis which is so powerful that it blunts our judgment and allows us to build within ourselves false hopes that distort our normal thinking so that we are not fully responsible.

Looking back on that day, after these many years, and realizing the appalling consequences that have resulted, I am, of course, as horrified at what I did as though I had been apprehended and punished, as I now realize I should have been; but, at the time—1932—while it is true that I was fifty years old and should have known better, there were extenuating circumstances, on which grounds I excused myself at the time and for the first few years that followed.

In the fall of 1932, the nation was at the very bottom of the worst financial depression that any of us of that generation had ever experienced. Those of our present population who were not mature at the time have no conception of the harrowing dread with which one dealing in financial matters looks forward to possibly endless years of financial losses and, ultimately, disaster.

San Diego, at that time, had literally thousands of vacant homes and apartments. There were hundreds of vacant stores throughout our business district. Bootlegging, crime, and gangsterism were at their worst in the nation's history.

Deep down in my heart, I knew better than to do such a thing, but I try to excuse myself with the thought that at that time I allowed myself to believe I was doing right, even though actually, of course, I knew I was doing wrong. This is the one act in my life which I would rather leave untold, but in fairness I believe it should be recorded because it might be a lesson, so to speak, causing others to pause on the brink, if necessary, and retreat before it is too late.

One other thought which I have kept before me all these years as a major relief to my inner self is that I did not commit this act alone, and for that I am thankful. Had I been solely responsible for what took place, I am frank to say I would not have wanted to live and watch the results.

I will not be a stool pigeon and give the names of any of my accomplices. I shall let them speak for themselves as their consciences dictate, but I feel that even at this late date, if I cannot begin to mend matters, I must and can at least clear my conscience.

On November 8, 1932, I voted for Franklin Delano Roosevelt for President of the United States.

CHAPTER XXXV

Dragging on the Bottom

IN THE EAST, the bottom of the Depression following the 1929 Stock Market Crash was in 1932. In San Diego, with no industry of consequence or other activity to be revived by the new Roosevelt Administration's spending spree, we continued to drift downward.

Since we could not sell any real estate, I was taking things rather easy, enjoying our Corte Madera "shack" to the utmost with our family and friends, and even toying with the idea that I might try my hand at short-story writing. After the very mild and rather depressing New Year's celebration for 1933 was over, I decided something should be done to at least stabilize the thinking of the owners of San Diego real estate, and to try to lay the groundwork for future activity. I suggested to James McMullen, then managing editor of the San Diego *Union,* that I write a series of articles on San Diego real estate for the Sunday papers.

At that time, Frank J. Belcher, Jr., was the head of all of the Spreckels companies, with offices in San Francisco, and at his request I was acting as "Real Estate Consultant" for the companies' real estate holdings in San Diego, which were then very large. I mailed a copy of my first article to Mr. Belcher, with the following letter:

February 28, 1933

DEAR FRANK:

The enclosed article is the first of a series I am preparing.

Yesterday, Tom Scripps said this article had brought back confidence in San Diego real estate to his whole family. He came in to pay his $500 assessment on his Point Loma Holding Corporation stock, which he had decided to drop.[1] This morning, the leading real estate man of Carlsbad told me he had already made one sale on the strength of this article.

You may remember in 1923 I wrote copy and prepared layouts for five large advertisements for the San Diego-California Club to be run in the Los Angeles *Times.* After this series of advertisements appeared, the unmerciful knocking of San Diego by Los Angeles people stopped.

---

[1] At that time I was Custodian for the Point Loma Holding Corp.

Those five ads changed the opinion of the residents of Los Angeles with regard to San Diego.

I believe this series of articles will do San Diego real estate some good.

O. W. COTTON

I ran the series every week from February 26, 1933, to October 1. They did not start a boom or any material real estate activity, but they did promote healthier thinking in the minds of the real estate owners and gave my office publicity that proved of lasting value when the pendulum began to swing the other way and real estate and homes could again be sold.

On March 4, 1933, the *Union* ran the following "Notice":

COTTON WRITES
ON S. D. REALTY

Oscar W. Cotton, San Diego real estate man who has been one of the most active in development of the city and back country for many years, is writing for the *Union* each week an article on local real estate conditions. What he says is backed by long experience and expert knowledge of the field.

Today's article, the second of the series, will be found on page 5 of the Classified Section. Everybody who is interested in real estate and the upbuilding of the city will enjoy reading it.

On March 12, 1933, my article was as follows:

JUST LET REALTOR UNEXPECTEDLY SAY HE HAS
CASH CUSTOMER, THEN WATCH ESTIMATION
OF LAND VALUE CHANGE

By OSCAR COTTON

Prof. Piccard arrived late at the Savoy Theatre to deliver his lecture "The Earth from Ten Miles Up." Ben Buker was making explanations, killing time. The audience was restless. I rose from my seat to suggest that I might speak on the subject, "Real Estate from Ten Miles Down" when, unfortunately, the professor appeared on the stage.

At the San Diego Realty Board meeting last Wednesday I was asked to tell about this real estate "column." I said to the realtors:

"I am glad to write these articles. It began to look like San Diego real estate was about to become an orphan, with no mother and no father—nobody to look after it or blow its nose—or horn, as the case might be.

"I am not going to write boom articles. I'm going to write pessimistic facts—stuff my readers will believe. When I get them to believing everything I write is true, I'll switch to a lot of hooey and they will believe that. You know how gullible people are; you ought to know. Nobody is so gullible as a real estate man. He buys more real estate at the top of the market than any client. He never drives his customers into deep water. He leads them up to his neck. More often than not he will look to his customers to pull him out."

Some folks think real estate is a dry subject. Say, I have sold town lots in San Diego that were so wet we could only show them at low tide.

On Sunday, 18 years ago, while we were selling a flat tract north of Old Town, a customer came to our office tent and said he intended to forfeit the lots he had bought the week before because he had been told that every time it rained his lots were under water.

The salesman took him across the road to meet an ancient resident whose word could not be doubted because for more than 40 years he had lived in that one spot and voted the straight Republican ticket. The salesman told him what his client had said. "No," said the ancient, "that is not true. In 40 years I have seen your lots under water only four times—about once every 10 years." That satisfied the customer. He kept the lots. Even in real estate the truth sometimes pays. However, one should not be too free with it.

The question before us today is, "Why do we want to own real estate? Is it just for the privilege of paying taxes?" Unless it returns an income, it certainly is no good to us. If, years ago, it did bring in an income, it probably does not any more.

The answer is, "We do not want to own it at all."

That is what we think we think. But, if you want to know what you actually think about the real estate you own, just let some realtor tell you unexpectedly he has a cash customer for your lot, then watch your estimation of the value of that lot change.

There are not many real estate buyers today; there never are in an accumulation period. There are fewer sellers. Numerous realty owners want to sell at 50¢ on the dollar. They think that is a bargain.

During the high prices we paid 60¢ a dozen for eggs that now cost 15¢; $2 wheat now costs 46¢; General Electric $100 stock costs $12 a share. Real estate at 50 percent of the old price is high. If you are obliged to sell your real estate under the present market, you must offer it at a bargain, the same as eggs and wheat.

If the man who was smart, or lucky, and held onto his cash wants to buy today, he is entitled to a bargain in real estate or stocks, and he can get it. But why should the owner sell?

In my office I have a panorama of San Diego harbor taken from a captive balloon in 1908. It shows three ships in the bay—one was John D. Spreckels' black yacht *Venetia;* that was before she was painted white.

The blocks from the waterfront to the business district of San Diego are dotted with shacks of the vintage of 1885, or are vacant. There is only one vehicle in sight on Broadway west of First Street. I cannot be sure whether it is an auto or a horse and buggy. It is parked in front of an old one-story frame building west of Union Street. There are 20 pedestrians visible and one streetcar. In those days Broadway (then D Street) was a heavily traveled thoroughfare for pedestrians. Most people walked to the Santa Fe Station. A grove of eucalyptus trees hides the old frame house where the Navy YMCA now stands.

Compare that picture in your mind's eye, with today. This morning I counted 90 ships in the harbor, not including 30 decommissioned destroyers tied at the base. I could not count the automobiles and pedestrians on lower Broadway—they passed in too large numbers. In a quarter century San Diego has changed from a village of "bay 'n climate" to a teeming city with an active harbor. The owner who today needlessly parts with his real estate is selling San Diego short.

This does not mean that the man who has overexpanded should doggedly hold on until he is wiped out. Far better that he lighten the load regardless of cost, the quicker the better. But for the realty owner who, like the golfer, can carry through, reward will be his on the 18th green.

In 1908 the plot on which the Spreckels Theatre Building now stands, 200 feet on Broadway by 230 feet deep, equivalent to more than nine lots, sold for $80,000 or $8,888 a lot. In 1927, the old Elks' property, 100 feet on Broadway by 70 feet deep, less than a lot and a half, directly across the street, sold for $165,000 or $110,000 a lot.

Sunday, March 26, 1933:

HUGE PROFITS IN LOCAL REAL ESTATE DEALS TOLD BY PIONEER MERCHANT; EXPRESSES CONFIDENCE IN FUTURE

By OSCAR COTTON

"In 1870 I bought a corner lot at Fourth Avenue and Fir Street from Father Horton for $100," George W. Marston said at the realtors' luncheon Wednesday. "Horton told me," he continued, "this was a $150 lot, but because I came from his home state, Wisconsin, he agreed to let me have it for $100. Some months later, I sold the lot for $150, so it must have been a $150 lot. In 1926, this lot sold for $5,000.

"At that time, lots on Broadway, Sixth, Seventh, and Eighth avenues could be bought for $500 each. The highest priced property was at Fifth Avenue and J Street. Later, Fifth Avenue and Broadway became the generally accepted center, and was regarded as the most valuable location. The Horton House on Broadway, where the U. S. Grant Hotel now stands, was then on the upper rim of the city.

"In those days, San Diego looked like a little windswept Arizona town. Houses were scattered. Even on Fifth Avenue, there would be only one or two buildings on a block. Most of the structures were one-story board stores with gable roofs and high, false fronts. More often than not, a building consisted of three stores; a grocery, a saloon, and a real estate office.

"Some of my real estate deals have been rather embarrassing. We merchants are not used to such large profits.

"About 1899 I purchased a block in Randolph Terrace near the present Mission Hills Subdivision, for $1,200. It was a good block. In 1913 I sold it for $13,000. I was embarrassed because I made 1100 percent profits in so short a time. Even in real estate I think 1000 percent should be sufficient."

Looking around the table, he added, "I assume there are no newspapermen present.

"In my later transactions I was more moderate. I purchased some blocks in Crittenden's Addition, east of Seventh Avenue for $10,000 and sold one-third of what I had bought to my brother-in-law, the late Dr. F. R. Burnham, for $10,000 so the two-thirds I kept cost me nothing. Judging by what you realtors tell us in your glowing advertisements about 'enormous profits to those who buy now,' this last transaction was quite modest.

"At another time, Burnham, M. Kew, and I purchased the northeast 100 feet on Fifth Avenue and C Street for $30,000. Later, I paid Kew $20,000 for his one-third interest. Then Burnham and I bought the adjoining 100 feet on Sixth Avenue for $75,000.

Evens Up Deal

"Finally, when I thought I should own the whole C Street frontage, Burnham charged me $150,000 for his interest in the two pieces. He figured he had more than evened up on our previous transaction, but I managed to sell the property to the Marston Company at a very satisfactory profit.

"After I had built my home on Seventh Avenue, I decided to buy the property across the canyon and develop it for rather nice homes. I asked D. C. Collier's advice, and he strongly recommended the idea. Collier owned some of the land. I bought his land and the rest from individuals and laid out an addition called Park Terrace. George Hawley persuaded me to change the name to Marston Hills."

This development was begun in 1923. Out of an original 74 lots, all but two are sold. Nearly 50 houses have been built, with building costs ranging up to $20,000. Among these are some of San Diego's most artistic homes.

Presidio Hills, above Fort Stockton, was George Marston's latest subdivision. Here he wanted to have the streets follow the old cow trails over the ridges. This proved practicable in only one instance: Presidio Drive follows the historic trail from Arista Street to Old Town.

a beautiful scenic descent. Presidio Hills is another of San Diego's highest-type subdivisions.

"Real estate," said Marston, "like all business, is fraught with joy, woe, failure, and success. I find we get less of woe and more of joy if we don't take life too seriously. I find, too, I can make more money in real estate on a rising market.

"San Diego, in the last decade, has made great forward strides. In some instances we have overreached, perhaps, but we have built well. We have a city of many attractions to those of high standards. We have, for the first time, an abundant water supply. We can look with confidence to the years ahead of us."

Happy is the man who can find his forte in San Diego.

Often I have had newcomers tell me frankly what the trouble is with our town, why San Deigo stands still while Los Angeles grows to more than 1,000,000 population. Others of less ego ask the question, "What is the matter with San Diego?" To these I answer, "There is nothing the matter with it." Nature has showered blessings upon San Diego. It is the finest place in all the world in which to live. It has grown with southern California. Our population has increased 800 percent in 30 years. The substantial businessmen of today are those who came 60, 40, 20, or even 10 years ago and established themselves in a small way, worked for and grew with the city, became, in fact, an integral part of our community.

The substantial businessmen of the future greater San Diego will be those who are here now, and those yet to come, who find their forte and work for and with the community. Cities are built by men.

Marston found his forte in San Diego, and for 60 years while he developed his business he worked indefatigably in the upbuilding of his chosen city. I could name a long list of other San Diegans who have done likewise in varying degrees. It is up to the individual. There are no silver platters.

In January, 1961, when I was doing additional work on this section of this book, although it had originally been my intention to use only the first two articles and the last one dated October 1, 1933, upon rereading the series, I found a number which divulge interesting sidelights on the early history and development of certain areas of San Diego. I believe all that I am including will be found of interest.

Sunday, May 28, 1933:

RAILROADS FOR BREAKFAST OLD DISH
IN SAN DIEGO'S EARLY DAYS

By OSCAR COTTON

Railroads for breakfast!

That is what we lived on in San Diego 20 years prior to December, 1906, when John D. Spreckels announced the building of the San Diego & Arizona Railway.

During that long period of hope, tranquillity, and not much else, there were so many earnest attempts made by leading citizens to get a railroad built from San Diego to Yuma that it became our daily habit to look for a new railroad announcement every time we opened the San Diego *Union* at the breakfast table. Occasionally we were disappointed.

During this period one steam railroad—not the Yuma variety—materialized. One morning in 1887, E. S. Babcock, president and owner of the San Diego Streetcar Company—horsecar system—announced the projection of the steam "belt line railroad" to City Heights. Starting at Eighteenth Street and B Street, this line was to extend up Switzer Canyon, Balboa Park, weaving snakelike, in and out, skirting hills and gulches, to City Heights, then back along University Avenue to a grand terminal at Normal Street.

Early Builders Had Grit

I admire the imagination of those early builders of San Diego. The town's small business district centered at F Street on Fifth Avenue. From F Street to Broadway many lots were still vacant. From Twelfth Avenue to the bay only scattering residences emerged above the sagebrush. Yet Babcock, backed by S. Stiner, A. Klauber, D. Choate, and F. L. Castle, promoters of a 1,000-acre town lot subdivision at City Heights under the name of City Heights Land and Water Company, completed this steam belt line railroad at a cost of $250,000 and operated five trains daily for nearly a month from Dec. 1, 1887, until the holidays.

In January, 1888, the boom collapsed and the railroad was abandoned.

In 1896, Julius Wangenheim came from San Francisco to make his home in San Diego. He was partner in the wholesale grocery firm of the Klauber-Wangenheim Company. Soon he bought the Bank of Commerce from R. M. Powers, and reorganized it into San Diego's first bank and trust company, the Bank of Commerce and Trust Company.

Wangenheim and Melville Klauber were offered a one-fifth interest in the City Heights Land and Water Company project for $500. Wangenheim could see no value in the 7,000 unsold lots that stretched two miles east and north from the city boundary and Laurel Street, but he and Klauber paid the $500 because, from past engineering experience, Wangenheim could see $800 worth of rails and ties that had not been salvaged from the old railroad bed.

Nine years later, in 1905, Harry Howard, promoter, and Barbee Hook, financier, offered to buy City Heights at the ridiculously high price of $40,000 with $4,000 cash to bind the bargain. At that time there were not a dozen houses in all the vast territory east of Thirtieth Street above Broadway.

New Trolley Track Built

When this deal was closed Howard and Hook, with T. A. and J. W. Rife and one or two others, reorganized the City Heights Land and Water Company into the Columbia Realty Company. The new company subsidized the building of a single-track extension of the San Diego Electric Railway Company's trolley line along University Avenue from Fifth Avenue to Fairmount Avenue and sold 25-foot lots by the hundred at prices ranging from $25 to $150 each.

In 1907, four or five families built homes in City Heights. In 1908 the streetcar line was completed. Then things began to happen. During the next three years upward of 650 homes had been built and were occupied—mostly huts and small houses fronting on excessively wide streets plowed through the greasewood and sage.

In December, 1911, I purchased for the Pacific Building Company, the remaining 2,000 City Heights lots from the Columbia Realty Company for $82,500. In 1923, we sold a 100-foot corner from this tract at Fairmount and University avenues for $15,000.

The population of City Heights and adjoining territory, which comprised East San Diego, increased from 2,500 in 1913 to 15,000 in 1924, and it was annexed to San Diego. The $25 sagebrush lots sold in 1926 for $1,000 a pair and up. The $150 car-line corners sold in four-lot groups for from $10,000 to $20,000. That was exactly 30 years after Klauber and Wangenheim paid $500 for their one-fifth interest in the original 7,000 lots.

Julius Wangenheim is now President of the Southern Title and Trust Company. Speaking on inflation and present-day financial conditions at the Realty Board luncheon recently, he said in closing:

"Things are bound to get better—but I cannot tell you how soon. This I will say, after the probable issue of billions of dollars of new money some people are going to buy real estate because they will want something tangible. There is probably nothing safer than well-bought San Diego real estate on today's markets."

I am sure of it.

Sunday, April 23, 1933:

OPPORTUNITIES HERE GREATER THAN EVER BEFORE—HELLER

By OSCAR COTTON

"I was carried away by the climate, but not favorably impressed with the possibilities of making money," said M. F. Heller, speaking of his first impressions of San Diego in 1889. "Even in those days of low living costs, after paying rent and providing for a family, there was not much left out of a $50-a-month salary. I was general assistant in a grocery store. When it rained I donned hip boots and a slicker and carried wet 100-pound sacks of coal through mud and slush. There were no paved streets or even board sidewalks.

"I bought my first grocery store in 1892. I purchased a horse for $15 and a second-hand wagon. I promised to pay for the stock of groceries and fixtures out of profits, and moved my establishment to a board and batten shack at Eleventh Avenue and F Street, where my rent would be only $5 a month. Having no credit, I solicited orders and got my customers to pay cash in advance, then drove to the wholesale house and filled the orders."

That was San Diego's first "cash and carry" store, but the wrong man did the carrying. It was tough going. The city was still on the downgrade from the big boom of '87. The population had shrunk from 32,000 to 20,000 and was still dwindling.

"To me," said Heller, "those were the most depressing years in the more than four decades I have lived here. Business houses were failing. Some of our leading citizens were leaving San Diego and going to Los Angeles—Frank Strong, of Strong & Dickinson; C. I. Stanton; W. J. Hunsaker; Judge Lewis R. Works, and many others. We could see no prospects of better conditions. The hardships of today do not compare with those of the early nineties. There were no welfare organizations— the poor got along as best they could.

"One of the bright spots in my early business career was when H. Jevne, Los Angeles grocer, came into my store and complimented me on its neatness. He said that if I would stay in San Diego and continue to run my business as I had started it, some day I would own a big grocery store in the center of town. Later, Simon Levi, local wholesale grocer, told me that if I did not establish a chain of stores in San Diego, someone else would. I profited by the advice of both of these gentlemen.

"The first San Diego real estate I purchased was a four-room home at 846 Twenty-second Street. It was a one-story frame cottage, with plastered interior, on a 50-foot lot."

With each increase in his family, Heller added another room. Finally, he ran out of ground, and in 1900 bought 100 by 140 feet at Twenty-fourth and B streets, then one of San Diego's finest residential districts, for $1700. He paid one-half of the purchase price in cash, and the balance in groceries.

Keeps On Buying

Heller's first real estate speculation was the 100-foot lot on which the garage of Western States wholesale grocery now stands, at the corner of Eighth Avenue and J Street. He paid $3,000 for this plot in 1903; later he sold it for $4,800.

"After that," said Heller, "whenever I had a few hundred dollars I did not need, I bought a lot or two. I felt my money was safe in San Diego real estate. The lots I bought for speculation I was always willing to sell at a reasonable profit. In real estate, as in the grocery business, I believe in quick turnover. I have often turned my grocery stock 30 times in 12 months.

"Once I bought a one-third interest in 10 acres on Point Loma from H. P. Wood, for $500, which I afterward sold for a shade under $5,000. But that was exceptional for me. I bought only what real estate I could pay for. I have never signed a mortgage.

"Since the beginning of the new century I have always had great confidence in the future of San Diego, but could not keep pace with such optimists as Judge Thomas J. Hayes, now deceased, who organized the San Diego 100,000 population club. I could never visualize so great a city here within my lifetime; our placid bay, highly improved and harboring 100 men-o'-war; the construction of our vast reservoir system; the tall downtown buildings; the development of Balboa Park and our great highways. San Diego has so far surpassed my fondest dreams that I stand in awe and admiration of its accomplishments.

"When I bought my first real estate the sum total of San Diego's apparent assets were 'bay 'n climate and hope'—part of the time only 'bay 'n climate.' Now we are on a substantial foundation. The opportunities in San Diego are far greater today than ever before."

In 1905, Heller, in partnership with Samuel I. Fox, built the Fox-Heller block, 100 by 100, at Fifth Avenue and E Street. They leased the lot on the basis of 6 percent interest on a $100,000 valuation plus taxes. This, like Heller's other real estate investments, turned out to be a profitable venture. The building housed the main Heller grocery store and the Lion clothing store for a quarter of a century, when it was razed to make way for the present Crystal Palace.

I have known Mat Heller nearly 30 years. During that long period I am sure he has devoted at least half of his time gratis to the welfare of San Diego, the development of which made possible his success.

He is another of our substantial local businessmen who cast his bread upon the waters. In 1929, 37 years after his first business venture, Heller sold his 42 grocery stores to the MacMarr chain. Now, under the corporate name of Heller Investment Company, he deals largely in San Diego improved real estate. He has ridden with San Diego over smooth and rough seas since 1889. Together they have always come through. As evidence of his never varying faith in this city's future, I know of two good properties he has purchased for his company within the last 12 months.

The nearest semblance to a public speech I ever heard Heller make was in a recent Board of Directors' meeting that had sat too long. Suddenly, without warning, he rose to his feet and, while all present sat in awed silence at the phenomenon that was about to take place, he said, "Gentlemen, I move we adjourn."

Sunday, June 25, 1933:

SAN DIEGO MUST KEEP HARBOR SAFE TO RETAIN NAVAL SHIPS

By OSCAR COTTON

Today I have to tell you how to vote. As father said to his offspring out in the woodshed, "I'm sorry to do this, but it's for your own good."

Personally, I should prefer to keep out of politics, but Donald C. Burnham, president of the Realty Board, said I must instruct my readers on the vital questions before us. I'll do it, but it's the bunk. The readers of my column are the most intelligent of all the San Diego *Union* subscribers; they know how to vote.

For instance, on the $150,000 harbor matter, Proposition Number Two, on the city ballot. All of my readers know that if San Diego can increase a $1,500,000 annual payroll to $3,500,000 by dredging a few thousand yards of mud from the bottom of the bay, to make room for more ships, it would be good business to do it.

If we want more government ships in our harbor, we must have the harbor deep enough so the ships can float around in it as they do at Long Beach, where four of San Diego's seven cruisers are now spending their days and nights, and $500,000 per annum each.

Cruisers Belong Here

If we can get these four cruisers back here where they belong, by investing only $150,000 to make a berth for them, we had better do it before our dear old Uncle Sam gets tired waiting, and sends the admiral of the fleet and the other three cruisers from San Diego to park with the rest of the gang at Long Beach. This is exactly what Uncle will do before next January if we don't get busy.

For years our Chamber of Commerce boasted that San Diego harbor, with its 22 square miles of surface, was big enough to float the navies of the world. That was before they tried it out. Now we find the admirals and captains of these navies of the world are more interested in the depth of our harbor than they are in its width and length. There is a technical objection to allowing a modern cruiser to rest on the bottom of the bay, even at low tide.

On the strength of our boast about the size of the harbor and a few millions of dollars spent in dredging, mostly by the U. S. Government, we got 100 warships to live at this port. If we were satisfied with 100 ships, we would not need to spend any more money, but we are not satisfied. What's more we should not be satisfied. When a man is satisfied with himself, he is just sitting around waiting for the undertaker to come and get him. Cities are like men.

I would be almost willing to bet $1,000,000—my third million—that everyone of my readers will go to the polls on Tuesday and vote "No" on Proposition No. 2 on the City ballot.

Take Your Time

One thing I do want to say about voting Tuesday: Take your time. There are many different kinds of ballots to vote on and many different ways to vote—I mean on some you vote "No," on others "Yes," and in one place on the state ballot you merely stamp an X in the left-hand circle.

If a busy businessman of high intelligence starts down the line on a zigzag run, he is liable to zag where he should zig and get all his marks in the wrong squares and circles. Take your time.

Our new City Council is making a sincere effort to lower taxes. A couple of weeks ago I sat in on a council meeting and watched that honorable body wield the ax on the budget. I am telling you it made my old heart thump to see the fat chips fly. The tide has turned. Taxes are going to be lower. It will take time, but we are definitely headed in the right direction. Lower taxes mean higher real estate values; higher realty values mean prosperity for San Diego.

On Saturday night, June 17, Mrs. Cotton and myself were guests of Col. and Mrs. Ed Fletcher at the reopening of Pine Hills Lodge, near Julian, under the new ownership and management of Mr. and Mrs. Fred Kruger.

The Lodge opened with a flourish and, as would be expected of the new owners, a delicious dinner was served. Many prominent San Diegans were present. The Krugers only recently purchased this Lodge with its 11 acres of mountaintop at a price that some day will yield them a handsome profit on their investment.

The following morning, after a bountiful breakfast, we enjoyed one of those thrilling Fletcher back country tours. Down Banner Grade to the desert, then up steep mountainsides to his charming "Eagle's Nest" in a crotch among the peaks overlooking beautiful Warner's Ranch and Henshaw Lake.

Thinks in Large Figures

Ed thinks in large figures. As we flash past meadows, forests, and lakes, with an expansive wave of his free arm he will say, "I own 400 acres here; I own three miles of lake frontage there," or stopping in a green meadow, he might exclaim, "I own all of the land you can see from here to the top of these surrounding mountains, 6,000 acres."

Fletcher is one of San Diego's most interesting men. He came to this city in 1888. When he arrived he had in cash $6.10. From this capital he deposited $5 with M. T. Gilmore in the San Diego Trust & Savings Bank. Immediately after making this deposit he asked Gilmore for a job and got it. Ed was then a lad of 14, but already he had been "on his own" in life for seven years. He knew his way about.

Now, Ed owns many thousand acres of San Diego County's finest lands with miles of constantly flowing streams and tree-covered mountainsides. To see the result of this man's vast accomplishments and to realize that practically all of his success has come about through dealing in San Diego real estate gives a comprehensive picture of the realty opportunities that exist here.

Some day a bronze monument will be erected in Balboa Park to Col. Ed Fletcher, and under it placed a tablet with a list of the great dams and boulevards he has built and other of his outstanding achievements. For the moment I shall drop down from these exalting peaks to Grossmont, where Ed has been selling lands in startling volumes. To be exact, in the last two months he sold 18 villa sites of from one to five acres each.

Approaching this tract on our homeward run, Ed told me that as a result of these sales eight new homes were to be built. Then he jammed down on the foot brake, skidding all four wheels. "Look!" he said, "There are the first three new houses already under construction." Sure enough, there they were.

It is a privilege to spend a day in the front seat of an automobile with Ed Fletcher and let him dream his dreams aloud. He sees in his valleys, his mountains, and forests, such opportunities as most of us would be too modest to dream of, even in our sleep. Today he is planning developments not only for the next prosperity era which is to come, but also for the one following.

After a day with Fletcher no one can doubt that he who owns good San Diego real estate has hitched his wagon to a star.

Sunday, July 9, 1933:

JEWELRY FIRM BUYS PROPERTY TO SOLVE INVESTMENT PROBLEM

By OSCAR COTTON

In Lytham, Lancashire, England, in the eighties, J. Jessop heard of the beautiful orange groves and big real estate profits in southern California. For verification of these glowing tales, he subscribed to 26 California newspapers, among which was the San Diego *Union*. In 1890, Jessop brought his wife and four sons to San Diego—the San Diego *Union* had scored.

A jeweler by profession, Jessop purchased some land near Miramar and established himself as a dry farmer. At that time there was quite a settlement of dry farmers from many walks of life, except farming, on the Linda Vista mesa surrounding Miramar. It was a settlement of happy, congenial folks in search of health and a mild climate, both of which they found.

The farming was not successful. The only water was from shallow wells which dried up during the years of drought. This meant a trip to Mission Valley once a week to fill the water barrels. One day, while Jessop was plowing a field and his eldest son, Armand, was following the crooked furrow, the team got tangled in the harness and stopped. One horse turned and bodly stared at Jessop. This was too much. "You see, Armand," said his father, "even the horses laugh at me." Soon after this the family moved to San Diego and the jewelry firm of J. Jessop & Sons was established.

Jessop rented a house for his family, although he could have got it for nothing had he driven a bargain, as there were hundreds of empty houses in town with no prospective tenants.

San Diego city water was pumped from Mission Valley, but not filtered. Armand well remembers his mother holding in her hand a glass of newly drawn water and watching three small polliwogs swimming happily in the sediment, and her emphatic remark: "This water is not fit to drink."

Even during these trying years, when many formerly prominent residents gave up and left our city, neither Jessop nor any member of his family ever regretted coming to San Diego. From a small beginning, his jewelry business gradually expanded as one by one his five sons arrived at maturity and a place in the store was found for each.

Later Jessop moved with his growing family to Coronado because the balmy climate across the bay proved soothing to an asthmatic condition. It was because of asthma trouble that Jessop, on recommendation of his physicians, came to southern California. In time, the Coronado climate entirely cured this ailment.

Despite his admitted failure as a dry farmer, Jessop believed in the ownership of land. He even kept the old dry farm on Linda Vista mesa. The family owns it today. As he began to accumulate a cash reserve over immediate merchandising requirements, Jessop bought San Diego lots. He considered close-in business properties best for permanent ownership. Property once bought he never sold except to reinvest the proceeds in other San Diego real estate. This policy he continued until his death in 1932 at the age of 82. His five sons have pursued the same policy. Today the firm of J. Jessop & Sons owns some of San Diego's finest downtown business property in what is known by realtors and merchants as "the hot spot."

A few days ago, on talking to Armand Jessop, now senior member of the firm, I heard one of the most interesting and remarkable real estate stories I have come across since I have been poking my nose into other people's business. I found a story startling even to a realtor. It is a story I never expected to get from any source, a story so strange that once heard it will never be forgotten. Here it is:

The firm of J. Jessop & Sons has made large profits through buying San Diego real estate at or near the top of the bull markets.

Bought at Top

For example, late in 1910, Jessop's paid $80,000 for the southwest corner, 100 by 100, of Sixth Avenue and B Street. This was the top price at which this property had ever been offered. The northeast corner of Eighth Avenue and Broadway, 100 by 100, was purchased at the height of the boom in 1912 for $130,000. The B Street corner sold for $125,000 and the Broadway property brought $250,000. During these years of ownership, these properties averaged a satisfactory income on invested capital.

With a part of the profits from the sale of these two corners, the firm bought the lot on Fifth Avenue between Broadway and C Street where Jessop's jewelry store now stands. Speaking of their latest purchase and other real estate transactions, Armand Jessop said, "We have kept all of the capital in our business that the expanding community would justify and have consistently invested most of our surplus in San Diego real estate. From time to time we have tried other types of investment, but always found real estate by far the best; in fact, the only profitable investment outside of our own business.

"Even our last purchase, this Fifth Avenue property, which we bought early in 1927 at the very top of the market, is still the best investment we could have made. From offers we have turned down recently, I believe we could sell this property today, or could even have sold it last year, for as much as we paid."

Investment No Worry

There is truth in the old saying, "It is more difficult to keep money than to make it." Jessop's have found the answer. They buy good San

Diego real estate when money for investment is available. They hold this real estate through depressions and sell in periods of expansion only when it appears that their capital position may be improved. Jessop's never hurry in or out of their real estate deals or look for "quick profits." They have no worries over investment problems.

There are business properties in San Diego today that can be bought on a basis of 6 to 10 percent net income on present low rentals. Capitalists, large or small, who are letting these opportunities slip by are asleep at the switch.

As of November 1, 1961, the descendants of J. Jessop and their inlaws number more than sixty. The firm of J. Jessop & Sons operates six jewelry stores in San Diego city and county, with a total staff of two hundred; an outstanding organization—a tribute to J. Jessop, and to San Diego's progress which made such a development possible.

Sunday, August 6, 1933:

YOUNG SAN DIEGAN WINS REPUTATION WITH DANCE ORCHESTRA, THEN TURNS TO BUILDING "HACIENDAS" AND FURNITURE

By OSCAR COTTON

Cliff May is one of the most interesting young men in San Diego. At 15, while in high school, he organized a professional dance orchestra; when he was 17 his orchestra furnished dance music for the Coronado Hotel. For eight years, San Diego's dancing public delighted in Cliff May's orchestra. While only a boy, Cliff had become an institution; his position was secure. Then Cliff took up architecture—walked out on his attained position and started mixing concrete. His friends were shocked. Cliff was happy, but to understand why we must go back four generations.

Cliff May is the great-great-grandson of Miguel Estudillo, who built the Estudillo house at Old Town, popularly known as Ramona's Marriage Place. He is the son of Mr. and Mrs. C. C. May, 3342 Albatross Street. His mother, before her marriage, was Beatrice McGee. Her sister, Jane McGee, has for 33 years managed the Las Flores Ranch at Santa Margarita. This historic place was built in 1812, and was at one time owned by Don Pio Pico.

Much of Cliff's boyhood was spent at this old Las Flores home, at the family's adobe "Condor's Nest" at Pala, and at the ranchhouse of his cousin, Cave Couts, near Vista.

Cliff learned to love the easy, quiet life of seclusion behind heavy adobe walls. As he matured, enjoyment developed into an ambition to give San Diego a true architecture of early California days, modernized to fit present requirements.

Designs Furniture

To date, Cliff has built two houses. I did not see the first. It was sold before I heard about it. I did visit the second. It is at 4669 East Talmadge Drive.

Descriptions are tiresome, besides, it is not what one sees in this "Hacienda," it is what he feels that takes him back a hundred years. The customs that steeped into May's soul through four generations have found expression in the handmade spools of the movable sun-couch in the patio, the rawhide strips that lace together the burlap bedspreads, the adzed window frames, and the adobe-finished corner fireplaces.

Such care has been lavished on each minute detail as can be given only by a lover of his art. Every piece of furniture was designed by Cliff and made by hand. The floors of the individual rooms follow the contour of the lot. When one closes the street door behind him and enters the patio, he instinctively pulls down into low gear. The world is on the other side of a heavy wall.

While I marveled at the harmony of the brick-red tile in the kitchen, two boys came in to look. I like boys. Excepting girls, I like them best. But I was glad when they left. I wanted to enjoy the restfulness of the place and Cliff May's quiet voice as he told me of his thoughts and plans.

Building Third House

Within a week after my visit to Cliff's second "Hacienda," it was sold. He is building his third on Alta Mirano Way in historic Presidio Hills above Old Town.

Of entirely new design, this third "Hacienda" has the same delightful character of its predecessors, the atmosphere of early California. Although the plaster is scarcely dry, newly planted shrubs and trees have been set out with such care they look at home in their new environment.

Cliff keeps open house every day from 2 to 5. In the mornings, he might be found at work with his tools, or a lead pencil, sketching the design for a heavy chair or stand. I am betting on Cliff. San Diego has lost an artist in dance music, but gained one architecturally. He has ideas and courage. Like the avocado, these "Haciendas" are adapted to our climate. They give character to San Diego and add to the already long list of reasons why one should live here.

Please note that May's "Haciendas" sell as fast as they are built. To a real estate man that tells volumes. Prospective home buyers want the newest thing in design and appointments, and when they find it they will pay.

If your wife wants a modern home, sell your old house for what it is worth and buy her a new one. A new home will cost less than a new wife—much less—and be more practical.

If you will figure depreciation and obsolescence on your old house, its present worth will surprise you.

Rule Shows Worth

I know a man who has had his old home on the market continuously since 1920. He and his wife wanted to build a modern home, but he was never willing to admit to himself the depreciation on the old house. Today this place would not bring half what he could have got in 1926. If he keeps it until the top of the next boom, he will get very little more than he could sell for today. There can be little appreciation in the actual value of an old house.

If you would like to know what your present home is worth, figure the number of square feet on the floor plan and multiply by $3 to $3.50, depending on the class of construction, then from the total deduct 3 percent for each year the house has been built, for depreciation and obsolescence, to this add a fair today's appraisal for your lot. Make no allowance for past expenditures in remodeling or upkeep.

This is only a general rule, but it will average out pretty well. If the results of such investigation make unpleasant reading, you can burn the sheets of paper with your figures together with this article. Then you will have your old value back again.

New homes bought or built now will sell for more money later because present building and lot costs are low. More than 100 new homes are under construction in San Diego. It will pay every home owner to drive around and inspect some of them. Also, it will pay you to investigate the present marvelous lot bargains.

Twenty-five years later, I received the following letter:

Cliff May Associates
CUSTOM HOMES FOR MODERN LIVING

13151 Sunset Blvd.,
Los Angeles 49,
California
GRanite 2-9576
July 15, 1958

Mr. Oscar W. Cotton
2900 Nichols
San Diego, California

DEAR MR. COTTON:

As busy as you were, twenty-five years ago you took time off to write an article about me and my first ranch house I was building out in Talmadge Park.

I appreciated it so very much and it was only last week when I was going through my scrapbook that I came across the delightful article, and I realized then how negligent I have been in not writing you sooner to thank you for the wonderful boost you gave me these many years ago.

I have just completed a new book which is being published by Lane Publishing Company called *Western Ranch Houses* by Cliff May and under separate cover, am sending you a copy with my sincere thanks for your friendship all these years.

Haven't seen Bill, John, or Jane for many years, but have noticed John's important work with the Realty Board and Bill's work with the Republican Committee.

Dad is still doing fine and still lives in the same house on Albatross Street.

The next time I am down would like to stop by and say hello to to you. With kindest regards and best wishes, and hoping this finds you in the best of health, I remain,

Sincerely,
CLIFF

Shortly thereafter, the book *Western Ranch Houses* arrived. One hundred and seventy-six pages, picturing seventeen of the most delightful, livable homes, exteriors, interiors, and furnishings, it has ever been my pleasure to review. It made me wish I were young enough to want to build a new home. The book is prefaced by a short history of the southern California ranch house—how it began, and why, with pictures of ranch homes and scenes in the 1850's.

Today, Cliff May has become an institution. Homes he has built, both large and small, number in the thousands and span a large part of the United States. Some individual homes cost upward of a quarter of a million dollars to build. Our son, William, tells me Cliff flies his own plane from job to job when they are widely separated, and carries a Dictaphone beside the pilot's seat and dictates as he travels. To all but Cliff May, his achievements are phenomenal. (And try as I would, I could not even learn to play the slide trombone!)

Sunday, October 1, 1933:

MISSION HILLS HISTORY RELATED; 25 CENTS ACRE PAID FOR FIRST TRACT

By OSCAR COTTON

I like to sit within the marbled enclosure among the vice-presidents of the First National Trust & Savings Bank and, with dignity, nod to passing acquaintances and one-time clients. It is good advertising, and free.

The other day, while visiting with Vice-President Johnston O. (Jack) Miller, and keeping one eye on the aisle not to miss anybody, by way of making conversation, I asked:

"Jack, how did you happen to come to San Diego?" His answer made me forget the passers-by and listen to what he said.

Jack learned to walk in the first house erected in Mission Hills, the fine old home built by his grandmother, Sarah J. Cox, on Orizaba Street, the highest point on the southern slope of this entire area. This home was built simultaneously with the erection of the Coronado Hotel in 1887. For many years the Cox home was the only edifice in that entire district. Shopping in San Diego, by the occupants of this house, meant a trip by horse and carriage down the hairpin grade to Old Town, then by steam train to Fifth Avenue and L Street. There one boarded a horsecar, or trudged through the dust or mud up Fifth Avenue to Marston's store at F Street.

The building of the Miller home by Mrs. Cox on this particular point was the culmination of a dream of Jack's great-grandfather, Henry J. Johnston, for many years captain of the Pacific Coast Steamship Company's old sidewheel S. S. *Orizaba,* which, under his pilotage, brought passengers and freight to this port from San Francisco. As the *Orizaba* rounded Point Loma on one of San Diego's 356 days of sunshine in 1868, this high Mission Hills promontory, overlooking the great expanse of sea, so impressed Captain Johnston that he resolved to buy it for his home when he should retire. Immediately after making fast his ship, Johnston proceeded to the courthouse in Old Town and bought the finest 60 acres of marine-view property in all Mission Hills and paid $15 cash—25¢ an acre—the price of land then prevailing in new San Diego.

Sixty acres being more land than the captain wanted for his home, he sold half of his purchase to the first mate for $7.50. At his death, the captain's 30 acres passed to his widow, who bequeathed it to their daughter, Sarah Cox. The street on which the Miller home fronts was named in honor of the old sidewheel steamer, *Orizaba.*

About 1904 I drove out over this remaining 30 acres with Mrs. Cox, who wanted me to put on a high-class subdivision and sell the lots for $1,000 each. She took me to the knoll her father had dubbed "Inspiration Point." I was forced to agree that it was well named, but I thought the property too far out ever to amount to much in my lifetime. I was entranced by the dear lady's enthusiasm.

Percy H. Goodwin, in company with his father, N. M. Goodwin, C. H. Swallow, and others, organized a syndicate in 1907, bought 60 acres adjoining Sarah Cox's property on the north and laid out the Mission Hills subdivision. By that time, this district was showing considerable life; the Catholic cemetery was established across the canyon from Washington Street; M. Hall had a citrus grove on Trias Street; there was an olive orchard on Fort Stockton Drive, where the old Mission Hills Congregational Church now stands—some of the old olive trees may still be seen in this neighborhood—and there were two or three small dairy and chicken farms almost within eyesight of each other, on a clear day. As a climax to these activities, Miss Kate Sessions had moved her nursery from Balboa Park to occupy the four blocks north and east of Lewis and Stevens streets.

First Restricted Area

An old road, extending from Fourth and University avenues to Old Town and northern points, wormed its way over hillocks and through hollows, serving these few scattered inhabitants.

The original Mission Hills map was filed January 20, 1908. Later, George W. Marston, Charles Hamilton, and John Kelly, plotted 22 acres adjoining this first subdivision on the west. Marston named "Arguello Way" after a prominent Spanish family who owned a large rancho at the lower end of San Diego bay. Arden Way was named for Arden Forest, in Shakespeare's *As You Like It*. Sentiment mingled with the desire for financial gain in the early beginning of Mission Hills. Percy and his crowd determined this was to be San Diego's finest residential district, and boldly recited in all deeds that no house should cost less than $3,500. Mission Hills was San Diego's first restricted subdivision.

It took optimism to visualize $3,500 homes in this inaccessible, wind-swept district, miles from the nearest streetcar line, through the grease-wood and dust, in places a foot deep. While the tract was in the making, Percy and his young wife, May, spent their Sundays driving over the new subdivision staking lots. May drove the horse and buggy with the lot stakes, and Percy, with a heavy hammer, drove the stakes.

Those were the days of the passing of the horse—the horse and buggy would pass the automobiles stranded by the roadside—but not for long. Before the sale of Mission Hills was over, big seven-passenger Fords and Stanley Steamers whizzed prospective purchasers to the tract at 12 and 15 miles an hour. Occasionally a complete round trip from the firm's office at Fourth Avenue and B Street would be made without having a puncture or blowout or any mechanical trouble.

Goodwin's syndicate paid $36,000 for their 60 acres—$600 an acre—and sold individual lots at $800. L. E. Fuller bought the first lot and built the first house at the southwest corner of Sunset Boulevard and Sheridan Way. At the outset, aside from its promoters, Mission Hills had few friends. With a city of only 30,000 the new subdivision was too far from Florence Heights to be taken seriously. First Avenue and Washington Street was the residential deadline. Success finally came with the extension of the San Diego Electric Railway Company's No. 3 car-line to Lewis and Stevens streets, late in 1908. From then on things began to happen.

High-Class Residents

All told, there are three official Mission Hills subdivisions comprising less than 100 acres, but for the last 15 years, real estate men have advertised Mission Hills houses and lots for sale from Spruce Street to Mission Valley and from Fifth Avenue to the bluffs overlooking Old Town.

The City Planning Commission classifies the boundaries of the Mission Hills-Hillcrest district from Georgia Street west and from Upas Street north and credits this section with a population of 19,358 in 1932, or two-thirds of the population of the entire city when the first Mission Hills map was filed.

The building of homes and the planting of trees and shrubs, which grew vigorously in the rich virgin soil, soon formed effective windbreaks. The contoured streets with pleasing names, and the building restrictions proved good drawing cards. From the first, Mission Hills has enjoyed a high personnel of residents.

Lot values increased rapidly—100 to 300 percent in the first three years. Later they were to go much higher, $5,000 and up for the best view lots. Percy recalled that one of the original $800 lots sold within two years for $6,500. He said the generally accepted price for the $800 lots was $2,500.

Capt. Henry Johnston bought 60 acres in this district for $15 in 1868. Sam Fox sold 40 acres at Washington and Hawk streets for $100 an acre in 1895. Goodwin's syndicate paid $36,000 for their 60 acres in 1907. Today there are 100-foot corner lots in some of the business centers of this so-called Mission Hills district that could not be purchased for $50,000. There are, too, some fine lots in Mission Hills that can be bought today dirt cheap. History repeats—big profits have been made in Mission Hills by those who could look clearly into the future; big profits again will be made by those who take advantage of present opportunities. You can't go hog-wild and buy lots promiscuously, or with your eyes shut, and make money. But there are profits ahead for the careful investor who doesn't wait too long.

CHAPTER XXXVI

I Introduce a Congressman

IN 1933, our Congressman George Burnham was running for re-election. His nephew, Donald C. Burnham, asked me to introduce George at a Realty Board luncheon. I was happy to be asked to officiate on this occasion because, like all who knew George, I always enjoyed his company and was delighted to be of some small service to assist in his re-election.

George Burnham was in no sense a politician, but he was a delightful gentleman to know and to meet. He was a handsome fellow, with a most pleasing smile and manner, always full of humor and a good story-teller.

For San Diego, the year 1933 was the blackest twelve months of any year following the 1929 Stock Market Crash. We were still slipping downhill, month after month.

My remarks on that August 9, 1933, were as follows:

Our Worthy Chairman is quite a joker—asking me to introduce our own United States Congressman, George Burnham, to his home town colleagues. It would have been more sensible to have asked Congressman Burnham to introduce me.

I hate to be made a monkey of in such a public place.

You all know Congressman George Burnham. You all voted for him, didn't you? Everybody I know, did. The men voted for him because we wanted more U. S. Government money spent in San Diego, and the ladies voted for him because—well, men, take a good look at him, if you want to know. It's that irresistible appeal. Personally, I hate men like that, but I never allow jealousy to influence my vote.

Aside from this "irresistible" business, I like George. He is good company. He doesn't rant like John E. Rankin, Lewis McFadden, and some other Congressmen. Burnham accomplishes his ends like Admiral Tarrant manages the Navy—by strategy. Even in small matters, this characteristic in George is outstanding.

Once I went to Chicago with George and our Mayor, John Forward. We were entertained aboard H. H. Timken's yacht. Before lunch, the steward always sent up an enthusiastically refreshing appetizer for each guest, and one extra for the last man to arrive aboard ship. George showed his strategy by always being the last man.

I first met George Burnham in his real estate office on E Street, between Fourth and Fifth avenues, when that location was in the midst of San Diego's financial district. That was in 1904, when San Diego's total population was not over 22,000—and Washington, D. C., seemed almost as remote as the moon. On that day, little did I suspect that I should ever be called upon to introduce George Burnham as United States Congressman to his colleagues in San Diego, a city of 160,000 respectable citizens, and real estate men.

At that time, although San Diego County extended to the Colorado River, we did not have a Congressman from this vast territory. The Congressman who represented this district was Milton J. Daniels, from Riverside.

Those were days of small beginnings—a $50 commission was worth working for. A large percentage of the properties to be sold were within walking distance of the office. If George wanted to show a lot in Florence Heights or National City, he could rent a horse and buggy from Adolph Levi's stable for $1.50 for half a day. The real estate commission schedule, when George was in business, was 5 percent of the first $5,000 and 2½ percent thereafter. Now we get 5 percent on $50,000. I mean, we should get it if we were to make a deal. I think George got out of the real estate business because he thought the new commission schedule was too high.

In all these years I have only one criticism of George, and I am going to state that publicly. He should have made it his business, back in Washington, to have the "Exterior" Department set aside two hundred and fifty billion new paper dollars to buy up all of the distressed real estate in San Diego County and get it off the market. Then we real estate men and our clients could have taken these two hundred and fifty billion new paper dollars and started something worth while. If George had done that, we would not need to worry about the N.R.A., or the Q.Z.X., or anything else. I would like to take this opportunity to suggest this move for the next session of Congress in December.

We have all kinds of Congressmen back in Washington, from the Tom Blankton type from Texas, who storms his way through, to the George Burnham type, who beams through like the sun after a storm. You can't down that type of Congressman.

I remember, on a warm day in August, in the early stages of the World War, when the government was considering building some concrete ships in San Diego, George Burnham and myself, and several other prominent citizens, took the Schofield Brothers, the engineers who had been selected to build these ships, for a drive through our back country. These were the days of open cars. In order to exhibit the best of the scenery, we put the top back. As we neared Descanso, the sky began to cloud over. Our guests, being from the East, were apprehensive. But loyal optimist, George, assured them it never rained in San Diego in the summertime; that we could count on our climate if nothing else. He said that was why the government picked San Diego as the place to build these ships, because we had 10 months out of every year without rain.

At that moment, the sky opened up like it did the day after Noah completed the Ark. Everyone got drenched. We had to open the side doors to let the water run out of the tonneau. Right through this terrible storm, Burnham stuck to his story. In the end, he must have convinced our guests, because they went ahead and built the ships.

That is why I voted for George Burnham for Congress. I figured that a man who could convince a group of hard-boiled engineers that it was not raining, while it was actually coming down like a flood, would be the best convincer we could get to be back in Washington.

I don't know how much time George gave to his real estate business, but I do know that, through all these years, he was more often than not to be found at the Chamber of Commerce or on some committee, and when I was in Washington during the war, our then Congressman, Billy Kettner, told me there was only one man in San Diego to take his place in Congress, and that was George Burnham.

I remember when General Strong and other high military officials came to San Diego to look over the Linda Vista Mesa as a possible site for a cantonment. George Burnham was in the party of four or five San Diegans sent out to bring home the bacon. George may have been the chairman of the committee—I don't remember. I do know he went back to Washington and sold Congress the site for the Marine Base and helped persuade them to take the site for the Naval Training Station.

Like all real estate men, George, by nature, is modest and retiring. He prefers telling good stories to talking about himself or his business. So I will tell you he was honored in Washington by being placed on the Committee for the District of Columbia, which is virtually a councilmanic board for the government of the capital city.

He was also appointed on the Foreign Affairs Committee, which is one of the mot desired committees in Congress. Such rapid progress is a high compliment to the popularity of the new Congressman. It comes to Congressman Burnham as a result of his years of effort in San Diego for the city's development, and his large circle of acquaintances among the high naval and military officers and Washington officials.

As soon as opportunity offered, Burnham, resigned his post on the Foreign Affairs Committee, to accept a place on the Naval Affairs Committee. This committee offers far less prestige to its members, but is of great value to San Diego. In George Burnham, San Diego has a Congressman who may always be counted on to put our city's interests ahead of personal advantage—CONGRESSMAN GEORGE BURNHAM.

CHAPTER XXXVII

Our Second Exposition

EARLY IN 1934, or it may have been late in 1933, Frank Drugen suggested that San Diego hold another Exposition, using what remained of our beautiful old Exposition buildings in Balboa Park, and possibly adding some new ones. The idea took like wildfire.

A strong committee of leading businessmen was formed. Three hundred thousand dollars was subscribed (verbally) by the city, county, and half a dozen of our largest financial institutions, with the understanding that a total of a half-million dollars be raised. Frank Drugen was given five thousand dollars in expense money and told to go ahead. He hired a manager for the Exposition. They made wonderful plans; announced them, and invited everybody to subscribe. However, since six millionaires and institutions had volunteered to subscribe more than half the total, the rest of the business community sat back to "Let George do it." Aside from the $5,000 in expense money, not one dollar was pledged officially.

It was really a pitiful situation. San Diego needed a shot in the arm as badly as ever before in its history. Here was the hypodermic, ready to give it, and absolutely nothing was happening, with month after month slipping by. One Friday, a committee asked me if I would take the chairmanship and raise the money. I told them I would give them an answer the following Monday morning. I took the week-end, at Corte Madera, to think about it.

About twelve years previously, I had had a near nervous breakdown. The circumstances contributing to this near collapse had had to do with the raising of the funds required for the second year of the San Diego-California Club's activities.

The San Diego-California Club had been such a stupendous success that when it came time to raise the $150,000 for its second year Duncan MacKinnon, who was then president, determined that he would omit all the "folderol" and, instead of putting on a campaign, he would merely call a luncheon meeting of the members and let them all subscribe. That was indeed a new and simple way to raise money and I was most apprehensive, but we went ahead and called the meeting. Everybody was most enthusiastic about the Club and the grand job it was doing for San Diego. They paid for their luncheons and applauded the speakers and the fine reports, but they did not subscribe any money. The San Diego-California Club was "my baby," so to speak, and it was so absolutely necessary that we keep it going that I got a small group of former workers together. We gave it everything we had, and finally raised $125,000 for the second year.

Up to and including that campaign, whenever I put my shoulder to an enterprise I put my whole life, thought, and energy into it. I never spared myself, day or night. I took my worries home with me, took them to bed, and woke up with them early the next morning, and then started all over again.

Raising that second year's fund for the San Diego-California Club under those conditions was the last straw. After it was over, I was "fit to be tied." I telephoned Dr. Homer H. Oatman, at that time one of our leading physicians and surgeons, and a warm, personal friend. He listened to my story and sent me to Dr. H. F. Andrews.

Dr. Andrews heard my recital: My food would not digest; my head felt numb on the left side I was unable to sleep, and I was wondering if the "end" were near. When I had finished, he took over and he talked to me for an hour. He had me come back for another hour's lecture three times a week for two months. Then he told me to go back to my office and go to work, but that when 6:00 P.M. came, I was to close my desk and forget all about business until 8:00 A.M., the next day.

I never would have believed that I could do it and still conduct my business, but after my two months' coaching by Dr. Andrews I started on a new life. Fifteen years later, I wrote a twelve-page letter on the subject, "Man Can Master Himself," which pulled a good friend of mine back from the brink of nervous prostration and has helped many others.

My reason for taking the weekend to think over whether I would tackle raising the half-million dollars to finance the proposed Exposition was twofold. First, I wanted to figure out exactly how I would proceed, and, second, I wanted to be sure, in my own mind, that I could do it. For twelve years, I had been following Dr. Andrews' advice to the letter. My head had cleared up; my health was good. I wondered if I should tackle this job, because it would mean eighteen hours a day for two or three months. On the following Monday morning, however, I told the directors I would raise the half-million dollars for them, provided I would have the full direction of the campaign in every particular. They agreed unanimously.

On July 1, I took charge, and I was most fortunate in securing Carl Dustin, an excellent professional campaign manager, and my old friend,

Tom G. Armstrong, who had carried on the San Diego-California Club so successfully for me, to act as publicity man. For several years, Armstrong had been operating a very fine advertising agency in San Diego. Starting with twenty workers, we increased our personnel until at the final meeting we had over four hundred.

At our first workers' meeting in August, I called their attention to the building permits, which for the month of July for the entire city of San Diego, were for exactly seven houses! Imagine it! Seven houses for the entire city for a full month, when our Pacific Building Company alone, back in 1912, had started thirty new houses in the first thirty days! I told them I believed July would go down in history as the low month in the home building in San Diego for this period, but in our first meeting in September, I had to retract that statement—in August, the total permits issued for new homes amounted to six!

This was a most interesting campaign. Everybody wanted the Exposition, but during the first thirty days we hardly got a subscription! The San Diego daily papers, encouraged by the Exposition Management and the Chamber of Commerce, kept a generous stream of stories on the front pages day after day, telling what wonderful things the Exposition would do for San Diego. The general public and "should-be" subscribers considered this wonderful windfall well on its way. Why should they dig down in their pockets and part with their hard-earned dollars?

Finally, I asked Frank G. Belcher, president of the Exposition, to call a meeting of the heads of the three newspapers: the San Diego *Union;* the *Evening Tribune;* and the San Diegan *Sun;* and the secretary of the Chamber of Commerce. I told them that if they were really going to have an Exposition, they would have to do two things: First, they must not print another line about the Exposition in any of our daily newspapers for ten days; and second, they must give the Exposition, free, a one fullpage advertisement, which I would write. When they finally became convinced that something drastic must be done or we would not be able to raise the money, they all agreed.

Within three days after all publicity had stopped, our "should-be" subscribers began asking each other what had happened to the Exposition? Before the ten days' waiting period was up, the whole town was at a nervous tension. During those ten days I perfected my organization for the final push, and wrote my ad.

For years, we have heard it said over and over that in writing ads you must be brief. I have never believed it. I think that what you must do is to get your reader's attention, and hold it. That is what I did in my ad.

Many years later, I was sitting beside Worth Wright, who was then the classified advertising manager of the San Diego *Union-Tribune* Publishing Company, at a luncheon meeting. We were discussing how much copy could be put in a newspaper advertisement. Afterward, I mailed him a copy of this Exposition campaign ad, and received the following letter from him:

DEAR MR. COTTON:

Thank you very much for letting me see the full page advertisement which was run prior to the 1935 San Diego Exposition. It was powerful copy and, although there were some 2,500 words, the advertisement measured up to all standards of effective advertising. We would like to have had our Mr. Bradley[1] see it, but he is attending a Bureau of Advertising meeting in Colorado Springs at this time.

With best regards, I am,

Cordially yours,
UNION-TRIBUNE PUBLISHING CO.,
WORTH WRIGHT
Classified Advertising Manager

Here is the ad:

DO YOU WANT AN EXPOSITION?

This week you must be prepared to answer that question.
Twelve o'clock noon next Friday is the deadline.
Answers must be in the form of regularly signed subscription cards.
If the answer is to be "Yes," there must be delivered to President Frank G. Belcher on that day and at that hour, the full half-million dollars in signed subscriptions.
Otherwise, there will be no Exposition.

On July 20, nearly two hundred businessmen met at dinner at the U. S. Grant Hotel and voted unanimously to work for an Exposition in 1935. The City Council, Board of County Supervisors, and seven San Diego businessmen and large institutions pledged $300,000 contingent on the total necessary sum of one-half million dollars being raised.

Since that memorable night we have been perfecting an organization to intelligently present to the businessmen of San Diego the general plan for holding this Exposition and to solicit their individual aid.

This week three hundred San Diego businessmen will leave their stores and offices to call upon you for your answer to this greatest

---

[1] Lester G. Bradley was then, and for many years thereafter, the president, publisher, and general manager of the Union-Tribune Publishing Company.

of all undertakings for our city in more than two decades. Your individual answers will determine whether there will be an Exposition.

Exposition Hangs by a Thread

Today the proposed 1935 Exposition hangs by a thread.

Our entire community is so exuberant over the thought we are going to have an Exposition that the matter has been dismissed as an established fact.

You would be surprised how many people have said, "If you don't get all the money, Baron Long will put up the balance," or "Los Angeles wants this Exposition as much as we do—you can get all the money you need up there." One intelligent person said, "Isn't it grand we are going to have an Exposition? I am so happy because you already have $300,000. Now we won't have to subscribe much."

Such talk is ridiculous. We cannot get any more money from Baron Long or from any of the other heavy subscribers. We cannot go to Los Angeles and beg subscriptions to stage an Exposition in San Diego. The only excuse for such suggestions is that those who make them are not thinking what they are saying.

If you and the other businessmen and women and interested citizens do not take seriously to yourselves the raising of the balance of this half-million dollars, there will be no Exposition. A half-million dollars cannot be raised in San Diego unless you will do your full share.

Please Get This Straight

All subscriptions must be based on a total of one-half million dollars being subscribed. We must have all, or none will be available.

True, we have $300,000 to start with, but remember that eliminates the large subscribers and places the burden for all of the balance of $200,000 on the rest of us. There is no Santa Claus left to fall back on to make up a deficit if we close the campaign Friday noon with only $450,000.

Either we will have an Exposition or we won't—there will be no halfway measure.

The last $50 subscription is as vital to the success of this enterprise as the first $50,000, and every man and woman who does his or her proportionate share can have an equal pride and gratification in the 1935 Exposition—*if we hold it.* This is the second biggest job ever tackled for San Diego. The first was in 1909, when our city, with 39,000 population, passed the hat for $1,000,000 for our last Exposition, and got it!

President Belcher, realizing the shortness of time, has been pressing to hurry the campaign. The Corporation treasurer, Emil Klicka, has been pounding the directors' table with his powerful fist and insisting that we step on it, and the officers and directors have been equally insistent.

We have held back until now only because we wanted to be organized to blanket the city with a full staff of volunteer solicitors, and because we wanted, when we start, to be able to show you facts, figures, and reasons why this is your Exposition.

Now Is the Time to Act

Last Wednesday night three hundred businessmen who had pledged their time to solicit your subscriptions met for definite instructions, received their individual assignments, and started making calls.

In addition to making their own generous subscriptions these solicitors are giving their time free—every one of them—in the hope that we can hold an Exposition in 1935, lift San Diego out of the worst depression in more than forty years, and again start us on the road to prosperity. When these solicitors call on you, please set aside your own business and give them your undivided attention and help.

In our work so far we have asked and received freely from the busiest businessmen in San Diego their full time on all occasions in the work of organizing this campaign. No San Diego businessman's own business is as important to him as the holding of this proposed Exposition.

Building Permits Are Barometer

We know that, while undoubtedly the low point in the depression for the United States was passed in the summer of 1932, and that for two years conditions elsewhere have been improving, here in San Diego they have been getting worse, until our building permits for July reached the lowest on record—only seven new houses for the entire city, and one of these houses cost only $600. In 1912, when we were getting ready for the last Exposition, one building company took out 20 to 30 individual house permits a month. In 1926, San Diego's building permits were more than $1,500,000 per month.

The history of our city for the last 67 years, since Father Horton bought San Diego's main business district for 26¢ an acre, shows five depressions with durations of from two to nineteen years each. History also shows that we have never emerged from one of these depressions except through some gigantic effort, such as the building of a railroad, large community advertising, or the staging of an Exposition. Never have we drifted out.

We have now been drifting into this present depression for seven years. If we do not use the proposed Exposition as a ready-made and waiting vehicle to pull us out, how long will we continue to drift? Two years? Five years? None of us know.

1940—San Diego—250,000

With scores of leading businessmen I am giving my time free to try to make this Exposition an accomplished fact. I take the stand that this proposition is of more consequence to you than your business, because if we do not hold this Exposition there appears to be nothing ahead for San Diego but stagnation for a period of years; while if we do put this Exposition over and follow it up with a united community and continued advertising, there is no reason why we should not show a population for the 1940 Census of 250,000.

It is within our power to transform San Diego from one of the darkest to one of the whitest spots on the business map of the United States. The holding of this Exposition is the first and foremost link in the biggest chain that ever pulled a community out of the mire.

In the years to come if this fund is raised, you will count your subscription as the best-paying investment in your business career. Subscriptions large enough to put this campaign over can be made in most instances without material inconvenience to subscribers—they can be made in seven monthly installments and figured as that much additional advertising. To subscribe $100 will cost only $15 a month.

Reverse Your Binoculars

The businessman who is not willing to make any reasonable sacrifice necessary and subscribe his full share to insure the success of this project, or who holds back to see what his competitor will do before subscribing, is viewing this Exposition through the wrong end of the telescope. He has not yet visualized the bigness of this opportunity.

It is not what your competitor may do, but what you subscribe that will mean success or failure of this project. Had the first seven large subscribers waited to see what the rest of the community was going to subscribe, there would not have been even a prospect of an Exposition.

This is a good time for every man to stand on his own two feet, use his own head, and view the plan as a whole, and then, if necessary, plunge a little bit. There is a tide in the affairs of cities as well as men, which, taken at the flood, leads to fortune.

Florida's Biggest Season

After several years' staying at home on account of the world depression, people are again going places. Last winter was Florida's biggest season. California is next in line, but hundreds of thousands of visitors come to Los Angeles who never see San Diego. If we hold an Exposition we will get practically all of the California tourists, besides thousands who will come especially to see the Exposition. An Exposition will give all travelers a reason to choose California as their objective and to come to San Diego.

San Diego, a city of 165,000 with its many cultural advantages, its new boulevards, and places of amusement, is a vastly different city from the San Diego of 1915. As a place to live it will appeal to a far greater number. Those who stay or come back will buy homes, or lots on which to build. Building homes for new residents will bring prosperity—it always has.

How the $500,000 Will Be Spent

There is not another city in the United States that could stage an International Exposition for only half a million dollars. Half of this $500,000 is to be used in promoting the Exposition; the other half is to be reserved for running expenses during the Exposition period. In addition to this will be the gate receipts, which should be double what they were in 1915, when they totaled $550,000. We will also have receipts from the sale of space, estimated at over $200,000—so I am forced to agree with Donald E. Hanson, comptroller of the Spreckels companies, who said:

"We have gone into the Exposition budget thoroughly. We have gone over the books of San Diego's 1915 Exposition. It is our opinion that every cent advanced to this fund will be returned to all subscribers, and that if it was in the form of stock, it might pay a dividend."

The Spreckels companies subscribed $50,000.

But this business of returning the money is of comparatively little consequence. The real point is the enormous profits that will accrue to San Diego city and county business by the carrying out of a program of expansion that should give us another 50 per cent or more increase in population by 1940.

By carrying out such a program every subscriber should get back through indirect profits ten, twenty, possibly fifty, times his investment.

What Kind of Exposition

The question is often asked, "What kind of Exposition are we to have?"

We are not going to have any kind of Exposition unless we get one-half million dollars in subscriptions.

If this fund is raised, no one need worry about the kind of Exposition we are to have. That feature is in competent hands.

Zack Farmer, who so successfully conducted the Olympic Meet at Los Angeles in 1932, is to be the manager of the California Pacific International Exposition—if held.

Mr. Farmer said: "From all parts of the globe will be assembled the strange and picturesque wonders of faraway scenes, peoples, homes, industries, quaint customs, all phases of life abroad.

"Industry and commerce, businesses of all kinds, are contributing to the spectacle of man's versatility that will be spread before the millions of visitors. Unusual and striking exhibitions will tell to the world the triumphant story of the progress of commerce.

Magnificent Setting

"There is probably no setting in all the world quite so beautiful and adaptable for an Exposition as vast and picturesque Balboa Park with its delicate spires and graceful frescoes, its long, winding walks through a forest of luxuriant trees and exotic tropical foliage.

"Blending with the theme of culture and beauty will be the saga of scientific achievement, from the cloistered savant toiling laboriously in his tiny workshop to the drama of progress as enacted in the laboratories of the great scientific institutions of the world. There will be atmosphere at the California Pacific International Exposition."

If we hold this Exposition in San Diego next year, it will be a gem unsurpassed; an Exposition with an irresistible appeal to the outside world; an Exposition that will delight all who see it.

Like automobiles and airplanes, expositions have been refined in the past twenty years since our own last bow to the world. The Exposition of today is a live, virile, moving thing that makes the heart beat faster and brings the visitor back through the turnstiles again and again. Every time a visitor goes through the turnstiles of our Exposition we tie him closer to the possibility of San Diego citizenship.

International Flavor

It is expected the flags of fifteen nations will float from as many masts in San Diego's 1935 Exposition—if we hold it. The management—the best the West had to produce—is working long shifts on preliminary work, getting ready to leap forward on September 15, if you say the word.

The management, Mr. Farmer and J. David Larson, have been straining at the bit since our meeting of July 20 because the time is exceedingly short in which to make plans, secure exhibits, and build and equip a World Exposition to be held starting May 29, 1935. That is the last possible opening date if we are to secure Chicago exhibits. It is only because of the Chicago exhibits, which we can get as a nucleus, that it is possible to stage an Exposition in San Diego for so comparatively small a sum as $500,000. Our last Exposition cost more than three million dollars, and it required five years to build.

Great Forward Stride

The building of this proposed Exposition holds promise of being the greatest forward step in San Diego's development in nearly two decades.

The Exposition will pour into San Diego city and county many millions of dollars of new capital which will lift businessmen and firms to a new plane. It will bring to our city many men of wealth and vision who otherwise might never see San Diego.

It will weld the city and county administrations and the businessmen into the most powerful organization for the advancement of San Diego

Historical Collection, Title Insurance and Trust Company, Union Title Office, San Diego, California

THE 1935 EXPOSITION: The BOTANICAL BUILDING and its lovely reflection in the lily pool. Allowed to fall into disrepair after 1935, the building was completely restored during 1960–61 and now houses a vast collection of tropical flowers and plants.

THE 1935 EXPOSITION: Spanish dancers and lovely *señoritas* on the balconies added to the atmosphere.

THE 1935 EXPOSITION: The California Tower and other beautiful Exposition architecture at night, with reflections in one of the lagoons.

Historical Collection, Title Insurance and Trust Company, Union Title Office, San Diego, California

THE 1935 EXPOSITION: The beautiful Firestone Fountain located in front of the rotunda (not shown) of the Ford Building. The sprays were sometimes twice this height, and at night were beautifully illuminated.

Historical Collection, Title Insurance and Trust Company, Union Title Office, San Diego, California

THE 1935 EXPOSITION: View along El Prado, with the California Tower and the dome of the State of California Building in the background. The cone-shaped trees extend east along El Prado from Sixth Avenue to Park Boulevard. At Christmas time, each one is now draped with Christmas lights, and El Prado becomes Christmas Tree Lane.

Laura Anna Cotton, a recent photograph.

Violet and Oscar W. Cotton—fiftieth wedding anniversary, May 9, 1957—at the home of their daughter, Jane, and their son-in-law, Willis H. Fletcher.

Violet and Oscar Cotton with their family, May 9, 1957: (*seated in front*) Betsy Cotton, Mary Fletcher, (*seated, second row*) Diane Fletcher, Violet and Oscar Cotton, Peg Cotton, (*standing*) Joan Cotton, Elizabeth Cotton, Margaret Cotton, Susan Fletcher, Jane Fletcher; (*in rear*) William Cotton, John Cotton, and Willis Fletcher.

city and county that this southwest corner of the United States has ever witnessed.

In his address on July 20, G. Aubrey Davidson, chairman of the Board, said: "There was never a more united people in the history of this country than we had in the days of 1909. If we can bring about that condition again, which I am sure we can, it will be worth while, and it will be worth the cost of the entire Exposition if we can have the entire community pulling for the general happiness of the people."

It Pays to Advertise

Advertising pays when you have something to advertise. No amount of advertising of San Diego today could be made to pay sufficient returns to justify its cost. But if we hold this Exposition we will have something to advertise, and with this Exposition $50,000 in advertising will do more for San Diego, to put us again in the limelight of the world, than would one million dollars without the Exposition. Never has San Diego had such an opportunity.

Of the hundreds of thousands of those who come to our city and get into the spirit of living conditions here through visiting again and again our beautiful Balboa Park, many will stay. Others will return home only to come back, and all will sing the praises of San Diego far and wide. They cannot help it.

The 1935 Exposition, if held, will scatter over the United States hundred of thousands of walking salesmen for San Diego. With such a widespread sales organization, a united city and county can capitalize on this outstanding opportunity and, by advertising, keep a continuous stream of new population flowing into San Diego for a period of years.

San Diego's Opportunity

The lure of southern California will always bring to our state the people of means from the entire nation. But Los Angeles looks small to a man from New York or Chicago, and San Diego, with only 165,000 population, is beneath his notice. That is why we get only a sprinkling of the vast number of visitors who come annually to Los Angeles. But during the Exposition period we will get practically all of the better class of tourists.

THIS PROPOSED EXPOSITION IS SAN DIEGO'S OPPORTUNITY. WHEN THE SOLICITORS CALL, BE READY. HELP THEM PUT THIS OVER.

CALIFORNIA PACIFIC INERNATIONAL
EXPOSITION COMPANY

G. Aubrey Davidson, *Chairman of the Board*
Frank G. Belcher, *President*
O. W. Cotton, *General Chairman and Campaign Director*
—*$500,000 Loan Fund Committee*

Hon. George Burnham, *Vice-President*
Joseph E. Dryer, *Vice-President*
John F. Forward, Jr., *Vice-President*
John L. Fox, *Vice-President*
Guilford H. Whitney, *Vice-President*
Emil Klicka, *Treasurer*
Roy E. Hegg, *Secretary*

DIRECTORS

Walter Ames	William D. Frisbie
G. W. Anderson	Herbert L. Jaffee
Fred L. Annable	Fred Lockwood
Dayton L. Ault	Baron Long
Elwood T. Bailey	Theodore C. Macaulay
E. S. Bernard	Samuel E. Mason
A. C. Bartlett	William R. Wheeler
Donald C. Burnham	Albert V. Mayrhofer
W. B. George	David N. Millan
Asher E. Holloway	Samuel S. Porter
Thomas M. Hurley	William F. Raber
Harry E. Callaway	Douglas Young
Walter M. Casey	Albert E. Scott
O. W. Cotton	Wynne L. VanSchaick
Frank Drugan	Harry Warburton
Samuel I. Fox	Lane D. Webber

We ran this ad in the middle of August and we closed the campaign on the nineteenth day of September with oversubscriptions of nearly $200,000. The most successful money-raising campaign of that character ever held in San Diego up until that time. That was the beginning of another tremendous upsurge in San Diego's growth and prosperity.

The summer and fall of 1934 the entire United States was still in the doldrums from the Wall Street Crash of 1929, and the fact that little old San Diego, a city of 165,000 people, could raise nearly three-quarters of a million dollars by public subscription to build an Exposition, went through the country like wildfire.

Immediately following the closing of the campaign for funds, the Exposition Management took over and began the development of a new Balboa Park, and the community, as it had done before in preparation for the 1915 Exposition, started a clean-up and a paint-up campaign to give the city a "new look."

CALIFORNIA PACIFIC INTERNATIONAL EXPOSITION
San Diego
Headquarters: Top Floor, U.S. Grant
Hotel, San Diego, California

September 26, 1934

DEAR MR. COTTON:

Acting under instruction of the Board of Directors, at its meeting on September 25, I have the honor to convey to you, on behalf of the California Pacific International Exposition, sincere thanks for your successful leadership of the Fund-Raising Campaign, which, to date, has provided more than $700,000 for the promotion and operation of the Exposition.

Faithfully,
CALIFORNIA
PACIFIC INTERNATIONAL
EXPOSITION
FRANK DRUGAN
Executive Secretary

SAN DIEGO CHAMBER OF COMMERCE
Organized 1870
San Diego, California

September 26, 1934

DEAR MR. COTTON:

The following is an extract from the Minutes of the meeting of the Board of Directors of this organization held Thursday, September 20:

"On motion by Director Burnham, seconded by Director Dryer, and carried, a resolution was adopted thanking and commending Mr. Oscar W. Cotton for his successful efforts in behalf of the 1935 Exposition loan fund campaign and endorsing his proposed five-year plan."

We would like to add to this extract from the Minutes that the officers, directors, and staff of this organization were exceedingly proud of the splendid way in which you handled this campaign for the raising of funds for the Exposition. The way in which the campaign was conducted not only redounded to the fame of San Diego, but also to the credit of you personally as a most valuable civic leader and worker. Those of us who have had the pleasure of being associated with you in the past in civic work are particularly gratified at the splendid work that you have performed, and to the congratulations and best wishes of this organization I desire to add that, personally, I feel you have played a most important part in bringing to San Diego a new era of growth and prosperity through the medium of this Exposition.

With all good wishes,

Very sincerely yours,
SAN DIEGO CHAMBER OF COMMERCE
By: T. C. MACAULAY, *Executive Manager*

THE FIRST NATIONAL TRUST AND SAVINGS BANK
of San Diego
Oldest Bank in San Diego

Lane D. Webber
Vice-President   October 8, 1934

MY DEAR OSCAR:

Your most friendly letter of recent date, with its good wishes and thanks for my assistance in the Exposition fund campaign, is much appreciated. What little I was able to do was done cheerfully and with the zeal of a long-time resident and an Exposition enthusiast.

Recognition and commendation for the startling success of the campaign belong to you personally and the little group of men who made possible this remarkable showing. To you and them, I doff my hat and offer my most sincere congratulations and thanks.

May I express the hope that the fruition of our dream and efforts will exceed even the high mark set for our undertaking.

With warm personal regards

Sincerely yours,
LANE D. WEBBER

DANCIGER BROTHERS
W. T. WAGGONER BUILDING
FORT WORTH, TEXAS

October 1, 1934

DEAR MR. COTTON:

I would appreciate very keenly your kindness in sending me a copy of the San Diego *Union* of September 20, describing what I consider a glorious day for San Diego. It is hard to believe that quiet, sedate, lady-like San Diego could rise to this occasion. By this action, she has demonstrated that she is made of the proper mettle, and her people deserve a world of credit for having, at a trying time like this, put over one of the most difficult feats capable of being accomplished. With this spirit San Diego should even surpass her two hundred and fifty thousand goal by 1940.

If it were not for such men as you and your able lieutenants, I feel satisfied she never would have made the grade. You have done a marvelous piece of work and deserve more credit than the people will ever be able to bestow. The work which you have done and are now doing will, of course, redound not only to your credit, but to the advantage of thousands of San Diego citizens. I hope you get more than your share. You deserve it.

Please accept my congratulations for a fine piece of work magnificently accomplished.

Sincerely yours,
DAN DANCIGER

Mr. Don E. Hanson,
208-A Union Building
San Diego, California   September 26, 1934

DEAR MR. HANSON:

I cannot wind up my duties as General Chairman of the California Pacific International Exposition half-million-dollar campaign fund without expressing to you my sincere apreciation of your splendid cooperation.

In the years to come, I believe we will each of us look back on this campaign as an epoch-making event, the turning of the tide for San Diego; a campaign in which the part we all played will be recalled with pleasure and satisfaction.

We received 3,275 pledges with a total of $700,647; an oversubscription nearly 100 percent in excess of our required goal of $200,000. This is a marvelous achievement for a city of 165,000 population at the bottom of the depression. This success was attained only through the combined efforts of more than four hundred workers, and to all these workers must go the credit.

In addition to the splendid results from your solicitation of funds, your work on the Speakers Bureau was of outstanding value because you covered the field which no one else on our Speakers Bureau was equipped to do.

While putting over this Exposition Fund, you, together with the other campaign workers, have instilled a new spirit into San Diego, a spirit that can be fostered and made to carry our community to new heights in development and prosperity.

I have enjoyed every hour of every day in my work with this "gallant 400," as the San Diego *Sun* termed our campaign organization. It is with keen regret that I step out of the chairmanship which has brought me so many new friends and acquaintances and cemented old friendships more firmly.

Please accept my hearty thanks for the time and effort you gave to this great cause.

Cordially yours,
O. W. COTTON
General Chairman & Campaign Director

As is usual on such an occasion, scores of heart-warming congratulatory letters and messages poured in from all quarters.

CHAPTER XXXVIII

Criticism

IN 1934, Frank J. Belcher, Jr., was the general manager of all of the Spreckels companies, with headquarters in San Francisco. When the holding of this Exposition was first suggested and the Spreckels companies were asked to subscribe $50,000, Mr. Belcher said they would do so provided the Exposition's directors would employ Zack Farmer as manager, to stage the show. Mr. Belcher had been connected with a Los Angeles Olympic Committee a year or two previously, and had seen Zack Farmer make an outstanding success of holding the Olympic Games in Los Angeles. He knew Farmer could do the job.

Farmer was employed, and the first thing he did was to start bringing men from Los Angeles and elsewhere, whose capabilities he knew, to get the job done. This brought down on his head and on the heads of the entire Management and Board of Directors, the most severe criticism by many of San Diego's businessmen. Two months before the Exposition was scheduled to open, criticism of the Management had developed to such an extent that the Management was devoting half its time trying to combat the criticism, and the other half to building the Exposition.

Finally, the Board of Directors determined to give a dinner party for all of the men and women of the press, of San Diego city and county, and explain to them why this hiring of these men from Los Angeles and elsewhere was a necessary procedure. I was asked to make the speech. President Frank G. Belcher called the meeting. The party was held in the Gold Room of the U. S. Grant Hotel. There were 135 members of the press present.

One meeting did the job. The enlightened press sold the community and the criticism dried up throughout the county within a week. Here is the "persuasion":

CRITICISM—CONFIDENTIAL—OFF THE RECORDS

Most criticism is based on lack of information or lack of thought and analysis of the individual problem with its relation to the whole.

Undoubtedly all of you have heard the Exposition Management criticized because they have brought outsiders to San Diego to build our Exposition. Within the past ten days one man stood up in an Exposition directors' meeting and made the positive statement that out of 211 executive employees, more than one hundred were outsiders.

That was like throwing a bombshell in the audience, and it cut the Management who were present to the quick, not because it was true, and it is true, but because the speaker did not explain why this was done. Probably he himself had never analyzed this problem of "outsiders."

One day when the Exposition was still in the formative stage, a prominent banker said to me, "I think it is a mistake to bring in outside men to stage this Exposition, because they will not have the San Diego viewpoint." I asked him who there was in San Diego who could do the job, and after a few minutes he said, "Well, I guess you are right; there isn't anybody in San Diego who could do it."

If any of us in this room had an intricate mechanical job to be done, we would select the best mechanic we knew and then we would allow that mechanic to select his own tools.

Zack Farmer came to San Diego to build for us an Exposition in nine months. He looked over the ground, made his plans, sent for his tools, and went to work. His tools consisted of more than one hundred men and women.

It is not because these "outsiders" have more intelligence than we who have lived here for the last quarter century that Zack Farmer brought them here to do this job, but because their past experiences have fitted them to do the specific things which must be done and done quickly if we are to open this Exposition on May 29th.

Crazy with the Heat

Within two days after I announced my intention of using the word "if" as a basis for raising the Exposition Campaign Funds, J. David Larson, executive manager of the Exposition and Mr. Farmer's right-hand man, wrote a two-page letter to Mr. Belcher telling him that I was all wet, that my program for carrying on the campaign would be a detriment to the Exposition, and was not necessary. He said it could be handled in other ways just as well, etc., etc. After the campaign, I went to Mr. Larson's office and told him I would like him to tell me specifically how he would have done it. Larson burst out laughing and said, "I was crazy with the heat!"

But when it came to laying out the floor plans in our old Exposition buildings, apportioning space for the different kinds of exhibits, determining what prices to charge exhibitors, and how to arrange the selling force, who to solicit, and what to sell them in order to get them to come here and exhibit, and planning all of the thousands of small and large but all-important details that are necessary to the success of a great enterprise such as this, I want to tell you that Larson was a past master.

Ticket Sale

You will all remember that when we started the campaign for funds $300,000 had already been promised. We needed only $200,000 additional, presumably. During the early stages of the campaign many San Diegans suggested to me that we abandon the scheme, which to them seemed impossible, of raising this money by subscription, and instead put on an annual ticket sale.

No doubt $200,000 could have been raised in this way, but I foresaw, as did all those connected with the Exposition Committee, that we would need a ticket sale later. My only fear was that when the time came to sell these tickets I would be asked to do the job.

Had I been asked to put on a ticket sale for the campaign, I would have gone to work in much the same fashion as I did in the campaign for funds. I would have sold those tickets all in San Diego. Frankly, it would never have occurred to me that an advance ticket sale for a San Diego Exposition could successfully be carried on anywhere except in San Diego.

Harry P. Harrisson

One night at an Executive Commitee meeting, Zack Farmer introduced his ticket salesman, Mr. Harry P. Harrisson, another "outsider," this time from Illinois.

Before Mr. Harrisson had talked to us five minutes about his proposed plan, I realized that we in San Diego were going to learn something about how to sell tickets. Mr. Harrisson has been selling tickets for the last twenty years. I believe there is no question but that he is the most expert ticket seller in the United States. He sold millions of tickets for the Chicago World Fair.

He has contracted to sell a million souvenir tickets for our San Diego Exposition, and the startling thing about his program is that he expects to sell, and will sell, at least three-quarters of a million of these tickets outside of San Diego, and every time he sells ten thousand tickets in San Francisco, or Chicago, or elsewhere, he has made of every purchaser of those tickets the best possible advertisement not only for our Exposition, but for San Diego.

The secret of Mr. Harrisson's success in what would otherwise be an impossible task is that he gives a 50 percent bonus to the ticket purchaser by adding a 25-cent concession coupon to each souvenir ticket and then he makes selling agencies of the churches, societies, clubs, stores, banks, and newspapers. In this manner, Harrisson gets for San Diego and the Exposition the advertising by the individual purchasers and also page after page of display advertising in the newspapers by the selling agencies.

J. W. Robinson Co.

For example, the day after these tickets were put on sale in Los Angeles, the J. W. Robinson Company ran a quarter-page ad in the Los Angeles *Sunday Times* devoted exclusively to the San Diego Exposition and the sale of these tickets. You have doubtless seen some smaller advertisements already in San Diego papers by the Marston Company and others. The work Mr. Harrisson is doing for our Exposition and for San Diego will be invaluable. There is no question in my mind but that he will sell a million tickets.

An Investment

Who in this room would ever have thought of such an idea as buying souvenir tickets to the Exposition as an investment? Mr. Harrisson in two minutes convinced me that these souvenir tickets can be bought by the institutions who are handling them not only as a safe investment, but as a profitable investment as well. This is true because of Harrisson's general plan on which his ticket selling is based, the concessions coupon bonus that goes with the ticket to the purchaser, the limited number of bonus tickets to be sold, stopping of the sale before the opening of the Exposition, and their wide distribution. After reviewing Harrisson's plan of sale, I have no doubt but that these $2.50 books of souvenir tickets will sell for $3 before the end of the summer. Like Zack Farmer and J. David Larson, Mr. Harrisson is another past master in his particular line.

Passes

I have heard the thought expressed that it was a mistake that the Exposition Management was not issuing passes for advertising purposes. This is merely an unfounded rumor. A few days ago, Zack Farmer told us that he had already prepared a list of more than eight thousand newspaper men and women to whom passes would be issued. The Management plans to be most generous with the distribution of passes to newspaper people and publishers, but, aside from this particular class, it will be "thumbs down." Every officer, director, and every member of the Executive Committee will pay for his own ticket to the Exposition. The first eleven annual tickets have already been purchased by the Executive Committee.

$3,000 per Day

It will cost $3,000 per day, or $90,000 per month, to run this Exposition. It cannot be operated without a gate. The gate cannot be given away. We are inviting the nation to come to San Diego and see America's great show of 1935. We must give them entertainment when they come. We cannot do this without a gate. It is legitimate to give passes to the press, because it is the press that is helping us to make this show, but it will not be possible to give passes elsewhere and conduct the show, and they will not be given.

Great American Prerogative

I want to repeat and emphasize the statement of the director who said that Farmer had brought to San Diego more than one hundred outsiders to stage this Exposition. He did bring these outsiders. He has them here. They are the tools with which he is successfully building the greatest Exposition ever held by any city in the United States of our population. With these tools he is building this Exposition in nine months.

Anyone who speaks in criticism of the Management's bringing "outsiders" to San Diego to build this Exposition or of Byllesby and Company in sending Colonel Raber to manage the Gas Company, or of the Southern Pacific in sending Fred Annable to manage the San Diego and Arizona Railroad, or of the Scripps-Howard Newspaper Syndicate in sending Al Bartlett here to manage the San Diegan *Sun,* or dozens of others of our leading citizens, is simply using the great American prerogative of talking without thinking.

The fundamental which they overlook is that San Diego is made up of outsiders, and the object of holding this Exposition is to bring more outsiders to build a bigger city.

How Many Natives?

Please let me have a showing of hands of all of those who were born in San Diego. The rest of us, then, are "outsiders." If San Diego waited for the birth rate to build the city, it would be a slow process.

Last year when we put up $700,000 we only started the Exposition. The real financing was done by outsiders, exhibitors, and concessionaires, from Los Angeles to New York, to the tune of millions of dollars to match our $700,000, and these millions of dollars were brought to San Diego through the organization of an inside ring of "outsiders."

As an outsider, I would say, "God bless the outsiders. Let us have more of them. Many more. Let the outsiders who now live in San Diego join with the natives to bring more and yet more outsiders to live among us, and build our city to a population of at least 250,000 by 1940.

$4,500 Printing Job

I have heard criticism expressed of the Management because a $4,500 printing job was given by our Management to a Los Angeles concern. This act was above criticism. It so happened that work could be turned out by the larger facilities in Los Angeles in one-third the time it would have taken in San Diego, and time was all-important.

Exposition Programs

The Exposition programs will be printed in Los Angeles. That will probably be citicized, but it is above criticism, because the Los Angeles firm who is taking this job is so well equipped to handle it that they are paying the Exposition Company a large cash bonus for the privilege of doing so. This could not be done by any San Diego firm. To make sure of this we canvassed the town first. The Exposition needs that cash bonus to help run the show.

Only a Few Highlights

I am only touching on a few of the highlights of some of the things you may have heard about, to give you a peek-in on the picture.

Mistakes

Sometimes the Management is wrong. I know of mistakes that have been made in conducting the Exposition up to the present time. Other mistakes will undoubtedly be made in the future, but outside of those of us who are now in this room, there are only a few people in the entire United States who do not make mistakes. H. H. Timken recently said to me, "A man who is right 51 percent of the time is a success." Fifty-one percent, mind you, and that from H. H. Timken.

One day recently one of the directors of the Exposition took fifteen minutes to tell me of the mistakes made by the Management, and I had to agree with him that these mistakes had been made. I was beginning to get depressed as the total piled up, when finally he cut the discussion short by saying, "But they are making a success of the Exposition."

That is the answer. The Management is building America's Exposition in San Diego in nine months. We are doing it largely with outside capital. All the Pacific Slope, partciularly the southwest portion of California will benefit by the holding of this great Exposition, but San Diego, the city where the Exposition is held, will be by far the greatest benefactor. We are being, and will continue to be, advertised as no city of our population has ever been advertised before.

Publicity

One clipping bureau which supplies us with possibly one-third of our clippings has reported to Mr. Belcher to date more than *90,000 column inches* of publicity, and this is just a starter; the big volume will come later. Now listen to this:

> THE GREYHOUND LINES—are spending
> in display advertising for San Diego
> and our Exposition, in newspapers
> and magazines: $200,000

THE UNITED AIR LINES: 50,000
THE SANTA FE RAILROAD: 100,000
THE SOUTHERN PACIFIC: 100,000
STANDARD OIL: 100,000
SHELL OIL: 100,000
FORD MOTOR COMPANY—Several hundred thousand dollars.
THE SAN FRANCISCO CALL-BULLETIN—is running full-page ads in 100 Middle West newspapers on an Exposition contest.

Many of our main exhibitors will do extensive Exposition advertising. Certainly straight advertising will pass the $1,000,000 mark.

The combined radio advertising will easily pass another million dollars.

All of these items and many more are in addition to the editorial publicity, news items, and write-ups.

$125,000

Now remember that as against this stupendous total the largest sum ever before spent in San Diego advertising in any one year was $125,000, and you can see what this California Pacific International Exposition actually means to us.

700 Percent Increase

Already the Exposition has achieved marvelous results in our return to prosperity. Building permits have been increased from six houses for the entire community for the month of August last year, to forty-eight houses for March this year—an actual increase of 700 percent on home building permits alone, to say nothing of apartments and other buildings.

You have never before seen this city so busy in our downtown district in the month of April, and this is only the beginning. The accomplishments of our Exposition Management have already outstripped our wildest dreams. The Exposition under this Management not only will produce prosperity in San Diego, but it has already done so. There have been mistakes—there will be mistakes; but the big thing is that the Exposition is going over. It is going over magnificently. In one way or another, we are all going to profit. We have hitched our wagon to a star; now let us keep our minds on that star and smile at the ruts and cobblestones in the road. If petty things loom, let us realize that we are looking through the wrong end of the telescope, and reverse our binoculars.

The Golden Chair

The coming Exposition will be the big show of the United States for the year 1935. We San Diegans will be sitting in the golden chair; we can offer our friends who come to see us this year the greatest possible entertainment at the least cost. The California Pacific International Exposition of San Diego will be the biggest and most magnificent Exposition ever held by any city in the United States of our population. Those who come will be charmed.

I hope every man in this room will begin immediately to plan how he and the associations to which he belongs can best capitalize on the Exposition and enjoy it. It is there for you—it won't come again for twenty years. I hope you cash in on your opportunity.

CHAPTER XXXIX

A Beautiful Exposition

THE EXPOSITION was beautiful. The floral effects were little short of breath-taking. Many fine improvements were added to Balboa Park, such as the Old Globe Theatre; the Ford Bowl, which has been a joy and delight for musical events every summer now for some twenty-five years, and many others. The Exposition ran for two seasons, and, by the time it closed for the last night, San Diego was again well on the way to prosperity.

I, personally, profited by the holding of this Exposition in several ways. First and foremost, I was a better man physically and mentally after ten weeks of eighteen hours per day than when I started. The answer for that was that I had learned to work without worrying. That in itself more than paid for my strenuous efforts. I renewed many old friendships and made many new friends.

I built and operated two exhibits for the Spreckels companies through both seasons, and that was fun, especially the "Sea Island Sugar Exhibit," with its animated doll mountain, its free movie theater, and the popular demonstration booth, where we served a delicious assortment of freshly baked cakes, lemonade, and hot chocolate, to demonstrate the Sea Island Sugar.

I had been most fortunate in securing Madeline Childs, a prominent housewife and one of San Diego's outstanding musicians and a "natural cook," to superintend the baking of the cakes. It was one of the most popular booths in the Exposition; we had our choice of the young society set of the town to serve the refreshments, and it was almost like a party every day.

Mrs. Childs, her assistant cake-bakers, and the young ladies serving were all blondes. One day a brunette came to me for a job, and I told her that, for this exhibit, we employed only blondes. She replied, "If you will advance me two dollars, I will be a blonde by tomorrow!"

When the gates were thrown open on the 1935 Exposition, San Diegans had a big surprise in store for them. The Exposition Management, under the direction of Zack Farmer, had done a splendid job. They had been able to obtain practically unlimited labor almost without cost through the then newly formed W.P.A., and they had done a wonderful job in rehabilitating all the beautiful old Exposition buildings. They were also successful in getting the Henry Ford organization to sign on the dotted line.

This was the "key" to our entire show. Ford built the Ford Building for his enormous exhibit, and then he built the Ford Bowl and engaged an excellent symphony orchestra for daily free concerts. In front of the Ford Building, a lovely, large pool, with a beautifully lighted fountain, was put in by the Firestone Company; Harvey S. Firestone was a very close friend of Henry Ford.

Another large reflecting pool occupied considerable of the quadrangle in front of the Fine Arts Gallery.

On the Opening Day, which was a bright, warm, sunshiny day, I was walking up the Avenue from the Spreckels Organ when I met James D. Forward, Sr., who was seeing our new show for the first time. Jim shook his head and had only one word to fit the occasion—"Fabulous!"

And so it was. The floral effects had been carefully planned and carried out by a past master on floral landscaping, and on every hand were huge beds of various flowers, with brilliant coloring, and in exquisite taste. There was no better expression than: "Fabulous!"

Bright sunshine warmed the sea breeze. There was block after beautiful block of flower beds, and with interesting exhibits in every one of the old and the new Exposition buildings, a big "Fun Zone" north of the Botanical Building (and even a Nudist Colony in the canyon off Laurel Street, adjoining the Electric Building), it really was a splendid show and most popular. I expect I spent half my time at the Exposition in the daytime and in the evening during the entire seasons. In some ways, the entertainment in the bright lights of the evening was better than daytime.

Attendance at the 1935 Exposition was nothing like what it would have been in times of prosperity; however, with the splendid publicity the Management obtained for us, it brought enough outside population to make a good start toward pulling San Diego out of another slump. Apartment houses and hotels which had been running with 50 percent or more vacancies were filled and had waiting lists. Home building, which had reached a low of six starts in August, 1934, jumped to fifteen in October, twenty-two in November, and, for the year 1935, there were 597 starts. By the end of the second year (September, 1936) business conditions in San Diego were good.

San Diego's population in 1930 was 147,995. It was probably less in 1934, but it jumped to 203,341 for the Census in 1940.

There were, of course, many contributory factors to this splendid record of accomplishment, but the Exposition and its outstanding opportunity for publicity certainly was a major factor. It was most gratifying to me to see San Diego again started on the upgrade, after five depressing years, and to feel that I had had a share in bringing it about.

CHAPTER XL

O. W. Cotton — Historian

EARLY IN 1936, Carl H. Heilbron decided to write the *History of San Diego County* and he asked me to write the history of real estate in San Diego County, and the history of the San Diego-California Club, and my own biography.

Upon receipt of my copy, he wrote me as follows:

CARL H. HEILBRON
Supervising Editor

History of San Diego County
under the direction of
THE SAN DIEGO PRESS CLUB
937 Sixth Avenue
San Diego, California

May 12, 1936

DEAR OSCAR:

The young lady from your office just delivered your article on the "History of the San Diego-California Club," and I have just finished reading it. It is wonderfully well done, and I am sure it will make interesting reading for everyone who is fortunate enough to secure a copy of our *History of San Diego City and County*. We will be able to print it it in its entirety without having to change a single word.

As indicated to you by telephone, we will be glad to give you an additional two weeks on the other articles suggested, and we can only hope that they will be as satisfactory and as fine as the one on the San Diego-California Club.

With the kindest regards and best wishes, I am,

Sincerely and cordially,
CARL

June 29, 1936

DEAR MR. COTTON:

We are just in receipt of your fine article on the History of Real Estate in San Diego County, and also your biography.

We want you to know how much we appreciate this fine cooperation on your part.

The article on the "History of Real Estate" is exceptionally well done, and we believe will be one of the outstanding articles in our volume.

With best wishes of the writer, we are,

Sincerely and cordially,
HISTORY OF SAN DIEGO COUNTY,
CARL
Carl H. Heilbron,
Supervising Editor

CHAPTER XLI

Our Last Buyer's Market

In 1938, in San Diego we were still working off the homes and other properties that had been taken under foreclosure of trust deeds after the collapse of the building boom of the late twenties. On Sunday, July 31, 1938, I ran a five-column ad full length of the page in the San Diego *Union,* which, as we reread it today, makes a most startling revelation. Frankly, if I did not have it before me now, in indisputable black and white, I would not believe it myself.

As I look at this ad, I remember the campaign perfectly, but I had forgotten that it was as late as 1938. On each side of the ad I printed a list: The names, addresses, and telephone numbers of all realtors in San Diego, Chula Vista, National City, and Coronado. Here is the ad:
(Reprint from the San Diego *Union,*
  Sunday, July, 31, 1938.)

TO HOME BUYERS
and Conservative Investors:

I have just mailed to your favorite real estate broker, whose name you will find herein, a list of 25 homes and income properties from my "hot" file with price range from $1,650 for a good 5-room, plastered house, complete with plumbing, 50 x 135 foot level lot, to a lovely, large, three bedroom home, two tile baths, nearly new, on a 60-foot lot in an exclusive district at $4,750. Some especially fine homes at higher prices. Terms to suit all pocketbooks.

Every home and income property on this list is "handpicked" from our file of over 2,000 listings. Every one is outstanding as to price, value, terms, class, view or some dominating characteristic to give it an irresistible appeal.

Each of these properties is newly priced by the owner for immediate sale under our new Cooperative Exclusive Contract plan which provides that properties so listed shall be placed through my office in the hands of all San Diego brokers for quick results.

As you read this ad, every real estate broker named herein has a complete description of every one of these 25 "hot" properties, and he or one of his salesmen can take you out immediately and show you any one that from the description he has sounds appealing to meet your requirements.

FOR EXAMPLE:

Magnificent harbor view, five rooms, 50x200 ft. very fine lots, four garages. $3,100. Will sell quickly.

$7,000. Investment property returning life income plus owner's apartment. No vacancies in last two years. Five rentals. 4 baths, 1 shower. Good district. 50x140 ft. corner. Total price $7,000. This is "Hot."

Exceptionally fine frame five-room home, good condition; complete furnishings except silver and linen. Some dishes included. Large rooms; 5¢ zone. Rented $35. Full price $2,575. Splendid buy.

Splendid value near McKinley School. Six large rooms, also extra room off garage. Well furnished. Paving paid. Excellent view, good house and all newly done over. Lot has 5,600 sq. ft. $3,950.

Two frame cottages, good condition, 125x125 ft. excellent lot-entirely fenced. Total price, $2,150. Beautifully planted. Houses well built, each has three rooms. Abundant room to build more cottages. Nothing else like this at anywhere near this price.

Nearly new 7-room stucco and tile. Very large rooms, three bedrooms, two tile baths. Gas furnace, two-car garage, 60x115 ft. lot, highly restricted district. Marvelous value at $4,750.

REMEMBER, we have 25 of these hot listings on this list.

Last month on our new Cooperative Exclusive Contract plan we sold for one client alone—the Home Owners' Loan Corporation—17 homes and investment properties in 17 days.

Many of the properties on this new list will sell like the proverbial "hot cakes" so if you want a chance at one, don't delay. Telephone your favorite broker immediately, for an appointment. First come, first served.

For your convenience, here is the list and phone numbers. Clip this ad for reference.

Or come to my office or telephone me, Franklin 7611, and I will show you some of the best bargains. I know them all by heart.

THERE ARE SOME HONEYS ON THIS LIST.

> O. W. COTTON
> REAL ESTATE
> COOPERATIVE EXCLUSIVE
> CONTRACT BROKER

524 B Street—Franklin 7611

CONSTRUCTIVE PUBLICITY

In 1938, I was asked if I would accept, if tendered, the presidency of the San Diego Realty Board. After giving the matter due consideration, I agreed. I was installed at the Annual Meeting of the Board held in the U. S. Grant Hotel on January 10, 1939. In my acceptance speech I said:

> It is indeed a pleasure to accept the honor that has been conferred upon me tonight, an honor of which any realtor may well be proud.
>
> This is the second time I have been so honored. As all of you will doubtless remember, I served as president of this Board in 1915—that was twenty-four years ago. It seems to have taken the Nominating Committee a long time to forget what kind of a president I was! However, I want you to know that I am not only highly honored, but I am most happy to accept this high office, and I shall endeavour to so conduct the affairs of the San Diego Realty Board that I may again be asked to be president, twenty-four years from now—which would be the year 1963. Beyond that, I will not offer any suggestions, because I think a third term is sufficient for any President! [NOTE: In 1939, Franklin Delano Roosevelt was being talked of for a third term.]
>
> Since I arrived in San Diego thirty-five years ago, somewhat younger than today and alone, the population of San Diego has increased from a little frontier village of twenty thousand to a vigorous city of nearly ten times that number. While I do not mean to infer that I am personally responsible for all of this tremendous increase in population, I will admit this much: I have brought to San Diego from Los Angeles one wife; we have two sons and one daughter, and if we count our grandchildren and their inlaws, I can today boast of a family connection in San Diego of more than one hundred! Just what the population of San Diego and this family connection will represent in another twenty-four years, when I hope to again be your president, I will not hazard a guess. Time works miracles!
>
> I am deeply appreciative of all the blessings that have been bestowed upon me in San Diego and particularly of the honor you have bestowed on me tonight.
>
> I thank you.

My reason for taking time to consider acceptance of the presidency was that I wanted to think out what, if anything, I could do to make the Board of greater service to its members and the community. When I had been president in 1915, San Diego real estate was so dead that nothing could be done to get the ball rolling. The plan I determined on for 1939 was one of public relations—to endeavor to build the confidence of the public in the realtors, and to help educate the realtors to inspire and deserve that confidence, and at the same time educate the "should-be" buyers of San Diego real estate on the present opportunities.

It was the psychological time to conduct such a campaign, because San Diego realty prices were still far below what they should have been, in view of the material advances in the city and county, and in the nation, made in the previous four years. At the last Board luncheon before the Annual Meeting, I offered the program:

The real estate business on the present hard market is a man-sized job. To make a success today, the realtor must work as he never worked before—he must think and perform. He must think out ways and means to make a deal and then he must up and at it before the half-baked idea gets cold. He must put everything he's got into every deal and then, before one deal is finished, he must have thought out another and be ready to plunge into that and stay with it. A realtor's job today is an endless chain of rough and tumble fight with a laugh at the end when he hits the ball and a tight-set jaw when he loses.

The real estate business is never easy. It is always fraught with new difficulties, ever-changing conditions, but on no previous market in San Diego have the minds of the investing public been so unsettled as today.

During the boom of 1925-27 you could sell downtown property on a basis of a net yield of 2 per cent and less. Today you can offer good properties at 8 to 12 per cent net with but few takers. Why? Lack of confidence.

There is a craze for building new homes. Only a few weeks ago real estate statistics showed 66 percent of home sales throughout the United States were new homes. Because of the F.H.A., and other low-payment, low-interest, high-loaning agencies, it is easier than ever before for the home seeker to purchase or build a new home, in many instances far beyond his means.

Very few of the new homes sold or built are dealt by realtors. Our business is largely in the sale of used homes, and home seekers don't want them.

A great many deals are lost to realtors because owners and buyers deal direct.

Many deals are lost because one realtor fails to boost the other realtor's deal.

Many deals are lost because the prospect asked his banker's advice, and of course, his banker said "No."

I am not such an optimist as to think we can correct all of these obstacles, but I believe we can go along way to correcting some of them and by so doing greatly increase San Diego's total volume of real estate sales.

This world is a fast-moving sphere. Every line of endeavor is up against ever-changing conditions which must be met and overcome before we ourselves are overcome.

The realtors who operate their businesses under the San Diego Realty Board's Code of Ethics, who take seriously their responsibilities to their fellow realtors and their clients, are far ahead of the old-fashioned brokers who do not even read the *National Real Estate Journal* and do not know how far behind the times they are.

Real Estate, particularly San Diego income real estate, is the best investment a client can make if he buys judiciously on the fairest advice of a realtor who is up on his toes and knows values, trends, and conditions.

The reason we are not doing a greater volume of real estate business in San Diego today is because of lack of confidence by the investing public and lack of knowledge on their part that the realtor is in a position to help them with their problems.

For three decades the realtors have been developing their business methods by the exchange of ideas among members, among boards and associations. The progressive realtor of today smiles to himself as he remembers his own methods of thirty years ago. The realtor has developed his business, he has raised his standards, he has helped his fellow realtor to do likewise, that all might prosper, but he has so far failed in one outstanding matter. He has not properly informed the investing public of this great transition.

The man who does not advertise is like the fellow who winks at his girl in the dark: The fellow knows what he is getting at, but the girl doesn't.

We realtors have been so busy operating our business and learning the new rules and ethics that we have not properly advertised this new realty method to the investing public. There is the weakest link in this great chain of the realtor from the individual realtor's office to the National Association of Real Estate Boards.

I believe the job ahead of us today is the education of the public— not the investing public only, not at all—but the public. We must drive home to them until they cannot fail to see the point that real estate is the best possible investment and that realtors are the agents who can show them the way to profitable investments.

Right here in San Deigo, at the southwest corner of the United States, the first port of call, where California began, the first city of its size to hold a truly beautiful and great Exposition, in 1915, the city that blazed the trail in organized community advertising, it seems to me is a fitting place to launch a program of education of the pubilc on the realtor and what he means to the community and to those who want to invest their capital where it will be safe and at the same time profitable.

About now you are thinking, "It sounds fine, but expensive."

Not at all. You cannot do this thing with money. It won't cost any of us a dollar in money.

I have already arranged to start a series of articles on this subject to be run weekly in the San Diego *Union,* beginning next Sunday.

Each of these articles will deal with a phase of real estate that will build public confidence in real estate itself, and will show by many examples how the realtor can help the investor; how the investor should seek out his favorite realtor in the beginning and solicit his advice on his problem.

Here are some of the titles:

> Old Homes vs. New Homes
> Real Estate Jitters
> Don't Shoot Your Realtor
> Where to Find the Home You Want
> What Net Profit Should San Diego Income Real Estate Yield?
> The Value to Home Seekers in Buying HOLC Properties
> When to Buy San Diego Real Estate
> How to Buy San Diego Real Estate
> Why Not Buy My Home Direct and Save the Commission?
> The Best Way to Sell Your Real Estate
> I'll Ask My Banker

When you step forward into a new field, you never know where the trail may lead. Before this, San Diego has taken the lead in matters that have rolled up like a snowball until they have affected cities in most nations of the civilized world.

Today the world is in such a state of upheaval that many businesses are groping in the dark and hoping for the best. It is just possible that a program of education that will guide the public into safe investments for their funds will not only prove to be an outstanding benefit to the realtors, but it may have a far-reaching influence in helping to turn the tide of sentiment from one of fear to courage.

These articles are to be written for the benefit of the investing public and realtors. Every realtor should read every article and clip it and put it in a scrapbook for reference when you have a hard client. If properly used, these articles will make and save you many deals.

CHAPTER XLII

National Recognition for San Diego

MY SERIES of real estate articles in the San Diego *Union* ran every Sunday for twenty-four consecutive weeks. How much good, if any, in public relations between local realtors and the real estate dealing public these articles accomplished was not visible to the naked eye, so to speak; however, they attracted widespread attention locally and nationally. Many were copied verbatim by the *California Real Estate Magazine* and many other real estate publications. Practically the entire series was published in the October, 1939, issue of the *Publicity and Advertising Magazine* of the National Association of Real Estate Boards, prefaced by the following editorial comment:

A SIX-MONTH EDITORIAL CAMPAIGN— PUBLISHED WITHOUT COST

Have you ever seen a complete and constructive real estate board campaign, one which is easy to read, and is interesting as well as informative?

Have you ever seen publicity in such a campaign that is valuable from the standpoint of the newspaper as well as the real estate board?

All or part of these questions may or may not be answered in the affirmative by you, but the series of 1,000-word articles, written by President O. W. Cotton of the San Diego Board and published weekly from January to June, 1939, in the San Diego *Union,* are of such value that, except for a few omissions, the entire series is herein reproduced.

We know, too, that after reading these articles you will, as we do, thank President Cotton for his fine work in acquainting realtors with some of the live, interesting, and educational facts surrounding his experience in the real estate profession; and for helping us all to more fully understand and realize the importance of bridging the wide gap that exists between real estate and the public.

We do not feel capable of selecting or recomending specific parts or sections of each article for your reading, but feel that the time required to read each article completely is a very sound investment. This series of articles is educational and informative, not alone from the value you personally will receive, but from the standpoint of the facts you will accumulate which you can recommend to others with whom you are associated. Then, too, this series will serve well as reference material in the preparation of advertising publicity for the individual Board.

When the *National Real Estate Journal* ran a cut of the titles of ten of the articles on one page, its accompanying article said in part:

There is always a lot of talk about constructive publicity for real estate boards and realtors, but sometimes the whole thing simmers down to good intentions. In San Diego, however, good ideas have been translated into effective action. President O. W. Cotton, of the San Diego Realty Board, has produced a series of weekly newspaper articles that seem to possess every attribute of a good public relations program. They are easy to read, live, interesting, and informative. More than that no newspaper editor could ask. They are as desirable from the editor's standpoint as from that of the Real Estate Board itelf. And that makes a publicity campaign worthy of anyone's serious consideration.

Recognizing that the publicity value of an article depends solely upon its being read, President Cotton has developed a fast, informal style of writing that gets its point across quickly and interestingly. He tells a good story in each article, and tells it in a way that will get it read.

What did he talk about? The facsimiles of clippings reproduced on the opposite page speak for themselves.

Then followed a series of quotes from the articles.

After a dozen or more of the articles had been published, the San Diego *Union* received the following telegram:

MR O W COTTON, PRESIDENT SAN DIEGO REALTY BOARD WROTE SEVERAL ARTICLES ON REAL ESTATE CONDITIONS STOP WILL YOU RUSH ME VIA AIR MAIL SPECIAL DELIVERY TEAR SHEETS ON EACH OF THESE ARTICLES STOP IF ANY CHARGES SEND BILL AND WILL REMIT IMMEDIATELY.

GEORGIAN AMERICAN, ATLANTA

After excerpts from this series of articles appeared in the *National Real Estate Journal* and *Freehold Magazine,* I received many enthusiastic "fan letters":

From New York City: "We wonder if we can reuse this material to help us in closing deals and in teaching our people how to close deals." —MARX REALTY AND IMPROVEMENT CO., INC.

From Boston, Massachusetts: "From one President to another, I am wondering if you will secure for me the weekly series of articles published in the San Diego *Union,* of which you are the author. I will gladly send a check for whatever the cost may be."—OLD COLONIAL INSURANCE COMPANY.

From Toronto, Canada: "As President of the Ontario Association of

Real Estate Boards I should like very much to get copies of the material you have been writing and publishing."—W. H. BOSLEY & CO.

From Chicago, Illinois: "Thank you so much for the newspaper articles which I have read with great interest and am passing around to all members of our staff, who likewise have found them very interesting and profitable. If the many splendid points you bring out could be embodied in a series of newspaper advertisements, it would be one of the very best forms of advertising that could be done."—EDERLIM REALTY CO., INC.

From Johnstown, Pennsylvania: "You have done just the very thing we have had in mind . . . we wonder if it would be possible to have your newspaper send us copies of each paper in which these articles appear. We shall forward money for the cost of sending papers, etc."—AMOS CAMPBELL & SONS.

At a convention in Los Angeles, a realtor from Monrovia and Long Beach told me with enthusiasm that his office had closed more than 150 deals on the strength of one of these articles, "The Real Estate Jitters."

Finally, after my term in office had expired, I put the series in book form and the San Diego Realty Board sold them throughout the state. One day my old friend, Ed Davis, then of Covina, wrote me that he was going into the real estate business and that he had gone to the Los Angeles Realty Board and asked the Secretary what books would be of most help to him. The secretary told him my book *How to Deal in Real Estate* was the best book of which he knew.

I received a postcard May 17, 1947, with the following message:

DEAR SIR:

It has been my pleasure to sit in on a course of instruction in real estate salesmanship given by Dr. Ives of the University of Southern California. He very highly recommends your publication entitled *How to Deal Real Estate.*

Please advise as to where to obtain a copy in this vicinity, or if necessary, to have one sent direct from you, include price, and oblige,

> M. B. STINNETT,
> 4901 E. 60th Place
> Maywood, California

One day my son, William, took a deposit of $1,000 from a good realtor friend of mine, Albert J. Jones, on an Offer to Purchase a lovely home in Mission Hills, San Diego, at about one-half what it was worth (which was the going rate on fine homes at that time). Early the next morning, Albert called me on the telephone and said he wanted to get out of the deal. He thought it was a mistake for him to buy the house. He said he would divide the $1,000 with William, if we would return his Offer to Purchase. I asked him if he could see me if I came over, and he said, "Certainly."

When I arrived, I sat down and admired the view of San Diego Harbor from his windows on the top floor of the California Theatre Building, and talked about the weather and one thing and another until he was relaxed and his mind was at ease. Then I asked him if he would take fifteen minutes to read an article in a book I was publishing, if I would send it over. He said he certainly would. I went back to my office three blocks away, and sent a copy to him by messenger, with the article marked that he was to read, "Real Estate Jitters."

Within an hour, Jones telephoned me that he would go through with the deal, and he did. Some years later, he sold the home for a price which was in the neighborhood of twice what he had paid for it. Here is the article:

REAL ESTATE JITTERS

After a man has definitely made an offer and put up his money in the purchase of a piece of real estate, in ninety-nine cases out of one hundred he gets the "jitters."

It doesn't matter whether it is a home, an income property, or a vacant lot, after he has once taken the step and had a night to sleep over it, he begins to wonder whether he has made a mistake. He forgets the salient points which were explained to him by the realtor, and which motivated his purchase; he remembers the dozen and one things which he forgot to ask about or which were explained to him and to which he forgot the answers.

He wonders if he paid too much for the property; if by angling further he might not have got it cheaper or if he had looked further he might not have found a better bargain. I should say that, in approximately nine cases out of ten, the next day after a man has made a real estate purchase, he thinks he would like to have his money back, if he could get it.

This ominous malady, the real estate "jitters," not only rattles the purchaser who pays all the property is worth, but it affects equally the man who gets the best bargain of the year in all San Diego. When I estimate that ninety-nine out of one hundred purchasers get the real estate "jitters," I want to include the realtors when they themselves make real estate purchases. I know, because I personally have been in the real estate brokerage business for thirty-five years and I get the real estate "jitters" every time I make a deposit to buy a piece of real estate for myself. I had the real estate "jitters" after making the very best real estate investment I ever made.

The real estate "jitters" is wholly mental. It has nothing to do with the value of the property or the kind of a deal the purchaser is making. It is a fear that takes possession of the mind of the purchaser after he has made the first plunge. That is why, in making offers on real estate, it is necessary that the purchaser put up a cash forfeit before the owner of the property will take his offer seriously because past experience has convinced most owners that a verbal or even a written offer without a substantial cash deposit is not to be taken seriously, and the reason for this is the real estate "jitters."

To my amazement, one of San Diego's foremost ministers told me one day that he never stood upon his feet to make a speech or preach a sermon without being so nervous at the outset that he could hardly speak. He went further to say that he did not believe a man could make a good speech unless he was nervous; that if he put his heart and mind into the undertaking it wrought him up to such a pitch that the performance reacted on his nervous system.

Real estate "jitters" come from nervous reaction, which is a letdown after one takes the first plunge into a new venture. After all the years of my experience in dealing with San Diego real estate for clients and myself, when I now personally make a real estate investment I endeavor to keep my head level, using my best judgment, and almost invariably purchasing through another realtor, because in that way I get not only the advantage of his additional counsel and advice but also, with him as a go-between, I get a better deal. I then go ahead and make the deposit, knowing full well that the next day I will wish I hadn't done so. Later, when the real estate "jitters" have worn off and the property I have purchased turns into the revenue producer that I had expected it would, I have a little quiet laugh at myself as I realize that the next time I personally make a real estate purchase exactly the same thing will happen again.

So let me give this warning to prospective purchasers of real estate— the next day after you have made your offer, or possibly three days later, since the nerves in some people work slower, don't be frightened when you get the real estate "jitters." Remember, if you have given full consideration to the property and consulted well with your realtor before making your purchase, that in the long run the investment will work out something like you expected it would when you put up your deposit. Remember that you are only one of the ninety-nine out of one hundred who get the real estate "jitters" every time they make a purchase and that if it were possible to throw up this deal over which you are now having the "jitters," the same "jitters" would come back to you with new vigor when you make your next purchase.

In contemplating an investment in San Diego real estate, than which there is no better investment for San Diegans, consider well what you are doing before you put up the deposit. Go over all points carefully with your realtor, secure his full counsel and advice, and then go straight ahead.

Remember that San Diego is in southern California, a place where more people want to come to live than ever get here; a place that has a future of double and treble our present population; of increased realty values and wonderful expansion in years of prosperity.

Remember that each bull market for the last seventy years has carried San Diego real estate values higher than any previous boom, and that the time to make real estate investments is on the way up, not at the top when everybody is buying.

"Faint heart never won fair lady,"—or battles, or financial success. The real estate "jitters" comes from a faint heart. So when you get it, take it and smile. Hold to your course and when good old San Diego blossoms into a new prosperity, you will thank me for this warning.

The final article of the series was published June 18, 1939:

ABOVE THE CLOUDS THE SUN IS STILL SHINING

When a man has finished what he has to say is a good time to stop talking. This might also be considered with regard to members of the fair sex, but I shall not go into that.

We are living in a grand country in this United States of America and we are fortunate. Recently a realtor friend handed me a clipping from the classified advertising columns of a London newspaper. Here it is:

Claygate, Surrey: Waterloo 25 Min.; L2,750.—Charming Family HOUSE set in beautiful grounds; frontage 100 ft., with possession; 7 bed, 4 reception, spacious garage for 4 and cottage; plenty storing room, and *shelter from air raids;* refined. Freehold.— Write Side, Lynton, Foley Road, Claygate. Esher 684.

Those four words, "shelter from air raids," said a lot. We take our individual, local, and national problems seriously, but if we compare, with some of the other nations, our mode of life, our freedom of speech and actions, our latent power that is our best guaranty of security, we cannot fail to realize that our troubles are small indeed.

We American are a high-strung, nervous race. Frightened at every shadow. If it isn't war or other pestilence, it is the political administration or labor strife which furnishes an excuse to the capitalist to hoard his money, without interest, because he has not the courage to buy good real estate. Fear—that is what is eating folks today—mostly fear of ghosts and there are no ghosts.

Those with courage, who have planned their course and leisurely made their investments in good real estate or are now making them, have found great peace of mind. They are taking a broad, long-range view of local, national, and world conditions, and they believe that in the future as in the past the labor, business, and political situations will shift to a more settled state and that this great nation, its states and cities and their back country, will again move forward on the broad platform of the greatest good for the greatest number.

I believe these believers are right. Forty years ago, socialism and the labor unions were the frightening cry of the "bogy" man. During those forty years our whole business and political structure has been changed. I do not believe any fair-minded man or woman would want to get our national clock back forty years. "Isms," reforms, depression waves come and go, but our nation goes on and the capitalists, small or large, who have put their money in their homes and in good income-bearing San Diego real estate, paid off their mortgages, and hold it clear, are today in strong financial position.

I am one of those who has been watching these changing conditions for these forty years. I used to get all hot and bothered about every new "ism" and political change. Many years ago I developed a friendship with a gentleman who had made a financial success and gone broke at the age of forty. He came back and at ninety left a fortune running well into seven figures. One day when the political situation looked blackest for capital, I asked him what he thought of the future and he replied, "Well, Cotton, I find these matters generally work themselves out."

Recently a young man in his early thirties, who has been in business only since 1929 and to whom all past bull markets are but hearsay, said, "You hear a lot of talk about good times but I think we are in good times right now. They don't need to get any better to suit me. I think the old-fashioned booms will never come again." Possibly three weeks later another friend of mine, a gentleman who has seen more cycles of bull and bear markets than I have ever seen said, "We are headed for inflation and nothing is going to stop us." "Well," I answered, "what then?" "We'll still be here," he replied. Both of these gentlemen are pursuing their respective courses as they see them. They are determined, conservative, and serene; they are living in the present but with confidence in the future.

"Hope springs eternal in the human breast." Also does discouragement, but like the "real estate jitters," these unsettling wide fluctuations of sentiment are largely mental. As the man or woman who makes a success in any undertaking, the successful real estate investor must determine on a course and stay put.

It will be a long time before this world comes to an end or the United States sinks to the bottom of the ocean. Those who wait until all arguments are settled before making their investments are going to have a long wait and lose a lot of good income and increment on their capital.

The thought which prompted the writing of this series of articles was to give to the real-estate-minded public a better understanding of the problems in the buying, owning, and selling of real estate and to furnish a manual for the realtor with which to illustrate the vital points in the various phases of the transactions.

While the series was written with a San Diego, California, background, the problems which confront us here in the southwest corner of the United States are the same problems which confront the realtors and the public in all of our progressive cities.

In pointing out the advantages to be gained by the layman in discussing his real estate problems with his realtor, I have not intended to convey the impression that your realtor is infallible. Of course, realtors make mistakes the same as our doctors, lawyers, and businessmen make mistakes, but, in the law of averages, prospective investors and owners of real estate will gain the maximum profit through cooperation and establishment of confidential relationship with their realtors, thereby securing their full help, advice, and guidance.

Though sometimes he may be wrong, the realtor's knowledge and experience on real estate matters is worth vastly more than the superficial opinion or sentiment of the layman who does not have the background of training and experience of the realtor.

There are many separate real estate fields and realtor specialists, but, even in a comparatively small city, the local realtor, through the publications of the National Association, of which all realtors are members, has access to detailed information on the best and most approved methods of sales and all types of real estate management throughout the entire United States. An "up on his toes" realtor in San Diego should be able to give you the same quality of service the New York City realtor gives his clients. We have this information here in our San Diego offices for you if you want it.

In behalf of the San Diego Realty Board, I want to extend our sincere appreciation to the San Diego *Union* for its splendid cooperation in the prominent display of this series of articles. The broad vision of its owner and editor in matters of civic and national value is too well known to need comment from me, but the subject of real estate transactions might easily have been sidetracked by a publication with an editorial staff of less understanding.

I should also like to express appreciation for the pages of splendid publicity given San Diego and this series by the *National Real Estate Journal, Freehold,* and the *California Real Estate Magazine.* I am free to confess that national recognition of these articles, "fan" letters, and words of commendation from my realtor colleagues and friends acted as a material stimulant and gave me encouragement while buring the midnight oil in their production.

The enthusiastic and highly complimentary "fan mail" I received from leading realtors from all parts of the country, with requests for copies and permission to republish the series, was most gratifying:

HOME OWNERS' LOAN CORPORATION

Regional Office   Pacific Building
                                   San Francisco

DEAR MR. COTTON:

Here is a copy of a Memo received by me from Mr. Ward Cox, my Assistant in Charge of Property Management for this Region.

I thought you would be interested to note the excellent effect which your booklet, so kindly sent to me and distributed by me among our people, has had among the technicians in our organization charged with handling our properties.

I share their own conclusions about it, and thank you again for remembering me.

With regards,

JAMES TWOHY
Regional Manager

HOME OWNERS' LOAN CORPORATION

Pacific Building   San Francisco
MEMO   August 17, 1939
To: Mr. James Twohy,   *Subject:* Mr. O. W. Cotton's Manuscript:
    Regional Manager   *How to Deal Real Estate*

On the whole, this is a very interesting series of articles. It is my opinion that Mr. Cotton has gone further into the many fundamentals of the real estate business than any similar treatment of the subject which I have read.

Mr. Cotton, as president of the San Diego Real Estate Board, and because of his interest in the California Real Estate Association, as well as national real estate affairs for a good many years, has naturally emphasized consultation with a realtor, who, as you know, must be a member of the Association before he is permitted to use that title.

I have passed this valuable treatise on to my deputy, Mr. Lee Taylor, also to Mr. O. H. Peterson, Regional Supervisor of Sales, and his assistant, Mr. W. B. Adams. Each one has read it with profit and enthusiasm for its matter-of-fact handling of an important subject.

There are many interesting articles in the group, particularly the one on "I Will Ask My Banker." From my own experience, I believe that all of us in the real estate business have been up against that re-action and have not only been subjected to the points which Mr. Cotton so ably brings out, but also to the uninformed opinions handed out "willy-nilly" fashion by paying tellers, clerks, etc., in various banks.

In my opinion, his article on "Old Homes versus New Homes," as well as the article on HOLC properties, bears out our reconditioning program, and to a certain degree substantiates it, in that our program not only recaptures obsolescence, but secures "eye-appeal" which is even more important from a salesman's point of view.

I believe that every salesman can profit from reading Mr. Cotton's articles not only once but many times.

WARD COX
Assistant Regional Manager
in Charge of Property
Management

JOHN C. HALEY & SONS
Madison, Wisconsin

DEAR MR. COTTON:

I have just completed your latest booklet *How to Deal Real Estate,* and have enjoyed it very much. I am now passing it through the office for our men to read, and I am sure they will get a great deal of good out of it. I can see where the articles were a big help to the business when run by the leading newspaper.

I notice that you have copyrighted these articles. Would you mind if we used these articles, making the changes where necessary for our local community, in our local paper, in somewhat the same method that you did? This is a lazy man's request, and if you have any objection to it don't hesitate to say so. Your articles are well done, and it would save us the bother of making up our own articles to help educate our public. Perhaps I have no right to ask this, but as you have probably had the same request from other individuals for other cities I presume you have a policy worked out.

I have an unusual personal interest in your articles, for the reason that I have seen San Diego grow. Mrs. Haley and myself spent ten weeks at La Jolla in the winter of 1920 and 1921. We have very pleas-ant memories of Point Loma, the Coronado Hotel, and your city parks. We have been there twice since then and have noticed many changes each time. I had no idea the city was as large as it is until I had com-pleted your articles.

Awaiting your reply and thanking you for your tremendous interest in helping the real estate business in a general way, I am,

Yours sincerely,
HARRY B. HALEY

Then, of course, there was "the Other Side of the Picture." In reply to a request, we sent the book, *How to Deal Real Estate* to one party with the usual bill enclosed. When we did not receive a check in due course, another bill was sent with the notation "Undoubtedly overlooked." The book and the bill were returned promptly. Across the face of the bill was written the following note (to avoid embarrassment I am not using the names on the bill):

No, I didn't overlook it—why do you bill Mr. A_____ for something he didn't order? From the way your ad read I had no idea you would turn around and soak me $1.00—if your ad had read that you were charging $1.00, I would feel differently about it. I am returning your book under separate cover. I haven't even looked at it.

MARYBELL G. S_____
with MR. A_____.

CHAPTER XLIII

The Brokers' Institute, N.A.R.B.

IN 1943, Leroy Ackley, of Los Angeles, President of the Brokers' Institute of the National Association of Realty Boards, asked me to conduct a campaign in San Diego to increase the membership in the Brokers' Institute. I accepted, and mailed the following individually addressed and personally signed letter to all our members:

SAN DIEGO REALTY BOARD
San Diego, California

August 29, 1943

DEAR _____:

At my own personal expense I am mailing to you and the other realtors of San Diego $100,000 worth of these letters, FREE!

I want you to join the Brokers' Division of the National Association. Not that it matters to me—it doesn't. Not because the Brokers' Division needs more good members—it does, but that does not matter, either. I want you to join because one year's membership in the Brokers' Division will be of greater value to you than anything else you can possibly buy for $5.

I say one year, because you will never drop out of the Brokers' Division after you join, if it continues half as good as at present. These Brokers' Division bulletins are meat from cover to cover. They get right at the heart of real estate dealing and show the best ways to perform every phase of the business. It's great stuff. I would not stay out of it if it cost $50 a year. The last issue was a "wow." It told enough between its two covers to make a successful real estate salesman or broker out of anyone but a blockhead, and that is only one issue of nearly a dozen we will get this year.

There are one hundred realtors in San Diego who are not members of the Brokers' Division. If you heed this letter and subscribe now, your membership will be worth at least $1,000 to you. I am just as sure of that as I am that my membership has already paid me back several thousand dollars. Remember, only realtors can join. Brokers who are not realtors must struggle with their own problems, while the members of the Brokers' Division know how other realtors, from New York to Los Angeles, are successfully batting 100.

Last week, the Long Beach Board sent in six new members. Salt Lake City, with thirty-two board members has twenty-eight Brokers' Division members. San Diego should have fifty at least.

This is not propaganda—I asked for it. I wrote Chairman Leroy Ackley and asked him to send me one hundred copies of the enclosed leaflet, because I want you to join. Right now, while it's hot, tear off the coupon on page four of the enclosed Brokers' Division leaflet and mail it to Secretary John N. D. Griffith with your check for $5.

If this investment does not pay you $1,000 cash value returns (20,000 percent), I'll buy you a drink. This is an investment—not an expense. Do it now.

Yours for the best in realty service and profits,

O. W. COTTON

I was not particularly pleased with the results, although percentage-wise, it looked good enough. It increased the membership from six to eighteen, or 200 percent. However, Ackley was delighted with the letter and had it used in part or in full again and again. When his term of office drew to a close, he suggested that Joseph Laronge, of Cleveland, Ohio, the incoming president, offer me the regional vice-presidency of the Southwest Division, which included California, Arizona, Utah, Hawaii, and the Philippine Islands.

Ordinarily, the regional vice-president was supposed to travel through-out his district, and talk to the individual Boards to build up membership in the Institute. I knew this, of course, and I knew that it would not be practical for me to carry on such a campaign. I did not want to shirk my responsibilities, however, so I accepted the honor with the mental reservation that I would carry on a "sit-down" campaign for members and do the job by correspondence. I carefully worked out a program and then began a series of circular letters to each of the seventy Realty Boards in my district, with a letter to each board president asking his suggestions for a local committee chairman.

While I was lining up these chairmen, I wrote a letter to every member of our San Diego Realty Board, again inviting them to join the Institute. I then sent copies of these letters to each of my new chairmen, suggesting that they send copies to all members of their respective Boards. I followed up this first letter with a series of about five letters in all. It made a sweet campaign, and surprised a lot of old-timers.

The *California Real Estate Magazine* for September, 1944, said:

CALIFORNIA LEADS IN BROKERS' ENROLLMENT

California is leading the nation in the campaign for new members to the National Institute of Real Estate Brokers of the N.A.R.E.B.

At the Institute Conference in Chicago in January, the Southwest Region, including California, Utah, Nevada, and the Hawaiian and Philippine Islands, was given a quota of 102 new members to be secured this year. As this issue of the *California Real Estate Magazine* goes to press, this region has already sent in subscriptions for over 300 new members, 200 of which were from California alone.

A recent letter from Joseph Laronge, president of the Institute, gave 775 as the total new members for the entire United States. This would give California 20 percent of the total to date.

Actually our California campaign is just getting under way. Maurice G. Read, sales manager of Mason-McDuffie Company of Berkeley, is state chairman for northern California, and Stewart B. Crebs, C.P.M., of Los Angeles, is chairman for southern California. Hobart C. Brady, of Wichita, Kansas, is national chairman of the 1944 Membership Committee.

Invitations have been issued from San Diego to one member of every California real estate board to act as local chairman for his board and invite Broker Institute membership to all local realtors.

For a "sit-down" campaign it was a dandy. I do not remember the final figures, but we led all other districts in the United States by a wide margin, capturing the prizes for both number and percentage. I believe our final report was about 400 percent of our quota.

I had been elected to the directorship and the regional vice-presidency for a three-year term; however, I did not feel that I could afford that much time. I also felt that it would not be fair to be on the Board and not attend meetings, so I gave the Institute everything I had to offer for one year, and then, with my final Report, sent in my resignation. I wrote Leroy Ackley to that effect, and received the following letter in return:

LEROY ACKLEY
161 South LaBrea Avenue
Los Angeles 36

December 14, 1944

DEAR OSCAR:

My hearty congratulations for your wonderful handling of the 1944 membership drive for the Southwest Region. It was most gratifying to me to see you come through as the winner of the prizes.

I am leaving next month for the committee meetings in Chicago, at which time I will consider the matter of your resignation. You see I am on the nominating committee, and if you resign, I might turn right around and have you re-elected.

With all good wishes,

Sincerely,

ROY

(Leroy Ackley)

At the Annual Meeting of the Board of Governors of the National Institute of Real Estate Brokers on January 25, 1945, President Joseph Laronge said:

In Los Angeles, I had the pleasure of congratulating our vice-president, Oscar W. Cotton, on his exceptional job in expanding the membership on the West Coast. He feels he should not continue in his capacity as vice-president for the remainder of his term, and has thus tendered his resignation. His efficient manner of operation was a credit to the Institute, and we will certainly feel the loss of his work. We have on file an outline of the way he organized his committee, and the hints contained therein will be helpful to us in future campaigns. I am proud to say we closed the year with a membership of 5,657—a net gain of 1,304 members.

CHAPTER XLIV

A Home in Seclusion

In 1943, I contracted with Harold Bell Wright to sell his "Quiet Hills Farm" near Escondido. At that time, we were in the midst of World War II, with gasoline rationing and all of the other discouragements, and I therefore took particular pains in preparing an eleven-page brochure describing the property and its advantages.

It was an easy brochure to write, because Mr. Wright had taken a beautiful knoll to start with, and had produced a charming "gentleman's estate" of sixty-six acres, with almost every luxury and convenience anyone could want. I mailed a copy of my proposed brochure to him for his approval, and received the following letter, which, coming from Harold Bell Wright, was most gratifying:

HAROLD BELL WRIGHT
Quiet Hills Farm
Escondido, California

December 20, 1943

DEAR MR. COTTON:

I would not like to say that you had missed your calling, but I am familiar with the work of many professional literary men who cannot hold a candle to you when it comes to the art of descriptive writing. The fact is, your prospectus has darned near sold the place to my wife, which, you will allow, puts me in a most embarrassing position. Evidently a counterirritant, as the M.D.'s say, was indicated, because the main pipe from the well to the reservoir busted. We repaired the damage without too much trouble and in the process recovered from the effect of your eloquence—so Quiet Hills Farm is still for sale.

As to using the name "Quiet Hills Farm," I am content to leave that to your judgment.

One detail in your prospectus provoked a comment. Under "Expanse of View" you mention "The valley with its stream of crystal water." Well, with your closing paragraph in which you quite properly sidestep all personal responsibility for your statements, I think I should and do—hereby deny all responsibility for said "crystal stream." True, there is water in the creek channel the year round. But it honestly exceeds my imagination to call it a crystal stream. And I don't want the lucky person who falls under the spell of your salesmanship to hold me responsible for your eloquence.

But now, having registered my position, I am content for you to use your own judgment in this also.

I am wondering in what papers you are placing your ads.

Have not yet heard from Wilson. We are having fine rains in this neighborhood, as you probably know. The hills are greening and the silvery (no, crystal) stream is roaring.

Mrs. Wright joins me in regards and all good wishes.

Sincerely,
HAROLD BELL WRIGHT

I appreciated this letter, not only because I so thoroughly enjoyed Harold Bell Wright's books, but also because in my short acquaintance with him, I discovered him to be one of the most delightful gentlemen it has ever been my pleasure to know.

William sold "Quiet Hills Farm."

CHAPTER XLV

Home Is Where You Make It

DURING THE BOOM in houses of 1920, we were happy to sell our old South Park home and move to a rented house on Front Street, between Kalmia and Laurel streets. When we made this move, we had no immediate plans except to be back in the section of town where our friends lived. As it turned out, we lived there twenty-four years; in 1926, the owner of the house died and we purchased it from the estate, remodeled it to suit our family's needs, and were most comfortable.

In 1928, we built our lovely mountain cabin, and, for the next twelve years, we divided our time between our town house and Corte Madera. It was a fine way to live and raise a teen-age family. Looking back on those years, there is little I would have changed. Our town house was convenient, and our Corte Madera cabin was a grand place to entertain, and many "Good Old Days" were enjoyed by all members of our family and our friends.

With the outbreak of World War II, all of this was changed. We had to give up going to Corte Madera (one hundred miles a round trip) because of gasoline rationing. Our friends with homes in the vicinity were not much better off. However, War Bond drives and various war activities kept us so occupied physically and mentally that we had little time to think of Corte Madera. It was the summer of 1944 before we could begin to sense that the war was nearing an end.

By that time, the atmosphere of our household was entirely changed. Our family, Jane, John, and William, were all married. There were now just two of us in a house built for five. The neighborhood, too, was rapidly changing; old homes were being remodeled into apartment houses.

One day, I heard about a house facing on the bay, on Point Loma. We went to see it. One look was enough. It was exactly what we wanted, and we made a deal. We have been in that house for seventeen years now, and figuratively speaking every day has been a delight. It has been a lovely home in which to entertain our friends, and in August, 1959, our granddaughter, Joan, chose our garden for her wedding.

The damp climate on Point Loma is not as good for either Violet or me as was, for example, Corte Madera, but we are only twenty minutes from town, and the views from our front windows and the terrace of the hundreds of boats passing daily, the miniature yacht races, and the myriads of various colored lights on Shelter Island and in the city beyond, give a day and night panorama far ahead of anything we saw in London, Paris, Venice, Nice, or anywhere in the United States.

Although we do not own a boat, we were invited to join the San Diego Yacht Club, which is almost like a second home, with good things to eat, no "help" problem, and almost always some of our friends or our family in the dining room at dinnertime.

Many, many "Good Old Days."

CHAPTER XLVI

Again We Can Travel!

AT THE START OF World War II, I was driving a twelve-cylinder Packard —4½ miles per gallon of gasoline. When gasoline was rationed, my car was valuable mostly as an antique ornament! In 1943, I bought a used Ford for twelve hundred dollars—twice what it was worth, but it made fifteen miles to the gallon, which helped. Still, we had to watch every mile. Late in 1945, with the end of the war in sight, manufacturers were promising new cars for sale after the turn of the year, so I sold my Packard to Marvin K. Brown-Cadillac, Inc., while any old car could be sold at a premium, and got my name on the priority list to get the twenty-first new Cadillac to be delivered in San Diego.

Prices on new cars were still restricted to the prewar prices, "plus extras." My new, five-passenger, four-door Cadillac sedan cost $1,900 "plus"—the "plus" being for extra equipment since the old prices. In my case, the "plus" items totaled $1,175; so my new car cost $3,075 complete with automatic transmission, window operators, an extra tire, etc., etc., etc.!

It seemed almost too good to be true that we would again be able to buy gasoline without coupons, and to travel for pleasure, but "sure enough" it came to pass! On Tuesday, September 10, 1946, Violet and I and the brand-new 1946 Cadillac started for Boston.

It was an exciting trip. The main objective was to pay a call on my brother, Dr. Albertus Cotton, of Baltimore, Maryland, who was nine years my senior. We left home about 11:00 A.M., had lunch by the roadside just off Highway 395 near Bonsall, and spent the first night of our journey at the Riverside Inn. We had been across the United States by train, but this was our first trip by automobile.

We spent the second night in Las Vegas, where we had a good dinner, saw a couple of excellent shows, and watched the "jackasses" lose more money than they could afford to lose on the so-called "gaming" tables, although, insofar as I could see there was no "game" to it—just straight losses.

The delightful "Last Frontier" Hotel where we spent the night, is situated on what was then the western fringe of Las Vegas. In this and other first-class hotels, the elaborate gaming rooms were in the main buildings, but in the town proper, the saloons and gambling houses were right on the street.

At 5:15 the next morning, we really got on our way, and, to our amazement, when we drove through town at 5:30 A.M., every one of them was going full blast! The "suckers" were standing or sitting around the tables, watching every spin of the wheel and marble as though their fortunes depended on the outcome. It seemed so silly; it was really almost nauseating.

But once away from the city and the roulette wheels, the air was clear and refreshing. The sun, when it came up, was bright and warm; the new car purred over the paved roads, and we practically had the highways to ourselves. That day, we traveled nearly the length of Utah, in a northeasterly direction, staying overnight in Provo, and then on up delightful canyon grades to the platcau of southern Wyoming.

Fifteen years earlier, we had taken our then teen-age family on an automobile trip from San Diego to Denver, Colorado, and then north from Denver through a portion of Wyoming to Yellowstone National Park. But this was different!

About the time we hit Highway 30, we were at an altitude of eight thousand feet. There were no higher mountains to be seen in any direction. The air was light, and we had the sensation, as we sailed along over mile after mile of open country, of being on top of the world.

We spent one night in Cheyenne, a night in North Platte, and then we were halfway across the United States. Our route took us through Omaha, Des Moines, Indianapolis, Cincinnati, and, almost before we knew it, we were in the "Deep South"—Huntington, Lewisburg, and Williamsburg. In Williamsburg, we spent several delightful days in tours of the rebuilt historic buildings, walking about and enjoying the atmosphere and the southern accents.

We drove over the beautiful new Parkway to Jamestown. To us, it seemed the "Parkway" was well named—every mile was like our own Highway 395 through Balboa Park, before the Crosstown Freeway was started. Jamestown today is merely a name, but to walk about the remaining walls of those old buildings and realize that you are actually standing on the banks of the James River, at the point where the first permanent settlement was established in North America in 1607, is a thrilling experience.

After our Rocky Mountains, with all their grandeur and gorgeous beauty, the Blue Ridge Mountains of Virginia seemed rather tame, but seeing is believing. Now we know something of what the famous Blue Ridge Mountains and the Valley of the Shenandoah look like.

We stayed one night at the New Willard Hotel, in Washington, D. C., and then on to Baltimore to my brother's home. Brother Bert and his wife, Florence, had a lovely old home situated on a twenty-acre knoll overlooking other lovely old homes, and surrounded by acres of trees and verdure.

Bert, a highly respected orthopedic surgeon, spent some time daily at his office and his favorite hospital. His assocate, Dr. Harry L. Rogers, and Florence's niece, Mary Campbell, and her husband, lived close by. Bert and Florence had a man and his wife to look after their everyday needs —cooking, housekeeping, gardening, and chauffeuring. Florence's charming little niece, Mary Jean Lovelace, and her husband and baby spent considerable time at Brother's home, where I gathered she rather took over and managed the household. All in all, it was a most happy life for Bert, Florence, and their two Airedale dogs.

One evening during our visit, Florence gave a party and we met a group of their interesting friends. One day we drove to Washington, and to Annapolis, and another evening they took us to dinner at a favorite restaurant where they started the meal with the enormous, fresh Baltimore oysters! Oh boy! It was a week always to be remembered.

I felt our parting keenly. Bert and I had always lived thirty-five hundred miles apart. This was only our fourth meeting, and it might, I realized, easily be the last, which proved to be the case.

The drive to New York City was uneventful, but it was strenuous driving through the city. We drove on to Boston, over another marvelous Parkway, even more beautiful than the one in Virginia. A friend asked me how I got along driving in Boston, with all its crazy zigzag streets, and with two or three names for the same street, depending on how far you drove. I suprised him by telling him I had no trouble whatsoever. I simply stopped at each intersection and asked a policeman.

While in Boston, I did commit one social error. One evening about dusk, we were walking trying to find a certain restaurant which had been highly recommended. I left Violet and tried to ask a young lady who was passing. She gave me one frightened glance and hurried on, without a word. Being sixty-four, I was quite complimented.

Leaving Boston, we headed for home via Poughkeepsie, in a heavy rain. The roads were paved, but narrow and crooked. There were no "Speed Limit" signs, but none were necessary; thirty-five miles per hour was as fast as anyone could do with reasonable safety as we threaded our way in and out and around the beautiful hills, all in gorgeous autumn coloring. We were having a wonderful time, but San Diego seemed a long way off!

Coming west from New York City, we hit the new Pennsylvania Turnpike. Then we did get a thrill—two wide lanes each way, smooth and straight—seventy miles per hour permitted and expected. There was very little traffic and all traffic at the same speed. This was really something, and as we put the miles behind us, the sensation was almost like flying. It did not seem possible that San Diego was eight days away! At that time, the Turnpike extended from the State Capitol at Harrisburg, west to Pittsburgh, 160 miles.

About ten miles east of Pittsburgh, we had to turn south and again reduce our speed to thirty-five miles per hour. Once again, San Diego seemed very remote. However, it was a wonderful time to travel. We had very little rain, and as we got further south we had mostly warm autumn days and cool nights.

At Lexington, Kentucky, we drove out to the Calumet Farm to see Whirlaway, the fabulous race horse and the world's largest money-winner —$561,161.50 and still going strong. At Calumet Farm, I parked on a wide driveway in front of the Administration Building and stepped inside for information. There was no one in the office, but in a few minutes, as I stood wondering what to do next, a young lady came in and said, "Do you want to see the horses? Right there," pointing to a side door. Then she was gone. Delightfully informal. Made me feel right at home.

We followed her directions and saw the great Whirlaway and many other beautiful horses, all in immaculate barns. There was one attendant in some of the stables, and none in others. It lookeed like a wonderful life for the horses—I could not help but think how fortunate to be a horse instead of a steer!

The "Farm" comprises about twelve hundred acres, all in beautiful rolling hills and dales, matted in the famous Kentucky bluegrass, and divided by miles of white fences. The entrance is through a long, park-like lane, bordered by ornamental trees that form an arch over its center. The pavement is of amiesite.

Kentucky appeared to be one vast lawn, broken only by an occasional Colonial home surrounded by mile after mile of white fences dividing the bluegrass fields. It was with sincere regrets that we left Kentucky and headed for Paris, Tennessee, and then the most interesting Hot Springs, Arkansas, and after Hot Springs, Dallas, Texas, and another thrill.

We enjoyed all of our trip—loved most of it. We particularly enjoyed the great profusion of trees and shrubbery that banked all the highways in the East and South, but as we neared the great state of Texas, trees and shrubs became more and more sparse, until suddenly we were again on the Great Plains, where we could see for miles in every direction—the "great open spaces." It was a wonderful sensation—like sailing into a new world.

We stopped at the state line and picked up a leaflet on Texas' speed laws from the State Patrol. The highways through Texas were straight and fast. After a couple of days in Dallas, we headed for San Diego.

Except for the few instances I have mentioned, the highways were nothing compared to those of today, but traveling was far simpler because of lack of traffic. The main "gripe" we had on this trip was the great number of large trucks on the roads. These trucks traveled at forty-five miles per hour; the speed limit was fifty-five or sixty miles per hour, so in order to pass one of them on a two-lane highway, we would have to drive near the white line, peeking around the truck until we had a clear road ahead for at least a half-mile. Then we would signal, step on it, and drive "like crazy" until we could turn back into our lane. Every time you passed one of these big trucks, you got a thrill, and it kept going all day! We thought, "Won't we enjoy a trip like this some day when, and where, they have four-lane highways?"

Sad to relate, now that we have the beautiful four-lane (and even six- and eight-lane) highways, there are so many cars the congestion is worse than ever! And we are sixteen years older. (That, of course, is confidential.)

Charting our trip in red on a map made an interesting picture. Our route led northeast from San Diego to southern Wyoming, southeasterly to Williamsburg, Virginia, north to Boston, and southwest to Texas and San Diego. We crossed our own trail once—at Cincinnati, Ohio.

CHAPTER XLVII

Beautiful Western Canada

IN 1947, Violet and I drove to western Canada. We took Highway 395 from San Diego to Mono Lake, driving the last twenty-five miles in second gear only. On the Sherwin Grade, north of Bishop, the hydromatic transmission went on the blink, so we limped along as best we could to our old favorite, Tioga Lodge, and the next morning continued to limp to Reno, Nevada, where they made temporary repairs which they hoped would get us to Portland, Oregon.

While repairs were under way at the garage, I walked over to the "Divorce Mill," which in other states is known as the "Courthouse," to see "how it was done." I wandered into a sizable courtroom, where court was in session. The judge was on the bench, apparently intent on a letter or something he was writing. A young woman sat alone in a chair in the front row. Her attorney stood before the court, making a speech from his notes or "brief." The court reporter was taking notes.

After about five or more minutes of monologue by the attorney (during which time the judge continued his writing), the attorney abruptly stopped talking. The judge nodded his head, the attorney turned to his client and nodded, then passed a paper to the judge. The judge signed the paper, the attorney motioned to his client, she rose, and went with him toward the entrance door.

I followed a few paces behind to see "what next." Outside the courtroom, the young lady ran—actually, not figuratively—across the corridor and into the arms of a handsome young "Number Two." Looked like it might be fun, but I passed it up and went back to see about my car.

The repairs were only temporary, but they did give me two gears in place of one and assured me we would make Portland, where they had a new transmission for us. All in all, it was pretty fine service, and we had an excuse to see Reno, an interesting little city with the Truckee River running through it. It's wide open, of course, with gambling and nightclubs, but not the "glamour" of Las Vegas—more on the order of a mining camp. The principal gold mine apparently is located at the Courthouse!

The next day, we crossed the great Sacramento Valley on two gears as promised, on Highways 40 and 20, bordering for a surprising number of miles on beautiful Clear Lake, then to Highway 101. In the late afternoon, we pulled into the parking area of the delightful Benbow's Resort Hotel, at Benbow, for a rendezvous with my little sister Laura, who had motored north from San Francisco for a visit.

Violet and I had stopped at Benbow's a few years before on our way to the Redwoods and Eureka with the Lester R. Budrows. We wanted another day there, and we wanted Laura to see it. It is a fine, comfortable old hotel on a hillside in a great pine forest. The beautiful Eel River flows on one side of the lodge, then crosses the valley and forms a sizable lake to the west, with the mountains of the Coast Range for a background. A nine-hole golf course is available, with a herd of sheep for a mowing machine. Meals are delicious, with fresh berries and tree-ripened fruits three times a day. It is an environment that tempts the traveler to give up the rest of his trip and just stay on and on.

After two nights and one delightful day, we persuaded Laura to follow us to Portland to "pick up the pieces" in case our Cadillac fell apart. Quite a joke on me—Laura was driving my old 1941 Ford. Before noon, we arrived at Eureka and Humboldt Bay where, by prearrangement, we had a get-together with son John and his entire family: Margaret, Peg, Larry, and Joan, who were driving south from a vacation and sightseeing trip to Victoria, British Columbia, Canada.

Eureka was not on John's route home, but I had arranged this meeting because I wanted John and his family, for once in their lives, to taste fresh Humboldt Bay crabs! The feast we had at that luncheon was worth a two-hundred-mile trip to anyone! Enormous, live crabs, dropped in boiling water, chilled, and served. Boy, oh boy! And if you have any room left, a slice of freshly caught, broiled Columbia River salmon.

John was late because of blasting on the Highway, but we waited, and drooled rather impatiently, and ultimately we all got together for the big feed and a talk-fest, and then went our respective ways; Laura and the Ford continuing to follow me, and Violet dividing her time between the Ford and the Cadillac.

Our next stop was at Gold Beach, at the mouth of the Rogue River. A few days before we started on this trip, Wesley Hall, who is a great trout fisherman and has fished many times on the Rogue, told me that the scenery at the lower end of the river just must not be missed. He said we should stay two nights at Gold Beach and take a boat trip from Gold Beach to Agness and back. He said, "This is a 'must,'" so I took a large envelope out of my pocket and wrote across the top: "Agnes." The next morning when I changed my suit, I put that envelope on my dresser. That evening at dinner, Violet looked across the table at me and said, "Oscar, who is 'Agnes'?"

Owing to our car troubles, I decided to postpone our visit to Agness until some future trip, but the proprietress of the lodge assured us that Agness, a river town and not a personage, actually did exist and was about three hours by boat up the beautiful Rogue River.

We made it into Portland, where the Cadillac Agency installed a new transmission, and gave the car a tune-up. The next day, we saw Laura off for San Francisco, and then we headed on north.

It often happens that as soon as you cross the boundary line, you sense that you are in another country. That feeling was strong as we approached Victoria by ferry from Port Angeles. There above, and straight ahead of us as we pulled into the dock, was the beautiful Empress Hotel, and to the south the buildings of Parliament. There was a different "tone" from any city in the United States. It was beautiful and impressive.

The Empress is a lovely hotel. Immediately upon arrival, we were taken to our two delightful rooms, overlooking the beautiful gardens, and were told that the dinner hour was 7 P.M. We dressed leisurely and took the "lift" down to the dining room floor, and here, at 7:30 P.M., we got our first Canadian surprise.

The lobby was half-filled with guests, waiting for the "second table." The custom, we learned, was to be on hand in the lobby fifteen minutes to half an hour before mealtime, and then when the doors were thrown open all file into the dining room. Latecomers waited for the second opening. There were no reservations.

The food and the service at the Empress were tops. At four o'clock, afternoon tea was served in the Lounge. All of the personnel were Canadian, including the shoeshine boy. All were courteous and spoke with that slightly different "Canadian accent."

While we were in Victoria, I wanted some cash. When I made my wants known to a teller at the bank, we were shown to a reception room, and then shortly taken to the office of the vice-president. He proved to be a gentleman of the old school, who visited with us for fifteen minutes; invited us to his club for tea, and finally authorized the cashing of my check. Wherever we went in western Canada, from hotel maids to "Mounties," all were most courteous.

It was also interesting to note how many had their eyes open for a job in the "States." One bellboy had it all figured out that a bellhop in a good hotel in the States would earn about two and a half times what he made in Canada.

On a little sightseeing and shopping excursion, I bought a heavy black and white sweater, made by Canadian Indians—an excellent garment which I am still using—and this is 1962.

At the Hotel Vancouver, in Vancouver, we did not fare so well. Arriving after dark, we were told our rooms were not ready and to come back after dinner. Inasmuch as we had had our reservations confirmed for some months ahead, we were somewhat taken aback. We had a good dinner, returned to the desk, and were given the same answer. Finally, at 9:30 P.M., I told the clerk we must have our rooms. He found that he did have one room ready and sent us to one room so small that there was hardly room for our luggage and ourselves. We were most uncomfortable. Years later, I realized it was my own fault. I had not given the head clerk a ten-dollar tip.

When Violet and I were planning our European trip in 1957, an experienced world traveler told us that she and her husband traveled all over Europe the year before without any hotel reservations. She said that upon arrival, when asking for accommodations, she always handed the hotel clerk an American ten-dollar bill, and that during their whole trip they had to sleep in a hotel lobby only once—generally, they got the best accommodations the hotel had to offer.

Such a system seems rather extravagant and unnecessary, but on occasion recently when I have, in emergency, tried it, I have been amazed at the results. Hotel clerks both at home and abroad seem to like our ten-dollar bills, especially if they are new and crisp. They bring out the best in disposition that the hotel clerk is capable of displaying!

From Vancouver, we motored to Seattle, where we were entertained royally by Di Ette Stewart, with cocktails at her home, and a dinner party at her club, meeting some of her delightful friends.

Early the next morning, with several bottles of fresh goat's milk in our refrigerator, we headed for Spokane. This was a most interesting day. As we left Seattle we drove over the two-mile-long pontoon Highway 10, over Lake Washington, and then through the greatest apple and cherry country in the world. From Spokane, we headed for our ultimate goal: Lake Louise and Banff.

In 1957, when we returned from our European trip, friends would often ask, "Which country or city did you enjoy most?" That is a very difficult question to answer. There is so much to see that is interesting, entertaining, and beautiful, throughout all Europe, that one cannot pinpoint one city or country as "tops" above all others.

So it is with our great mountain chains in the western United States and Canada. As we motored through the mountains of Utah, Colorado, the Yellowstone, and passed the Grand Teton Range of Wyoming, we did not believe that we would ever see anything comparable elsewhere, but as we traveled mile after mile through the beautiful mountains of western Canada, we realized our planned trip was far too short.

We were told that Jasper, Canada, was a "must." The resort there is owned by the Canadian Pacific Railroad. When we were planning our trip by motor, we could not get reservations, so we passed it up. While in Seattle, our friend Di Ette Stewart, who knows her way around in the Northwest, secured reservations for us for one night, the plan being to cut one day and night from our stay at Lake Louise, and drive 150 miles up and back, to Jasper. Lake Louise was so delightful and thrilling and rest-ful, we decided to stay there and loaf, rather than spend two more days traveling over the not-too-good mountain roads. Looking back on those glorious days, I realize we made a mistake. The scenery in that country is so grand and inspiring, one can never see too much of it.

In planning our trip, Banff intrigued me for several reasons. The pic-tures of the hotel were so thrilling that I wondered if it could be possible such a mountain resort existed—and I wanted to play the Banff Springs Golf Course. For fifteen years after we built our cabin at Corte Madera, I played very little golf; some years, not any. Always a poor player, I finally got so I could hardly hit a ball with a wood club! But I had heard so much and seen such pictures of the Banff course, laid out among the towering pine trees and bordered by the beautiful Bow River, I knew I wanted to play it, so when we packed the car, I put in a light golf bag, my golf shoes, and iron clubs.

Banff was all and more than it had been advertised. The hotel was magnificent—a towering building two or more blocks long, with palatial lobbies, dining rooms, and terraces, excellent meals and service. We were taken to our rooms immediately upon arrival, our suite being on the front of the building overlooking the swimming pool, the golf course, the Bow River, and the valley surrounded on three sides by tall mountain peaks in heavy forests—a thrilling picture.

The next morning, I took my golf bag with my old iron clubs with the hickory shafts, and with Violet for my "gallery" sallied forth. The Num-ber One Tee is at the side of the Clubhouse and about twenty-five feet above the rapid, gurgling Spray River. The first drive is over the river.

In addition to Violet, there was already a small gallery standing beside the tee, admiring the magnificent panorama of river, valley, trees, and mountains that stretched out before us. There was nothing to wait for, so I teed up my ball, took my Number One iron, and drove a beautiful ball—for me—well over the river and down the middle of the fairway! The one man in the gallery remarked on the hazard from this first tee. I answered casually and seriously that all you had to do was to drive a long, straight ball. He looked at me as though he thought I was a jackass to make such a remark, but refrained from further comment, as Violet and I started down the path toward the bridge to follow the ball.

I was feeling unusually fit that morning, and my good first shot having stimulated my ego and confidence, for me I played very well. I do not remember my total score, but I played one beautiful hole I shall never forget! Be sure you have the picture: The weather was perfect—mild sunshine, moderate temperature, and a gentle breeze. The fairways led deeper and deeper into the magnificent pine forests, and they were good turf fairways. The hazards were moderate, and the greens were perfect.

On the 570-yard, 5-par hole on the first nine, I was on the green in four, and about twenty feet from the cup. As I took my putter and approached the ball, a tallyho of tourists pulled up and stopped on the road close by. I did not look toward the tallyho to see if I was the attraction, but calmly took my stance, and, as good luck would have it, sank my putt.

As it turned out, that was an important event in my life. Even after the ball dropped, I did not look at the tallyho, but, as I heard no talking and the driver drove on after my putt, I assumed he had stopped on my account. In any event, my heart gave an extra beat as the thought went through my mind that "If I can shoot par on a 570-yard hole with my irons, there is no reason why I should not take up golf again."

In a manner, that was a turning point in my life. When we returned home, I started playing at the lovely little course they then had in La Mesa. The climate was good for me, and later, when the La Mesa course was subdivided, I started playing the Palms Pitch and Putt Course, in Mission Valley, with Albert E. Scott. When the Mission Valley Country Club was organized, I joined, and divided my golf time between the big course and the driving range.

One day, while sitting on the bench at the driving range watching "Another Golfer" practice, I was so impressed with the manner in which he could "call his shots" to a small gallery and then invariably execute them, that I inquired who the gentleman was. I learned that he was Olin Dutra, the Club's head "pro."

I immediately put myself under his tutelage, and, for the first time in my life, learned how golf should be played. I do not recall how many lessons I took, but I kept on until Dutra told me he could not teach me any more and suggested that I practice what I had been taught and come back for an occasional "brush-up." Sad to relate, all of his instruction did not materially improve my score, but the knowledge he gave me of what I was trying to do, and how the game should be played, was worth many times the cost and effort. It has made golf a great pleasure to me as well as a great benefit to my health and disposition.

CHAPTER XLVIII

When Were the "Good Old Days?"

AT A DINNER PARTY one night my dinner partner said, "San Diego isn't what it used to be in the 'Good Old Days.' "

"When were the 'Good Old Days'?" I asked her.

She replied, "Back in the nineties, before everyone was in such a hurry. When the town could not grow, so nobody tried to do anything about it. Everyone lived his or her life in peace and quiet. Everybody knew everybody. There was no servant problem. People were not striving every minute for the Almighty Dollar. Our pleasures were simple: tallyho, and beach parties, and boating in the summer, and home parties at night when the weather was cool. We did not have much, but we were satisfied with what we had." As a young lady, she had lived on one of the many beautiful lemon groves at Pacific Beach.

The guest on her left thought San Diego was at its best in the early twenties: "When we could forget about World War I," he said, "and we were not handicapped by wartime regulations. When prosperity was just ahead for us, and everybody was having fun." He had been about thirty then; married, and with a young family.

The guest on my right thought that 1912 to 1915 were the "Good Old Days," while the city was growing healthily, "but not wild." Those were the days before we believed we could ever be in the First World War, the days when the first Exposition was being held and we were having gay social parties every night—and such parties! She had been in her thirties during those days; healthy and happily married.

To her right, the guest thought the "Good Old Days" were after World War II. "The city was big enough to be interesting," he said, "and to attract more interesting people." He added that we had just finished the second "World War to end all wars." Taxes were high, but that was only tempo-rary, because since there were to be no more wars, our military and naval expenditures could be cut to a minimum and all that extra tax money would be retained and enjoyed by the individual. At that time, he and his wife were in their early forties, with many friends their own age.

So it went, around the table; a most interesting and instructive topic. The "Good Old Days" for each particular guest were the days when he or she was full of life and vigor, free from worry, with congenial friends and enough of the comforts of life to make them contented with their environment and enable them to look to the future with optimism.

I am sure for that, for many San Diegans, the middle and the late twenties were "Good Old Days." The horrors of World War I were behind us; prosperity had returned; the city was expanding in every direction. No clouds were apparent on the horizon. San Diegans were enjoying life.

Among the newcomers to San Diego at that time was Baron Long, who for a number of years had operated a "Palace of Entertainment" most successfully in a suburb of Los Angeles. When he first arrived, Baron Long purchased and personally operated the U. S. Grant Hotel. Later, with some associates, he acquired the Agua Caliente Hot Springs across the Border in Baja California, Mexico, only a few miles east of Tia Juana, as Tijuana was then called. At Agua Caliente, he built a race-track, a large and magnificent hotel, a beautiful night club and gambling casino. Today, except for betting on the races and the *jai alai* games, gambling is prohibited in Mexico, but in the twenties it was not only legal but officially encouraged.

Tia Juana was then a typical little, dried-up Mexican village, with a few frame houses and many shacks. There were several curio stores, a number of saloons with roulette tables, wheels of fortune, and slot machines, but not much to attract tourists except the excuse to cross the "line" into Mexico and gamble.

Baron Long's Agua Caliente Hotel was built around a patio, and in a separate building were several beautifully appointed gaming rooms, a large and most pleasant dining room with a dance floor, and there was always alluring dance music. The food was excellent and the prices were moderate, because the profits were made at the gaming tables.

The floor shows always included top Mexican singers and dancers, with their fresh Mexican costumes, and tambourines, and, to cap the climax, concluded with a pretty and graceful little "fan dancer," who would weave her way through the crowded tables to the dance floor, with her two fans and a timid little smile.

Many delightful evenings were spent by San Diegans at Agua Caliente during those lush years. After dinner and the entertainment, we would enjoy the beauty of the gaming rooms, saunter through the "classy" jewelry and gift shop, and possible leave a few dollars on the roulette or birdcage tables or at the "Wheel of Fortune." For many San Diegans, those were "Good Old Days," never to be forgotten.

Tia Juana did have one excellent restaurant at that time, Caesar's. It was there that the famous "Caesar's" tossed green salad originated, which is to be found on every menu in this part of the country. Today, it is brought to you on an individual salad plate, or in an individual salad bowl; however, when a salad was ordered at Caesar's Restaurant in Tia Juana, a small table was wheeled alongside your dining table. On it reposed a large bowl of tossed salad greens and all of the ingredients for mixing, including a small bowl of fresh, raw eggs. Caesar himself would perform the ceremony of the mixing, one of the last acts of which was to break a raw egg over the concoction and finish the "tossing"—whereupon the waiter would take over and serve a most tasty salad. Caesar's was another good excuse for San Diegans to go to Tia Juana, because everything he served was tops, and in addition to the entrees available on this side of the Border, at Caesar's one could almost always have venison steaks or quail on toast, served with good Mexican beer, or the very best imported liquor of your own choosing.

San Diego has changed quite a bit since I arrived here in 1903—many, many ways for the better; some for worse, but that does not mean that "Good Old Days" are past and gone! Not by any means. I had a "Good Old Day" today, May 23, 1960, and I am far past my teens, my twenties, my thirties, or my forties, et cetera, et cetera AND ET CETERA!

My alarm awoke me at 5:30 A.M., after a good night's sleep. I played eighteen holes of golf with a congenial friend, Lester G. Bradley. I shot a "46" on the first nine holes, with three 20-foot or longer putts. Lester drives the electric cart; I keep the score. Lester likes to ride all the way; I walk about one-third of the course.

I had a good luncheon at home; went to the office for three hours; then home, and a shower, and took Violet to Lubach's for a delicious dinner. Returned home for a quiet evening with magazines, conversation, and scribbling. I feel, as some would say, "like a million dollars." I call it "tiptop."

Yes, the town is bigger than it was in 1903—bigger by more than fifty times—and I have to be alert every second when driving my car about the city, but I enjoy being alert, and my 1958 Cadillac is more "alert" than was the three and one-half horsepower "Merry Oldsmobile" with a shaft to steer with, which I drove all over the dirt roads north of B Street and east of Seventh Avenue, fifty-seven years ago!

Not only has San Diego changed, but so have living standards, environments, knowledge, and thinking. It is too bad that the atom bomb and the hydrogen bomb were ever discovered, but they were, and have been developed until it is possible that the entire civilized world might someday be exterminated. So what? It will do no good to "stew" about it, so let's forget it as much as we can when we are not reading the daily newspapers, and have FUN.

Last week, we went to two delightful parties. One was a small, formal dinner party at the lovely home of Mr. and Mrs. Guilford H. Whitney. The table was a picture, with exquisite hand-embroidered linen, and silver, china, and decorations to match, and the dinner was delicious, with consideration for the diet of each of the guests. The other was a larger, informal party, at the home of Dr. and Mrs. James F. Churchill, where we visited with our friends over cocktails for two hours then gravitated to a delicious smorgasbord in the dining room, where each of us selected what he or she could, or should, or wanted to, eat. These parties were as different as any two parties could be, and I told Violet afterward that each was as delightful a party as could possibly be given. "Good Old Days," May, 1960.

On Sunday, July 24, 1960, Violet gave a "brunch" at our home for about fifty of our family and music-loving friends. Lyall Barbour played works of Mendelssohn, Chopin, and Mozart on Violet's Steinway grand in the living room. Afterward, we sipped refreshments and nibbled a few hors d'oeuvres on the terrace and watched the dozens of launches and sailboats pass until "brunch" was ready. A Sunday never to be forgotten.

The same can be said of a formal cocktail and dinner party at the Point Loma home of Mr. and Mrs. James D. Forward, to celebrate their fiftieth wedding anniversary. For hors d'oeuvres, there was caviar covering a huge slab of Philadelphia cheese, and crackers, and after a delectable dinner we enjoyed Irish coffee in the living room. After coffee, there was a contest with prizes for the one who could give the most correct answers to the following questions, all ending in *-ty* within fifteen minutes:

(1) The best policy? (2) The soul of wit? (3) What killed a cat? (4) Which never faileth? (5) Mother of inventions? (6) Heat, power, and light? (7) The Four Hundred? (8) Forever and ever? (9) A national possession? (10) The spice of life? (11) It is only skin deep? (12) First and always?

The answers are: (1) Honesty; (2) Brevity; (3) Curiosity; (4) Charity; (5) Necessity; (6) Electricity; (7) Society; (8) Eternity; (9) Nationality; (10) Variety; (11) Beauty; (12) Priority.

The guests were all old friends of twenty to fifty years, some longer. What could be more delightful? Certainly another of the "Good Old Days."

Norman Vincent Peale has an excellent recipe for "Good Old Days." He does not spell it out that way—that is my interpretation. I carry a typed copy of it in my wallet as a reminder and, when I remember to use it, it helps a lot. In case you do not know it, here it is:

The Way to Happiness: Keep your heart free from worry. Live simply, expect little, give much. Fill your life with love. Scatter sunshine. Forget self, think of others. Do as you would be done by. Try this for a week and you will be surprised.

CHAPTER XLIX

Here and There

"JULIUS CAESAR" PAYS OFF

IT WAS the twenty-ninth day of January, 1960, at the Mission Valley Country Club—the second day of the big P. G. A. Tournament. I had recently had the flu and was not too steady on my feet, but I particularly wanted to see Gene Littler tee off. To go from the temporary parking field past the driving range, it was necessary to step over a three-foot rope. I stepped over with my right leg, but as I swung my left foot the heel of my shoe caught in the rope.

The instant I realized I was going down, my old *Julius Caesar* training of sixty years ago, on how to fall gracefully, flashed across my mind in one word: "RELAX!"

I relaxed and went down in a heap, but got up without a bruise, muttering to myself, "Pretty good for seventy-seven years!"

A SWEET LOVE LETTER

It was Christmas morning, 1944. Violet and I were in front of the tree, opening packages. The Love Letter accompanied a package, and it was written for her by the young lady's mother. It was addressed to: "Gampy from Susan, with Love." I quote it in full: "I like you. You're funny.—Susan Fletcher."

LEST WE FORGET

Occasionally, when Violet has some suggestion of particular importance, she will write me a memorandum on a scratch pad I keep on my chiffonier. One beautiful spring morning, when I came back to my room from the shower, I found the following message: "Oscar: Good morning! Now that it's warmer again would you . . ."

I read the message several times and then wrote my answer in a bold hand: "Yes, definitely!—O."

While shaving, I thought the matter over and wondered why she would ask such a question, so I added to the page a question of my own: "Why not?"

As I dressed, it seemed to me the whole proposition was rather vague, so I added another note: "However, I think I should have more information!"

Believe it or not, that evening, when I returned to my room, I found to my amazement that, without further explanation or comment, she had written in heavy and indisputable letters: "You nut!"

THE ROYAL HAWAIIAN

In 1952, we had a delightful trip to Honolulu on the *Lurline*. We had smooth sailing for five days each way. She is an excellent ship, with excellent cuisine.

We were met at the dock in Honolulu by our old friends, George and Lulu Parker, and Madeline Childs. We stayed at the well-named Royal Hawaiian Hotel, where everything was tops—including beautiful Hawaiian music and songs, with one deep, bass voice we shall never forget.

The Parkers drove us around and across the Island, through miles of pineapple fields, and then to their home on a hill high above the city. Madeline Childs entertained us royally at her home on another hilltop, with Hawaiian music and native dancers.

We ate our fill of delicious, ripe pineapples, right from the field, and we drank the fresh juice from the spigot at the Dole Pineapple Plant. I played golf in Honolulu. On the Island of Hawaii, we were taken up to see the volcano, which was then smoldering.

In Honolulu, I was surprised by the many coconut palms along the sidewalks. I inquired if it were not dangerous for pedestrians, and was quickly informed that "The Chamber of Commerce takes care of that."

I asked in what manner, and was informed that "If a coconut should drop from a tree and hit a tourist on the head, the Chamber of Commerce would send a check for a hundred dollars to his widow."

One evening after we had been in Honolulu for a few days, the manager of the Royal Hawaiian, Mr. Stephen W. Royce, who had arrived that day from the Mainland, gave a cocktail party to the hotel's guests. When asked to say a few words to the assemblage, he responded most cordially, giving us interesting and some amusing incidents. One I remember concerned a period when, during a hotel strike, some fifty young ladies from the Junior League volunteered to do chambermaid duty so that the hotel could remain open.

They were instructed that, among other duties, they should knock on each door at 9:30 P.M., and if there were no response, to knock a second, and a third time. If there were still no response, they were instructed to open the door with a passkey, go in, and turn the bed down and give the room night service.

One night, one young lady went through the knocking performance, and after her third knock and no response, she unlocked the door and went in, arriving just as the occupant was pulling his shirt off over his head. In rather a surprised voice, the young lady reeled off her speech: "I'm your volunteer—I've come to turn your bed down and give you night service!"

When we were there, there was no strike on, but we moved with caution, nevertheless. One evening, a young chambermaid came into my room about 10:00 P.M., to give "night service." She came within four feet of me, and then stopped and stood there staring for fully half a minute. Then she said, "Excuse me staring at you, but you look just like my father! He's dead, of course."

FANCY BEES

Arthur A. Church, one of Violet's dear uncles, lived on an orange ranch in Duarte. In addition to fine navel oranges, he produced the most delicious honey, made from orange blossoms. He also had a large apiary in southern Nevada. In appreciation for his sending us a five-gallon can of orange honey for Christmas, 1930, I wrote him the following:

January 28, 1931

DEAR ART:

For the past month, I have been intending to drop you a note to tell you how much we are enjoying the honey.

There is such a difference in honey! This is very much the same as some you sent about four or five years ago, which was, I think, the finest honey I ever tasted. This is going some, because I have tasted honey every time I have had a chance for nearly fifty years.

A friend had breakfast with us the other day and had put some in between each hot cake on the stack, and then poured it over the top until I looked in the pitcher to see how much was left (by way of a hint). Anyway, he started to eat, smacking his lips so that our neighbor looked out of her window to see what was going on. He, too, said he liked this honey better than any other he had tasted, and I said I could readily believe it. There is a saying, "Actions speak louder than words." Now I know what is meant by that—the smacking of lips from eating hot cakes and honey.

My friend asked me how you got such fine honey. He is an ignorant type of man—you know the kind—raised in New York City, and does not know the difference between a common house bee and a hornet. I had to explain to him that you were a breeder of fancy bees, the same as other people breed race horses, and that the best honey came from the highest type of bee, the same as the richest milk comes from a Jersey cow. Any fool should know that, of course, but I did not say that, as naturally I did not want to hurt his feelings.

He is one of those fellows who would expect to get navel oranges from a seedling tree, and then, when he was disappointed, take a table-spoon and a saucer and go out and try to get a dish of honey from a yellow jacket's nest, which both you and I know is not practicable.

However, I told him I was going to write you, so he asked if I would please get you to tell me what kind of bee it is that lays this particular kind of honey, so that any time he wants to smack his lips so it can be heard a block, he can ask for honey made by that particular breed of bee.

He told me that, in New York State, they raise a quackless duck, and that he had heard there was a breed of bee which could neither buzz nor sting. I told him I thought these would be only the very old bees.

Since January 15, when the Duck Season closed, when we walk near the lake at the Corte Madera Ranch, large flocks of big ducks fly low over our heads, and quack and laugh and offer all manner of insults that a duck could think of.

Best regards, and again, many thanks.

                                                                    OSCAR

CHAPTER L

Proposition "F"

ON A BEAUTIFUL, sunshiny day in August, 1950, I received an invitation to have lunch with Jack L. Oatman, at the Cuyamaca Club. This sounded like a nice invitation, so I accepted with alacrity. As it turned out, it was not so nice.

At the last meeting of the State Legislature in Sacramento, it seemed a Bill had been passed by both Houses authorizing cities to condemn and take for public use any property their City Councils chose to take, to be used at that time or in the future, for off-street parking, and, in the interim, such properties could be rented or leased for any purpose desired. There was now a movement afoot by a small group of downtown businessmen to have that new law approved by the City of San Diego.

World War II years had been lush years for San Diego's downtown merchants. Our population had increased tremendously; every available house and apartment was filled, and thousands of temporary housing units were built by the government. A large percentage of our population, both old and new, was making money as never before and spending it freely. As yet, there were no suburban shopping centers of any consequence, and few people had either the time or the gasoline coupons to go to Los Angeles, so downtown San Diego reaped a harvest.

However, immediately after the war, new suburban shopping centers sprang up like mushrooms, and in most instances offered free parking. Residents in these outlying districts started doing a large part of their shopping near home to save time, gasoline, and parking fees. From 11:30 A.M., until 1:30 P.M., some of the closest-in parking lots in downtown San Diego would be full, owing largely to the many luncheon meetings and clubs. This gave rise to a popular cry by former shoppers that "they only came downtown when they had to, because there was no place to park.

Finally, a material number of our leading merchants in the downtown area came to the conclusion that our beloved "Downtown" was doomed unless and until we had more off-street parking. A "Downtown Committee" was organized, and called the "City-Wide Committee for Off-Street Parking." Hamilton Marston was chairman. Its express purpose was to have this new state law made a part of San Diego's city laws, so the city could acquire unlimited lots or blocks and make cheap or possibly free parking available to all.

Before we parted with Jack Oatman at the Cuyamaca Club, we had formed ourselves into a Committee known as the "San Diego Committee for the Defense of Free Enterprise" and had subscribed to a $5,000 budget to oppose this most unfortunate piece of legislation, which was to be voted on at the coming election. I was asked to act as chairman, and I promptly accepted and went to work.

The downtown merchants took the stand that "since the city furnished the streets for the autoists to drive on, it was also the city's duty to provide a place to park at the autoist's destination."

Our Committee's contention was that furnishing automobile parking in the downtown area was a private enterprise, the same as were the stores and other businesses. We said that it was vital to the downtown district that more parking spaces be added from time to time, and that if allowed to expand without fear of condemnation or tax-free competition, private enterprise would do the job and provide ample parking as needed.

We circularized the owners of downtown real estate and got together a committee of about seventy realty owners and businessmen. We subscribed and spent about $10,300. We put on a campaign that was a honey —and we "snowed" Proposition F under by more than two to one.

That was twelve years ago—November 7, 1950, and nobody has ever suggested that we try on that shoe again.

CHAPTER LI

Another "Good Old Day"

JULY 2, 1953, was a "Good Old Day" for me, and I think it was for my family. William and John gave me a "coming out" party—a party to celebrate my fiftieth year dealing real estate in San Diego.

The party was held in our offices in the Orpheum Theater Building, where I had been since 1928. Elizabeth Cotton (Mrs. William O.) had decorated the walls with pictures of various subdivisions, buildings, and other of my activities that brought up old memories. It was most pleasant to be greeted so heartily by so many good friends, both old and new.

During the party someone asked me, "How do you like San Diego?"

I replied, "I like it so much that I have decided to stay and make San Diego my home."

There were many wonderful expressions of good wishes, both personally and by letter and telegram, which built up my ego no end!

THE BILTMORE HOTEL
Los Angeles

Baron Long	Charles Baad	Edward S. Bernard
President	Managing Director	Manager

DEAR OSCAR:

By golly I wish I could be there for your party celebrating your 50th Anniversary in the Real Estate Business in San Diego.

To hell with that—I would just want to be there to toast the man who is responsible for San Diego as it is today.

I feel quite sure in my heart that if you hadn't taken off your coat, rolled up your sleeves, and gone to work back there in 1934 and kept slugging, making us raise the money necessary to insure the Exposition, the fair city of San Diego would not be as "fair" as it is today.

Please accept my regrets that I cannot attend. It just so happens that we will be doing so much business at the Biltmore I can't get away. Otherwise, I'd be there with my best bib on.

Fifty thousand congratulations to you. You deserve them all.

Sincerely,
EDWARD S. BERNARD

In 1934, Baron Long was the owner, and Eddie Bernard was manager, of the U. S. Grant Hotel, in San Diego.

THE FIRST NATIONAL TRUST & SAVINGS BANK
OF SAN DIEGO

Anderson Borthwick   June 25, 1953
President

DEAR OSCAR:

In this morning's mail I received a notice of your Fiftieth Anniversary as one of our leading Real Estate Executives, on which achievement I would like to extend to you my sincere and most heartfelt congratulations.

Your name and your actions have always stood for integrity, reliability, and fair dealings, and I feel that you are deserving of a great deal of praise and respect for the splendid part you have played during all these years in making our community a better place in which to live.

All my associates in the bank, who have been great admirers of yours, join me in extending to you every good wish for continued success, health, and the happiness which you so fully deserve.

Sincerely yours,
ANDY BORTHWICK
President

SWING SCHARNIKOW & STANIFORTH
Attorneys at Law
San Diego 1, California

July 3, 1953

MY DEAR OSCAR:

I was very much pleased to see and participate in the tribute paid you yesterday by your fellow townsmen on the occasion of the completion of fifty years as a realtor in this community.

Your spacious offices were crowded throughout the reception hours with the best known men in town, drawn from all walks of life—business executives, social and professional men and women and public officials, but especially the old-timers who have been in the van of every fight, every drive, and every movement to push forward the growth and development of this city and to make it a better place in which to live. These men who have been closely associated with you in your civic and business work and in your social and professional activities and who therefore know you best—all these gladly paused in their busy workday lives to troop to your offices and, by their presence, testify to their esteem and high regard for your sterling character, the fine life you have lived, and the constructive work you have done as a citizen of this community and to bespeak their warm personal affection for you as a man and a friend.

It must have been a pleasure to your fine family to have joined with you in receiving this well-deserved tribute from your many friends. You can well be proud of your attractive wife and fine children, every one of whom ranks high among their own group and command the respect of all who know them. They, too, I am sure, feel very proud of your outstanding record, your good name, and the wonderful reputation you have among all who know you.

With best regards, and best wishes for many, many more years of health, happiness, and a justifiable satisfaction in a life well lived, I am,

Sincerely, your friend,
PHIL D. SWING

Phil Swing was U. S. Congressman from 1921 to 1933, and "Father" of the Boulder Dam project.

CHAPTER LII

A Parking "District" Is Proposed

IN 1954 a new Downtown Committee was formed, comprising many of San Diego's top-flight merchants and bankers. It was called the "Parking District Survey Committee." Hamilton Marston was chairman. In the beginning, it was ostensibly for the purpose of determining what was fundamentally wrong with our downtown district, and what could be done about it.

The downtown merchants were feeling acutely the continued material loss in "pedestrian traffic" in the downtown area and, to cap the climax, so to speak, Sears, Roebuck & Company moved its big store from Sixth Avenue and C Street to Tenth and University avenues, and surrounded their new store with twelve hundred free parking spaces.

Various surveys were made by this Committee, but they always came up with the same answer: There was not enough off-street parking, and that was the major cause of all of downtown San Diego's financial ills. After due consideration, it was determined that the central forty-eight blocks in the heart of downtown should be formed into a "Parking District." At the request of this district, the city would condemn two full city blocks and two half-blocks, and build four multistory garages.

Finally, the "Survey Committee" had an elaborate fifty-page brochure prepared, with sketches of the proposed garages and elaborate figures compiled by "experts" showing how the project could be carried out at a cost of something over $5,000,000 and would "solve" our downtown parking problem with 1,082 stalls to start with, and stating: "When this initial program has been financed and has a successful operating record, then additional facilities can be created as required."

The cost of the land and the buildings was to be financed by the sale by the city of Revenue Bonds against the district; the garages were to be operated at cut rates, to be tax-free, and losses in operation were to be made up by assessment against the entire district.

One day I dropped in to see a good Republican friend of mine who was one of the leaders of this movement, and when I referred to the proposed project as "socialized parking," he interrupted me to say, "Now, Oscar, don't call this scheme 'socialized parking'!"

"Ed, we can't call it anything else," I said. "You propose to have the city condemn and take nearly four solid blocks at the four strategical districts around the business center. You propose that the city will build these parking garages, and rent the parking spaces at less than the present cost of parking. These garages will be tax-free, and the losses in operation will be paid by the taxpayer."

My interests in San Diego real estate were largely downtown, so when I was asked to take the chairmanship of the "Downtown Property Owners' Protective Committee," I accepted.

This was a long, hard battle, from February, 1955, to January, 1958, and I hated every minute of it. Many of my very best friends, men for whom I had the highest respect, were on the other side. They had become convinced that the only way to save our downtown was to have greatly increased parking. They knew it would cost millions of dollars, so, in line with the example set in Washington, D. C., we should have the "government" do it. In this case, the governing body was the city.

Through a circulation campaign to the property owners in this district, we got together a committee of 125, mostly downtown property owners. Our Executive Committee was: Phillip F. Bartlett; E. A. Brelin; Arnold S. Cosgrove; Joseph C. Ewing; Theo. Fintzelberg; A. A. Frost; Capt. Oakley J. Hall; Mrs. Marjorie F. Hutchinson; Evan V. Jones; Herbert C. Kelly; Baron Long; Lee Packard; Mrs. H. R. Peckham; George Riley; A. Paul Sutherland and Leroy A. Wright. Our job was to convince a majority of the owners of real estate within the forty-eight-block boundary that it was not necessary to encumber and assess their property for this project, because if it failed private enterprise would do the job, and do it better and far more profitably for the entire community. Since this was purely an educational effort, the campaign did not require much cash.

It was another "Sit-Down Campaign." All in all, over the three-year period 1955 to 1958 as chairman of our Protective Committee I wrote and sent to all property owners in the downtown district a total of thirty-four letters, of from one to nine pages. Also, Herbert C. Kelly, a large downtown property owner and a member of our Executive Committee, wrote sixteen letters. One of my letters read:

DOWNTOWN PROPERTY OWNERS PROTECTIVE COMMITTEE
521 Orpheum Theatre Bldg., San Diego 1

February 21, 1957

To DOWNTOWN PROPERTY OWNERS:
The four garages proposed by the Parking District Survey Committee to be built on four downtown blocks to be condemned by the city are to be TAX-FREE.

In their communication mailed to downtown property owners on December 15 last, the Committee stated: "Property to be acquired has a total assessed valuation of $470,000 from a District total of about $24,000,000.—about 2 percent.

But in this analysis they have overlooked the fact that the proposed *garage buildings* will be TAX-FREE.

The tax loss would be on the assessed value of *land* and *buildings*— approximately $1,750,000—nearly 8 percent of the total, or around $108,000 PER YEAR.

In the same paragraph, the Parking District Survey Committee states "After these bonds are retired, the city is estimated to enjoy each year an income from the garages more than ten times the taxes on the proposed sites."

Again, the Survey Committee has overlooked the fact that in acquiring these garages the city will have paid in losses from meter revenue $100,000 per year plus the city and county losses in taxes of $108,000 —or a total of $208,000 per year for 31 years.

In other words, in 31 years, when these bonds are retired, the city will have paid approximately $6,500,000 for four 31-year-old garages that only cost, when new, $5,500,000 and if you add the loss of interest at 3 percent, you will get a total cost of $9,900,000.

In place of an "income more than ten times the taxes," which the Survey Committee expects the city to "enjoy each year," at best it could be a very meager return on the actual cost. It might quite conceivably be that these 31-year-old garages would be outmoded as 31-year-old automobiles and airplanes are today, in which case the garages might be a liability.

If you carry your figures through to a conclusion, you will find that even the city, under condemnation, cannot get "something for nothing."

AND DON'T FORGET, THIS $6,500,000 IN LOSS OF TAXES AND PARKING METER DONATIONS IS GOING TO BE MADE UP TO THE CITY IN FULL BY AN ADDITIONAL $6,500,000 TAXES THAT YOU AND THE OTHER SAN DIEGO TAXPAYERS MUST PAY.

Also there is the small matter of 50 cents per $100 valuation annual assessment that all of the *owners of land within the assessment district* will have added to their tax bill. On $24,000,000 valuation, this will amount to another $120,000, per year, or $3,720,000 in 31 years, *not* counting interest.

And all this cost to taxpayers is for only the first four garages with 500 additional hourly parking spaces for shoppers over what we now have.

Suppose after the parking authority is appointed they should decide our downtown needed 5,000 more hourly parking spaces in place of

500. You would then multiply all of the above tax increases by ten, for a total of $136,000,000.

Probably the members of the Parking District Survey Committee, when presenting their petitions, will say such a statement is ridiculous. If so, please read the next paragraph carefully:

THE PARKING AUTHORITY OF SAN FRANCSICO PUBLISHED A STATE-MENT IN 1956 THAT BASED ON THE 1954 DEMAND DOWNTOWN SAN FRANCISCO NEEDED TWENTY-SIX THOUSAND MORE PARKING SPACES—NOT 500 MORE, NOT 5,000 MORE, BUT, TO QUOTE THEIR EXACT FIGURES: "26,549 MORE."

Is it any wonder that the Chamber of Commerce of the United States has taken a positive stand against socialized parking? I will tell you more about that in my next letter.

DON'T SIGN THE PARKING DISTRICT SURVEY COMMITTEE'S PETITIONS.

O. W. COTTON
Chairman

As you read this, it may seem to you that I am using more verbiage than is justified by the project, but it seems to me that it is of value to record an outline of it, because it was an important milestone in San Diego's twentieth-century history—Was this city to have a reasonable amount of "Free Enterprise" parking, or unlimited "Socialized" parking?

In the midst of the campaign, Graydon Hoffman, vice-president of the Bank of America and also a member of Hamilton Marston's "Survey Committee," made the announcement that the Bank of America had purchased the 100 by 200 foot corner on Seventh Avenue and E Street adjoining the bank, and would build a six-story and basement garage, to accommodate the bank and for public use. Shortly after that, the "Financial Advisors" notified the "Survey Committee" that the financial picture was changing, and that it would probably not be possible to finance their project without secondary financing, which the Committee would have to subscribe.

Soon after these happenings, a member of our Committee, Evan V. Jones, whose main business was operating parking lots and garages, returned from an extensive tour of the United States. He told Graydon Hoffman of a man whom he had met in Detroit, one George A. Devlin, who was probably the nation's largest builder and operator of parking facilities, and suggested that he might have some useful suggestions for the Bank of America Garage.

As a result, Graydon Hoffman employed Mr. Devlin, who came to San Diego and, as Graydon later told me, within an hour he realized that Devlin had a fund of information on building and operating parking facilities that would be most valuable to San Diego. He invited Hamilton Marston and his Committee to luncheon, and presented Mr. Devlin.

Before the luncheon was over, Devlin had convinced the Committee that its scheme was entirely outmoded, and had sold them on the idea of organizing a company and building their own garage as a private enterprise. After the meeting, a number of the party walked over to inspect the parking lot at Seventh Avenue and C Street, and decided then and there to buy the property and to build a multistory garage, with stores on the first floor.

On April 12, 1958, I wrote all members of our Committee as follows:

DOWNTOWN PROPERTY OWNERS PROTECTIVE COMMITTEE
521 Orpheum Theatre Bldg., San Diego 1

August 12, 1958

TO ALL MEMBERS:

On January 28, an announcement was made by Mr. Hamilton Marston, that a group of downtown San Diego businessmen, largely from the Parking District Survey Committee, had formed a corporation to be known as "Metropolitan Garages, Inc.," for the purpose of building a multistory garage on C Street between 7th and 8th avenues.

This garage is to be owned by this new corporation and operated by it or by a professional operator, as all other San Diego garages and parking facilities are now operated, on the free enterprise system. The parking facilities will be on the upper floors, and the ground floor will be leased for stores, thus preserving for business use the valuable C Street frontage.

This project as it is being planned by these gentlemen is one of the most forward single developments that has come to downtown San Deigo in many years. It will give the very heart of our downtown district a splendid parking facility and the building of this facility by this group of downtown merchants and businessmen, to be operated as a free enterprise institution, will encourage other downtown owners and groups to build other parking facilities.

Our Executive Committee has delayed taking official action on this matter until we felt assured the project would be carried through as planned. Recent developments seem to indicate that these gentlemen are fully determined to proceed along the lines contemplated, which would make it appear that there is no longer any necessity for our Committee.

The Executive Committee of our Downtown Property Owners' Protective Committee have asked me to take this opportunity to thank each of our members for their loyal support to our free enterprise movement. I am sure we can all feel that the educational program carried on by our Commitee has been of great value to our city and its future prosperity.

I enclose herewith a statement by our treasurer, Evan V. Jones, of Receipts and Disbursements of funds in our campaigns, and I also return herewith to each subscriber his share of the unexpended balance.

Sincerely,
O. W. COTTON
Chairman

The Parkade, as this new parking facility is named, and the new Bank of America Garage are both wonderful assets, and, as our Committee foresaw, other facilities have already been erected and others are planned.

1955 to 1958 were strenuous and mostly unhappy years for me—not many Good Old Days—but, without our Committee's efforts to educate the property owners, there is no doubt but that San Diego would now be under a system of socialized parking.

I have never asked, but my guess is that today even the proponents of the two plans for socialized parking are not unhappy with the present system.

CHAPTER LIII

That Wonderful Game Called "Golf"

THERE COULD NOT BE a more fitting description for a game than the current phrase on golf: "Golf Is a Challenge."

After my series of lessons from Olin Dutra, I played regularly twice a week, and worked on the driving range and putting green at Mission Valley Country Club at least twice a week as well. But I could not learn to play golf. I kid myself and tell my family that it is because of my health I spend so much time on the golf course, but confidentially just between you and me, I do it because I hope, the next game, I will play better. I never do, but I still sincerely believe I will.

Two-thirds through my series of lessons, I thought the end was in sight. I had the game licked. I was going to play in the "80's" and I decided to write a book on golf to teach the other duffers how to take fifteen strokes off their game. I invited Dutra to edit the book. Then, to my utter dismay and chagrin, I found that, no matter how much I learned about how to hit the ball, I could not do it!

Recently, I played with a young man from Scotland and he quoted a saying that would have fitted me perfectly: "He who can, plays; he who can't, teaches." But I do get great enjoyment from the game; meet lots of nice folks, and, all joking aside, it has been and is better than any pills for my health.

At a party one evening at the home of Clark M. Cavenee, Clark said he would enjoy joining me at the Mission Valley Country Club for a 7:00 A.M. game on Saturday. That suited me fine, and for several years, right up until the day before his death, we teed off regularly at 7:00 A.M., almost every Saturday morning. I did not learn much about how to play golf from Cavenee, but he was good company, and occasionally I picked up some pointers from him on what to say when I made an unusually bad shot!

One fine day in Washington, D. C., Clark had been paired off with the then Assistant Treasurer of the United States. Before teeing off, his partner asked Clark what they should play for, and Clark replied, "Whatever you like."

The Assistant Treasurer said, "Two-fifty a hole?"

Clark said, "O. K!"

At the end of the game, Clark had been ahead by two holes and the Assistant Treasurer said he would write him a check. Clark was surprised that his new friend would not have $5 in his pocket, but when he handed him the check, it was for 500!

"Wait a minute," said Clark, "I was playing for $2.50, not $250, a hole." And he handed back the check.

To Clark, however, no game of golf was a game without a stake, so we agreed on 25 cents a hole and adjusted our handicaps between ourselves, based on the last game—not very orthodox, but it worked out.

One Saturday, I had a wonderful streak of luck, and Clark was entirely off his game. At the 16th green, he was down nine holes. In disgust, he took two new dollar bills from his wallet and a quarter from his pocket, and threw them at me, turned, and stalked off the course. On Monday, I wrote him as follows:

Clark M. Cavenee,
Bank of America Building,
6th & Broadway,
San Diego 1, California

December 15, 1954

MY DEAR SIR:

It pains me beyond words to express, but my real estate conscience compels me to send you this score card and—what pains me even more —to return to you herewith your overpayment to me last Saturday.

When you literally began throwing money at me from various directions, I became so confused and overwhelmed I did not consult the score, but merely gathered in my honestly begotten new riches, and, with head high and chest expanded, went on with my excellent game. It was not until I sat down to my bookkeeping that I discovered your net loss was on seven holes, and not nine.

I feel confident you will believe me when I tell you it is with heartfelt regrets that I enclose herewith my check for the overpayment.

Insincerely yours,
O. W. COTTON

Clark promptly responded:

CLARK M. CAVENEE
625 Broadway
San Diego 1, California
Member: New York Stock Exchange

December 17, 1954

Mr. O. W. Cotton,
524 B Street
San Diego 1, California

DEAR SIR:

I just received your insulting letter. It reveals very clearly your character. Let me point out only two of the many revealing facts in your letter. Our game took place on December 11. In your letter you try to claim that you were very honest in your error and imply that you corrected the error at the earliest possible time. You say you corrected it when you "sat down to my bookkeeping." It certainly was a long time after the game before you "sat down." Of course, the fact is that probably Violet found the card and noticed your error and, after much persuasion, induced you to do the best you could to cover up the matter.

The second revealing circumstance is that you write on the face of the check that it is for "ONLY FIFTY CENTS." I am sure that you have confidence in my integrity and would not for a moment believe that I would raise the amount of the check. Therefore, the only reason that you wrote the check the way you did was that if it had been even fifty-one cents, you would have overdrawn your account. I therefore had my agent immediately cash the check because it so clearly reveals your financial situation.

My first reaction to your letter was that you should be shot forthwith, but, being of a noble and forgiving nature, I reconsidered the matter and reached the conclusion that the only proper reaction was to cry rather than be angry about it. Therefore, I have had several really good cries.

I have concluded that you are really not responsible for your acts, and I am going to propose to Violet that I will pay one-half of the cost of placing you in a mental institution, that is, provided you agree in advance that you won't keep on living forever.

Yours truly,
C. M. CAVENEE

One Saturday in January, when my playing was unusually bad, Clark suggested that I had better go to a "pro" and learn how to swing a golf club. I took his advice, and then wrote him as follows:

Mr. Clark M. Cavenee
Bank of America Bldg.,
San Diego, California   January 25, 1955

MY DEAR SIR:

In view of your insulting remarks to me about my golf swing, I went down to Chula Vista this morning and took a lesson from Charlie Heaney, and I have to report to you that this golf pro said there is nothing whatsoever the matter with my swing, except that I am not going back far enough or following through. He also advised that I stand closer to the ball before hitting it, and farther away after it landed. He advised, too, a somewhat different grip than I have been using, and suggested that I keep my eye on the ball before whaling at it.

So you can plainly see that you were entirely out of order when you criticized my golf swing.

After my lesson, I went to the practice range for an hour, and I hope to go there for two or three hours each day until I meet you on Saturday morning. Please remember also that I have a handicap and come prepared for whatever eventualities might come about.

I am, my dear sir,

Yours very truly,
O. W. COTTON

CLARK M. CAVENEE
625 Broadway
San Diego 1, California
Member: New York Stock Exchange   January 27, 1955
Mr. O. W. Cotton,
O. W. Cotton Company
524 B Street
San Diego 1, California

YOU POOR, WRETCHED, SO-CALLED MAN:

I just received your very welcome letter of January 25, 1955. Its contents were very gratifying to me. One of the noblest aspirations of man is to improve himself. Your letter proves conclusively that you are spending much time, money, and effort in a more or less hopeless effort to improve yourself. It is of course regrettable that you are not seeking to improve yourself mentally, but, as I understood it, you gave this up as an impossible task about fifty years ago. However you deserve credit for still trying to improve yourself physically in a much more lowly way—namely, golf.

I will meet you on the field of honor on Saturday morning. Bring with you a good supply of handkerchiefs. You will need them.

Yours truly,
C. M. CAVENEE

For the next few weeks, I had a run of good luck.

Mr. Clark M. Cavenee,
Bank of America Building
San Diego 1, California

February 14, 1955

DEAR MR. CAVENEE:

It has just come over me again for the third or fourth consecutive week what a wonderful world this is in which we are living.

As I walked down the street this morning headed for the First National Bank, to make my weekly deposit of my golf winnings, I called to mind what a friend, W. W. Whitson, said to me many years ago:

"Cotton," he said, "it is all very fine to be president of the Chamber of Commerce and the Rotary Club and to make fine speeches, but when all is said and done, the real test is, 'What is your note worth at the bank?' "

As the weeks go by and my bank account is increasing, it seems to me that I can detect a little more affability in the "Good Morning" and the handclasp of the officers of this great institution, the First National Bank, which leads me to believe that my friend was probably right. So in view of the fact that you are so largely responsible for this wonderful state of affluence into which I am entering, I thought it only fitting that I drop you this little word of appreciation, so that you may know that I am thinking of you on other days besides Saturdays.

Some people are of the opinion that there is an element of luck in this game of golf. My personal belief is that it is almost wholly scientific. Of course, I have accepted the handicaps for the last few weeks because of your insistence. Now that the scores have changed and it is necessary for me to give you a handicap of five for next Saturday, I will try to do so with the same cheerful smile that you have had, but frankly I am hoping that the net result at the end of the game will still enable me to make my weekly trip to the bank and continue to hold my credit rating.

The only real regret that I have had in the last month is that we were not playing for $250 a hole, as you tell me was your custom when you played with the Assistant Treasurer of the United States.

Looking forward hopefully to next Saturday morning, and with all good wishes for your health and prosperity, which in turn I trust will make possible my continued prosperity, I am,

Very truly yours,
O. W. COTTON

CLARK M. CAVENEE
625 Broadway
San Diego 1, California
Member: New York Stock Exchange

DEAR MR. COTTON:

In view of the arrogant and deprecatory letter which Mr. Cavenee received from you today, we, as loyal employees, thought it about time someone advised you of the extreme financial straits Mr. Cavenee finds himself in. You state that your bank account in the First National Bank has been increasing by leaps and bounds. On the other hand, Mr. Cavenee's bank account in the Bank of America has been completely depleted. It is with extreme pain that we await our employer on each Monday morning to see his red-rimmed eyes and completely worried expression. We know he is wondering how he will be able to meet his payroll obligations on Friday. Thus, you see, it is no longer a matter between you and him, but of us, his employees, as well.

You stated in a prior letter that you had spent an entire week practicing on the golf course for your encounter with Mr. Cavenee. He, of course, has never used such an underhanded trick as this. We have, however, prevailed upon him to discontinue trying to make ends meet here in the office and go to the golf course each day to perfect even to a higher degree his excellent form in preparation for your next meeting.

This failing, perhaps more drastic measures shall be taken—such as engineering a breakdown of elevator service in our building, stopping same between floors for a few days—on one of your infrequent trips to the barbershop. Please do not consider this as a threatening letter. We merely want you to realize what the situation actually is.

Mr. Cavenee knows nothing of our desire to help him by writing you this letter. We trust it will be kept in strict confidence.

Yours truly,
EMPLOYEES OF CLARK M. CAVENEE

MVQ
PT
ES
HMT/DT

Mr. O. W. Cotton
Orpheum Theatre Bldg.,
San Diego, California

February 21, 1955

M.V.Q.; P.T.; E.S.; H.M.T.; D.T.,
C/o Clark M. Cavenee,
Investment Advisor
Bank of America Building
San Diego 1, California

DEAR M.V.Q.; P.T.; E.S.; H.M.T., AND D.T.:

I was very pleased to receive your communication of February 15 and glad indeed to know that Mr. Cavenee has such a loyal staff, but, frankly, I am not the least concerned over Mr. Cavenee's financial status.

When he pays his golf losses, he pays in brand-new, crisp, paper money that looks as though it has been printed by the United States Government, but it has a crisper feel and fresher smell, which, confidentially, makes me suspicious that he has a press of his own locked up in some closet unbeknown to anyone but himself. A time or two on the course he complained about his feet bothering him and, putting two and two together, I concluded that this was probably caused by standing long hours overtime working at his press.

They caught an old fellow down South a year or two ago who had been making just enough dollars bills for his own needs for twenty-five years or more, so I know it is possible to get away with this if a fellow is smart, and, regardless of what I have ever said to or about Mr. Cavenee in the past, I have never claimed that he is not smart, but I do sometimes wonder if it would not be just as easy and much more profitable to print his bills in $10 denominations, then he would not have to work such long hours at the printing business, which would be much better for his feet and would also give him additional leisure for the more honorable pastime of golf.

If, as you claim, Mr. Cavenee's bank balance is at low ebb, it is probably because he is careless in money matters. Last Saturday, for example, as we finished our game, he pulled out his large roll of new bills again and peeled off what he figured was coming to me, and strode off from the 18th green to the clubhouse. By the time I had figured out what his actual debt to me was, he was gone and I found that again he had overpaid me by 25 cents. If he handles all financial matters as he does his transactions on the golf course, your conclusions might have some foundation. But, insofar as I am concerned, I have been a realtor for more than 50 years and no man who has been dealing in real estate half that long could possibly have left any semblance of a heart or sympathy. I explain this to you so you will understand that, when next Saturday at 7:00 A.M. arrives, I shall again go after Mr. Cavenee's money, be it regular U.S., or counterfeit—although possibly I should not use that nasty word—and get every dollar I possibly can, just as though he had one thousand honest dollars in the bank.

Just to illustrate to you what a grand and exciting game golf can be, under certain circumstances, last Saturday I took from Mr. Cavenee four straight holes in a row—talk about fun! ? !

I must close now so I can be at the First National Bank with Saturday's winnings when the doors open.

Gleefully and Hopefully yours,
O. W. COTTON

CLARK M. CAVENEE
625 Broadway
San Diego 1, California
Member: New York Stock Exchange

February 26, 1955

Mr. O. W. Cotton
2900 Nichols Street
San Diego, California

HONORED SIR:
Penniless, creditless, voiceless, broken-hearted, and cowering in fear, I hereby acknowledge that indubitably I must be your willing slave from now to eternity.

Yours truly,
C. M. CAVENEE

CMC:DT

O. W. COTTON CO., Realtors
524 B STREET
SAN DIEGO 1, CALIFORNIA

March 30, 1955

Mr. Clark Cavenee
Bank of America Bldg.,
San Diego, California

MR. CAVENEE:
At last, my dear sir, I have found you out. I can see through your whole scheme. You did it purposely, with malice of foresight and with the deliberate intention of intimidating me so that I would lose my nerve in your august presence, and likewise my money at the ridiculous rate of $250 a hole.

I am embarrassed beyond words to express that I could be so taken in and never even suspected your perfidy—I am using plain language, my dear sir, because you deserve it. You were perfidious!

I admit also that I was a dope and fell for it—but who would not? When you are decked in a starch-bosomed shirt and in the company of your charming wife, you have every appearance of an honest man. You could fool anybody, so I am not to be laughed at or sneered at because in my immaculate innocence and belief in the goodness of all things—even humans—I only look for the good and noble characters in all my so-called friends.

But let me tell you this, my dear sir, once and for all when I do finally discover that a supposedly tried and trusted friend has betrayed me, has taken advantage of my younger years[1] and unusual sense of moral justice, when once my eyes have been opened, they are opened— wide.

You doubtless remember the boy who took his father's friend around to his dog kennel to show him his beautiful "New Deal" puppies, born that day—and a week later he took the same friend around and showed him the same puppies which he called his "Republican" pups—and the friend said, "But I thought you said they were 'New Deal' puppies!" "Ah," said the boy, "that was last week. Now they have their eyes open."

You will, of course, remember that when I returned from Canada last year you greeted me with the news that you had been playing some wonderful golf—sinking long putts, etc., etc., etc., and one day you actually had a score of "79!"

Well, in this instance, your rascality succeeded. You made me so nervous I played at least 10 strokes worse than I should on every game. Just trying to putt in the presence of anyone whom I believed could play like that made my hands tremble, my heart throb, and my knees knock together.

But, my dear sir, on last Saturday after you abandoned our game and strode off the 15th tee like a man in seven-league boots, with your poor caddy trotting along trying hard to keep up and still pull the heavy cart containing more clubs than any self-respecting or honest golfer should have, I added your score, and it came to—what do you think? *79!!*

Instantly that rang a bell—79! Then it all came to me—of course you played a "79" while I was away, but you did not tell me you played only 14 holes!

Listen, Mr. Cavenee, I am not afraid of any man or beast who shoots a 79 in 14 holes—so from now on I am going into our game to win! With my head up and chin down, I am going to do all the things the pros do, and I am going to teach you a lesson you will not soon forget, so that the next time you try to intimidate a friend you will pick on one your own age.

On next Saturday, my dear sir, you watch my score! I will give you

---

[1] Clark Cavenee was sixteen months my senior.

the six strokes all right because that is what our scores demand, but I am going after you and your money as I have never gone before, and there is an old saying, "You get what you go after when you go after it to get it."

I felt most unhappy last Saturday because when you paid me my honest gains I could see you still had money left! Next Saturday, please bring your checkbook—and come prepared to play 18 holes.

I gleefully sign myself to you, my friend, as an out-and-out Republican with my eyes open—wide!

Devotedly,

O. W. COTTON

DEAR SIR;

I take my pen in hand
To beg of you to understand
Why I, who was too proud to beg,
Now come to you on bended leg

And add my plea (oh, do not laugh!)
To Clark's and all his office staff—
I, too, am starving day by day
Because of what you make Clark pay.

Our little dog, our darling pet,
Is starving too, because of debt—
Our little cocker sadly gnaws
On ancient bones, and wrings her paws.

When you open up your locker
Do you think about our cocker,
While you take your balls and tees from off the shelf?

Oh, Cotton, Mister Cotton,
How could you have forgotten,
You might sometime suffer poverty yourself!

Signed: CLARK'S WIFE

Mr. Clark M. Cavenee
Bank of America Bldg.,
San Diego 1, California

March 1, 1955

DEAR MR. CAVENEE:

I capitulate!
You have broken my heart of steel.

It was the poetry that did it. When I read the verses by "Clark's Wife," and came to the lines about the dog, I could not take it.

The thought of that poor little dumb beast—I am sure I don't know why a dog is called, a dumb beast with all their yapping and barking—gnawing his little paws, etc., etc., and etc., I realize I do not have the strength of character with which I have always credited myself.

So please accept the package I am sending you with my heartfelt sympathy, and from now on I will do all in my power to lose an occasional hole for your dear cocker's sake.

Looking forward with sadness to Saturday and the future, I am, my dear sir, your depressed and disheartened, but noble, friend.

Sincerely,
O. W. COTTON

I sent the above letter, with a package of dog food, by messenger. On March 12, 1955, the following was received at home, via Special Delivery:

The O. W. Cotton Co.

SIRS: You cannot ever know
How much your package of Gro-Pup
Eased my pangs, and cheered me up.

Dear O. W. Cotton Co.!
You have spared me grief and woe
By your amazing self-control
In letting Clark win just one hole—

Oh, O. W. Cotton Co.,
Honestly, I love you so—
I'm all choked up—I'm all agog
To lick your hand!

With love,
CLARK'S DOG

CHAPTER LIV

Love and Honor

ANOTHER "Good Old Day" never to be forgotten was May 9, 1957, when all our family gave Violet and me a party to celebrate our fiftieth wedding anniversary. This party was at daughter Jane Fletcher's home on San Gorgonio Street, Point Loma.

Just before the party, who should walk in but granddaughters Joan Cotton, from the University of California at Berkeley, and Susan Fletcher, from Stanford University. They had flown down, unbeknown to their families, to give us all a surprise and make the party perfect.

The guests numbered several hundred. The "eats" were superb, and we all had a perfectly wonderful time. Many of our friends have since told us they never attended a more delightful party. Of course, Violet and I felt that way about it. Again and again, we have been complimented on what delightful little hostesses our granddaughters were!

In the San Diego *Union* of May 11, 1957, Eileen Jackson wrote in part:

GOLDEN WEDDING CELEBRATION

The guests who gathered on Mr. and Mrs. Willis Fletcher's Point Loma terrace Wednesday to toast to the golden wedding anniversary of Mrs. Fletcher's parents, Mr. and Mrs. Oscar W. Cotton, looked over a Riviera-like setting to a shining city which they all had helped to build. Nearly every guest at the party, like the honored ones, had had a hand in perfecting the vista or was a descendant of a visionary pioneer. The party was hosted by the Fletchers, and by Mr. and Mrs. Cotton's sons and daughters-in-law, Mr. and Mrs. John Cotton and Mr. and Mrs. William O. Cotton. The day was as golden and cloudless as the occasion, bathing the terraced garden and the blue harbor with a lingering sunset.

Fair as the yellow roses on the loggia and other congratulatory bouquets in the house (including gold carnation leis flown in from Honolulu by Mrs. Madeline Childs, formerly of this city) were the honored guests' bevy of six beautiful granddaughters. As a surprise to their grandparents (and to their own parents) Miss Susan Fletcher, Stanfordite, and Miss Joan Cotton, student at UC at Berkeley, flew in on a late plane from their campuses. Mr. and Mrs. John Paul Scripps, who happened to be at the airport when the collegians arrived (they were waving Bon Voyage to Mrs. Ludell Benbough and Mrs. Cy Oberg, who had tickets for New York City) and brought them to the party after a stopover at Mrs. John Henry Fox's where they pressed their party frocks (black taffeta on Susan and black linen on Joan). Other grand-daughters at the party were Miss Peggy Cotton, in pink chiffon trimmed with pink satin (her ankle accessory was a ski accident bandage), Miss Betsy Cotton in a full-skirted voile print, Miss Mary Fletcher, in a green and white cotton print, and Miss Diane Fletcher, in a lace-trimmed blue cotton.

WATER COLORS MATCH DECOR

Mrs. O. W. Cotton, never lovelier, wore her hair piled modishly high and ever-so-slightly blue-washed to match her soft French blue chiffon model. Mr. Cotton's blue-haze tweed suit seemed woven to match. Mrs. William O. Cotton's pink dress, subtly patterned in white, was jeweled and drawn to back fullness. Mrs. Fletcher, who received congratulations on her new water colors (some prize winners), which had been hung to match the party decor, wore a beige linen dress with white-lace-over-beige cummerbund. Mrs. John Cotton's pastel silk or-gandy was embroidered in black and shot with a metal thread.

Among the out-of-town guests at the party were Mr. and Mrs. Reeve Gartzmann and Mr. and Mrs. August Sensenbrenner, formerly of San Diego and now of Los Angeles.

Mr. and Mrs. A. E. Holloway, who were at the party, left yesterday for their Pine Hills home. Mrs. Holloway and her sister, the late Mrs. F. Tudor Scripps, were the first San Diegans to call on Mrs. Cotton when she came here as a bride 50 years ago. Mrs. Holloway was then Miss Violet Jessop. For the party, she wore a white, gold, and aqua floral raw silk print under a white fox wrap.

Among the many congratulatory messages were those from the honored guests' grandsons, Larry Cotton, who is an electronics tech-nician in Kaiserslautern, Germany, and Ensign James Cotton, USNR., who is stationed in the Philippines. Mr. and Mrs. John Cotton plan to visit Mr. and Mrs. Larry Cotton in Europe within a year.

Many heartwarming messages received from our friends helped to make the party one we shall never forget.

Following the party, Violet and I completed plans for our "Second Honeymoon"—a trip to Europe by air and water. From time to time, Violet and I had talked of a trip to Europe, but as the years passed I found it increasingly difficult to avoid colds and stomach upheavals when away from home, so we never got past the "talking" stage. Early in 1957, Violet developed an eye condition which would require an operation, possibly within a year, so when, in March, she suggested we go to Europe, the thought occurred to me we had better go. It might possibly be "now or never." I went immediately to the American Express Company, and had them suggest a three months' itinerary for our approval and made our reservations.

This proved to be by far the best "hunch" in my total of eighty years. Every day was a new and intensely interesting adventure. We both enjoyed good health. I had no trouble whatsoever with my diet and I gleaned many pointers on the preparation of good, wholesome yet tasty foods which I would never have learned in the United States.

After our return, I put together an 80-page book, *Europe—1957*, consisting of my letters to "Dear Everybody" edited by Violet, telling of our delightful experiences. From Venice, I wrote:

GRITTI PALACE HOTEL
Venice
September 2

Now that I have been in both, I can speak with authority. Nice is more thrilling than a nudist colony.

With its crowded, mile-long strand, opportunities for trifocal observation are more than 100 to 1 in favor of Nice, and, to further enliven the panorama, both girls and men change from street clothes to swim suits and back again, right on the beach.

The cobblestone beach (there is no sand at Nice) is about seventy-five feet wide. There is only one single line of breakers at the water's edge. Paralleling the beach at an elevation of possibly eight feet is a 40-foot-wide esplanade. Along the front of this espalande are two or three rows of various types of lounging chairs.

Knowing that certain members of my family would be interested in conditions as I found them here, I cheerfully paid 15 francs for the privilege, and took a front-row seat. I always think of my family.

The most fashionable swimsuits for girls in Nice consist of two economically designed brassières.

I have always considered the saying, "Clothes make the man" as a gross exaggeration, but during my four days in Nice, having carefully noted many hundreds of these swimsuits the young ladies are wearing (so that I could write you about them, of course) I am forced to admit that these stylish modes do bring out the personalities.

We arrived at Nice in the evening, so the first performances we saw were after the swim.

The changing of clothes by the men I did not find interesting. They merely slip on a long-tailed shirt, and under this screen, slip off the swim trunks, pull on their shorts, and tuck in the tails of the shirt. Some of the more conservative first wrap a large bath towel around their waists.

The girls use various methods. Sometimes they start by fastening a white bra on the chest below the wet one, then they adroitly slip the white one in place and remove the other.

During this first stage, the "model" faces the ocean with her back to "Spectators Row." Then she puts on a blouse, drapes a skirt over her head, fastens it around the waist, slips off the lower bra, and steps in her stepins and sandals.

Early the following morning, after paying another 15 francs for a seat, I found that the strip-tease, or undressing process, is just as simple.

At first, an observer may be disappointed because the girls are so clever, but after a time, he concentrates on the beauties of his surroundings, individually and collectively, and a generally good time is had by all.

Sometimes a man will hold a large towel around a girl while she changes. Sometimes half a dozen or more young people will come in a party, changing in singles or in pairs, laughing and chatting. This custom certainly simplifies the old-style procedure of going to a bathhouse.

Of course, every girl who wears a smile and a couple of skimpy bras is not a raving beauty, but some that we saw would stack up mighty well with the Rockettes of New York City fame, and in one of the front chairs you would be a good quarter of a mile closer than the front row, first balcony, of the Radio City Theater. Again, I speak with authority.

I did not happen to notice what type, style, or color suits the men wore, but they must not have been very good, because, so far as I could observe, nobody paid any attention to them.

Occasionally along this mile of beach, some hotel owner has built a sun shelter about 10 feet wide, right in front of and below the esplanade. Some of the girls from these hotels sneak under that shelter and change. Stingies!

One evening, we spent an hour on the esplanade at Cannes, possibly twenty miles west from Nice. Here, the beach was all sand and looked like it had not had a high tide for years.

This beach was crowded. Water and sun-bathers occupied nearly every square foot of sand. Most of them were under beach umbrellas or shelters. Everybody seemed to be having a good time, but it was not nearly as pleasing as Nice. For us, one hour was enough.

Back of the esplanade in Nice is a wide, four-lane street, divided by a wide parking strip planted to palms and other trees, shrubs, and flowers, and bordering the street, 20- to 25-foot sidewalks. Classy hotels line this street in either direction in one grand, curving sweep. The effect is most pleasing. It is no wonder we have heard so much about Nice. It deserves all the good things that are said about it.

A 20- to 25-foot sidewalk sounds like an extravagance, especially since the city provides a 40-foot esplanade on the other side of the street, but in Nice as in many other European cities, wide sidewalks are fenced off and used as cafés.

In front of the hotel in which we stayed, only about three or four feet next to the curb was in use as a sidewalk. All the balance was used for dining. In good weather, these sidewalks cafés are the most popular places to eat.

The climate while we were in Nice was close to perfection. A little too warm in the bright sun for some, but delightful for me, and always a fresh, cool breeze. The hotels are excellent; not the best food by any means, but old-type, luxury hotels, large rooms, and top service.

We stayed at the Hotel Ruhl, which is centrally located for almost everything, and had reserved for us by the American Express Company a gorgeous suite of three rooms, top floor, on the corner facing the ocean and entire coastline. Each room had a balcony overlooking the beach and park with its grandstand, and at night, music and dancing—never a dull moment.

We took an evening bus trip to Monte Carlo and two nightclubs, and to bed at 3 A.M. The nightclubs were not much, but it is always interesting to see how people in other countries do things. They did not differ greatly from American nightclubs.

Monte Carlo was rather flat. A splendid layout, beautiful buildings and grounds, and an entrance corridor of Italian marble pillars that to me were almost breath-taking.

The gambling hall, or I should say, series of large halls, is an enormous place. Large room after large room, so the few tables operating that evening were almost lost in the big expanses around them.

The walls and tile floors were dingy, and the entire appearance was as of a has-been, now being operated solely for the revenue it would produce.

There was no entertainment or music; in fact, there was nothing to cheer up the losers. The players were merely supposed to sit, walk, or stand at the tables until their money was gone, and then go home. Even the dealers who raked in all the chips did not seem to be having any fun. We did not "play," if that is what you call it.

This is quite a town, Monte Carlo, with good-looking stores, and across the street from the Casino a hotel with a splendid-appearing restaurant. But to me, Las Vegas has Monte Carlo beat four ways for Sunday—whatever that means.

The highlight of our trip to Nice was our last day. Mrs. Lot Ensey ("Kate" to us—formerly Jane's UCLA college chum, "Billie" Zeiss) picked us up at our hotel in a beautiful new Volkswagon, and took us **for** a two-hour drive over the old upper, lower, and middle Corniche roads, above, below, around, and through Monaco and Monte Carlo. For its length, by far the most scenic drive we have had on our entire trip. Perfectly gorgeous pictures at every breath-taking turn of these crooked, but splendidly paved roads.

Castles in ruins—castles and palaces in use, including the palace where the Princess of Monaco (Grace Kelly) and family now live. Beautiful Mediterranean homes, on steep hillsides below the road, and above, tier after tier. It was a glorious drive by a splendid driver and charming hostess.

When our heads were so full of this rugged scenery (or, as Kate so aptly puts it, "untamed country,"), we thought we could take no more, she parked in front of another Mediterranean-type building overhanging a cliff, with the comment, "This is where we live." We walked down two or three flights of stone steps to the first floor and onto an open terrace, and there before us was the harbor of Nice and all of the mountainsides, surrounding. Practically a replica of the gorgeous pictures we have seen of the French Riviera in *the National Geographic* Magazine and in many enticing travel advertisements.

Kate looked over the rail with a possessive smile and a wave of the hand to Michel, her ten-year-old son, who, with several other boys, was swimming in a rough little cove possibly another fifty feet below us in the rocks, that made us think of the coves at La Jolla.

We sat for a while drinking in the glorious view and sipping French champagne. Michel, as fine a young man as you would want to meet, came in to say hello, and had to leave to get ready for a basketball game that his mother was taking him and several friends to that evening.

Kate is just as sweet as she was as "Billie." Teeming with vitality and sparkling with fun. It was wonderful to spend the afternoon with her. Captain Lot Ensey is scheduled to become a rear admiral, which made it a special reason why we should drink champagne. At present, he is with the Sixth Fleet.

With this warm and pleasant memory of Nice, we boarded the Italian train the following morning, to Italy.

We had an eight-hour train trip from Nice to Milan. About four hours along the rugged coast to Genoa, then inland through the mountains to Milan. And when I say, "through the mountains" I mean "through the mountains."

At first, the tunnels came only occasionally; then they came quicker and longer; then the open spaces were only occasional; then we hit one tunnel that lasted twelve minutes, which reminded me of a ride through the Newhall Tunnel when I was twelve: A young lady about my age sat beside me and insisted on poking her head out the window through the entire tunnel. Remembering my chagrin on that occasion, on our ride to Milan I did not try any monkey business.

Milan, a city of 175,000, is largely manufacturing, but I presume they use electric power, because there is no smoke or smog. It was a little mistry most of the time—enough to spoil sightseeing, but no smog.

We had a two and a half hour auto trip to Lake Como. The drive through the city was rather monotonous, but to me it was worth it. Lake Como is beautiful. At the end of our trail, we stopped at the Villa d'Este, a lavish old hotel on the lakeshore, surrounded by lovely gardens, part of which were formal and of unusual beauty. Around the edges of the lake are large homes, partly hidden by trees.

Our driver told us that one hour more along the western shoreline would reward us with even more beautiful scenery, but we declined. We had made up our minds before we left home that we would not try to see everything.

En route to Lake Como, we stopped at the Santa Maria della Grazie Chapel, to see the original painting of "The Last Supper" by da Vinci. It was interesting to see, but the room in the Chapel was so poorly lighted that very few of the features of the party were clear enough to be impressive to me. Probably it is because of the faded condition of the picture that they keep the place so dark.

The Milan Cathedral is stupendous. It dwarfs every other cathedral we have seen, even in London or Cologne. They tell me there is one larger in Rome. I don't see why. This one at Milan is big enough to hold a dozen services at one time, without getting in each other's way. As we stood under these tremendous arches and looked toward the sky, we were again wonderfully impressed by the engineering skill that enabled the builders of that age to put together this beautiful, skyscraping structure that has stood all these years.

The streets of Milan are wide, some with four lanes, plus room for four lanes of parked cars, plus a parkway down the center for a double streetcar line. No parking problems here.

We left Milan about 1:00 P.M. of the third day, and headed for Venice. Venice—the fabulous city I had dreamed of for sixty years, at least—and now we were on our way.

We passed through lush farm country, along the southern shore of Lake di Girda, through Verona, Vecenza, and Padova, and, as we passed, they all looked the typical Italian city, with massive, multi-storied buildings jammed up against each other—a few outstanding in size and age. An occasional castle, and in the distance, at one point, an old wall with towers extending up the hillside to another castle. The realization that in all these fantastic scenes we were looking at the real thing, and not at a Walt Disney reproduction, made every mile more interesting.

And then we arrived at Venice! A launch—not a taxicab—was waiting. Our bags were put aboard and we started to plow through the waters of the Grand Canal.

The trip to the Gritti Palace-Hotel was all too short. We crossed the Grand Canal and then wove in and out through narrow waterways and back again to the Grand Canal and to the steps of the hotel. A short, but exciting ride.

After dinner, we walked about just to get the feel of the place. Every step through this silent city was a new experience. As I write this, we have been here two nights and two days, and every hour of each day to me is as thrilling as our first.

I had supposed it would be necessary to get in a gondola to go any place, but I guessed wrong. I am sure one could walk fifty miles in Venice and never have to use a boat or retrace his steps.

The main business district is in and around the great Piazza San Marco, an enormous square probably 300 by 600 feet or larger, and now at the height of the tourist season, alive with people walking in every direction from early morning until I have no idea what hours at night.

Today, we saw a seven-year-old boy on a small bicycle. Occasionally, you will see a man pushing a small, two-wheeled cart, but, aside from that, if anyone wants to go any place, he walks. To get over the waterways (and they are everywhere), you climb up a dozen steps and down the other side.

Some of the streets are quite wide, possibly 25 feet; no sidewalks, of course. Some are 6 feet wide, and they twist and turn about at right angles and then again at left angles and then over another bridge, and then you wonder where you are.

Many of the store windows are dazzling. Especially those displaying their blown glass, practical glassware, ornamental glass pieces, comics, and many truly beautiful pieces. I saw two cute little glass birds I might fall for unless I stay off that street. The displays of blown glass inside some of the larger stores are fabulous.

This noon we went inside the Basilica San Marco (St. Mark's Cathedral), and here again we found an entirely new, or I should say different, architecture and appointment. The domes are rounding, and all in gold, and again we were amazed and thrilled.

We had a delicious lunch at the Royal Danieli, on a fourth-floor terrace overlooking the waters just beyond the entrance to the Grand Canal.

I have been surprised at the tremendous crowds of people we see everywhere in little old Venice. But today, I discovered that Venice has a population of 265,000, not counting tourists. No wonder the streets are teeming with people. Also, this is Venetian Regatta Week.

Yesterday, they had the Gondola Parade, a colorful pageant held every year since the twelfth century.

We were lucky and had seats at a table on the hotel veranda. For several hours, the Grand Canal was alive with gondolas, large and small, and of many colors and decorations, intermingling with powerboats. Quite exciting to a boy from the country. (When I was four, I lived on a ranch.)

As we walked about these narrow streets, past gleaming shop windows, through plazas, narrow alleys, and over footbridges with never a sound of a city except the shuffling of feet on marble slabs and the voices of the throngs, I found myself thinking, "This is it!" The ultimate in a city.

On the morning of our fourth day, I took a brisk three-mile walk across the Grand Canal and to parts of the city I had not seen before, and did I get a surprise! I found out how the residents of Venice get their supplies! I happened, by chance, to pass a wide street set up with temporary marketing stalls. Following this street, I discovered another, and then several more.

There must have been at least half a mile of open markets—sometimes two rows, sometimes four rows of stalls—along a street all piled high with fruits, vegetables, fish, meat, etc., and from several canals, gondolas were still unloading tons more. It is simple enough when one stops to think of it. This market is centrally located, and residents come from all over Venice to buy their produce for the day or week.

At home, the automobile has caused the general public to nearly forget they have legs, or having them, why they were hung from the hips and for what purpose. But in Venice everybody walks, or stays home, and since there are no delivery wagons, housewives "tote" their food supplies home and think nothing of it. Even at the early hour I was out, I saw many women homeward bound with baskets and bundles of supplies.

When I say Venetians either walk or stay at home, that is only true as pertains to going from place to place around and across the two islands.

As we sat at dinner on the terrace overlooking the Grand Canal our first evening, we noted possibly twenty large passenger boats, loaded with people, passing back and forth. I supposed there were more American tourists, and I marveled at their number and wondered where they were going. I discovered later that these boats consist of "bus service" and they ply the Grand Canal by day and through the night, stopping at every "port" first on one side of the Canal and then the other. They also go on to the mainland at Lido, and other ports.

Our last evening, we had occasion to use this bus service and found it most satisfactory. We walked from a side entrance of our hotel around one building and there we were at a landing dock and a "bus" just drawing up. I paid 35 Lr. each for a ride to Rialto, a station about three-quarters of a mile from our takeoff landing. In real money (at least it is more real to me than their 1,000 lire bits of paper) the ride cost about ten cents for both.

We found some nice places to eat in Venice. Harry's Bar—a one-room affair about 20 by 40 feet, not counting the kitchen. We got inside just once for a perfectly delicious meal. The bar was packed three deep with customers, and we could hardly find standing room, everything was so jammed.

Since I had phoned for reservations, the young hostess finally had a special round table about 2½ feet in diameter put down beside a larger, crowded table, and we were seated. There were probably sixty people in that small room. The waiters had to actually force, and I mean force, their way through the crowded rom to give any service at all. Once a glass of water on our table was knocked over into my lap, and a little later a glass of beer was turned over on our table in Violet's direction. It was great fun, but you could not hear yourself think, let alone talk.

Harry's Bar has been advertised by Ernest Hemingway and put on the "must" list by Fielding, and it deserves it. Every bite we had there was delicious. We tried two other times to get in, but could not make it.

Taverna La Fenice also was tops. This is a large place with many tables inside and under a canopy in the street. We had two meals there. They were so good I told the proprietor I would stay for a month if he would give me a job in his kitchen so I could learn to cook La Fenice style. He raised his eyebrows and said, "You want me to pay you to learn to cook? Never. How much you pay me if I let you work in my kitchen?"

We had a fish salad with Hollandaise sauce, which included several kinds of fish, shrimp, lobster, and I would like to know what else. It was superb. I had large, green macaroni stuffed with spinach and something else that was wonderful, and the tenderest breast of chicken you could imagine, partly fried in butter, then baked in cream and wine sauce. This restaurant had a long menu, and everything we tried in two meals was superb.

On our last evening, our grandson, Lawrence Cotton, who is now stationed in Germany, and his lovely wife, Ginger, came and took us to dinner at the Restorante Al Graspo de ua' Albergo. Their menu was longer than their name. It had 125 items, costing from 150 to 180 lire each. Their specialty was fish. They served everything from sole to squid. I did not try the squid, but we all had a splendid feed and one long to be remembered. It was fun to have one last and delightful visit with Lawrence and Ginger. This time we really said good-bye, and I startled

Ginger by showing her (not telling her) what I had learned during my four days in France, in that regard.

I think it is broadening to one's character to learn the ways of people in other lands. Take, for instance, France. You must always kiss a lady's hand when you greet her, and then kiss her on both cheeks when you part. That is where that saying originated: "Parting is such sweet sorrow . . ."

On Tuesday, September 2, we were lucky and got tickets to hear Artur Rubinstein give an all-Chopin recital at Al Teatro la Fenice, which, translated for U.S. consumption, means "The Beautiful Opera House in Venice." It was beautiful. Boxes around the entire theater, seven tiers high. It was great to be there at such a performance and, of course, the concert was tops and Rubinstein was most gracious and generous to his enthusiastic audience.

Another lucky break: We had just started to walk across St. Mark's Square on our last day, when the chimes in the old campanile struck 2:00 P.M., and from under the colonnades came a man with a 10-gallon can of corn, to feed the pigeons. Boy! oh boy! Was that a sight! Before we realized what was going on, we were a third of the way across the Piazza, and when he started throwing grain, pigeons flew past us a mile a minute in all directions, and within a foot of our heads. No exaggeration. Thousands of them.

It reminded me of stories my father used to tell about the flights of wild pigeons in Indiana. How they would actually shut out the sun for hours while they were passing over. They were not that thick here, but I am telling you it was a whirlwind for about ten minutes. Then back they flew to wherever they came from. Ten gallons of corn in ten minutes—and not a kernel left.

As the motorboat took us back to our train on the morning of our fifth day, it was a different picture we carried away than we had the day we arrived.

Venice is a city unique: no smoke, no dust, no automobiles, no streetcars, no horses. In many ways, the lives of the Venetians are vastly different from the rest of the world. Imagine living in this year of 1957 without ever riding in an automobile.

Insofar as we could see, the Venetians are a happy people. I enjoyed our stay in Venice tremendously.

HOTEL MEURICE
Paris
September 20

Paris is Paris.

A city of parks, trees, plazas, fountains, monuments, cathedrals, art museums, operas, theaters, nightclubs, high-priced restaurants, and then start all over again.

Five million people, fifty square miles, 90,000 sidewalk trees, not counting parks. Here, streets not tree-lined are streets; where tree-lined, they are avenues. Most of them seem to be avenues because, most of the time you are getting about on foot, or otherwise, you are on avenues lined with beautiful horse chestnut trees, or another tree known by a different name that looks exactly like the horse chestnut, and has chestnuts all over it. So figure that one out.

But there are lots of thing to figure out over here. One is where in heck the Frenchmen who cannot keep their government solvent get the cash to pay the high prices for food and everything else I have priced so far.

I was rather shocked to pay 5,850 lire and a tip in Rome for nothing much to eat plus a five-piece orchestra, for a dinner in what is overrated in my opinion, by Fielding, as one of the "Great Restaurants of the World," but when we come to Paris, we pay more than that dollarwise for less to eat, at a sidewalk lunch, and no music. Most of the people we saw at these expensive places were French.

Except at our hotel or on bus trips most of the people we see everywhere are French. Even at the Folies Bergère, where we went last night, I should think at least a majority were natives, and at the ballet at the palatial Opera House the night before. I should guess at least 80 percent.

Our hotel rooms overlook the Jardins des Tuileries. After lunch today, I walked through these Gardens, and told Violet I had counted over two million kids playing every imaginable game from riding burros to sailing boats in the little lake, apparently made exclusively for that purpose. Besides children, there were many adults, mostly reading, knitting, chatting, or just lounging. It made an interesting, restful picture. Everyone seemed happy.

The Folies-Bergère is a pleasing theater with good acoustics, and the first four rows in the orchestra circle the most comfortable, lounging, down-cushioned seats I have seen anywhere.

We had heard many conflicting reports on the show, from good to lousy. I enjoyed it. We had been advised to ask for seats in the second row, which we did, but the American Express had tickets for us in the first row. The second, third, or fourth rows would have been much better. The first row is right over the orchestra pit. We got too much cool air and the music was too loud. The choruses are not trained like the Rockettes; the voices are of no consequence; there is considerable horseplay that is "horsy" and one act should be taken out and put in one of the low-class nightclubs; but the show runs from 8:30 until nearly midnight with only one moderate intermission and, with the above exceptions, it is bright, colorful, and lively.

They display many shapely figures, most of them partly clothed. The costumes worn are bright and pleasing, the stage settings are elaborate, and there is something going on every minute. The girls who cannot afford costumes go through their parts as nonchalantly as though they were in evening gowns or the Nice-type swim suits. They are there to dress up the show, and they do just that. The show has a few specialty acts that are good, and on the whole to me it was well worth an evening, even though I was not one of the men chosen from the audience to go up on the stage and show the slightly but brightly costumed blond mistress of ceremonies how the men in their hometown kiss.

It is something to stand by the rail in the beautiful Hôtel des Invalides, and look down upon the exquisite, polished brownstone tomb, on a pedestal in the center of the beautiful rotunda, and realize that inside that tomb lie the remains of Napoleon Bonaparte. To me, it was far more impressive than any other tomb I have seen.

Not far from des Invalides is the enormous Place de la Concorde, where Louis XVI, Marie Antoinette, and many others were guillotined. It is a beautiful square now, with statuary and fountains, but it must have been messy in 1793.

All that is left of the Bastille is one eight-foot-high pile of stone. In front of this, as your bus drives by, the guide tells you over the loudspeaker to look at the brown outline on the pavement of the Plaza, and you can see where the front towers of the Bastille once stood.

We entered the Cathedral of Notre Dame on Sunday morning, just as services were concluded. People were pouring out as we went in. The pipe organ was playing, and I wondered why the congregation did not sit and listen to the music. But when we got under the main arch, I decided the organ was probably being played to clear the cathedral. The walls are bare, and the echoes were positively the worst I have ever heard, and so continuous that two or three new chords would be blasted out while the chords just played were still bouncing back and forth from wall to wall. Suddenly, the music stopped. Then, a few vibrations later, the echoes stopped, and all was quiet except for the muffled foot-shuffling of the few hundred people (probably mostly tourists) moving about the cathedral.

Notre Dame is situated on an island, the Ile de la Cité, dividing the Seine River. On this island, a block from the cathedral, is the exquisite Chapel of Sainte-Chapelle, built in 1240, and particularly noted for its beautiful stained-glass windows. Adjoining the chapel is the Court of Justice.

As we walked through the great halls of this court, we passed, and were passed by, some men and one woman in full-length black robes with white pleated bibs about ten inches long hanging from the neck. Upon inquiry, I learned that the men and the woman so dressed were lawyers.

Across the river, and about three blocks from the Notre Dame, we found the famous restaurant, La Tour d'Argent, which served us one of the best meals we had in France. The main dining room is on the second floor. All floors and stairs are heavily carpeted, and the walls are covered with red velvet. It was delightfully quiet after our experience in Notre Dame, and the food was superb.

Avenue des Champs-Elysées, for possibly two-thirds of a mile between the Place de la Concorde, above mentioned, and L'Arc de Triomphe de L'Etoile, is something to see and see again. My guess is that this avenue is at least 300 feet wide—about four times the width of a San Diego downtown street—and so heavily tree-lined you have the feeling you are looking at a wide street cut through a park.

As you turn on this avenue during a reasonably busy hour of the day, you find yourself moving in four lanes of traffic. There are no street markings, however, and to your left, coming toward you, are four more nearly solid lanes of cars. On either side are two or more lanes of parked cars under the lines of trees, then forty- to fifty-foot sidewalks, which are sometimes used in part for additional parking, but more often for sidewalk cafés.

In front of one classy hotel, I counted five rows of tables on the sidewalk, plus twenty-five feet or more width for pedestrians.

L'Arc de Triomphe is a massive and pleasing arch at the summit of this beautiful Avenue des Champs Elysées. On the floor in the center of the arch burns the Eternal Flame for the Unknown Soldier.

Radiating from the circle surrounding the arch are twelve tree-lined avenues. I walked up and down part of the charming Champs Elysées and rode its entire length many times, always with increasing pleasure.

At almost every turn in Paris, you will find a park or at least a large plaza, a church, or a monument. When we drove to Versailles to see the Palace and the beautiful formal gardens of Louis XIV, we were less than half a mile from L'Arc de Triomphe when we entered the Bois de Boulogne, an enormous park with forests, lakes, and a full-sized racetrack, and miles of paved boulevards winding through the park in all directions. It is amazing, the vast amount of land in Paris that is devoted to parks, and they are all beautiful because they have so much rain.

Most of the shops in Paris, as in the rest of Europe, are small. We went into one glove shop in one of the good business districts. The entrance door was not more than thirty inches wide—so narrow, in fact, that, after looking in the window, we had quite a time finding it. When we got inside, we found a store not more than 12 by 20 feet in size, lined with shelves with boxes of gloves, and with a counter almost full-length, three clerks and three customers ahead of us. They carried good stock, and Violet got a nice pair of gloves.

Another high-class glove store a few blocks away was even more interesting. To enter this store, we had to turn off the main business street into an alley (or "byway," as they are termed in Paris), then into a small hall with an elaborate old, winding stair. At the head of the stairs, a door led us into a series of small rooms, literally filled with boxes, counters, stools, customers, and clerks. The counters were piled high with boxes opened and not yet put away, and when a clerk was free, she brought out more gloves in boxes and opened them on the pile in front of us.

Apparently, many of the modern stores in Paris today are in buildings erected for large homes for wealthy residents some generations back, as it is quite common to find entryways similar to the above, to many of the prominent stores. Also, quite often these narrow alleyways, or "byways," lead to an old court, which now serves as an entryway to a number of shops or stores.

The streets of Paris range all the way from the beautiful 300-foot-wide Champs Elysécs to many one-way, 30-foot streets with two sidewalks and parking on each side. But even these narrow streets do not faze the taxi drivers, who go pell-mell between the rows of cars, missing everyone by at least four inches.

Most of the streets of central Paris arc onc-way, so in order to diive eight blocks to a given point, the driver may have to take you three times that distance. At first, you are suspicious he is merely adding mileage against you, but after you learn more about traffic regulations and taxi-cab drivers, you realize such is not the case. In the first place, they have to follow the one-way streets and, in the second place, they have other cute little ways of collecting extra tips from greenhorns, so they come out all right.

I asked a guide on one of our bus trips, "How big is the Louvre?" He was stumped. It is enormous! You walk block after block on any one wing, then go upstairs and start over. "Upstairs," mind you, means fifty or more steps. We spent the best part of two days in the Louvre. and looked at (it seemed to me) about eight thousand beautiful paintings. That was all the time we could spare in Paris for Art, which was just as well, because I have a feeling if we had spent two more days and seen even seven thousand more pictures, I might have become confused.

I am not quite sure why Susan calls her mother "Rembrandt." I studied carefully all of his self-portraits in the Louvre and many elsewhere throughout Europe, and I see no resemblance to Jane whatsoever. If Susan thinks her mother paints landscapes like Rembrandt, I will agree with her on that. Landscapes by both Jane and Rembrandt are beautiful. On the other hand, Jane's work in Abstracts is far superior to any such works I could find by Rembrandt.

I do not pose as an Art critic, nor do I aspire to being one, but having studied carefully something less than a million paintings in most of the art galleries and museums in Europe during the past three months, it would seem I should have gained some slight knowledge on this subject.

I like to consider Art not only from the artist's point of view, but also for its practical pruposes. For instance, when I get into a taxi, I try to explain to the French driver that I want him to take me to the Eiffel Tower; I say it ten or twelve times, and if he still looks blank, I take from my pocket a map with a picture of the Tower, and instantly his face lights up and he pronounces it in French or something, and we are off.

At our table in the restaurant of the *Queen Mary* (the beautiful dining room is called the "restaurant"), one of our table companions told of a couple of friends of hers who spoke only English, yet they motored through Europe on their own and got along fine. It seems that, for several months before leaving the United States, they clipped and put into a carefully indexed loose-leaf book, pictures of all the hotels they wanted to stop at, and pictures of all the principal foods they wanted to eat. When they went into a restaurant and were presented with an enormous menu, all in French, or Italian, they simply fished out and handed the waiter a picture of "Ham and Eggs," or whatever food they wanted. That is putting Art to a practical use no artist ever dreamed of!

We enjoyed a good lunch on the first landing of the Eiffel Tower. It was a beautiful day, and after lunch we walked around the outside rail and enjoyed the view. We did not take the excursion to the top. I looked up and pictured myself standing there on the small end of almost nothing, with only very thin air to bolster my courage, and thought, "Why punish myself like that for one more view?" So we saw Paris from 150 feet up and enjoyed our day. The top of the Tower is more than 900 feet high.

I never cease to be surprised at the lack of flies, mosquitoes, gnats, etc., throughout Europe. Even as far south as Rome, we have never been in a hotel room with screens. We leave the windows open all day and all evening with the lights burning brightly, and never a mosquito and only an occasional fly. They must all be in California. It certainly speaks well for our climate.

I presume that because of so much rain, there is very little dust. The streets are generally clean. I have not seen a mechanical street sweeper. The only evidence of street sweeping is an occasional man with a bundle of brush tied on the end of a four- or five-foot broom handle, who brushes the debris along the gutters by holding the broom contrivance in front of him, brushing with a sidewise motion. In looks most primitive and ineffectual, but it is the general practice and seems to do the job.

Among other things that are different here are: Sheets—which are a heavy, coarse linen, and at least nine feet long; Blankets—which are

longer than are generally found at the hotels at home; Bath towels—
in place of six-foot-long bath towels, here they furnish a smaller than
average towel, and two enormous bathrobes made from heavy bath-
towel material. I never did figure out how to use one.

One of the most unique features of Paris is the waiter service in a
leading hotel. As soon as you are seated by the headwaiter or one of
his assistants, you are presented with a large menu printed entirely in
French. Then, standing over you with his pencil poised menacingly, he
starts asking you what you will have. You point to one item and ask
what it is, and he rattles off something in French-English, which you
cannot understand, and says, "You will have that?" and starts to write
it down.

If you have courage, you say, "No! No! No!" emphatically. He looks
disappointed, and you start on the next item. If, after three or four
items from a double page of forty or more, you become discouraged
and tell him you have heard many wonderful compliments on the fine
foods at this hotel or restaurant and ask him what he would recommend
as one of their specialties, he will answer by naming whatever food he
thinks Americans eat, generally, and then, without waiting for your
answer, writes it down on his little 4 by 6 inch pad. If you are of hardy
disposition and temperament, you may have him cross that one out and
start once more, but keep in mind he is fighting every minute, and keeping you at top speed in your thinking.

Finally, after the third or fourth trial, in desperation you agree to
something. He finishes his scribbling on his little pad, puts it on your
table, and rushes off to some other part of the dining room, and you sit
and wonder what you are going to get to eat, and when, and what good,
rare French dish you might have had if you had only known how to
get it!

After a time, your waiter comes and reads the little slip and goes
away. Then his assistant comes, and the busboy, and each reads the
little slip and after that comes action. The busboy changes your silver,
takes away your plate, and brings another exactly like it, places a serving table next to your table, and possibly brings you rolls and butter
to keep you entertained while the headwaiter and his assistants carry
out the same performance at two or three other tables around the room.

About the time you determine to leave and go somewhere else, or
be satisfied with just a roll and butter, things really start to happen. The
busboy brings in your dinner on more silver-covered dishes than you
thought any busboy could carry, stacks them on the serving table, and
runs back for more. When I say "runs" I mean "runs." Sometimes you
will see as many as three busboys running back and forth around and
across the dining room, fetching implements or food to the various
waiters preparing to serve the main courses from the serving tables to
the diners.

On the serving stand is a double silver-plated rack with two alcohol wicks. The waiter or his assistant lights both burners and puts your plate over one blaze to warm, while he heats part of your main course, which has just come hot in a covered dish from the kitchen, over the other flame. After about seven seconds, he proceeds to serve your dinner on the still cold plate, and then before you have tasted a morsel to be sure it is all right, and before you are sure all of the meal you have ordered has been served, you look around to blank spaces. Your waiter, assistant waiter, and busboys are already bustling and rushing about to give similar service to other tables around the dining room.

If something is missing, as, for example, salt, it is just too bad, unless you don't mind sitting quietly for ten or fifteen minutes after which time someone, from headwaiter to busboy, will pause at your table long enough to fill your glass with more of your bottled water than you want, and ask if everything is satisfactory, and beat it before you can make him understand you want salt. On the other hand, should you reach for the water bottle to fill your own glass, the headwaiter or one of his assistants will be there and take the bottle out of your hand by main force, if necessary, and finish the pouring.

Please understand this not exaggerated. This is the customary service you get in most of the leading hotels and restaurants in Paris. If you don't like it, you can go elsewhere, or come back another time and get the same kind of service. The headwaiter is first, last, and always a salesman. His job is to sell you a bill of goods as quickly as possible, and then get away.

My greatest disappointment in Paris was the food. Generally speaking, it was mediocre. Only twice in eight days were we served French bread as good as is made every day in San Francisco. Of course, the fault may have been partly mine. Having heard so much about the French cuisine, I expected uniformly good cooking at top hotels and restaurants, and undoubtedly we would have had better luck if we had spoken French and had had the patience to bicker with the headwaiters and not allow ourselves to be rushed.

We did have several meals that were delicious. Lunch at La Tour d'Argent, dinner at the Ritz Hotel, the Hotel Plaza-Athénée, and several other meals, all of which were fully up to our highest expectations, so we know excellent French food is obtainable.

One of our table companions on the *Queen Mary* who spends considerable time in Paris, told me that the famous French cooking is to be found now mostly in the homes. He said that, generally speaking, all public eating places have become too commercialized.

Our three-hour trip by private auto to Versailles was most interesting, through the heavily wooded Bois de Boulogne park, and the suburban countryside with the walled-in homes and the quaint hamlets.

To me, the impressive thing about the palace was its enormous size and the magnificence of its formal gardens. These gardens, with the pools, the exquisite statuary and fountains, the surrounding forests with their long avenues between the stately trees, and the lakes, were all so lovely we were glad indeed we had not missed the trip. The same was true of Paris.

While making our plans for this European tour, we had heard so much about how little regard the Parisians have for Americans, and how they rob the tourists. It made us wonder if possibly we might skip Paris. Now that we have spent eight days here, I would say most emphatically it would have been a great mistake to spend three months in Europe and not go to Paris.

From the drive to the city at 10:00 P.M. from the airport, until we left, there was not a dull moment. We found nothing but extreme courtesy from all of the Parisians with whom we came in contact, with the exception of one taxi driver, who got excited through a misunderstanding. We enjoyed the beauty of the city, with its tree-lined avenues, parks, statuary, and many beautiful buildings, the National Opera House, one exquisite ballet, and should have liked to have heard an opera. We had lovely hotel accommodations and most courteous treatment throughout. In short, we enjoyed Paris, and I might even have suggested that we skip one boat and stay over another ten days, if it had not been for my horrible dream.

Never in my life before have I taken seriously any dream I have had or have heard anyone tell about. But this dream, three nights before we were to leave Paris, was so frightful and vivid I could not help but feel it might possibly be a premonition of what might actually happen if we prolonged our stay.

Late last year, I read a book by John P. Marquand in which the author had several of his finest characters so brutally and disgustingly murdered that, for days after, I would awaken at 3:00 A.M., in a cold sweat. It took weeks to get the horrible story out of my mind.

This dream affected me the same way, only worse, so from that time on my main objective has been to get back to San Diego and prove to myself that it was only a dream and not a premonition. Here is my dream, and it stands out as clear and horrible in my mind today in broad daylight as it did at 2:00 A.M., ten days ago: I dreamed I was on the Number One Tee on a golf course, and to save my life I could not drive my ball more than fifty yards!

The seven-hour trip by train from Paris to Cherbourg was lovely. As we approached Normandy, the rain stopped and the sun came out, so we saw all of that rich butter and cheese country at its very best. Green, fresh, and bright. Many of the old towns seemed, from our point of view, to have escaped major bombing damages. The old stone farmhouses and groups of houses with barns and haylofts attached looked as they might have 150 years ago. So before it got dark, we felt we had seen enough of this part of France to get the feeling of the country. It made a most satisfying exit through a beautiful land.

The English-speaking driver who took us from our Hotel Meurice to the railroad station gave us another picture. He said he had lost everything he possessed in the war, and what he could not understand was that, before the war, the French franc and the German mark were of equal value. The French had won the war and the Germans had lost, but now it took 100 French francs to equal 1 German mark.

Owing to too much wind, we were told the *Queen Mary* could not dock, so we were taken out to her in a tender—a powerboat possibly 200 feet long. The trip took less than an hour. Some of the passengers complained mildly, but to us it was merely another link in the chain, and when we came aboard the *Queen,* I am sure everyone heaved a sigh of pleasure. She is delightful.

This is September 30. We land in New York about 12:30 P.M., tomorrow.

The entire trip has been almost as smooth as glass. The slight motion we have felt has not been enough at any time to make even me reach for my bottle of pills. When I get back home, I am going to see if my druggist will take them back.

I do not see how one could ask for a finer ship in every respect—comfort, convenience, excellent food, and a marvelous and courteous crew from purser to cabinboy. It is like being with a crowd of friends, and, to top all, we were seated at a table with four delightful and interesting people—an English couple and an American couple from New York.

October 1

Now the picture aboard ship is changed. Bags are packed and in the aisles, or are en route to the baggage rooms on deck. Breakfast is over and we have said our good-byes to our table companions, just in case we should not meet at lunch. Most of the passengers are on deck to get a first look at the Statue of Liberty, the New York harbor traffic, and the one and only skyline of lower Manhattan.

At this point, the *Queen Mary* plays it safe. As against an average speed of 27 knots at sea, we now make about 3 knots, and as we approach the piers a large tug comes alongside to nose us around. Soon another tug slides up, then you walk around the deck and find there are five large tugboats: two pushing on the bow on the starboard side, one on the port side to see that she does not turn too fast, and the others on either side toward the stern. Again, to a boy from the country, more thrills.

We pass the rather sad-looking *Mayflower II* tied up at a wharf. She showed plainly the ordeal she had been through. Another big liner was towed out from another wharf and headed for the sea, passing us on our starboard. Then we passed the American liner *United States,* which had docked a few hours ahead of us. A beautiful ship, she looked a little small compared to the *Queen Mary*—actually, the *United States* displaces about 30,000 gross tons less than the *Queen Mary.*

By now, we were just inching our way in, so we took one more good eyeful of the famous skyline of tall buildings, and then went down to the "restaurant" for a quick lunch and a last glass of goat milk, returning to the deck after we had docked and possibly half the passengers had gone down the gangplank.

Continuous belts carried two streams of bags to the dock, where porters with carts took them to Customs. We were asked to open two bags—we had six altogether—one we opened was only clothes; the other had all the packages containing our purchases, which brought forth the comment from the Customs officer, "I guessed right that time!"

We must not have looked suspicious, because he fumbled through each one for "just a few fumbles" and then said, "O.K." I locked up, and he put stamps on each bag and a chalk mark, and I was off to get a porter.

In less than an hour from the time we walked down the gangplank, we were comfortably seated in a "taxicab" at least twice as big, and four times as comfortable, as the European variety, and listening to our driver talk unadulterated "American" while he drove us through the great canyons between the skyscrapers, to our hotel.

Although the World Series was starting the next day, they gave us very nice rooms at the St. Regis. We had tickets engaged for *My Fair Lady*—and San Diego, our family, and our friends were only eight hours away!

Epilogue

THE CALENDAR says I am getting old, but I don't feel that way.

Recently, I invited the family for a get-together—seventeen, not counting the great-grandsons—and surprised them by personally preparing and serving the dinner: Baked Beans à la Bisbee; Filet Roast Beef; Sliced Cucumbers, marinated two days in "Oscar's Special French Dressing"; Asparagus Tips on Lettuce with Mayonnaise; Hot Boston Brown Bread; Hot Rolls; Ice Cream and Cake.

My father left us at the age of sixty-two; Mother at fifty-eight. My sister Florence, at fifty-three, and sister Shellie at eighty-four.

Laura, at seventy-five, is still—shall we say—"active"? She lives in Berkeley and enjoys driving her friends over the Bay bridges and highways, daytimes or nights. She conducts a choir of twenty voices of young ladies, ages sixty to eighty-five. One day in March, 1961, we received a most enthusiastic letter from her, telling of having sold one of her recent oil paintings to a party in whose establishment it had been hanging on a rental basis for some months. This letter also contained the rather startling news that she had that day ridden her bicycle five miles!

My wife, Violet, left us and her many friends on December 10, 1961, after a confinement of seven months. Toward the last, life held so little for her, she was ready. A few days before the end, as I sat beside her bed, holding her hand, she said, "I will not tell the children, but I know the end may come any time now, and I am not afraid." Her passing left a void that cannot be filled.

San Diego has continued to grow and expand, far beyond my wildest imaginings: Population increase in sixty years—1900: 17,700; 1960: 573,000—and apparently just started. Teeming new business centers surrounding the city at Mission Valley, Clairemont, Grossmont, Lemon Grove, National City, and Chula Vista, and now a plan for the complete redevelopment of our downtown, with multistory skyscrapers, Convention Hall, Civic Theater—practically a new city. But why not? In spite of occasional smog and growing traffic congestion, San Diego and vicinity is still the grandest place to live in the entire United States—and the United States is the finest country in which to live, in the world.

In 1904, I drove my horse and buggy from San Diego to Pacific Beach in fifty minutes. In January, 1962, our granddaughter "Betsy" (Elizabeth Jane Cotton, William's and Elizabeth's daughter), an airlines hostess stationed in New York City, had a week off. In five hours, she was with her family in San Diego for the entire week, and in another five hours she returned to her base.

We are indeed in a different age. The opportunities are with us today, as they were in 1903, but fast-moving and vast by comparison!

O. W. C.